The Internationalization of Higher Education

A volume in
Contemporary Issues in Higher Education
John D. Branch, *Series Editor*

Contemporary Issues in Higher Education

John D. Branch, *Series Editor*

Black Experiences in Higher Education: Faculty, Staff, and Students (2023)
Sherella Cupid and Antione D. Tomlin

The Internationalization of Higher Education

Concepts, Cases, and Challenges

edited by

Marina Apaydin
American University in Cairo

John D. Branch
University of Michigan

Michael M. Dent
Sunway Business School

Otto Regalado-Pezúa
ESAN University

INFORMATION AGE PUBLISHING, INC.
Charlotte, NC • www.infoagepub.com

Library of Congress Cataloging-in-Publication Data

A CIP record for this book is available from the Library of Congress
http://www.loc.gov

ISBN: 979-8-88730-169-3 (Paperback)
 979-8-88730-170-9 (Hardcover)
 979-8-88730-171-6 (E-Book)

Copyright © 2023 Information Age Publishing Inc.

All rights reserved. No part of this publication may be reproduced, stored in a retrieval system, or transmitted, in any form or by any means, electronic, mechanical, photocopying, microfilming, recording or otherwise, without written permission from the publisher.

Printed in the United States of America

CONTENTS

1 Introduction 1
   Marina Apaydin, John D. Branch, Michael M. Dent,
   and Otto Regalado-Pezúa

2 Transnational Higher Education, the Emergence of Local
   Professional Bodies, and its Impact on Developing Countries:
   The Association of Chartered Certified Accountants 19
   Sivakumar Velayutham and Ajantha Velayutham

3 Exploring the Use of Universal Design for Learning to Reduce
   the Pedagogical Tension Created by the Internationalization
   of the Higher Education Classroom 35
   Frederic Fovet

4 Governance and Internationalization in European Universities 51
   Francisco Valderrey, Íñigo Arbiol, and Mike Szymanski

5 Coopetition in the Internationalization of Higher Education 71
   Rauno Rusko

6 Internationalization in Higher Education in the Confucian
   Heritage Culture Region: A Case Study of Japan 89
   Bradley D. F. Colpitts

v

7   Proximity in International Teaching Collaborations:
    The Case of INTENSE 105
    *Tine Lehmann, Veit Wohlgemuth, Aleksandar Erceg,
    Sunčica Oberman Peterka, Menno de Lind van Wijngaarden,
    and Annette Ammeraal*

8   A Critical Review of Transnational Education Partnerships
    in U.K. Higher Education Institutions 119
    Eun Sun Godwin, Jenni Jones, Joshua Whale, and Tanya Mpofu

9   Increasing the Internationalization of Business Education by
    Utilizing Visiting Instructors 141
    Joan Lofgren and Oleg V. Pavlov

10 Internationalization at the Semi-Periphery: Alternative Forms
    of Practice and the Determinants of Adoption 157
    Başak Topaler

11 Management Education: Internationalization, Accreditation,
    and the Pandemic 175
    Michael Osbaldeston and Adriana Kudrnová Lovera

12 Critical Success Factors of International Education Programs 193
    Laura Colm, Brandi DeMont, and Amanda Swain

13 Exploring the Intercultural Challenges of Internationalization
    Within Higher Education Institutions in the United Kingdom:
    A Pilot Study 209
    Cheryl Dowie

14 Legal Risk Abroad: Examining Trends in Extraterritoriality
    and the Application of U.S. Federal Law 221
    Sara Easler and Susan Bon

15 Internationalization of Higher Education: The Challenges
    of Facilitating Critical Thinking Among Culturally Diverse
    Student Populations 237
    Andriy Kovalenko and Rosemary Richards

    References 251
    About the Contributors 301

CHAPTER 1

INTRODUCTION

Marina Apaydin
John D. Branch
Michael M. Dent
Otto Regalado-Pezúa

THE INTERNATIONALIZATION OF HIGHER EDUCATION

"We talk about globalization today as if it's some great big new thing, that we've all just discovered. But there's really nothing new about it." So declared Jacqueline Winspear (2016), author of the best-selling series of Maisie Dobbs mystery novels. And intuitively, it rings true because globalization—the relentless force of political, social, and economical integration—has seemingly been in play since the dawn of human existence.

This anthology is premised on a similar declaration—that when it comes to the internationalization of higher education, there is likewise really nothing new about it. Indeed, as summarized by Dirlik (2012), "Students have been attending 'foreign' universities, and universities have been recruiting 'foreign' students, since the origins of the university" (p. 49). In other words, the internationalization of higher education is as old as the university itself.

The Internationalization of Higher Education:, pages 1–18
Copyright © 2023 by Information Age Publishing
www.infoagepub.com
All rights of reproduction in any form reserved.

Consider the University of Karueein, for example, which, as the world's oldest higher education institution, has welcomed Muslim students from across the Islamic world since its founding in 859. The University of Oxford welcomed its first international student, Emo of Friesland, in 1190 (University of Oxford, n.d.). And Sultan Ulug Beg, the 14th century ruler of a vast area of Central Asia from Kyrghyzstan to Afghanistan, built one of the world's first observatories in Samarkand along the Silk Road, thereby attracting astronomers from far and wide to study the skies (Golden, 2011).

The internationalization of higher education, however, is more than simply the presence of foreign students. In medieval Europe, scholars often spent their sabbaticals abroad, enjoying time in "Oxford, Tübingen or the Sorbonne to pursue their scholarly activities and access the vast resources of the university libraries" (Harris, 2008, p. 352). Latin, which was the *lingua franca* of higher education until the Renaissance, facilitated the itinerant scholar's rambling from *studium* to *studium* (de Ridder-Symoens, 1992). It is not surprising, therefore, that the European Union chose the name ERASMUS (European Community Action Scheme for the Mobility of University Students) for its student exchange program, a nod to one of the most famous academic wandering minstrels.

At the end of the Middle Ages, the university lost its academic universalism, becoming an instrument of the state. Indeed, its newfound purpose was to serve the ideological and professional needs of the emerging nation-states of Europe (Scott, 2000). Kerr (1994) characterized this period as the "convergence model" in which "education, and higher education, not only came to serve the administrative and economic interests of the nation-state but became an essential aspect of the development of national identity" (p. 27). It was during this period that the university also gained its new identification with science and technology.

As these emerging nation-states gained power, national systems of higher education also began to emerge, and these systems were subsequently exported. Johns Hopkins University in Baltimore, for example, adopted the German discovery-oriented approach to higher education, and became the model for the modern American research university (Johns Hopkins University, n.d.). The export of national systems of higher education, however, was more often another facet of the European colonization of Africa, Asia, and Latin America (Knight & de Wit, 1995). Although primarily in service of national interests, it also led to the sharing of scientific ideas, and reignited academic exchanges.

The years immediately following World War II triggered an explosion in higher education (Seidel, 1991). Indeed, half of the world's universities have been established since 1945. In the United States in particular, higher education was linked to a broader social equity agenda which aimed to expand educational opportunity and access. Spurred by the G. I. Bill (1944) and the civil rights movement (Newfield, 2011), this agenda led to the massification of higher education and, correspondingly, an almost Fordist assembly-line approach to teaching and research (Scott, 1995). But as highlighted by Scott (2000), the golden age of universities also coincided with the height of the Cold War and consequently a kind of nationalism, which, he argued, resulted in (using Kerr's language) a re-convergence.

The 1960s and 1970s, however, saw a rekindling of the internationalization of higher education, despite—or perhaps because of—the Cold War. Both the United States and the Soviet Union began to support international exchange for economic and political motives, resulting in a new form of educational imperialism. The Chicago School of Economics, for example, had a profound impact on the macroeconomic policies of Chile—the effects of which can still be felt today. Or consider the legions of African engineers, doctors, and scientists who were educated in universities and institutes across the Soviet Union. The People's Friendship University (now of Russia), for example, was founded in 1960, with the express purpose of educating citizens of developing nations.

The internationalization of higher education in the 1960s and 1970s was also spurred by the de-colonization of the developing world, the rapid expansion of higher education globally, and the changing role of the university from a center of intellectual pursuit to a training facility for human resources (Knight & de Wit, 1995). This internationalization took on a decidedly north–south geographical axis, with students moving (usually one-way) from south to north, and staff and technical assistance in the opposite direction. The consequences were both positive (e.g., the spread of scientific developments to the south) and negative (e.g., brain drain from the south).

The forces of globalization which erupted in the 1980s prompted a new twist on the internationalization of higher education. Indeed, the sense of urgency which accompanied these forces resulted in more internally oriented international activities at higher education institutions—for example, cross-cultural training and new area studies programs—which were intended to nurture the "international-ness" of staff and students (see, e.g., Gacel-Ávila, 2005). This urgency was captured concisely in *A Nation at Risk* (the landmark federal evaluation of American public elementary and secondary education which was commissioned by then-President Ronald Reagan): "Our unchallenged preeminence in commerce, industry, science, and technological innovation is being overtaken by competitors throughout the world" (National Commission on Excellence in Education, 1983, p. 1). In higher education more specifically, the concern over America's global competitiveness led directly to the Centers for International Business Education (CIBE) program, "created under the Omnibus Trade and

Competitiveness Act of 1988 to increase and promote the nation's capacity for international understanding and economic enterprise" (U.S. Department of Education, 2016, n.p.).

The 1990s, however, ushered in another era in the internationalization of higher education, in which education itself is considered a product which can be packaged and sold internationally (Cudmore, 2005). Now most known as *transnational higher education*, this international trade of higher education was triggered in the United Kingdom, for example, by Tony Blair, who launched a worldwide campaign to increase the number of foreign students in British universities (Ayoubi & Massoud, 2007). Likewise, government changes in higher education funding encouraged Australian universities to begin offering their degrees internationally (Currie & Newson, 1998; Smart & Ang, 1993), especially in the markets of Southeast Asia. The inclusion of education as a tradable product in the World Trade Organization's (WTO) 1995 General Agreement on Trade in Services (GATS)—the culmination of the Uruguay Round of negotiations which began in 1986—gave "additional momentum to the process" (Anandakrishnan, 2008, p. 199).

Transnational higher education is now a multibillion-dollar industry (Alderman, 2001); trade in higher education accounts for 3% of global services exports (Vincent-Lancrin, 2005). Recent decades have witnessed an explosion in the number of universities going abroad. Weill Cornell Medical College, for example, was opened in Qatar by the United States-based Cornell University in 2001. The Open University Business School of the United Kingdom now has more than 30,000 students in more than 100 countries who are studying by distance education (Open University, 2014). And higher education ranks as Australia's fourth largest export behind coal, iron ore, and gold (Group of Eight Australia, 2014).

Doubtless, the COVID-19 pandemic has impacted (and perhaps even accelerated) the internationalization of higher education. One of John's former MBA students, for example, was accepted to the doctoral program at the University of New South Wales in Australia. However, the Australian borders were closed before he could relocate, thereby forcing him to proceed from his home in Malaysia. It's more than 2 years later and he continues to work on his research "at a distance."

THE CALL FOR CHAPTERS

It was against this historical backdrop of the internationalization of higher education that we, the editors, proposed this anthology to the publisher. Upon approval, we issued a call for chapters that explored the substance and scope of internationalization in the context of higher education. Potential authors were prompted with (but not limited to) possible chapter topics:

- International institutional branding
- International student recruitment
- International academic recruitment
- Foreign branch campuses
- Educational hubs
- Internationalization policies
- Virtual exchange programs
- International practicum/internship programs
- Internationalization modes
- Internationalization theories of higher education
- Cultural challenges in the internationalization of higher education
- Curricular innovations for internationalization
- Student mobility
- Legal issues in the internationalization of higher education
- Internationalization platforms, apps, and other technologies
- Patterns of internationalization in higher education
- Ecological/environmental implications of the internationalization of higher education
- The politics of internationalization in higher education
- Case studies of institutions which reveal innovative approaches to the internationalization of higher education

Any chapter proposal, however—irrespective of the topic—was required to address both *internationalization* and *higher education* explicitly. Potential authors were also guided by three broad but interrelated themes:

1. *Conceptual:* What is internationalization in the context of higher education? Are there different types of internationalization? What are the essential characteristics or features of internationalization? Answering these types of questions will sharpen the definition of the internationalization of higher education. Chapter proposals were evaluated, therefore, on their contribution to our understanding of the *nature* of the internationalization of higher education.
2. *Theoretical:* What are the antecedents and consequences of internationalization in the context of higher education? Why does internationalization occur? Whom does internationalization benefit/harm? Answering these types of questions will help to explain the internationalization of higher education, raise its significance, and extend its predictive power. Chapter proposals were evaluated, therefore, on their contribution to our understanding of the *mechanisms* of the internationalization of higher education.
3. *Practical:* How is internationalization executed in the context of higher education? What are the best practices of internationaliza-

tion? Which lessons can be learned from internationalization? Answering these types of questions will illustrate the internationalization of higher education. Chapter proposals were evaluated, therefore, on their contribution to our understanding of the *applications* of the internationalization of higher education.

THE EDITORS AND THE INTERNATIONALIZATION OF HIGHER EDUCATION

As editors, we bring our own perspectives to the role, which are based on our own experiences with the internationalization of higher education. We have our own disciplinary backgrounds, which come with their corresponding approaches to internationalization. And we have our own philosophical assumptions about teaching and learning which, in turn, influence our views about the internationalization of higher education.

Marina

For a professor of international business, my origin was not very international. I was born in the closed confines of the Soviet Union, where the word "international" was mostly associated with communist movements in Latin America and Africa (which to us was a remote place where pineapples grew on palm trees). Soviet people did not have the right to travel outside their own country, and most people were not even aware of what a passport was. As a result, my first exposure to the possibility of "internationalization" even existing, was seeing Columbian international students taking courses at the university. These students were required to study Russian before they were able to continue their studies within their respective fields. But within a year, through their hard work, they became fluent enough to be able to study medicine, electromagnetic waves, and so on... all in Russian. Most of these students also knew English or French, in addition to their native languages. Their grit inspired me, and I decided to learn English, French, Italian, and Spanish, in parallel with my major in unmanned aerial vehicles (UAV) at the university. This decision was the first of many which defined my professional and academic life going forward.

Being one of the few engineers who could speak four foreign languages, I was approached by many international companies which were interested in establishing businesses in the virgin economic landscape of the USSR at the dawn of the Perestroika. Consequently, I had many opportunities to practice these languages, and to observe capitalism in action. And in a couple of days of working with foreign companies in the USSR, I was able to earn the same salary as my father earned annually. My economic windfall, however, was overshadowed by my discovery that the salary of my fresh Harvard graduate boss was 133 times greater than my salary. It was—as we say in academia—"a significant difference." My boss, however, was a good mentor, and with his help I was able to join the MBA program at UCLA, which was funded by the Edmund Muskie fellowship. So began my international journey.

At that time, UCLA was one of the few American universities with a large number of international students. I was able to merge fully into the multicultural mosaic on campus; on Soviet campuses, contact with foreign students was not promoted, and was often monitored by state agents. Los Angeles was truly a melting pot of many cultures, open to be explored. As a result, for my first post-MBA job I moved to Jeddah, Saudi Arabia, where my passion for the Middle East was born.

Unlike the United States—where reality was close to my expectations—the Middle East was shocking. As an example, I had come from an atheist Soviet society, but found myself in a Kingdom where religion was central to people's everyday. Consequently, my experience in Saudi Arabia, then Bahrain, and finally Egypt, was full of cultural discoveries, thereby prompting me to learn yet another language, and to complete another master's degree at UCLA in Near Eastern language and cultures.

This "learning as a lifestyle" led me to complete my PhD degree at the Richard Ivey School of Business at Western University in Canada, with a focus on organizational learning. I then took up a directorship at the cultural arm of the United Nations, UNESCO's World Heritage Centre in Paris. After concluding my brief diplomatic career, I finally settled into the field of university education.

Since joining the Academy in 2009, the topics of my research and my teaching interests have always been highly international. My two principle locations have been Beirut and Cairo, although I have traveled around the Middle East to promote interactive teaching methods. I have published several peer-reviewed publications on this subject. And I have shared my professional experience with many students.

In 2019, I had the opportunity to participate in a highly innovative virtual exchange program which was conducted under the aegis of the U.S. State Department Stevens Initiative. The program is a collaboration between four universities from the United States, Lebanon, Egypt, and Libya. Students from these universities meet once a week in a virtual classroom to discuss cultural issues in international business, and to learn how to work together, despite the geographic (and cultural) distance. Doubtless, this was an extremely enriching and rewarding experience for everyone involved. Not only that, it was the perfect format to weather the educational restrictions which were imposed by COVID-19. Eventually, our multicultural students merged into a global alumni association, and we the professors, became friends and co-authors (as evidenced by this anthology).

Early in my academic career, a mental framework which I made for myself has become a way of life. I call it the 3A approach: awareness, analysis, and action. Indeed, I have become aware of the things which I "didn't know that I didn't know", which I then analyze for their utility, and eventually explore in practice. Internationalization was a completely foreign concept to me during my early years in the Soviet Union. Then I analyzed it during my time in the United States and the Middle East. Eventually, I enacted throughout my professional and now academic career.

Recently, a graduate exchange student from Belgium asked me an interesting question: "What was the most important life changing decision you ever made?" Without hesitation, I can confidently say, it was the choice to work anywhere, with anyone... the decision to live an international life without borders.

John

It might be shocking that a university professor who has lived in, worked in, or traveled to 89 countries worldwide started life as a unilingual, unicultural kid from small-town Canada. Indeed, until the age of 23, my life was very insular, provincial, and unsophisticated... unless you count the Grade 10 road trip to Florida with my father and closest friend Sean Burns.

In 1992, however, after the successful completion of Year 1 of my MBA, I secured a spot with fourteen classmates in the new international internship program. It was 1992, and our Polish-émigré assistant dean organized a 12-week combination of study and consulting in Poland. For the first 2 weeks, we studied economic re-organization and re-structuring at the Warsaw University of Economics, and enjoyed cultural activities in the evenings and on the weekends. For the remainder of the internship, we scattered to various cities throughout Poland to help state-owned Polish companies which were floundering in the new market-driven economy. It was the most transformational 12 weeks of my life.

For the consulting gig, I was paired with another engineer who hailed from Newfoundland, Canada. We were stationed in a medium-sized city in north-central Poland. Our company manufactured truck and tractor tires, and was part of the state rubber products behemoth which, during the socialist period of Polish history, provided the country with not only tires but also hot water bottles, kitchen spatulas, and even condoms. Garry had worked for 2 years in a Michelin manufactory in Nova Scotia, Canada, so he was well-versed in tires. My 8 years of evenings, weekends, and summers at the foundry in my hometown likewise made me a good match for the company.

Our posting was in the marketing department. Two days into the job, however, revealed that it was not much of a marketing department at all. Remember that this was 1992, less than 2 years after the democratization of Poland. The managing director of the company knew nothing about marketing, because the manufactory had operated for many decades under a centrally planned economic system. But he did know that foreign companies had marketing departments. So 2 weeks before our arrival, he created a marketing department.

There were five employees in the marketing department. Jerze, the chief of the marketing department, was an engineer by training, but had most recently spent some time in the commercial (sales) division. Another man, whose name I cannot remember, spent the summer essentially trying to figure out how Microsoft EXCEL worked. Two Polish interns just sat around and read the newspaper all day. The only employee who did anything remotely marketing-like was Alicja, a recent graduate of the Faculty of Foreign Languages of Toruń University. Her job was to purchase company knick-knacks—such as pens, cigarette lighters, and little sewing kits—all of which were emblazoned with the company logo and address, for the purposes of trade fairs and other sales events. Alicja was our host, and she spoke English beautifully.

This lack of marketing meant that our summer was spent teaching marketing to Jerze and Alicja, with Alicja translating for Jerze. Garry realized early on that he was not a teacher. He understood the material, but just could not teach. He could not find examples in the Polish streets around him, or take the new (and I do mean new) concepts of marketing and make them understandable to these "students." I, on the other hand, excelled. Garry looked at me one day when we were laying on our single beds in the tiny room of the Hotel Robotnichje (Worker's Hostel) and said, "You ought to be a teacher. You are really good at it."

I also learned that I could not only survive in a foreign country, but that I thrived on it. Alicja took us everywhere. The first weekend we drove to the lake district where the company had a lakeside resort for its employees, complete with fishing and boating equipment, sports facilities, and hiking and leisure trails. We took one of the small sailboats out for the weekend. There we were, under the stars on some tiny island in the middle of Lake Mikołaiki around a fire cooking Polish kielbasas, drinking vodka, and singing some camp songs—they in Polish and we in English. This was just the first weekend. I knew then that I needed international in my life.

I returned to Year 2 of the MBA program, now fully vested in the idea of becoming a professor. I began searching for doctoral programs in the United States. New Brunswick was a 17-hour drive from my home town, but I realized that I was ready to explore further afield: the United States. Plus, American business schools had a reputation as being the gold-standard for doctoral programs. My General Management Aptitude Test score was not exceptional, and, of course, my undergraduate average was mediocre at best. Despite my high grades in the MBA program, therefore, I doubted my ability to be accepted at a top-tier university. Consequently, I looked to medium-sized state universities with decent marketing departments, which were located in cities which seemed like interesting places for 4 or 5 years. The resulting list included the University of Nebraska, the University of Memphis, the University of Oregon, Louisiana Technical University, and the University of Arkansas.

Meanwhile, the University of New Brunswick had a visit from the dean of École Supérieure de Commerce de Rennes in France, who was eager to set up an exchange program with the faculty of administration. Garry and I, as two leaders in the MBA student council, offered to give the visitor a tour of the campus. After showing him the various buildings and historic sites, he asked us what we planned to do after graduation. Garry mumbled something about combining his engineering and management skills. I told him of my applications to doctoral programs. His eyes lit up.

His school was looking for a young marketing professor who would consider being the guinea pig for a new doctoral program. He said that he could offer a salary of about $25,000 per year for teaching a half-load of courses, and support research toward a doctoral dissertation for the remaining time. The school was located 2 hours from Paris. About 1 month, and several faxes and letters later, I had accepted the position, and was auditing a French-language module at the university.

I could keep going, regaling you about my 4 years in France. I am happy to share my story of the summer of 1993, when I taught the first marketing course in the first MBA program in the first business school in post-Soviet Kyrghyzstan. And I can certainly boast about the visiting positions which I have held at more than 40 universities worldwide, including the Stockholm School of Economics in Riga, the Zagreb School of Economics and Management, and Chulalongkorn University in Bangkok. But like Marina's story of internationalization (although in the "opposite direction"), my international academic life began as a result of a kind of epiphany. And then it blossomed through a mixture of opportunism, diligence, and sometimes sheer luck.

Michael

My interest in teaching and learning was kicked off at the age of 5. My first school was in Cornwall in the South West of England. I then transferred to another school in Yorkshire (in the North of England) after the first term. So, I had to learn to make new friends and adapt very early. A couple of years later, I moved to an English church school in another town, and then onwards to a grammar school on the Derbyshire/Yorkshire border. Hence, I had attended four schools by the age of 11.

At age of 13 (following my parents' divorce), I returned to Scotland (where I was born), to attend a Scottish high school. This brought a whole new set of problems. The first problem was when I arrived with a major handicap—an English accent. At that time (1966)—just after England had won the World Cup—being English in Scotland was hazardous to your health. Even the language threw me. I was accused (falsely) of giving someone a "keeker," which I assumed meant a good kicking, but turned out to mean I had given someone a black eye. Trying to talk my way out of that when I did not properly understand the context was not easy.

Most readers might assume that Scotland and England are really just the same country, but I can assure you that they are very different... religion, just for starters. I remember going to my first football match in Dundee and being asked by a group of older boys if I was a "Proddy" or a "Cathy." A quick mental calculation suggested that I had a 50% chance of getting the answer incorrect, so I told them my name, said that I was visiting, and then changed the subject by asking where the best place to watch the match would be. Slightly confused, they gave me advice, and then let me pass.

The differences between an English grammar school and a Scottish high school were manifold. To give but one example, let me mention the subjects which were offered. I liked history, geography, biology, English language, English literature, and German. I found that I could not take German unless I was good at French (which I was not). Geography, history, and biology clashed, so I had to drop one. And English literature did not exist! Thus, straightaway I had a major non-commensurability problem. My education took a major hit as I had to master new subjects (physics & chemistry), whilst losing those subjects which I enjoyed. My O grade results were not great, but I stumbled on into the fifth form successfully. Getting English universities to recognize my Scottish Highers did not prove to be a major issue, but it subsequently confused many HR departments. I began to realize that the internationalization of education was fraught with pitfalls.

I was unable to enroll in a degree program in England because my parents were fighting over alimony, and my Father would not complete the necessary financial declaration. So instead, I took up a job offer with the Automobile Association studying for an HND. I then used that to take a 1-year top–up program with the Institute of Marketing (as it then was) for a diploma in marketing. I used this qualification to get on an MSc program at City University which I completed part time, thanks to my employer. Whilst doing post-grad research at London Business School, I taught at a local technical college and the University of London.

I had learnt that gaining qualifications could be achieved by hard work over a long time... but that the clever way was to build on what you already had and look for credit exemptions. I was able to apply this knowledge in my (limited) aviation career some years later. I received my private pilot certificate in the United States, and easily converted this to a UK PPL. I added the UK IMC to my UK license and used my training to then take the full FAA (U.S.) Instrument Rating. All of these got me on to a commercial pilot course in Warwickshire, where I also got my instructor's ticket.

Although I had mastered the technique of moving seamlessly from one administration to another, language continued to be a problem. TSVC means thunderstorms in the vicinity of the airport, but the U.S. definition of vicinity is different to that in Europe. Low approach in the United States does not mean fly lower; it means do not land! I came across this language confusion again just last month. A colleague was asked to be involved in a pilot project by a French company. He assumed that this was a test of the water type exercise in which he would play some minor role. It turned out that in French this meant to pilot (as in to fly) an entire major product launch.

After a few very enjoyable decades in the corporate world, I exercised my plan to move into academia before it was too late. Once again, I came up against all sorts of non-commensurability problems. In Malaysia, the passing grade for a master's degree is 60% (please do not ask me why). Consequently, to ensure that my university and our British partner do not offer different grades to the same student, we had to develop a complex conversion formula, which led to much discussion over rounding, decimal points, and so on. I also worked with universities in Nepal and Vietnam, and of course the credit hours calculation were completely different in each country.

I have worked as a "fly in fly out" instructor in Vietnam and collaborated with staff flying in from the United Kingdom to Malaysia to conduct 3-day or 4-day seminars for our MBA students. So, I have experience with both sides of the coin. In both cases, relationships and working practices with tutors turned out to be the bane of my life.

In terms of culture shock, I have made a large number of big errors. I nearly offered a desk clock to our most important clients; in the Chinese culture, this means that your time is up and I want you to die! I survived teaching in the National Islamic University in Kuala Lumpur. I did commit one major faux pas there, but fortunately my students understood (and tolerated) my sense of humor and decided not to report me.

In my current role as head of marketing at Sunway Business School, I report to an American, and have Australian, Japanese, Iranian, Korean, Malays, Tamils, and Malaysian Chinese as work colleagues. Some of them still struggle with my Scottish jokes. Undaunted by the less-than-aligned environment, I set out to reclaim the space from didactic intent, and to recast it as a space for discussion and problem-solving. I did this by using the data projector to introduce tasks to students, expecting them to use peers to their left and to their right to discuss the problems which were presented, and to negotiate solutions. As further technical options became available, I was able to bring laptops into the classroom, and to complement the sessions with VLE-based activities. Eventually, these VLE-based technologies were implemented before, during, and after the sessions, with face-to-face and online learning opportunities being meshed together in a sequenced design which I came to refer to as "woven learning." Core to the philosophy of woven learning is the provision of time and space for collaborative learning.

Otto

My affinity for international education began at a very early age, when I was studying at the Franco Peruano School in Lima, Peru, where I had the opportunity to interact with francophone classmates from all around the world who were in Lima for a year or two, while their parents were on international assignment. Coming into daily contact with classmates and teachers from so many different countries piqued my interest, and motivated me to study international business and, years later, conduct research on the topic with a special focus on global marketing and tourism management.

During my MBA studies at ESAN Graduate School of Business, I had the opportunity to travel to the United States on two short study trips to UCLA in Los Angeles and to Harvard in Boston. The opportunity to meet the researchers whose work I had read back in Peru, was eye-opening and helped to motivate me to continue my academic endeavors—but in a more international direction. The following year, I traveled to France to study a master's degree in marketing at the Université Pierre Mendeès France, and then a master's and doctorate in business administration research at the Université de Nice. I came to see at an even deeper level the differences in higher education in different countries of the world—which materials were used, how subjects were taught, and even the way in which students interacted with professors. There was so much to learn when researchers, teaching professors, and students from around the world interacted with one another. Indeed, this experience was what solidified my intent to focus on the internationalization in higher education.

In 2001, I was asked to be part of the team that founded the Center for Tourism Management at CERAM Sophia Antipolis, now known as SKEMA Business School. This center, which was funded by the European Union, brought together academics from all over Europe to conduct research, develop software for the international tourism industry, and teach tourism professionals who were obtaining their master's degree in tourism management. The 4 years during which I worked as a visiting professor at SKEMA were my first dive into on-the-ground experience of what international educational collaboration can look like from the professor's perspective.

As a professor, I have always sought out opportunities to work with colleagues and students beyond the borders of my own country. I have participated in academic conferences on different continents and have served as a visiting professor in Latin America (Mexico, Ecuador, and Colombia) and Europe (Spain and France). I have accompanied MBA students on short study trips to different campuses throughout Latin America, the United States, Spain, and China, and I have also given online guest lectures for audiences in India, Tunisia, and Puerto Rico. These interactions always prove fruitful and enriching, both to the students, to my international colleagues, and to me—providing opportunities for cross-pollination and dialogue in which creativity and innovation can come to the surface.

Always wanting to keep up with the times, I recently forged the Academic Network for Digital Transformation (Radigital) with representatives of six other business schools in Europe and Latin America. The purpose of this network is to collaborate on research of interest to the professional world, spread the findings to various parties, and create academic programs which specifically target the needs of the business community.

Since 2021, I have been on sabbatical in Cannes, France, where I have been able to conduct research, and teach courses on marketing and tourism in different French universities. I teach in both English and French. I am certain that my 5-year-old self would be smiling, knowing that he would grow up to provide to others exactly what he was experiencing at that age.

CONCEPTS, CASES, AND CHALLENGES

We received almost 40 submissions, covering a wide spectrum of topics in and around the internationalization of higher education. Authors were similarly varied—living, working in, or hailing from all corners of the globe. The subsequent review and re-submission process whittled the 40 submissions down to the 14 chapters which follow in this anthology.

A significant challenge when editing an anthology, however, is curating its chapters, even when they all share a common theme. In our role as editors, therefore, we teased out a variety of frameworks by first juxtaposing a number of different dimensions of the internationalization of higher education: a teaching versus learning focus, for example, a domestic versus international orientation, and a physical versus virtual delivery mode. We tried two dimensional frameworks, Venn diagrams, circles, xy plots, and even a pyramid.

In the end, however, we settled on a relatively simple categoriztion scheme as the framework for the anthology. Chapters 2 through 5 examine concepts within the internationalization of higher education. Chapters 6 through 10 present cases about the internationalization of higher education. And chapters 11 through 15 discuss challenges of the internationalization of higher education.

The Anthology, Chapter by Chapter

Chapter 2 by Sivakumar Velayutham and Ajantha Velayutham reveals the symbiotic relationship between transnational higher education institutions and global professional bodies. It begins by reviewing transnational higher education institutions and global professional bodies as multinational enterprises. Then, it traces the development of professional accounting bodies in Malaysia. Finally, it discusses transnational higher education institutions and global professional bodies as agents of globalization.

Chapter 3 by Frederic Fovet explores the use of universal design for learning to reduce the pedagogical tension which is created in the classroom by the internationalization of the higher education. It begins by identifying the need for the pedagogical inclusion of international students. Then, it introduces universal design for learning, and demonstrates how it can be used to support international students. Finally, it provides specific solutions which are based on Fovet's experiences.

Chapter 4 by Francisco Valderrey, Íñigo Arbiol, and Michal Szymanski establishes the link between governance and the internationalization of higher education. It begins with a review of governance in general, and university governance more specifically. Then, it presents cases of the governance of four European universities. Finally, it draws conclusions from these cases about governance and the internationalization of higher education.

Chapter 5 by Rauno Rusko views the internationalization of higher education through the lens of coopetition. It begins by enumerating the specific characteristics of universities. Then, it outlines the notion of coopetition, and discusses how coopetition has been applied to higher education. Finally, it summarizes the current state of coopetition in higher education, with a special emphasis on the internationalization of higher education.

Chapter 6 by Brad Colpitts examines Japan's internationalization reforms by situating them in the Confucian heritage cultural region. It begins by providing history and idiosyncrasies of Japanese higher education. Then, it establishes the shared characteristics of the so-called Confucian heritage cultural region. The chapter continues by identifying the unique challenges which Japan faces in its reform-oriented internalization efforts. Finally, it presents possible solutions which Japanese universities might implement to address these challenges.

Chapter 7 by Tine Lehmann, Veit Wohlgemuth, Aleksandar Erceg, Sunčica Oberman Peterka, Menno de Lind van Wijngaarden, and Annette Ammeraal profiles the EU-financed cross-border entrepreneurship development project INTENSE. It begins by overviewing the project, including the teaching approach which was adopted across all institutional partners. Then, it reviews the CAGE framework by Pankaj Ghemawat. Finally, it discusses the INTENSE project, using the CAGE framework as an analytical lens.

Chapter 8 by Eun Sun Godwin, Jenni Jones, Joshua Whale, and Tanya Mpofu reviews the transnational education partnerships in U.K. higher education institutions. It begins by characterizing the current U.K. transnational education partnership approach. Then, it reports host institution instructors and students perceptions of partner institution. Finally, it discusses implications for U.K. institutions, and proposes a new model of partnership.

Chapter 9 by Joan Lofgren and Oleg V. Pavlov probes the practice of visiting instructors using the case of Aalto University's bachelor's program in international business. It begins by introducing the "flying" faculty phenomenon. Then, it situates visiting instructors by reviewing the internationalization of educational services broadly, and export strategies of educational services more specifically. Finally, it details and analyzes the case of Aalto University's bachelor's program in international business.

Chapter 10 by Başak Topaler investigates the internationalization of higher education in Turkey. It begins by sketching the internationalization of Turkish higher education. Then, it derives a set of hypotheses about Turkish universities and their internationalization practices and outlines the research methods for testing these hypotheses. The chapter continues presenting the findings of the hypothesis testing. Finally, it discusses these findings, especially with respect to internationalization practices.

Chapter 11 by Michael Osbaldeston and Adriana Kudrnova Lovera pinpoints the challenge of accreditation of internationalization of higher education. It begins by identifying the unique context of management education and specifying the international criteria of EQUIS. Then, it advances several internationalization strategies which have emerged among business schools. Finally, it comments on the possible effects of the COVID-19 pandemic on the internationalization of management education and accreditation.

Chapter 12 by Laura Colm, Brandi DeMont, and Amanda Swain enumerates the critical success factors of international education programs. It begins by overviewing the study abroad phenomenon. Then, it ties the concept of the experience economy to higher education. The chapter continues with a profile of IES Abroad in Milan. Finally, it describes the key success factors and key pillars of experiential learning abroad.

Chapter 13 by Cheryl Dowie researches the intercultural challenges of internationalization within higher education institutions in the United Kingdom. It begins by tracing the historical development of the internationalization of higher education and underlining the need for research on its intercultural aspects. Then, it highlights the cultural challenges of internationalization within U.K. higher education. The chapter continues by outlining the research methodology. Finally, it presents results of the research, discusses its limitations, and suggests future trajectories for research on intercultural challenges of internationalization in higher education.

Chapter 14 by Sara Easler and Susan Bon spell out legal risk abroad by examining trends in extraterritoriality and the application of U.S. federal law in the context of higher education. It begins by identifying the legal challenges of study abroad. Then, it summarizes lessons which were drawn from litigation which has occurred in the United States. Finally, it makes recommendations for mitigating legal risk in study abroad.

Chapter 15 by Andriy Kovalenko and Rosemary Richards underlines the challenges of facilitating critical thinking among culturally diverse student populations. It begins by reflecting on critical thinking and the internationalization of higher education. Then, it pinpoints synergies between critical thinking and higher education. Finally, it discusses how to facilitate and assess critical thinking.

IN SUMMARY

This introduction to the anthology began with the declaration that when it comes to the internationalization of higher education, there is really nothing new about it. Indeed, the history of the internationalization of higher education is the history of higher education. That is to say, internationalization began when universities, colleges, and other institutions of higher education opened their doors.

Despite its lack of novelty, the internationalization of higher education is seemingly in a permanent state of flux. Indeed, both its substance and scope continue to transform and transfigure in concert with political, social, and economical changes. The fall of the Berlin Wall, for example, was accompanied by massive changes in the higher education of Central and Eastern Europe. Students whose educational opportunities had previously been geographically limited were suddenly crossing borders. Universities from Western Europe and the Americas "set up shop" in cities from Tallinn to Tirana. And scholars gained access to new ideas, nurtured new relationships, and discovered new pedagogical and research approaches.

The consequence of this permanent state of flux is that the internationalization of higher education—as evidenced by the number of submissions for this anthology—continues to be a subject of immense interest, to scholars and practitioners alike. Indeed, with each emerging variation on the internationalization of higher education comes theoretical and practical questions which must be addressed. As editors (and keen scholars and practitioners of international higher education ourselves), therefore, we are delighted to present this anthology on the internationalization of higher education. Its 14 chapters of concepts, cases, and challenges represent the latest take on something which at its core is, well, old. Enjoy!

CHAPTER 2

TRANSNATIONAL HIGHER EDUCATION, THE EMERGENCE OF LOCAL PROFESSIONAL BODIES, AND ITS IMPACT ON DEVELOPING COUNTRIES

The Association of Chartered Certified Accountants

Sivakumar Velayutham
Ajantha Velayutham

It is frequently argued that the internationalization of higher education is not a new phenomenon because knowledge transcends borders and research has an intrinsically international character. Internationalization has, however, assumed new dimensions towards the end of the 20th century.

Globalization has intensified competition among higher education institutions and transformed higher education institutions into self-funding autonomous institutions (Van der Wende, 2010). This context has contributed to new phenomena—transnational higher education, transnational educational institutions, and global professional bodies. These strategies are focused on transforming knowledge into service for revenue generation and a profitable enterprise for export. Education is marketed as any other service, and government support is available to education institutions similar to other exporters.

While there exists a considerable number of studies on the motivations, rationales, and strategies of transnational higher education (Knight, 2016; Wilkins & Huisman, 2012) and the global professional bodies (Briston & Kedslie, 1997; Faulconbridge & Muzio, 2012; Samsonova-Taddei & Humphrey, 2014), their contribution to globalization has been ignored. Furthermore, higher education is also closely related to professional control and migration. The influence of internationalization on these areas has also been under-researched (Bourgeault et al., 2016; Iredale, 2001). The objective of this chapter is to examine the impact of transnational higher education on professional bodies.

We propose a broadening of the research agenda of transnational higher education focused studies to better elucidate the critical role of transnational higher education institutions as agents of economic globalization. This role, we argue, ought to become a core theme in research given that transnational higher education institutions are not just organizations engaged in cross-border work and intra-organizational coordination. They are also highly active participants in the construction and diffusion of various institutions which facilitate and support economic globalization.

The above objective is achieved through an exploration of the symbiotic relationship between transnational higher education providers and global professional bodies. The chapter specifically explores the strategic alliances and joint marketing initiatives by the U.K.-based transnational higher education institutions and the U.K.-based global professional body—the Association of Chartered Certified Accountants (ACCA)—in Malaysia, which has been chosen for several reasons: First, because the authors are very familiar with its educational environment, but more importantly, because Malaysia has been at the center and is an early mover in transnational higher education and the global professional body among developing countries in both allowing the establishment of private higher education institutions and receiving full-fee-paying students from African and other Asian countries (Knight & Morshidi, 2011; McBurnie & Ziguras, 2001; Van der Wende, 2010).

The rest of the chapter is organized as follows. In the next section, we begin with an overview of the literature concerned with understanding transnational higher education institutions and global professional bodies as multinational enterprises. Section three expands the understanding of transnational higher education institutions as agents of economic globalization and highlights the symbiotic relationship of U.K.-based transnational higher education institutions and the ACCA in Malaysia. Section four briefly analyzes the impact and consequences of transnational higher education on Malaysia and lessons that can be learned with concluding comments in the last section.

TRANSNATIONAL HIGHER EDUCATION INSTITUTIONS AND GLOBAL PROFESSIONAL BODIES AS MULTINATIONAL ENTERPRISES

Transnational Higher Education Institutions

Education has always had an international dimension because knowledge transcends borders and research has an intrinsically international character. However, nation-states have usually exercised strong control over education and, more importantly, over educational institutions through funding and policies (Marginson, 2012; Neave, 2001; Scott, 1998). Prior to World War II, the proportion of students and staff who participated in international activities was also limited because international travel was not widely affordable and communication was limited. World War II had a major impact on internationalization because developed countries recognized that educational exchange and scientific cooperation could foster peace, and higher education was critical to economic development (Van der Wende, 2010). This contributed to the development of programs such as the Fulbright program, European Community Action Scheme for the Mobility of University Students (ERASMUS), and University Mobility in Asia and the Pacific (UMAP). These initiatives fostered student mobility programs and promoted their growth. The rationales for the internationalization in higher education included political, economic, cultural, and academic dimensions (Blumenthal et al., 1996).

Globalization, however, has had a transformative effect on the internationalization of higher education through both direct and indirect means. The major direct effects of globalization are the free trade agreements between countries, regional cooperation clusters such as the EU and NAFTA, and finally the establishment of a global trade organization—the World Trade Organization (WTO). Of particular importance to higher education is the General Agreement on Trade in Services (GATS) which came into effect in 1995 and was renegotiated periodically to extend its reach. GATS not only covers all types of services but also applies to all possible modes of delivering services, including" (a) cross-border delivery, (b) consumption abroad, (c) commercial presence, and (d) movement of natural services. GATS hence laid the foundation for transnational higher education or cross-border higher education (Arnold, 2005).

The indirect effect of globalization on trade and finance and the economic crisis of the 1970s (Fligstein, 2010) laid the foundation for the rhetoric supporting tax reductions, industrial reform, and corporate governance and executive compensation reform in the United States (Hacker & Pierson, 2010) and other countries, as well as the new public management reforms (Marginson & Considine, 2000). The common rhetoric is that industrial production and capital will flow out of the country if there is no tax reduction and public sector reform. The new public sector management reforms removed "collective agreements [in favor of] ... individual rewards packages at senior levels combined with short term contracts" and introduced private sector-style corporate governance, including using a "board of directors" approach to strategic guidance for public organizations. The above model was introduced extensively to public universities along with competition, decentralization, cost reduction, and output controls in OECD countries (Marginson & Considine, 2000; Slaughter & Leslie, 1997). Universities were allowed to charge fees, be less reliant on state funding, and increase intakes (Slaughter & Cantwell, 2012). Global competition and knowledge economics also led to nations seeking to attract highly skilled migrants for the knowledge economy. The aforementioned reforms promoted transnational education.

The above arrangements contributed to a shift in mobility from people (students, instructors, scholars) to program (twinning, franchise, virtual) to provider (branch campus) mobility (all forms of transnational education), and most recently to the concerted development of education hubs (Knight, 2014a).

> There has also been a shift from a development cooperation framework to a partnership model and to a commercial and competitiveness model in which traditional mobility approaches have been turned into a substantial, worldwide business of international student recruitment. Australia's relationship with international students, for example, has shifted from "one of aid to one of trade." (Coleman, 2003, p. 355)

In transnational education, learners are in a country different from the location where the awarding institution is based. Transnational education can take several forms, including distance education, franchised programs, collaborative ventures, and international branch campuses (Soliman et al., 2019). Since the beginning of the 21st century, the establishment of international branch campuses has accounted for most of the growth in transnational higher education.

The size of transnational higher education is substantial. As of December 2016, there were 247 international branch campuses globally (Cross-Border Education Research Team, 2017). The statistics indicate that the main providers of international branch campuses are the United States 51), the United Kingdom (28), France (13), Russia (13), and Australia (10; Cross-Border Education Research Team, 2017), and the main language of instruction of transnational providers is English (Wilkins & Urbanovič, 2014). Even higher education institutions from non-Anglophone countries that have entered the transnational higher education market have adopted English as the language of instruction. The main destination of international branch campuses are in China (32), the United Arab Emirates (32), Singapore (12), and Malaysia (12; Cross-Border Education Research Team, 2017). The last three countries have sought to position themselves as regional higher education hubs with incoming international students. In 2012–2013, 63 U.K. higher education institutions had 323,730 active enrollments in 2,785 transnational programs globally, which generated a total of £495.8m in revenues (Mellors-Bourne et al., 2014).

Global Professional Bodies

Just as U.S. and British universities influenced developing countries through student mobility programs, the early overseas influence of the British professional accounting bodies was through the export of British qualified accountants to overseas countries initially to the United States, Canada, and Australia and later to the colonies (India & Malaysia; Johnson & Caygill, 1971). These accountants frequently belonged to the Institute of Chartered Accountants of Scotland (ICAS)—which was formed in 1853—and the Institute of Chartered Accountants of England and Wales (ICAEW)—founded in 1880. On attaining independence, these accountants helped establish the local professional accounting bodies (Susela, 1999; Verma & Gray, 2006) with the support of the state just as the state established local universities. Examples of this include the formation of the Institute of Chartered Accountants of India (ICAI) in 1949 (Verma & Gray, 2006) and the Malaysian Association of Certified Public Accountants (MACPA) in 1958 (Susela, 1999).

The objectives of both the establishment of local universities and local professional bodies in the newly independent countries included economic development, poverty alleviation, and income redistribution, indigenization of knowledge, and the use of local language. To achieve this, the state enacted legislation (the Chartered Accountants Act of 1949 in India and the Malaysian Institute of Accountants [MIA] established by the Accountants Act of 1967 in Malaysia) whereby only members of the local professional bodies could call themselves ("chartered accountants" in India and "accountants" in Malaysia). In this context, the ICAI and MIA were both registration and professional bodies. The two bodies from their inception, however, continued to recognize members of foreign professional accounting bodies, principally those from the United Kingdom and Australia—although this action was not reciprocated.

Globalization, however, transformed the professional landscape in that national professional bodies had "to learn to co-exist with equally powerful and effective supra-national actors" (Faulconbridge & Muzio, 2012, p. 137). Globalization contributed to the emergence of global professional service firms which have sought to become world leaders in the development of practice methodologies (Robson et al., 2007); and claimed their place as global representatives for the accounting profession (Arnold, 2009; Suddaby et al., 2007). Similarly, systems of professional self-regulation (or co-regulation) at the national level has transformed the systems of global self-regulation, with global professional service firms being seen as having mutually compatible interests and agendas. Professional bodies' special relationships with independent global regulatory agencies have helped much in this regard, not least through providing funds to support their activities, participating in standard-setting, and/or influencing governance arrangements and structures (Humphrey et al., 2009; Loft et al., 2006; Malsch & Gendron, 2011).

The above developments have resulted in national accounting professions and their member bodies effectively losing the capacity for "self-determination" (Malsch & Gendron, 2011). Instead, such a capacity has been increasingly shared and re-negotiated within the cohort of new national monitoring and surveillance institutions as well as umbrella organizations established to coordinate their activities at a global level. Additionally, these developments required professional bodies to rethink their relevance and role in the milieu of the accounting profession, and the strategies of the national professional bodies and their potential global significance.

A report commissioned by the New Zealand Society of Accountants—now called Chartered Accountants of Australia and New Zealand (Wheeler Campbell Limited, 1993)—recognized the regulatory role of a professional association, not in the context of a profession but rather as an owner of a brand:

> We propose a conceptual framework which suggests that Society membership signals information about the quality of the services the consumer can expect. The ACA in this context can be seen as a brand, and brand reputation is the primary component of the Chartered Accountant product. (Wheeler Campbell Limited, 1993, p. 3)

The brand, they argued, provides important information about a product or service—based on perceptions of performance or reputation earned in the market—and reduces marketing costs to providers of a service. Velayutham (1998, 1999) argued that this represented the transformation of professional bodies into global franchisors of a brand.

More recently, the development of service branding has been referred to as the emergence of global professional accrediting organizations (Samsonova-Taddei & Humphrey, 2014). In addition, professional bodies have also formed global professional alliances to reinforce and garner benefit from belonging to a certain "global elite" set of national professional bodies, while others have sought to provide more "peripheral" bodies with the means to acquire a stronger voice in the arenas of transnational regulation (Samsonova-Taddei & Humphrey, 2014).

Briston and Kedslie (1997) observed that the end of World War II resulted in a dip in the export of British qualified accountants overseas due to the formation of overseas professional accounting bodies. They observed, however, that since 1970, U.K. accounting bodies have gained members overseas through the export of examinations. Briston and Kedslie (1997) identified the two major exporters as the Association of Chartered Certified Accountants (ACCA) and the Chartered Institute of Management Accountants (CIMA). They observed that between 1969 and 1989 the total membership of the five British accounting bodies (ICAS, ICAEW, Chartered Institute of Public Finance and Accountancy [CIPFA], ACCA, & CIMA) grew from 81,511 to 172,151—an increase of 111%. The individual growth rate for the five bodies was ICAS (51%), ICAEW (95%), CIPFA (102%), CIMA (164%), and ACCA (167%). During this period, the overseas Commonwealth membership of ACCA, increased from 1,376 to 10,250, causing the total proportion of overseas Commonwealth membership to rise from 11% in 1969 to 32% in 1989 (Briston & Kedslie, 1997).

At the end of 2015, ACCA had more than 188,000 members and 480,000 student members in more than 178 countries. Among these new members, more than 110,000 members and 400,000 students came from outside of the United Kingdom (ACCA, 2016). In recent years, ACCA has not been publishing its membership breakdown by country, although its membership has grown to 227,000 (ACCA, 2020). Based on the above statistics, one could argue that ACCA is a global professional body rather than a national accounting body located in the United Kingdom. Globally, CPA Australia has also attempted to become a global professional body with more than 155,000 members in 118 countries (CPA Australia, 2015).

For a long time, the ICAEW did not allow practical work experience to take place overseas, which hindered foreign membership. In 2002, the ICAEW expanded its training network outside the accounting profession and overseas. The result of this is that more than a quarter of its students came from overseas.

Accordingly, one can observe many similarities between transnational education and the emergence of global professional bodies. The two main sources of branch campuses worldwide from Anglophone countries other than the United States have been the United Kingdom and Australia; similarly, the two main global professional accounting bodies are from the United Kingdom and Australia. The delivery of higher education overseas through twinning programs and branch campuses by the United Kingdom and Australian higher education institutions facilitates the expansion of the United Kingdom and Australian professional bodies overseas. Similarly, ACCA has the highest number of members in Malaysia outside the United Kingdom (ACCA, 2016).

THE TRANSNATIONAL HIGHER EDUCATION—GLOBAL PROFESSIONAL BODY SYMBIOSIS IN MALAYSIA

Malaysian Higher Education and the Accounting Profession Before 1997

In Malaysia, the first professional accounting body formed following independence in 1957 was the Malaysian Association of Certified Public Accountants (MACPA), established in 1958. The dominant force behind the MACPA was the chartered accountants (CAs) from the United Kingdom and Australia, and the association sought to exclude qualified accountants from other professional bodies like the ACCA and Australian Society of Accountants (ASA) by stipulating the need to sit for entrance examinations. From 1958 to 1967 there was no legislation to regulate the accountancy profession. During this period there were calls for the establishment of an accountancy registration body by legislation from two main groups—members of foreign professional accounting bodies which were excluded and Malay groups which felt that Malays were excluded from the profession.

The Accountancy Act of 1967 was passed by parliament, providing for the registration of accountants and the establishment of the Malaysian Institute of Accountants (MIA). The MIA recognized 10 professional bodies (the ASA and ACCA included) and graduates of local public universities for admission purposes. However, MACPA continued to dominate the development of the accountancy profession as the MIA was content with the statutory function of registering accountants practicing in the country (Malaysian Institute of Accountants, 1987). In 1987, a majority of ACCA members attended the first Annual General Meeting of MIA and voted in a new council committed to turning MIA into an active regulatory professional body (De Freitas, 1992).

The May 13, 1969 racial riots marked a watershed in the history of the country and had a momentous effect on the country's economic and education policy. Following the riots, there was a change in the leadership of the country and the New Economic Policy was adopted to eradicate poverty and redress economic imbalances between the Malays and the non-Malays with the intent of reducing and eventually eliminating the identification of race with economic function (Selvaratnam, 1988). Higher Education was identified as the key agent in achieving the above objectives through the University and University Colleges (UUC) Act of 1971.

The UUC Act of 1971 provided the state with the power to determine student enrollment, staff appointments, curriculum development, and funding (Morshidi, 2009)—which it exercised extensively. In stages, Malay also replaced English as the medium of instruction in schools and universities. All English medium (national type) schools were converted to national schools, the establishment of new government universities was accelerated, and the establishment of private universities was banned. The only exception was that vernacular primary schools with government support and independent Chinese secondary schools were allowed to continue.

Following the May 13, 1969 riots and the implementation of the New Economic Policy, there was also a concern that Bumiputra (Malay, as distinct from other Malaysian groups including the Malaysian Chinese, Indians, inter alia) participation in accountancy was unsatisfactory and that greater effort was required to promote their entry into the profession. In 1972, the Accountants Act was amended to allow direct entry of local university graduates to MIA membership without requiring further examinations. The MACPA, however, continued to require all non-CA professional body members to sit for its examinations, which began in 1961.

Despite the rapid expansion in their number and size, the country's universities were still unable to meet the rapidly increasing demand for places in higher education, not only for non-Bumiputras, but also Bumiputras themselves. Many non-Bumiputra students—an overwhelming number of whom are of Chinese ethnic origin—who were unable to secure a place in vocationally oriented courses in any of the local universities, felt discriminated against and were drawn to obtain an overseas education (Selvaratnam, 1988). In the late 1990s, more than 100,000 Malaysian students were studying overseas.

In the 1980s, to alleviate the limited number of places in local universities and to reduce the huge outflow of foreign exchange, the government allowed local private institutions to offer bachelor's degrees and other qualifications of foreign universities through twinning and franchise arrangements (Morshidi, 2006). In 1996, the biggest changes to university education since 1971 were introduced. The Education Act of 1996, Private Higher Educational Institutions (PHEI) Act of 1996, National Council on

Higher Education Act of 1996, and the National Accreditation Board Act of 1996 were passed by the Malaysian Parliament, paving the way for different institutional structures and delivery of higher education in Malaysia. The package of laws provided for the liberalization and privatization of higher education to meet the demands for higher education within the country and converting the country into a regional education hub (Knight 2014b; Knight & Morshidi, 2011; Morshidi, 2006; Tham, 2013).

Before 1996, private higher educational institutions in Malaysia had no degree-awarding powers, and when local institutions offered overseas degrees through twinning or franchise arrangements, some parts of the program had to be undertaken in the degree-awarding partner institution (Morshidi, 2006).

Malaysian Higher Education and Accounting Profession Post-1997

The Asian Financial Crisis of 1997 and the devaluation of the Malaysian ringgit provided an important boost to transnational higher education. In 1998, the Ministry of Education allowed the "3 + 0" arrangement where the entire overseas degree could be done in Malaysia, and in 2003 the PHEI Act of 1996 was amended to provide for the establishment of branch campuses of foreign universities in Malaysia (Morshidi, 2006).

As pointed out earlier, before the introduction of transnational higher education to Malaysia in 1998, the ACCA already had a strong presence in the country. The ACCA membership in Malaysia mainly consisted of non-Bumiputras who qualified from overseas universities or who did not have a degree and completed the ACCA exams starting from the foundation level. The amendment of the Accountancy Act of 1967 in 1972 to allow direct entry of local university graduates to membership of MIA achieved its objective of increasing the number of Bumiputera accountants, but created two classes of accountants within MIA—MIA members who gained membership through membership of other professional bodies which is dominated by non-Bumiputra's, and members who gained membership through degrees from local universities dominated by Bumiputra's. Table 2.1 also highlights

TABLE 2.1 MIA Membership—Bumiputera (as of 2004)

	Bumiputra	Non-Bumiputra	Total
Professional	857 (4.2%)	13,844 (68.5%)	14,701 (72.8%)
Local Graduates	3,194 (15.8%)	2,312 (11.5%)	5,506 (27.2%)
Total	4,051 (20.0%)	16,156 (80.0%)	20,207 (100.0%)

Source: Susela (2010)

the large imbalance between the number of Bumiputera accountants (20%) and non-Bumiputra accountants (80%; Susela, 2010).

The establishment of the 3 + 0 arrangement, where the entire overseas degree could be completed in Malaysia, provided the ACCA with a new market for members. ACCA extended the same exemptions to graduates who completed the British 3 + 0 programs as graduates of British home universities in Britain. ACCA then began recognizing the accounting degrees of local private universities and offering the same subject exemptions to their graduates as it did to British university graduates.

The lack of uniform professional exams by MIA for all aspiring members has meant variations in the quality of MIA members, contributing to employers preferring members of ACCA, CPA Australia, and CIMA. This is reflected in ACCA having 12,521 members in Malaysia (the largest number outside the United Kingdom (ACCA, 2016). Following the report by Soliman et al. (2018), it was revealed that the chief financial officers (CFO) of publicly listed companies did not recognize the local professional accounting body (MIA) as keenly as they did qualifications from ACCA and other foreign professional accounting bodies. Membership of the Malaysian Institute of Certified Public Accountants (MICPA), while recognized by professional bodies outside Malaysia, did not receive special recognition, either by MIA or other government organizations. MICPA members, therefore, received the same recognition as other members of MIA affiliated with other professional bodies like ICAEW, ACCA, CIMA, CAANZ, and CPA Australia.

Aspiring accountants who desired nationally as well as internationally recognized accounting qualifications were also more attracted to membership in foreign professional bodies like ICAEW, ACCA, CIMA, and CPA Australia—as the qualifications were more recognized and portable overseas as compared to MICPA membership. Membership of foreign professional bodies identified earlier was particularly attractive to Malaysians with a desire to migrate overseas (Iredale, 2001).

Following the above attitude of CFOs, government agencies like Yayasan Peneraju and Talent Corp have started promoting overseas accounting qualifications among Bumiputras (Yayasan Peneraju Pendidikan Bumiputera, n.d.). Malaysian government universities have also sought ACCA recognition of their degrees so that their graduates gain exemptions when sitting for ACCA professional examinations. The popularity of foreign professional bodies is also evident from the statistics of new members admitted to MIA from 2012 to 2016 (see Table 2.2; MIA stopped publishing breakdowns in its annual report after 2016). As can be seen in all 3 years, new members admitted to MIA were dominated by ACCA and CPA Australia, with the ACCA proportion averaging 30%. The percentage of new members admitted to MIA from MICPA only averaged less than 1%.

TABLE 2.2 MIA Categorization of New Members by Original Professional Bodies and Government Universities

	2012	2014	2016
MICPA	15	13	13
ICAEW	12	19	25
ACCA	406	322	407
ICAANZ	22	7	4
CPA Australia	179	155	176
CIMA	39	29	34
Government University Graduates	1,044	676	772
Total	**1,717**	**1,221**	**1,431**

In 2009, MICPA ceased its examinations and signed a memorandum of understanding (MoU) with the Institute of Chartered Accountants Australia (ICAA) to deliver a joint professional accounting program in Malaysia, granting graduates of the program the eligibility to become members of both institutes, mutual recognition for members of both institutes, and collaboration in the organizing of thought leadership events in Malaysia. Following the merger of ICAA and the New Zealand Institute of Chartered Accountants (NZICA) to establish the Chartered Accountants Australia and New Zealand (CAANZ) in 2014, graduates of the joint program will henceforth obtain two professional qualifications and be entitled to use the credentials CPA (Malaysia) and CA (ANZ) as members of both institutes.

TRANSNATIONAL HIGHER EDUCATION INSTITUTIONS AS AGENTS OF GLOBALIZATION AND THEIR IMPLICATION FOR DEVELOPING COUNTRIES

Transnational higher education is usually seen as an outcome of globalization rather than an agent of globalization (Coleman, 2003; Knight, 2014a). The previous section shows that transnational higher education institutions, which are an outcome of globalization, may also become agents of globalization. Prior studies in critical accounting (Gendron & Barrett 2004; O'Dwyer et al., 2011) offer insights from the past into the role of accounting institutions—for example, the global professional accounting firms (the Big Four) in the globalizing of the world economy. Arnold (2005) provides a detailed analysis of the activities of the Big Four and their relationship with the World Trade Association (WTO). The author outlines how global accountancies have helped construct and deploy particular WTO-backed institutional arrangements (such as the General Agreement on Trade in

Services articles relating to domestic regulation) which in effect facilitate the international expansion of the Big Four and their clients.

The above overview highlights two major phases or regimes in the development of Malaysian higher education policy and the development of universities and professions in Malaysia. In the first phase between independence in 1957 and 1997, the state adopted policies to indigenize the Malaysian higher education institutions as well as the professions in the country. This included the adoption of the national language (Malay) by the local universities and public service as well as affirmative action policies to increase the number of Bumiputra (Malay) professionals. The policies contributed to a substantial increase in the number of Bumiputra graduates and their proportion in the managerial labor force (H. Lee, 2012). However, they also provided the perfect ground for the practice of personal influence or political patronage and corruption (Selvaratnam, 1988).

The post-1996 period after the Asian economic crisis can be considered the second phase of higher education and professional development in Malaysia. The Asian economic crisis exposed the weak corporate governance systems and affirmative action policies in Malaysia. The drop in the value of the Malaysian ringgit also put stress on a lot of Malaysian students' ability to continue their higher education in the United States and the United Kingdom. Malaysia decided to enter the transnational higher education market by liberalizing education, in general, and higher education, specifically. It was felt that the policy would help stem the outflow of valuable foreign currency and at the same time attract foreign currency into the country. In the above environment, local government educational institutions and professional bodies realized that Malay as a medium of instruction in schools and universities would not attract overseas students to Malaysia and changed their language policies.

Globalization makes the world of centers and peripheries more complex (Altbach, 1998a). The modern powerful universities and professional bodies currently located in the major (mostly Western) international academic centers have dominated the production and distribution of knowledge rank suggests that the higher education market is characterized by a winner-take-all environment. This situation is prevalent not only globally but also within countries. In recent years there have been exceptions to this with the emergence of world-class research institutions in Japan, Korea, Hong Kong, China, and Singapore because of their economic progress, but this is the exception rather than the norm. Altbach (1998b) argues that the entry price deters fuller integration. There are two major cost categories—first, investment in laboratory facilities, equipment, information technology, and databases, and second, attraction of high-quality academics. The two are closely related as the second is impossible to achieve without the first. As the Malaysian evidence indicates, the international mobility of instructors and students makes the ability of Malaysian universities to attract top talent very difficult—a prerequisite for world-class status. The ability of universities in developing countries to attract talent is also further compounded by the prevalence of nepotism and discrimination in developing countries (Iredale, 2001).

The Malaysian evidence indicates that developing countries which establish policies that promote transnational education can have serious implications for domestic socioeconomic objectives. First, the development of transnational education locally not only has an impact on educational institutions but also other local institutions—for example, professional bodies. The qualifications of local professional bodies become less attractive because they are only recognized locally; hence, they are not transferrable overseas and therefore impede the mobility of its members globally. This has contributed to the membership of local professional bodies like the MICPA stagnating, whilst the membership is growing within the MICPA (2016) and ACCA (2016).

Second, the government's ability to promote the development and usage of the local language will not only be constrained but also conflict with transnational education since students have a choice, and individuals who possess qualification from the English language higher education institution are not only more marketable locally but also globally as the Malaysian evidence indicates. Malay graduates from local public institutions where Malay is used extensively have a disadvantage not only outside the country but also in the local job market as highlighted by H. Lee and Khalid (2016). The future of many local languages in developing countries will become perilous.

Third, the Malaysian evidence also raises major questions on the potency of affirmative action policies. The Malaysian affirmative action policies were effective in the 1970s and 1980s because the state could control entry into institutions of higher education and therefore control the number of graduates overall—as well as in specific disciplines—and hence, to some extent, employment. Although control was never complete even then because of student mobility programs, it was on a very limited scale. Private and transnational higher education removes government control over entry into institutions of higher education making affirmative action policies impotent and probably counterproductive when the economically disadvantaged group is being favored.

CONCLUSION

Transnational education has become a feature of the education scene of many developing countries. While the forces, motivations, rationales, and strategies of transnational higher education have been extensively discussed, research regarding their relationship to professional work, professional standards, and professional bodies is scarce. Malaysia has been at the center and is an early mover amongst developing countries in transnational higher education in both allowing the establishment of private higher education institutions and branch campuses of foreign universities as well as receiving full-fee-paying students from African and other Asian countries.

This chapter highlighted the symbiotic relationship between transnational higher education providers and global professional bodies. The chapter specifically explored the strategic alliances and joint marketing initiatives by U.K.-based transnational higher education institutions and a U.K.-based global professional body—the ACCA—in Malaysia. The findings call for a broadening of the research agenda to better elucidate the critical role of transnational higher education providers as agents of economic globalization. More specifically, transnational education has a major impact on other institutions like local higher education institutions and professional bodies. It also constrains the state's ability to undertake affirmative action policies and specific language development policies, as in a globalized world, market forces are stronger than national government policies.

CHAPTER 3

EXPLORING THE USE OF UNIVERSAL DESIGN FOR LEARNING TO REDUCE THE PEDAGOGICAL TENSION CREATED BY THE INTERNATIONALIZATION OF THE HIGHER EDUCATION CLASSROOM

Frederic Fovet

CONTEXT AND INTRODUCTION

There are many obvious benefits to the internationalization of the higher education (HE) landscape in Global North (GN) countries. The GN is used in this chapter to broadly describe countries having attained a level of post-industrial development, which places them generically in a category of nations sharing similar characteristics and features in relation to the organization, modus operandi, and funding model of the HE sector. It is acknowledged that the Global North versus Global South terminology has limitations and can be increasingly challenged (Horner, 2020), but it does allow for the examination of important features of the HE landscape within a global sector with some homogeneous characteristics. This terminology and its use in this chapter also recognizes that internationalization of HE might have very different objectives and features in developing countries. Within this broad category of countries, beyond the clear appeal of increased revenue and sustainable development for these campuses (Buckner, 2019), internationalization of the post-secondary sector leads to the development of global citizenship (Massaro, 2020), cultural competency (Flammia et al., 2019), and social capital across border boundaries (Rathburn & Lexier, 2016).

Though marketing strategies aiming to steadily increase the percentage of international students admitted to GN campuses are effective and constantly improving, the inclusion of these students in the HE classroom has not kept pace (Moriña, 2017). International students face significant barriers in their access to learning (Agostinelli, 2021); many instructors on the other hand report feeling challenged by the specific needs of these culturally diverse learners (Wu et al., 2015). This tension increases exponentially as the percentage of international students rises sharply. The simplest way to conceptualize this tension is to identify the degree to which HE teaching has remained traditional and ethnocentric, despite a discourse advocating internationalization (Zelenková & Hanesová, 2019); this ethnocentrism creates very real barriers for international students as they arrive and attempt to adapt to the host institution (Wu et al., 2015). In some extreme cases this clash has become public, with instructors condemning the internationalization of the HE classroom (Worthington & Taylor, 2019), and this criticism has been perceived by universities as dangerous to their visibility and credibility (Knaus, 2019).

There is a need for rich and authentic pedagogical reflection to keep up with the tempo of internationalization, and for models to be developed to support instructors in their search for new best practices for inclusion in the internationalized classroom (Tran & Nguyen, 2015). This chapter will argue that universal design for learning (UDL) is uniquely positioned to fill this gap—supporting instructors as they shift away from a deficit view of international students and providing a sustainable framework for the authentic inclusion of international students in the classroom (Fovet, 2019).

The first section of this chapter has set the context and showcases the tension which currently exists within the internationalized HE classroom with regards to the pedagogical inclusion of international students. The second section introduces UDL and demonstrates the ways it can be used as a tool to support instructors and reduce this tension. The third section introduces and analyzes the phenomenological data drawn from the lived experience of the author to illustrate specific ways UDL offers immediate solutions to the current crisis faced by the post-secondary sector, as it increases the tempo of internationalization. The author was, for 3 years, academic lead on a Canadian master's program in education specifically catering to the needs of international students.

EXPLORING THE EXISTING LITERATURE

Before the chapter examines the use of UDL in the creation of inclusive provisions in a landscape of increased internationalization, this section reviews existing literature, which is useful to contextualize the reflection proposed here. The concepts examined here are crucial in navigating the observations to follow in the later part of the chapter.

The Internationalization of Higher Education

The internationalization of HE has rapidly increased over the last decade in the GN (de Wit, 2020). There have been many arguments for the rapid growth of this phenomenon. Internationalization is seen as conducive to (a) the creation of global citizenship on our campuses (Massaro, 2022), (b) the development of social capital across cultures and jurisdictions (Luo & Jamieson-Drake, 2013), (c) the acquisition of cultural competency (Alexiadou et al., 2021), and of course (d) the increase of cross-border travel and employment opportunities (Coelen & Gribble, 2019). It is, however, undoubtedly the economic argument that has been the main driver of HE internationalization (Loudenback, 2016). Revenue generated by the enrollment of international students is in many cases the only funding which allows post-secondary institutions to remain sustainable (Ansari, 2020; Bound et al., 2021). Internationalization of HE did not just happen organically; it has been generated by intense and strategic marketing campaigns, which target specific countries and, in many cases, use recruiting agents and local consultants (Collins, 2012; Robinson-Pant & Magyar, 2018). The theoretical underpinning of this drive is therefore firmly neoliberal, and this chapter examines the tension which exists between this neoliberal push and the pedagogical inclusion of international students in the classroom—a process grounded in critical theory (Buckner et al., 2021).

The commercial process of internationalization has the result of increasing international enrollment but overall little focus is placed on the pedagogical transformation that is required in HE in order to support the authentic inclusion of these students in the classroom (Guo & Guo, 2017). In many ways, the increased internationalization of the HE classroom ought to connect to the scholarship on critical pedagogy (Han & Zhang, 2021), critical race theory (Henry et al., 2017; Houshmand et al., 2014), and the decolonization of the curriculum (Charles, 2019). Instead, much of the work carried out in relation to the inclusion of international students in HE has focused on campus climate, social integration, and the overall perceptions these students have of the host campus, rather than their experiences with teaching and learning (Applebaum, 2019; Glass et al., 2014). Even when attention has been given to the social integration of international students on campus spaces, this reflection has remained fairly superficial and often amounts to mere lip service (Martirosyan et al., 2019) rather than to a genuine political awareness of the shifts in power dynamics which are necessary to offer these students the right of voice and empowerment (Zhang, 2017).

Inclusion of International Students

There are very specific barriers experienced by international students in the HE classroom. The literature focuses mostly on the issue of mastery in the language of instruction (Aizawa et al., 2020; Uchihara & Harada, 2018). International students might arrive in the host country with very strong academic backgrounds but they might not master the target language sufficiently at the time of their arrival to produce or access academic writing (Bradford, 2019; Trenkic & Warmington, 2019). This is the main reason why a negative stigma is so often attached to international students in HE. Regardless of their academic ability, the first impression of instructors is that there is friction when it comes to the immediate consumption of academic literature and to the production of formal academic writing (Macaro et al., 2018; Martirosyan et al., 2015; Pessoa et al., 2014).

Language mastery, however, is not the only hurdle experienced by international students. Often instruction and assessment is ethnocentric in nature and makes considerable assumptions as to the learners' familiarity with many teaching and learning practices (Gelb, 2012; Wu et al., 2015). There is often such an extensive use of the deficit model lens (Heng, 2018), and such a focus on the acquisition of the language of instruction, that in most cases little attention is paid to the fact that significant assumptions are made about international students' grasp of expectation and teaching staff at host institutions continue to fail to make these expectations more explicit (Agostinelli, 2021; Chen & Van Ullen, 2011; Yeh et al., 2021). Very few programs or courses take the time to unpack these expectations in a way which is not ethnocentric, or to formulate them in a way which is appropriately differentiated (Skyrme & McGee, 2016; Yefanova et al., 2017).

The ethnocentric nature and format of instruction and assessment is another problem faced by international students. Beyond issues of design, teaching can have the effect of making these learners feel marginalized and isolated. Microaggressions are a common phenomenon (Wong et al., 2014), and while marketing policies encourage increased internationalization of the classroom, mindsets have not always evolved; instructors are not always receptive to international learners, their needs, or their perspectives (Jin & Schneider, 2019). As a result, international students can be stigmatized in the classroom, made to feel ostracized, and generally are not offered optimal conditions for success (Freeman & Li, 2019). Negative attitudes towards international students can also be manifested by fellow students. This can affect learning when perceptions and attitudes of peers affect teamwork, collaborative learning, and socio-constructivist classroom objectives and processes (Khoshlessan, 2013; Straker, 2020; Zhu & Bresnahan, 2018).

UNIVERSAL DESIGN FOR LEARNING

UDL is a framework for inclusion which positions itself very differently than more traditional approaches such as personalized learning (Shemshack & Spector, 2020), individualized learning (Pino & Mortari, 2014)—both of which usually take the form of accommodations in a HE setting—or differentiated instruction (Jørgensen & Brogaard, 2021). These three traditional stances—while advocating for equal access to education—retain a deficit model view of the exceptional learner: the learner is seen as having needs that are unusual and require specific interventions. UDL on the other hand sees learner diversity as a given and encourages the instructor to prepare for it proactively, addressing it with the systematic use of inclusive design (Rao & Meo, 2016). UDL, in fact, importantly positions itself as the translation of the social model of disability into classroom practices (Fovet, 2014). The social model argues that disability is not an inherent characteristic of the individual, but is instead the result of a tension between individual embodiments and experiences, products, or spaces which are not designed to address and include these (Goering, 2015). UDL builds on this theoretical stance and argues that the burden—in inclusive education—is on the educator to design instruction and assessment with optimal flexibility so as to avoid this friction, or lack of it (Fornauf & Erickson, 2020).

In order to support instructors in this inclusive design process, UDL offers three user-friendly, common sense, and intuitive principles: multiple means of representation (offering optimal flexibility in the way information is presented to the student); multiple means of action and expression (offering the learner optimal flexibility in the way they are required to provide information, complete assessment, make contributions, demonstrate participation, and create content); multiple means of engagement (integrating optimal flexibility in the way instructors conceive and define learner engagement, and optimal flexibility in the way students are offered opportunities to create affective connections between the content of learning and their lived experience; Kennette & Wilson, 2019). These three design principles can be used separately or collectively; they can be applied to an analysis of either instruction or assessment (Rao & Meo, 2016). They enable instructors to identify the barriers that students might encounter in their access to learning, and to erode these with the use of a progressive inclusive design process (Dalton et al., 2019).

There has not been significant use of UDL in the context of internationalization of the HE classroom, but this is a field where scholarship is emerging (Fovet, 2019). There has definitely been some exploration of how UDL can support culturally diverse learners in a domestic context (Chita-Tegmark et al., 2012). There is also growing overlap between the scholarships on UDL and culturally responsive pedagogy (Kieran & Anderson, 2019; Pearson, 2015). It therefore seems logical and desirable that UDL ought to start being seen as increasingly more relevant in relation to the inclusion of international students in HE (Steunpunt Inclusief Hoger Onderwijs, 2021). It can be useful and immediately pertinent in reducing the tension that otherwise mounts between the neoliberal push for greater international student recruitment on the one hand and friction regarding ethnocentrism of pedagogical practices.

METHODOLOGICAL REFLECTION

The broad methodological lens adopted in this chapter is phenomenology. Phenomenology is an approach to research which focuses on the analysis of the lived experiences which individuals have of a phenomenon as a way of understanding how it is being perceived and addressed by those which it affects (Leonor, 2020). The subjective sensemaking of these individuals becomes the target of the analysis in such studies, as it offers researchers wider understanding of how individuals navigate the realities of social environments armed with the help of their lived experience (Petitmengin et al., 2019). Phenomenology is popular within the investigation of organizational processes and management of change (Gill, 2014); it has become increasingly useful in educational contexts (Webb & Welsh, 2019). In this chapter, it is the lived experience of the author as a stakeholder, having personally navigated the tension described above as an instructor and as an academic lead, that yields the observations and offers the themes developed in the analysis. The author's lived experience of the central phenomenon described here is relatively unique and exceptional, in the sense that I approached the obvious tension existing in the program through his lens as an accessibility specialist. This approach enabled us to avoid common instructor strategies and views, frequently grounded in a deficit model approach. The author's lived experience illustrates the needs of international students from the point of view of an accessibility professional, and provides a narrative that allows a rich and unusual analysis. The phenomenological analysis of auto-biographical narratives—as well as its use as a theoretical setting for the purposes of auto-ethnography—is common now in social sciences when authors have unusual and pertinent experiences with a phenomenon around which meaning making is ongoing (Pitard, 2019; Tawfik, 2021).

The author was an instructor for 3 years at a university in Atlantic Canada, and he taught principally on a master's stream in education (MED) catering mainly to international students. As an instructor teaching students who were new to Canada, he developed, within his practice, strategies to create inclusive conditions for these specific cohorts. He quickly came to realize the usefulness of UDL as part of these strategies. He had previously held a leadership position in accessibility on another campus during his PhD studies. In this role, he had been instrumental in rolling out UDL among faculties for a more effective inclusion of students with disabilities. UDL appeared as an equally effective framework in this new professional context, and the transfer of his reflection and expertise around UDL to the internationalized classroom was fairly seamless. Beyond his own professional reflection within his classroom, the author also held the role of academic lead within the Master of Education in question. As such, he had the opportunity to support contract instructors as they themselves addressed the realities of the internationalized classroom, often with great struggles. He was able to use UDL in supporting these instructors. This chapter represents a summary, a thematic coding, and an analysis of this lived professional experience.

USING UNIVERSAL DESIGN FOR LEARNING TO CREATE INCLUSIVE PROVISIONS WITHIN A LANDSCAPE OF INTENSIFIED INTERNATIONALIZATION

The author's experiences around the use of UDL in the internationalized HE classroom have been coincidental. Having just finished 4 years of intensive UDL rollout work from the perspective of accessibility, he shifted overnight to an instructor position overseeing a Master of Education stream catering principally to international students. The shift of the UDL strategies to the inclusion of international students was organic, intuitive, and fairly seamless. Few stakeholders in this landscape, however, are exposed to UDL scholarship and practice as a matter of course. This chapter argues that these opportunities must be increased rapidly and that this area of implementation must become a pressing focus for all campuses. This section illustrates the extent to which UDL can be useful in the inclusion of international students. It does not seek to position itself as an exhaustive description but rather offers the reader illustrations as triggers for reflection.

Avoiding Deficit Model Approaches With International Students

UDL has traditionally been used in the context of disability and impairment in HE (Dalton et al., 2019). There is no reason, however, why its use ought to be restricted to this context. UDL translates the social model of disability into action and, as such, it helps shift instructors away from a deficit model approach (Sharma & Portelli, 2014) and towards an inclusive design mindset, within which diversity is seen as the norm and the onus is placed on the educator to design instruction and assessment proactively in an accessible and inclusive fashion.

The process in practice includes shifting from a focus on individual learner exceptionality to a proactive scan of the learning experiences and an analysis of the potential barriers to full access to these experiences. It quickly became apparent to the author that this barrier analysis is very similar whichever dimension of learner diversity one considers. International students experience barriers to learning in the classroom which are very similar—if not identical—to those encountered by students with disabilities, but also those identified by Indigenous students, culturally diverse domestic students, first generation students, and students facing socioeconomic challenges, and so on. The deficit model approaches certainly impact the classroom experiences of international students, and the barriers which they face overlap with those experienced by many other diverse learners. UDL is therefore uniquely useful in shifting pedagogical mindsets in the internationalized classroom.

The rest of this section of the chapter will provide illustrations of the ways UDL can be useful to instructors as they reflect on ways to make pedagogy more hospitable and more inclusive for international students. For the purpose of convenience, these illustrations have been categorized using the three UDL principles as headings, but it is acknowledged that often a reflection on classroom practices uses the three principles simultaneously in ways which overlap, rather than in a way which is so sharply fragmented or categorized.

Multiple Means of Representation

This UDL principle usually—within the context of accessibility—encourages instructors to consider the use of alternate formats when presenting information to students. Reflection around representation, however, does not need to be limited to format and ought to extend to flexibility in content itself. Such design thinking will be essential to international students who might at times—for reasons of varying fluency in the target language—experience challenges with the terminology and formality of academic writing. A good example of how a UDL reflection can become immediately pertinent in this context involves the intentional use of the learning management system (LMS) to offer students multiple pathways to the essential concepts of a course. Instead of posting and archiving a single reading, the LMS can become a tool to scaffold and differentiate sources, offering international students multiple ways to engage with and master key content (Fovet, 2018). Readings offered on the LMS can vary in length, degree of formality, level of language, degree of conceptualization, and complexity.

Another key reflection involves the provision of class slides ahead of time (Smith et al., 2019). While there are concerns among instructors that providing slides in advance has an impact on attendance (Chipchase et al., 2017), this practice has proven to be key with international students as it allows them to use strength-based strategies to familiarize themselves with terminology, language, and concepts which might be novel to them ahead of class. This in turn increases engagement and participation (Macgregor & Folinazzo, 2018). The author has encouraged instructors within the program for which he acted as academic lead to offer slides ahead of class as a matter of routine. The author has observed that in many cases international students not only access the material to clarify language and terminology, but will often contact the instructor to address any gaps in concepts and readings they identify as being problematic in terms of their understanding of content or as requiring their attention ahead of the class. Instructors who engage with this practice quickly and organically shift from a deficit view of international students to a perception of them as engaged and committed beyond the norm.

Multiple Means of Action and Expression

This UDL principle is most frequently mentioned and used when it comes to redesigning assessment in an inclusive way (Morris et al., 2019). Offering flexibility and ensuring accessibility in the assessment format is important for all learners, but international students encounter specific challenges in this area and UDL will be key in terms of developing instructor awareness around this topic (Fovet, 2020a). It is, first of all, essential when grading rubrics to be as explicit and detailed as possible, as international students might not be familiar with assessment practices used in the host country. The reflection, however, must go beyond this initial basic task. The assessment directives themselves might involve a significant amount of implicit messaging, which is only grasped by domestic students.

These directives will not only need to be detailed and clear, but will also need to explain and unpack all terminology and concepts. Explaining these nuances in written, video, and audio format might offer optimal opportunities to reframe the expectations in slightly different ways and to eliminate all confusion (Fovet, 2019). The author has repeatedly had the opportunity to observe how even the most committed and culturally receptive of instructors might be using terminology or concepts in assessment directives which are unknown or misleading to international students; this, in turn, creates confusion and leads to failure, though there are in fact no hurdles to international students demonstrating the appropriate competency when they have a lucid and clear understanding of the objective. A simple example the author has encountered is how students in faculties of education are regularly asked to journal field experiences; they might not have had any prior experiences in their home programs of what journaling entails; nor might they yet have had time to gain the type of field experiences in the host country which the assignment targets.

Multiple Means of Engagement

Using this UDL principle in examining classroom practices is usually the design task that is met with the least resistance from instructors. Most instructors, indeed, feel they already consider how to engage learners in varied ways as a routine pedagogical process. Offering multiple means of engagement to learners, however, involves more than just diversifying tasks for greater student engagement. It requires instructors to reconsider the very ways they construe engagement and formulate their expectations in relation to it. Instructors usually quickly realize—when using this UDL principle as a lens to examine their practice—how narrow and teacher-centric their existing concept of learner engagement is. It becomes rapidly obvious to them that learner engagement can only be achieved when students have an affective investment in learning, and when course content connects in authentic ways with their personal interests and lived experiences.

For international students, this might occur authentically in even rarer occasions than for domestic students—as the curriculum is generally not designed with them in mind—and they might require even further flexibility and choice in order to be able to assert their preferences and establish their choices. UDL will be a key tool in shifting instructors away from teacher-centric views of the curriculum. The literature has already evidenced how using UDL supports instructors in creating more authentic connections with course content among culturally diverse domestic students. It overlaps significantly with critical pedagogy in this respect (Fovet, 2020b). An example of what this reflection might involve in the internationalized classroom is an increased awareness on the part of the instructor of how the core concepts of a course might need to be contextualized appropriately for international students before they are introduced. The author experienced for example how within an MEd program, several key course outcomes made no sense when international students had little practical understanding of the contemporary challenges observed in the Canadian K–12 sectors. This led to the creation of additional non-evaluated activities to allow these students to progressively grow their understanding of the North American K–12 classrooms and of the key current stakes which are of concern within this landscape. These activities included an exploration of the domestic educational press in weekly seminars and in the creation of a film club focused on movies from popular culture focused on schools—two forums where these students had the opportunity to deepen their understanding of context and to connect the course content to their own lived experiences.

REPERCUSSIONS OF THIS REFLECTION FOR THE FIELD

There are imminent repercussions emerging from this reflection, in relation to the strategic and sustainable development of the HE sector.

Developing a UDL Mindset Among Instructors

UDL has not thus far been used when supporting instructors who are teaching international students. There is therefore an immediate and pressing need for professional development around the use of UDL for international students. While effective resources related to the implementation of UDL in HE have begun to emerge, very little of this material addresses the needs of international students, and the focus remains primarily students with disabilities (Fleet & Kondrashov, 2019). A considerable amount of strategic work is therefore required before instructors become aware of the pertinence of UDL in this context and they grow competent in using it for this purpose.

UDL implementation and integration are, in any event, not simple and seamless processes in HE. There are many factors that make the adoption of UDL by HE instructors challenging. UDL implementation can be perceived as amounting to increased workload (Moriña et al., 2020). There can be fears that UDL necessarily requires extensive technological competency (Ableser & Moore, 2018). Instructors can also feel that the burden of inclusive design is too overwhelming, or they can be caught up in a deficit model vision of diverse students which hinders the adoption of UDL or social model approaches (Fornauf & Erickson, 2020). UDL adoption and implementation amount to a shift in mindset, which is complex, multilayered, and highly political. Addressing the hurdles inherently present in this process of change requires the use of an ecological lens, which offers advocates and promoters of the framework an adequate mapping of the numerous challenges (Fovet, 2021b).

Supporting International Students Through Transitional Friction

It would be naïve to assume that instructors are the only stakeholders who experience challenges when encountering UDL. Students might be unsettled when first introduced to UDL. Being offered more flexibility means having more choice, and having more choice means having to make more decisions. Although UDL is conducive to the creation of rich, fully accessible, student-centered learning conditions, at first it might seem daunting to learners. It can certainly be perceived as representing more work and effort. Learners can also feel disconcerted when they need to adapt to UDL practices for one class but are then asked to return to traditional directive teaching in other courses. As a result, they might at first be reluctant to fully embrace UDL and to explore it. This can be described as transitional friction.

It usually subsides quickly, but must be addressed explicitly. Transparent communication is essential. Students must understand the purpose and rationale of UDL implementation. There has often been poor communication occurring with the student body in recent campus initiatives related to UDL across North America, and this can threaten the successful implementation of the model. International students who are themselves often transitioning from teaching and learning models which are very different from those used in the GN can already be in a state of upheaval as they arrive in the host country and are adapting to the HE classroom. Being confronted with UDL in some courses but not others can be further unsettling to international students and they will require very explicit messaging to understand the process they are experiencing.

Creating an Osmotic Dialogue Between Instructors and International Support Staff

International support staff have traditionally been actively involved in addressing the challenges that international students can experience in relation to campus life, social interaction, accommodation, employment, demanding administrative tasks and requirements, and student affairs issues (Cho & Yu, 2015; Martirosyan et al., 2019). They have, however, always been very hesitant to tackle issues related to the pedagogical practices even if these might be essential to address when it comes to fully including international students. Hierarchical power dynamics, furthermore, make it very strenuous for these international support staff to engage directly with instructors.

It will be important to break these silos and create new practices and interactions that can support and ease frank discussions between these two groups of stakeholders (Glass et al., 2021). Support staff who support international students often have the most accurate understanding of the ways ethnocentric pedagogical practices are creating hurdles for these learners (Page & Chahboun, 2019). Instructors will benefit from an open dialogue with these staff members once such discussions are expected to take place, becoming more common practice (Stein et al., 2016). It would be fair to say that neither of these stakeholder groups currently has access to extensive or effective UDL resources. Both groups of stakeholders will therefore simultaneously have to gain mastery over the UDL framework, familiarize themselves with the terminology associated with it, and learn to use UDL as a common discourse to understand the pedagogical struggles of international students.

Contextualizing This Reflection in a COVID Landscape

The spread of the COVID-19 virus from 2019 to 2022 led to a world pandemic which caused campus closures, a pivot to fully online or blended instruction, and a major disruption of the process of internationalization of the HE sector (Woicolesco et al., 2021; Yıldırım et al., 2021). It has been easy for campuses to set aside the issue of the inclusion of international students over the duration of the pandemic, as most of these students were no longer physically present in these institutions. With a lack of mobility of international students came a desire on the part of campuses to dismiss many of the issues raised in this chapter.

This has, in many ways, had disastrous effects, as international students have continued to register for programs and simply remained at home—depending entirely on online instruction and assessment. The pandemic and the online pivot have considerably increased the gap that already existed in terms of inclusion between domestic students and their international counterparts (Day et al., 2021). International students have had to navigate hastily designed online teaching and learning, within which ethnocentrism has increased and become more pronounced. International students have also not had the same degree of support from student services and student affairs. This has led to increased feelings of isolation, and considerable challenges in the classroom (Yu, 2021). Ethnocentric classroom practices have been devastating and insurmountable for international students who have been attempting to adapt to new teaching and learning formats from a distance—and with very little support.

It is difficult at this stage to predict the lessons that will be learned in HE from the COVID-19 crisis, or how rapidly the internationalization of the sector will return to previous patterns. It is fair to assert, however, that the pandemic has greatly increased the dynamics and challenges described in this chapter. There will also be concerns that it might take many years before focus returns to the need to create inclusive provisions for international students through the use of UDL. It is regrettable that the inclusion of international students is no longer seen as a priority in the current post-pandemic landscape, as the online pivot of 2020 has also in fact shown the extent to which all instructors consistently play the role of designer of the learning experience, and have the power to make learners included or disabled. There is a missed opportunity here for any HE instructor reflecting on how to break free from perpetuated ethnocentric classroom practices. Many of the design choices instructors faced during the COVID-19 crisis indeed were made overnight, and with very little support; most instructors have become highly aware of the impact of the design on their practices on the inclusion of diverse learners, and UDL now appears as an extremely timely tool (Fovet, 2021a).

CONCLUSION

HE is currently in a state of disruption. Internationalization has been essential to the survival of the post-secondary sector and its sustainable development, but this phenomenon has also rapidly accelerated the need for transformation and metamorphosis, which was beginning to become apparent prior to the pandemic. This need for change is particularly apparent in the area of pedagogy. It would be difficult to claim that conventional HE pedagogy has any hope of surviving into the 21st century landscape, irrespective of the presence of international students in the post-secondary classroom, but the rapid internationalization of the sector has acted as an acid test and has demonstrated how inadequate and antiquated many classroom practices have become. The needs of international students will probably finally make evident the need for the adoption and rapid implementation of UDL in a landscape where the needs of students with disabilities have thus far been surprisingly insufficient to trigger systemic change. It becomes increasingly apparent, indeed, that if campuses wish to continue to rely on the considerable revenue which is generated by international enrollment—a source of funding which has proven irreplaceable during the COVID-19 pandemic—they will also need to simultaneously create genuine and systemic practices to ensure the inclusion of international students in the classroom. UDL will prove to be a key tool for this shift in mindset.

CHAPTER 4

GOVERNANCE AND INTERNATIONALIZATION IN EUROPEAN UNIVERSITIES

Francisco Valderrey
Íñigo Arbiol
Mike Szymanski

The internationalization of universities continues to move forward, despite the challenges of the crisis originated by COVID-19. The pandemic has caused human pain and economic destruction while accelerating processes such as the digitalization of enterprises and their repercussions in the disparity of income distribution and the technological divide among nations or entire segments of the population. The hardships of COVID-19 extend to most sectors of society, as happened with education, with pressure from underlying demographic changes and demands to increase the quality of teaching or to foster its alignment to the needs of the industry. The pandemic has taken a heavy toll on universities, with an abrupt decrease in the number of enrolled students, steep budgetary cuts, and a feeling of uneasiness of instructors and students alike (UNESCO, 2020), placing higher education (HE) at the mercy of unpredictable movements.

Notwithstanding those adversities, some universities have proven their resilience and continued internationalization. At the core of advances in the universities' internationalization process might stand those changes in governance which provide a competitive edge to some institutions. Indeed, adequate governance appears to propel some universities' growth or provide reasonable stability in turbulent times, but the question is whether or not facts might prove such a claim. Answering such a question is at the center of this chapter.

After the introduction, we briefly review the concept of governance and internationalization in HE before moving into a geographic scenario full of potential for analyzing the intersection of governance and internationalization of universities. Arguably, no other region offers a better opportunity for comparison than Western Europe. Such a region provides a suitable field for contrast due to its relevance to local dynamics with global impact. The region's HE systems have been subject to investigations for many years, facilitating longitudinal comparisons and the analysis of alternative models which still coexist. Regional integration processes which have created harmonized public policies in the European Union (EU) had less impact on coordinating HE models in the entire continent. Those differences become evident when pointing at the governance of institutions providing tertiary education, which has been an issue since medieval times. In fact, from their early start, European universities have followed different rules of operations and regulations. The fate of institutions of higher learning has been entirely different in the internationalization process, achieving remarkable results. Nowadays, universities across Europe benefit from sophisticated pan-European programs targeting student and instructor mobility across the continent. Those efforts aim to increase the offering of international exchange programs, provide administrators with further opportunities, and build a network of "super campuses" as champions of mobility, social impact, and inclusion.

Next, we address the relationship between governance and the internationalization of selected universities within the Western European context. We build upon previous investigations comparing the different models of governance in Europe to single out those factors which might turn into a strategic advantage. Specifically, we look to those characteristics which make those models unique, based on the review of university governance in Sweden, the United Kingdom, The Netherlands, and Germany. We focus on these countries which have achieved significant progress in governance and internationalization and might be considered examples for other nations with the same governance model. Some important nations are not part of the comparison and leading universities of the chosen countries. Therefore, we look at individual efforts from those institutions and the implied effects of public policies in those nations. The selected universities are Lund University in Sweden, King's College London in the United Kingdom, University of Amsterdam in The Netherlands, and University of Bonn in Germany. After a comparative review of the different HE models and the universities chosen as their representatives, we point at possible future developments and the factors which might change fundamental issues.

In the final section, we share some thoughts about the relationship between governance and the internationalization of universities in Europe. The results from this investigation might be relevant to researchers looking into the same topic. Globalization itself is shifting patterns towards more universally accepted models of governance and internationalization strategies of universities worldwide. Although the issue ought to be of interest to institutions of higher learning, a solid body of literature is not yet available. Therefore, we intend to provide valuable insights to the leaders of those institutions, researchers, and decision-makers in the realm of HE, even if our advice could be to analyze the issue at stake further.

UNIVERSITY GOVERNANCE AND INTERNATIONALIZATION

In addition to the previously stated pressures which have universities under siege, other forces have been reshaping the HE system for a long time. Such a system includes "all types of study programs or sets of courses of study at the post-secondary level which are recognized by the competent authorities of a State Party" (Sabzalieva et al., 2021, p. 4). It is undergoing a modernization process, with governance and internationalization at the center of the debate. This section clarifies some fundamental concepts about both topics, especially within the European context. After the conceptualization of governance and a presentation of the primary governance model in place in that continent, we discuss the internationalization of HE before sharing some thoughts about the possible intersection of those two elements.

Governance in Western Europe

Despite the popularity of the concept of governance, the use of such a term is relatively recent and initially was related to the proper administration of funds by international organizations no more than a few decades ago (Nanda, 2006). In its initial stages, governance conveyed the meaning of proper management of funds, linked to economics and politics. However, a more modern vision implies a holistic approach and a commitment to broader objectives, including sustainable development. Despite a more extensive view of its role in society, governance still relies on the power and authority over the allocation and management of resources in organizations, even if answering to internal and external stakeholders (Bratinau & Pinzaru, 2015).

Governance in HE is a rather complicated issue—often involving drastic organizational and strategic changes—but might provide universities the road map to meet their ultimate goals and even reach ambitious targets (Arregui-Pabollet et al., 2018). Despite the positive achievements, university governance comes at a price. The newly gained autonomy of universities from public control often entails the scrutiny of a multiplicity of internal and external actors. University governance includes "internal and external arrangements on how the institution is organized, planned, managed, and coordinated as well as the structures, frameworks, resources, activities, protocols, and processes used for achieving its objectives as well as its interrelationships with key stakeholders" (Chiyevo & Tirivanhu-Gwatidzo, 2016, p. 146). Universities—which are the backbone of HE—are compelled to justify their role in society through appropriate governance and ought not to escape from their responsibility to promote the values which represent the pillars of modern society.

The benefits of proper university governance are many, but its exact meaning is still subject to debate, as demonstrated by the different HE models still in place. A universally accepted definition of university governance is elusive, despite the many attempts and the permanent quest for benchmarking the efforts made by institutions of higher learning all over the world. The issue is no novelty, as early attempts to compare governance across universities started many years ago, including combined quantitative and qualitative approaches, although limited by the voluntary participation of the institutions subject to comparison (van Vught, 2008). Currently, there are different sets of sophisticated tools to elicit contributions from various sources, an approach which might be more widely accepted is the one proposed by the Organisation for Economic Co-operation and Development (OECD) "that goes beyond metrics to also focus on policy and practice benchmarking to tell the story behind the performance of higher education systems" (OECD, 2017a, p. 51), thus promoting action from policymakers across nations. Other voices point at the need to find convergence among the different governance models through alliances (Estermann et al., 2021), while many higher learning institutions and national entities combine solutions proposed across the globe.

Presently, four significant governance models prevail—unitary, dual traditional, dual asymmetric, and the German model—while many other nations have evident peculiarities. Briefly described, the unitary model could be described as one with only a single council responsible for all significant decisions. Second, the dual traditional model includes two governing bodies: One body with a limited size board takes strategic decisions, and a secondary body devotes itself to academic governance. Third, a dual

TABLE 4.1 University Governance Models in Europe, per Country

Country	Model	Country	Model
Spain	Dual Asymmetric	Iceland	Unitary
France	Dual Asymmetric	Republic of Ireland	Unitary
The Netherlands	Dual Asymmetric	Belgium	Unitary
Hungary	Dual Asymmetric	Sweden	Unitary
Croatia	Dual Asymmetric	Norway	Unitary
Finland	Dual Asymmetric	Denmark	Unitary
Switzerland	Dual Asymmetric	Poland	Unitary
United Kingdom	Dual Traditional	Portugal	Unitary
Italy	Dual Traditional	Germany	German
Austria	Dual Traditional		
Slovakia	Dual Traditional		
Slovenia	Dual Traditional		

Source: Bennetot & Estermann (2017)

asymmetric model of governance is formed by an executive board charged with the general management, whose members are appointed, suspended, and dismissed by a second supervisory board controlled by the government.

An imaginary map showing the different models of tertiary education in Europe will bear little resemblance to the political map of the 27 nations conforming to the EU (Olier et al., 2021). Such a map would be intriguing at best, as it will provide few clues about the underlying differences—whether explained by tradition, economic factors, cultural affinities, or other reasons of any kind. Table 4.1 lists selected countries according to governance models.

The Internationalization of Higher Education

Whereas university governance requires further academic consideration, the internationalization of HE has been the subject of constant analysis, bringing light to the phenomena from different angles. Since medieval times, many universities were open to foreign instructors and students exchanging knowledge and ideas regarding their origin. Throughout the centuries, higher learning was subject to fewer restrictions than many other activities, with minor limitations to the mobility of students and professors across borders. After World War II, the international exchange process began by institutionalizing exchange programs, scholarships, and recognition of overseas studies.

Different definitions described the phenomena, even though the meaning and interpretation vary notably (Sharipov, 2020). Under the academic lens, the internationalization of HE raised scholarly interest in different waves; after initial arousal in the 1970s and 1980s in the United States, the discussion centered in Europe during the 1990s and finally opened to the world as the topic was linked to globalization (Dagen et al., 2019). For a long time, the definition by Knight (2003) as "the process of integrating an international, intercultural, or global dimension into the purpose, functions, or delivery of post-secondary education" was widely accepted by international organizations, such as The European Association of European Universities (EAEU).

More recently, the EAEU has endorsed the conceptualization of the internationalization of HE as proposed by de Wit, Hunter, Howard, and Egron-Polak in 2015, stating

> the intentional process of integrating an international, intercultural, or global dimension into the purpose, functions, and delivery of post-secondary education, to enhance the quality of education and research for all students and staff, and to make a meaningful contribution to society. (p. 29)

The above definition clarifies that internationalization ought not to focus predominantly on mobility but more on the curriculum and learning outcomes, emphasizing the pertinence of analyzing university governance and internationalization strategy together. Although the universities' international element has grown in relevance, internationalization of HE as a driver which evidences and speeds up globalization has been often diminished, despite its long-term societal impact. As Sharipov (2020) expresses, "One of the forms of the manifestation of globalization is the internationalization of higher education, which has become one of the main educational policies of both states and Higher Education Institutions" (p. 136).

Despite the positive remarks on the internationalization of HE, some critical voices look at the possibility of an excessive homogenization of culture across the globe, the prevalence of business and political interests over the more noble purpose of building a better educational system based on academic collaboration (Knight, 2015).

Different models describe the internationalization process in HE, with scholars describing and labeling the stages differently. Nevertheless, the logical sequence appears to be similar in many scholarly proposals. According to Spencer-Oatey and Dauber (2017), there are four developmental stages of internationalization. The first stage is *pre-internationalization* characterized by a culturally homogeneous campus community. The second stage is *structural internationalization*, with first international actors (such as international students, instructors, and staff members) being introduced into the university community. However, the interactions between locals and foreign actors at this stage are still limited. The next stage is *community internationalization*.

When a culturally diverse university community embraces its new international culture, interactions between locals and foreigners are frequent, and everyone has an opportunity for personal growth. The final stage is *competency internationalization*, where the whole campus community (students, instructors, and staff members) is inter-culturally competent.

Strategies to pursue the internationalization of universities offer an ample range of possibilities, including general attempts to venture into other markets, "ad-hoc" movements, or different combinations which might lead a university to acquire a global status. Many European institutions act similarly as business enterprises establishing an entire campus overseas, developing or partnering local institutions, or building their facilities in a foreign land. However, a preferred model privileges networking and friendly agreements with partnering institutions (Kumar & Aithal, 2020). A fundamental difference lies between those efforts pursued by individual institutions. The strategies tend to be heavily differentiated versus a national approach to position universities under a common umbrella.

Governance and Internationalization: A Shared Destiny?

Two decades ago, OECD started analyzing HE institutions comparatively, and it has been reporting on the changing patterns of governance in HE institutions (OECD, 2003, 2021). Governments have been restructuring the HE systems in the context of political transformations, public policies, and reshaping reforms, undertaking key reforms in their governance models. Even though there have been relevant studies on universities governance—such as the ones exploring the relationship between governance and quality assurance and the impact on nation-wide guidance to help HE fulfill its mission effectively (Hénard & Mitterle, 2010)—there is a pending need to study the relationship between models of governance, their reforms, and the internationalization strategy. Although the universities' international element has grown in relevance, internationalization of HE as a driver which evidences and speeds up globalization has been often diminished, despite its long-term societal impact.

On the one hand, universities have been actively engaging in policies to increase their internationalization by pursuing a world-class status, reflecting on their governance model. As Yonezawa and Shimmi (2015) explain, the construction of "world-class" universities requires a resolute financial investment and a comprehensive renovation of university governance for a global context defined by diverse international relations (IR) actors. On the other hand, in the European Union context, Tamtik (2017) argues that studying a coherent approach to internationalization has been developing for decades as "a bottom–up process" in which the role of the universities' governing instruments has had a considerable influence. Regardless of the preferred approach, a globally accepted model needs a reinterpretation of universities governance systems to confront a complex international context.

CASES

In the absence of rigorous data to support a comparison of governance and internationalization of universities, we look into selected cases of European universities which might represent the main governance models in place. Although it is not possible to extrapolate the results to the thousands of HE institutions in the continent, it might give a starting point for future comparison. The national educational systems thus represented—Sweden, the United Kingdom, The Netherlands, and Germany—have already gone a long way to provide new proposals for achieving excellence in HE.

Within each nation, we selected well-known universities, although not necessarily the leading university for each country. Their best practices might be representatives of the most reputed institutions of their national field and probably similar to many world-class universities. The selected universities are Lund University, King's College London, University of Amsterdam, and Bonn. In Figure 4.1, we take the example of one of those universities to show the complexity of governance in any Western European university.

The following is a concise description of each selected university and an overview of their governance model and internationalization process. In the later part of this section, we provide some comparative data.

Lund University[1]

Founded in 1666, Lund University has been consistently ranked among the top 100 universities in the world. Lund University's governance model can be qualified as a unitary model with only a single council responsible for all significant decisions. This body is the university board, the university's highest decision-making body, and fulfills the mission of the university by supervising all matters concerning the university. The body includes a vice-chancellor, eight community representatives appointed by the government—of which one is chair of the board—three members of the academic staff, and three students.

According to its 2017–2026 strategy, Lund University's vision is to be a world-class university that "works to understand, explain, and improve our world and the human condition" (Lund University, n.d., p. 4). The strategic shift in its governance and goals intended to reach an objective:

Governance and Internationalization in European Universities • 59

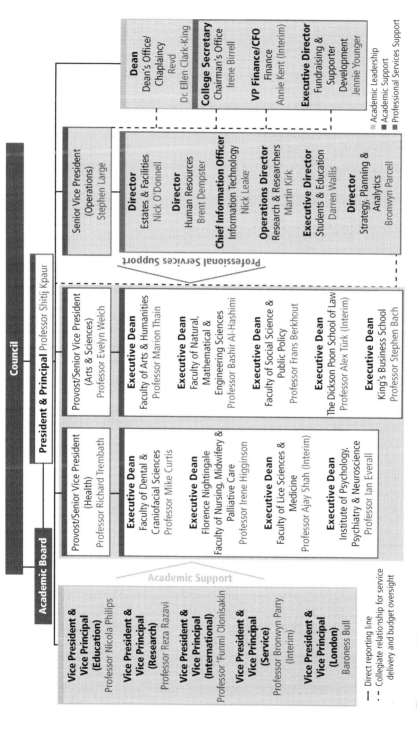

Figure 4.1 The complexity of the governance model of a European university. *Source:* King's College London.

developing its collegial leadership. The strategy established several development areas designed to improve its capacity to solve societal challenges in terms of goals. One of these areas, particularly important for this research, is leading internationally. The pro-vice-chancellor governs Lund University's internationalization strategy for external engagement, overseeing the entire university's internationalization, including those carried out by the different schools and faculties. Specifically, the pro-vice-chancellor supervises the Division of External Relations which works promoting collaborations, agreements, and programs. In addition to the centralized work of the division, the faculties and departments have their specific international collaborations.

The internationalization strategy seeks to promote continued development as an international university through four elements of specific objectives. First, sharing an international perspective and global engagement vision at a university level. Second, the improvement of international mobility for students and staff. Third, increasing the capacity of the institution for international students and staff. Fourth, promoting strategic international partnerships where the institution can actively participate with top universities worldwide. As examples of the last element, Lund University reinforces its investment to be present at transnational networking spaces such as Universitas 21 (U21)—a global network comprising 27 research-intensive universities in 18 countries (the focus is on stimulating student mobility through exchange programs and conferences); and the League of European Research Universities (LERU)—comprising 23 leading research universities in Europe which receive one fifth of all European grants for fundamental research.

King's College London[2]

King's College London is an internationally renowned university delivering exceptional education and world-leading research since 1829. With a mission to drive positive and sustainable change in society, the university is governed under a dual traditional model, with a limited-in-size board taking strategic decisions and a secondary body for the academic governance. The first of these two bodies at King's College London is the council, which is the supreme governing body of the college established under the charter and statutes and with its functions oriented towards strategic debate and decision-making. Among other functions, the council defines King's College's mission and vision, establishes management and monitoring systems, ensures that delegated responsibilities are clearly defined, and oversees the effective and adequate functioning of King's College. The council's powers and functions derive from the college's charter and statutes. The council's membership is various with two types of members: independent and staff. On the other side of its dual traditional model of governance, King's College is co-governed by the academic board, a collegium responsible—under delegated authority from the council—for the regulation of teaching, examination, and research carried out at the university.

King's College has prioritized internationalization in its strategy identifying the need to increase its role in a more interconnected, complex world. This internationalization strategy focuses on providing students with a critical thinking education, with the "character and wisdom to make a difference in the world around them" (King's College London, n.d., p. 4). As a general objective, King's Strategic Vision 2029 sets the aim to make "a significant and innovative contribution by serving the needs and aspirations of the [British] society and the wider world" (King's College London, n.d., p. 4). In terms of specific objectives at the internationalization pillar of the strategy, the university pursues to attract the best international talent, provide an internationalized curriculum, build and invest in strategic partnerships and international communities, and raise the university's profile in major global issues.

The academic board governs King's College's internationalization strategy through its international committee. Chaired by the vice president/vice principal, it brings together vice deans of International and Professional Services staff to provide the necessary considerations and decisions to govern and oversee all of King's College's international needs. To identify this university-specific international focus, an analysis of its internationalization strategy and its alignment with King's College's Vision 2029 is required. The document details specific objectives constructed upon three main pillars. In addition—as a crosscutting element of goals—King's College's vision for internationalization stands on two core values: a cultural competency (defined as the ability to see the world through the lens of others) and a global problem-solving mindset.

In terms of its specific objectives, the internationalization strategy settles various purposes. The university participation in strategic networks fundamentally summarizes them as a means of connecting its staff and students with international collaborators, the increase of research impact, the provision of innovative and unique educational offerings, the creation of opportunities to create global mindsets, and the ability to attract international students and staff.

King's College's international strategy's pillars first imply that students and staff ought to interpret and model a world-changing leadership. Second, the university needs infrastructure and processes. Third, its global reach builds on its capacity to join and energize alliances and networks. King's affiliation to international university networks offers its researchers and students various chances and facilitates debates on HE policy at global fora. Key memberships are the Guild of European Research-Intensive Universities consisting of 19 of Europe's most distinguished research-intensive universities, and UNICA—the Network of Universities from the Capitals of Europe, offering a network of 46 universities and constituting a forum to influence the policy and best practice in HE in Europe. Law Schools Global League commits to the globalization of law and its integration into teaching and research, and Circle-U works to develop an inclusive, research-intensive, and interdisciplinary alliance formed by seven partner institutions from across Europe.

University of Amsterdam[3]

Since 1632, the University of Amsterdam has built a reputation as a leader in international science and an innovation partner. As a result, the university is ranked periodically among the world's best universities globally.

Following a dual asymmetric model of governance, the executive board—formed by three members—is charged with the general management of the University of Amsterdam. Its members are appointed, suspended, and dismissed by the supervisory board. This organ also assesses overall governance and supervises the implementation of key planning documents, such as the strategic plan, the budget, the annual financial report, and the management and administration regulations. The Dutch Minister of Education appoints the members of this collegiate supervisory forum for 4 years.

The strategic plan, Inspiring Generations, sets out the University of Amsterdam challenges and drivers from 2021–2026, defining its core values, main challenges, and critical ambitions. The university seeks to promote its values through independent and engaged science that seeks to understand and serve the world, without political, religious, or other constraints. Throughout the last decade, the University of Amsterdam expects to tackle concrete systemic challenges in the national and international field of HE and research. The strategy identified as digitalization the right balance between rules and professional freedom, funding, talent management, open science, and societal trust.

The University of Amsterdam maintains a solid international positioning. Based on the assumption that globalization of the labor market requires highly qualified staff with intercultural competencies and experience, the university commits to work on four interconnected pillars in its strategic documents. First, to prepare undergraduate and graduate students for a future career in the global labor market. Second, the university collaborates with other international institutions in joint research projects which provoke international synergies. Third, to enrich the university's international vocation and its programs, the attraction of global talent is prioritized. Fourth, the university strategy clarifies the need to encourage internal and external collaboration to expand and strengthen international partnerships.

The University of Amsterdam works to maintain its membership in prestigious international university networks. Key memberships include: (a) the League of European Research Universities, a network of 23 research-intensive European universities and one of the primary lobbyists within the European Union, and (b) Universitas 21 (U21), which promotes student mobility through exchange programs, summer schools, and student conferences. The network also organizes conferences for early career researchers, helping them establish contacts and build up a network.

University of Bonn[4]

With global recognition for its research capabilities and programs since 1818, the University of Bonn has been one of the best research-led universities in Germany. The university's mission and vision promote education and democracy as fundamental for freedom of research and a prosperous society within a globalized world.

The University of Bonn follows a model in which a combination of three institutions interacts. First, the university follows the leadership of the rectorate, composed of the rector, the provost, and six vice-rectors, each with their areas of responsibility and assisted by the executive management staff. A key complementary responsibility is the design and overview of strategic objectives and the coordination for their implementation. Second, the university council is a governance body of the university created by the Higher Education Act of North Rhine-Westphalia. The tasks of the university council include advising the rectorate on its budget, supervising general management, issuing recommendations for the university's development plan, and electing its members. Third, the senate of the university is another central part of the governance system composed of the members of the rectorate, the deans of the university faculties, student, and staff representatives. The senate co-participates in the election of members of the rectorate, oversees the university statutes and regulations, and supports the drafting of the university's development budget plan.

The University of Bonn has reinforced its international vocation. This global perspective is deeply rooted in its mission "to promote research as a pathway to solutions to the great challenges facing our society [...] best achieved within a collaborative and innovative research culture which—crucially—is internationally networked" (Univesrity of Bonn 2022, p. 3). In terms of governance, measures convey a multilevel perspective. At a general university level, the vice rectorate for International Affairs and

International Office is the responsible unit, and at the disciplinary level, the responsibility lies on the faculties and cross-departmental organizational units. To fulfill this mission, the University of Bonn has designed a strategy (2025 Internationalization Strategy [University of Bonn, 2021]) which locates internationalization as a central element for the institution's future.

The university explains how its internationalization contributes to improving its quality and competitiveness across all areas of its institutional action, meeting the targets by 2025. First, the strategy settles its focus on the internationalization of academic research, which seeks to increase the proportion between German and international academics, increase the number of international research projects and European Union research funded programs, and expand the European and international research and innovation networks. The second action area is the internationalization of study offerings and teaching.

The objectives are the digital internationalization of study programs and teaching, the increase of English-language degree modules, and the number of incoming international exchange students at the undergraduate level. The third action area is the construction of its agenda for internationalization. Its objectives are to expand multilingual services in central administration, improve language and intercultural competencies of its staff, and develop existing internationalization structures within the faculties, departments, and institutes. The fourth action area is the creation of strategic partnerships and collaborations based in the city of Bonn. As objectives, the institution has planned to form a global network with strategic partner universities, including new partners, expand and develop bilateral strategic partnerships in research, teaching, and administration, and promote joint doctoral programs by 2025. The University of Bonn belongs to a significant number of international networks.

CASE COMPARISON

The four universities chosen for comparison belong to different governance models, although they share standard features, such as being all public and scoring exceptionally high on research output. Intuitively, it seems reasonable to think that the reasoning behind such coincidence is related to the methodology, which probably tends to favor those institutions achieving higher output on research. It is also worth mentioning that private universities struggle with research efforts in Europe compared to institutions with public funding.

Out of the five major university rankings—ARWU, THE Ranking, Webometrics, Methodology, and QS Ranking—we choose the last one. There is a heated debate about the benefits and limitations of each ranking. Still, the

QS Ranking is widely used and provides some indicators of the internationalization of universities, such as the international instructor and student ratios (Chowdhury & Rahman, 2021). The QS Ranking uses six comparative criteria—academic reputation, employer reputation, instructor/student ratio, citations per instructor, international instructor ratio, and international student ratio—assigning 20% of the total score to the category "citations per instructor." Half of the final score comes from a quality output, with academic reputation and employer reputation (Quacquarelli Symonds, 2022). In contrast, the other half might directly be a consequence of the availability of funds and perhaps other factors which tilt the scales favoring public universities.

Another striking similarity, probably without a logical explanation, is the total number of students, which is 22,454 to 30,541, as happens to the entire faculty, in the range of 2,829 to 4,216 professors. The international student's and international instructor ratios show an evident variation, ranging between 15% and 52%, and between 20% and 45%, respectively. The overall score and the rank show the differences among the four universities, with King's College of London leading with its 35 positions and 82 scores, versus the University of Bonn, which occupies the 226 positions with a 40.3 score in the same QS Ranking 2022. The fierce competition among prestiguous universities worldwide might suggest that the University of Bonn plays in a different league, considering is strong reputation. Table 4.2 shows the comparative results of the international profile of the four universities.

Probably from their inception, university rankings have endured severe criticism. Scholars look at those rankings from different angles and marvel at the striking differences in the results presented. The ranking score by *Times Higher Education*, QS by Quacquarelli Symonds, and the Academic Ranking of World Universities by Shanghai Ranking have a common denominator: a different interpretation for the quality of HE. Despite the

TABLE 4.2 International Profile of Case Universities

Criteria	Lund	King's College	Amsterdam	Bonn
QS Rank	87	35	55	226
QS Overall Score	63.8	82	73.8	40.3
Total Students	27,443	29,238	30,541	22,454
International Students	6,682	15,075	7,969	3,276
International Students Ratio	24%	52%	26%	15%
Total Instructors	3,040	4,216	2,829	4,207
International Instructors	1,111	1,885	980	834
International Instructor Ratio	37%	45%	35%	20%

Source: QS Ranking, 2022

apparent limitations, those rankings are proper tools for benchmarking universities. Sometimes the figures are not presented, although a bit of effort might lead to exciting results—like those shown in Table 4.2, which required detailed examination within the report.

Unfortunately, no similar instrument is available to benchmark the governance of HE. Scholars have pointed out such a vacuum for a long time, and consequently, exciting tools for comparing governance have surfaced over the years. For instance, the World Bank compares the governance of HE across the Middle East and North Africa, developing the University Governance Screening Card, aiming at the modernization of universities in that region. Such tools allow comparing those institutions on five dimensions: (a) context, mission, and goals; (b) management; (c) autonomy; (d) accountability; and (e) participation (Jaramillo, 2012). The tool allowed for extraordinary clarity on the presentation of the results. The model included relevant factors to measure and compare the commitment of each university to clear and positive goals, with full accountability of the governing bodies and management in academic and administrative matters. Additionally, the accountability for results, use of financial resources, and relationships with the community were also part of the model. Unfortunately, those advances in the measurability of governance have gained little acceptance.

Bearing in mind the absence of a standardized instrument to measure governance in HE we choose to identify some factors from the analysis of the four selected universities which might give us a picture of how governance might impact the internationalization process of those institutions. It is essential to state that we move in the realm of perceptions and from a convenience sample with no pretensions to extrapolate results to the four types of governance represented by those institutions. Thus, such comparison aims to spark the interest in developing quantitative and qualitative studies on that topic. Table 4.3 presents some data on the perceived actions taken by those universities in their internationalization strategies related to governance.

As mentioned when explaining the limitations of the comparison results shown in Table 4.3, the chosen criteria are subjective, hence must be taken with a grain of salt. The first criteria, "Centralization of Decision-Making," represents the centralization or dispersion of decision-making. In the case of Lund University, the answer is straightforward, as all power is heavily centralized. It does not happen with the other universities, where different entities provide a check and balance system. The second criteria, "Values Over Performance," might be implied by the declared objectives of each university, although such evaluation might underestimate the true purpose behind it. The third criteria, "Commitment to Universal Values," could be interpreted as the desire to adapt to other systems and models versus building internationalization strategies based on their own vision. The fourth

TABLE 4.3 The Perceived Relationship between Governance and Internalization

Criteria	Lund	King's College	Amsterdam	Bonn
Centralization of decision-making	High	Medium	Medium	Low
Values over performance	High	Medium	High	High
Commitment to universal values	Low	Medium	High	High
Networking and alliances	High	High	High	Medium
Empathy to foreign models	Low	Medium	Medium	Medium
Promotion of student mobility	Medium	High	Medium	Low
Promotion of instructor mobility	Medium	High	Medium	Low

Source: QS Ranking, 2022

criteria, "Networking and Alliances," are probably easier to measure upon results than on the much desirable declaration of joining networks to share forces and reach broader objectives. Whereas it is common practice for universities to state the value of alliances and partnerships, we measure this factor by emphasizing joining well-established international networks. The fifth criteria, "Empathy to Foreign Models," is implied by the declaration of the institution on what their ultimate purpose for internationalization is, whether it's for expansion of a model which the institution might consider solid, versus the declared intention of venturing into unknown areas where the university might acquire some new learning. Finally, student and instructor mobility promotion could be interpreted as the results from current ratios related to those factors, as stated in Table 4.2.

Once again, it is paramount to state that the previous exercise is highly subjective and based on a comparison of four universities. Nevertheless, the message is clear: It is imperative to create a set of tools which could allow the benchmarking of governance and the relationship of that factor with others, such as the internationalization of universities (Delgado-Márquez et al., 2011). Still, from comparing the four selected universities, it is not easy to visualize a superior governance model. Those governance models, though, might show some indisputable facts, such as the superiority of the British universities in global university rankings. Is such superiority a consequence of governance? It is to be proved.

CONCLUSION

The different models of governance in Europe establish alternative power-sharing structures in the European HE institutions. Their tradition and level of autonomy from public authorities have constructed a diverse panorama in strategizing, governing, and internationalizing HE. Despite their differences, the analysis of the selected universities shows that a mid-to-long-term strategy is crucial. Dynamized by the governing bodies, the plan is implemented through different institutional levels and layers, such as management offices, faculties, technical staff, among many others.

As part of their general strategy, all of the analyzed European universities identify the need to have an internationalization vector in their design. Its relevance in strategic terms is crucial. In every case, it is one of the fundamental pillars for fulfilling the university's combined mission/vision strategic objective: obtaining prestige and academic relevance as an educational institution. Therefore, it can be concluded that internationalization stands as a critical element for university reputation, and that the model of governance of the four analyzed universities has, a priori, no relevance/influence on the fact that the universities always give a sizable strategic relevance to their internationalization strategy. In addition to not identifying a clear connection between these four models of governance and the universities' internationalization, these models do not influence the priority axes of its internationalization strategy. The internationalization strategies focus on three significant priorities in all the analyzed cases: opening the university to international talent, exchange, and presence in high-level networks. Lastly, the analyzed institutions' four different models of governance do not influence, in these four cases, the execution of the internationalization strategy. Each university decentralizes the decision and management to a separate unit.

The previous statements might sound harsh to many universities, while they focus on improving their governance model and the success of their internationalization strategy. Nevertheless, their principals and governing bodies might find no rest until a harmonized and universally accepted set of governance criteria might prove that their efforts are heading in the right direction. Until such instruments are available, decision makers at institutions of higher learning might well continue making loud declarations on how governance is the cornerstone to transform into a genuinely international university. As never before, fostering good governance and internationalization are essential for the future of HE. The COVID-19 pandemic has accelerated the transformation of universities and questioned the nature of HE. Those changes are still unclear but intuitively it is easy to see how leading universities might succeed through individual efforts or collaboration with innovative institutions keeping pace with the demands of society.

NOTES

1. https://www.lunduniversity.lu.se/sites/www.lunduniversity.lu.se/files/strategic_plan_2017-2026-updated030517.pdf
2. https://www.kcl.ac.uk/about/assets/pdf/Kings-strategic-vision-2029.pdf
3. https://www.uva.nl/binaries/content/assets/uva/en/about-the-uva/organisation/organisatieschema_en.pdf
4. https://www.uni-bonn.de/de/universitaet/medien-universitaet/medien-organisation-und-einrichtungen/medien-gremien-und-organe/hochschulgesetz-vom-12-juli-2019.pdf

CHAPTER 5

COOPETITION IN THE INTERNATIONALIZATION OF HIGHER EDUCATION

Rauno Rusko

This conceptual paper focuses on coopetition as a tool for the internationalization of higher education (HE). Actually, this chapter will launch the coopetition concept in the discussions about internationalization of HE. The internationalization of HE has several coopetitive features, which this chapter will show and analyze combining two elements: (a) the contemporary coopetition discussions, where the role of public sector activities is rising and (b) the discussions and examples about internationalization of HE, where the role of coopetition is evident, but less studied—until now.

The internationalization generally, and especially in HE, is becoming stronger and stronger due to the Internet. The Internet, and social media as a part of it, is totally indifferent to international boundaries (Graham, 1999; Stier, 2004). Thus, territorial, local, or national identities have supposedly been substituted for mobile and cosmopolitan identities (Stier, 2004). This development has even strengthened because of the COVID-19 epidemic.

As a result, this chapter contributes by combining coopetition discussions with internationalization of HE discussions—providing new interesting perspectives. Although competition has been the main paradigm of management and marketing studies, contemporary literature expresses more and more cooperation activities and policy between enterprises. Thus, the two main paradigms of management and business, in this sense, are competition and cooperation (Padula & Dagnino, 2007). However, competition and cooperation are extremities and this duality does not cover practical activities of business entities somewhere *between* competition and cooperation (Rusko et al., 2018). Coopetition is a relatively new perspective, which takes into account the existence of simultaneous competition and cooperation between firms (or between other actors). Even with the remarkable practical importance, coopetition has not achieved the similar status of paradigm as similar to competition or cooperation (Bengtsson et al., 2010).

The initial coopetition discussions focused on firms and their relationships. However, gradually coopetition discussions and perspectives have grown and their relative importance among management practices and discussions have increased (Zacharia et al., 2019). At the same time, coopetition perspectives also cover public organizations, semi-public organizations, and networks between different kinds of organizations (De Ngo & Okura, 2008; Kylänen & Rusko, 2011). In other words, the coopetition framework contains micro-level, meso-level, macro-level, and even meta-level relationships (Rusko, 2018).

HE and universities have met several new tendencies during the latest decades. These tendencies are not parallel, however. The internationalization, privatization, marketization, and state intervention, for instance, are contemporary topics in the development of universities and HE (R. Brown, 2010; Furedi, 2010).

Thus, the studies and activities of the universities focus more and more on the same perspectives as the business studies and activities of the firms. Furthermore, the activities and financing of the universities are often based on public organizations, semi-public organizations, and networks—and they often have micro-level, meso-level, macro-level, and meta-level relationships with their stakeholders and competing universities. All of these features are also typical for coopetition discussion and perspectives. All in all, universities and their international relationships will provide a fruitful platform for coopetition studies though coopetition studies have so far nearly forgotten this kind of research area.

This theme, university coopetition—and especially international university coopetition—is a less studied area in the field of management and marketing studies. However, the different kinds of networks between universities are everyday practices in the academic world. Generally, cooperation between universities is a very fruitful research theme due to multifaceted structures of the universities. Despite the different backgrounds and structures of universities, they have various international cooperation channels and possibilities with each other.

The aim of this chapter is to provide initiative to focus coopetition studies properly on the universities, and especially on the internationalization of the universities. In order to achieve this aim, this chapter introduces different coopetition perspectives and contemporary international coopetition activities of the universities—the activities of which exist, but are not yet studied properly. Thus, one important aim of the chapter is to show several further studies of international university coopetition. Furthermore, this chapter introduces a new framework to map coopetitive perspectives of universities. This framework is also applicable to the other branches and coopetition contexts.

The chapter has the following structure: at first, specific characteristics of universities have been introduced, then coopetition—and especially the levels of coopetition (micro, meso, macro, and meta). After which follows the section, "Contemporary Coopetition Discussions About Universities," which introduces the rare already existing literature about university coopetition. After that are Outcomes of this study and the section, "Coopetition in the Internationalization of Higher Education." Finally, there are conclusions with several suggestions for further studies.

THE SPECIFIC CHARACTERISTICS OF UNIVERSITIES

According to Brusca and colleagues (2019), universities are knowledge-intensive organizations, which are strongly based on the use and development of intangible resources. Generally, universities are challenging research subjects for management studies. The financing and public status of universities varies even in the same countries and especially between the countries. In the world there are about 28,000 universities ("Ranking Web of Universities," 2019). For example, in India there were 3,944 universities and in the United States there were 3,257 universities in July 2018 (Figure 5.1).

Based on the ownerships and financing of the universities, the universities have three main categories: public universities, private universities, and universities—which have both the features of public and private universities, that is, semi-public universities (Thang & Quang, 2007). Due to different ownerships and financial background, the strategies and the general features of these universities vary significantly.

The general tendency in public organizations is new public management (NPM). NPM launches managerial business practices, efficiency, and performance to the public sector. Dai (2019) notices that analyzing performances of universities is never an easy task because the performance of

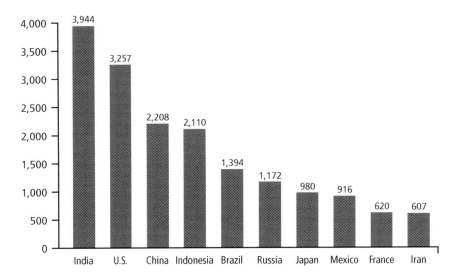

Figure 5.1 Top 10 countries number of universities. *Source:* Statista, 2019.

universities depends on many factors and some of them are highly correlated themselves. However, this NPM phenomenon also has effects on the aims and practices of initially public-owned and public-driven universities all over the world. In Ukrainian universities, for example, there have been neo-liberal reforms, such as internationalization orientation, marketization, managerial practices, and output-based funding schemes (Hlib, 2019; Oleksiyenko, 2014).

In the United States, for instance, in 2016 there were 4,360 active HE institutions. Total expenditure of U.S. public and private colleges and universities in 2017 was 608 billion dollars, of which 389 billion dollars was in public (63.98%) and 219 billion dollars in private colleges and universities (36.02%). Accordingly in 2007 total expenditure was 408.49 billion dollars of which 261.05 billion dollars was in public (63.91%) and 147.44 billion dollars in private colleges and universities (36.09%; see Figure 5.2). A remarkable fact is the static share of expenditure between private (36%) and public (64%) HE institutions in the United States.

Through the different structures and ownership of universities, their competitive advantage is based on the generally accepted criterions of performance, which are measured by numerous top lists. These lists and their outcomes vary, but they contain mostly the same measured variables, such as scientific publications, number of students, and efficiency, among others. These same features have effects on financing of the universities. Figure 5.3 shows one example from Finnish public financing structure of universities.

Coopetition in the Internationalization of Higher Education • 75

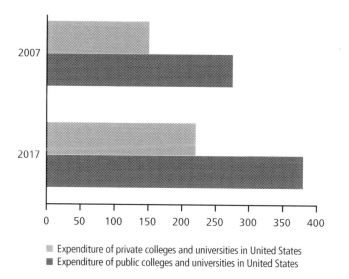

Figure 5.2 Expenditure of private colleges and universities 2017 and 2007 (in billion USD). *Source:* Statista, 2019.

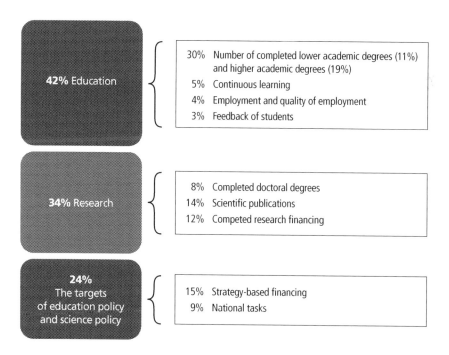

Figure 5.3 Finnish financing model of universities in 2021.

These kinds of structures, such as in Figure 5.3, cause strong competition among universities. In Finland, the government provides 1.6 billion euros to universities following the financing model in Figure 5.3. Consequently, Finnish universities are playing a kind of zero-sum game. There are only about 1.6 billion euros, which universities will divide among each other based on their relative efficiency in each category of financing model. The Finnish financing model does not encourage any cooperation between universities (that is to say coopetition) except scientific publications, where joint articles with two authors from different universities will yield twice as much as joint articles of two authors from the same university. This special detail will encourage cross-university cooperation. Competed research financing might also cause cooperation between different actors of universities due to the challenging application system of scientific financing: Often the competed financing presupposes joint research projects between universities. However, universities have also multifaceted cooperation between each other. Remarkable is that cooperation is focused on the same sectors, which are the relevant parts of public and private financing.

The prestige of university has effects on financing of universities. National and international ranking systems are an important part of the prestige of universities. University prestige is usually associated with visible markers of success—such as rankings published by institutional intermediaries (Dearden et al., 2019; Hazelkorn, 2015; Rindova et al., 2018; Torres-Olava et al., 2020). These rankings are some kind of game or competition between universities and these rankings have reflections on the HE and its financing. Many of these ranked universities have joint activities, such as student exchange, projects, and research activities. Thus, these ranked universities have competitive elements and cooperation with each other, that is they have coopetitive relationships.

The roles of universities and their tools to educate students have gradually changed. Marketizing is one of these changes. Technological change and digitizing have also changed the operational and strategic environment of the universities. For example, improved technology enables several forms of national and international distance educations (Gill, 2009). Massive open online courses (MOOC) collects students from different training programs and universities into the same courses (Vale & Littlejohn, 2014). These kinds of MOOCs are the sources of competition, but also the sources of national and international cooperation between universities.

DISCUSSIONS OF COOPETITION

Coopetition—Micro, Meso, and Macro Level

Coopetition discussions cover in a multifaceted way the different perspectives and levels of organizations and their interactivities. Coopetition discussions are mainly based on the decisions and actions of human beings, especially the entrepreneurs and managers of organizations (Rusko, 2019). Thus, in the discussions on coopetition, the role of human decision-makers and actors is important concerning coopetition relationships (Bengtsson & Kock, 2000). However, typically coopetition studies often regard these coopetition actions at the meso level or macro level (Tidström & Rajala, 2016), assuming that the decision-makers are firms, business units, organizations, or networks (Rusko, 2019). Thus, coopetition involves simultaneous interactions, regardless of whether their relationship is horizontal or vertical (Bengtsson & Kock, 2014; Tidström & Rajala, 2016). These three levels are possible to define several ways. Bengtsson and Kock (2000), for example, notice individual, organizational, and other entities whereas Tidström (2008) finds individual, organizational, inter-organizational, and network levels. Actually, individual and organizational levels are possible to call an "intra-organizational" level. However, an individual level is possible to call a micro level, intra-organizational and inter-organizational level are on a meso level, and networks are on the macro level (Dagnino & Padula, 2002; Tidström & Rajala, 2016).

Several coopetition studies emphasize the relevance of coopetitive actions on different levels—even at the same time (Bengtsson et al., 2010; Dahl et al., 2016; Tidström & Rajala, 2016). Tidström and Rajala (2016) notice that especially strategy as practice with coopetition perspective is focused on all these three levels. However, in some studies, even four levels have been introduced, that is, micro, meso, macro, and meta level (Chim-Miki & Batista-Canino, 2017) whereas in some studies coopetition has been introduced with two categories, such as micro level and macro level (Bengtsson et al., 2016).

Brandenburger and Nalebuff (1996/2011) introduced in their textbook of coopetition a value net, which contains five PARTS; namely the organization, competitors, customers, complementors, and suppliers. According to them, value net contains symmetries: customers and suppliers play symmetric roles, and competitors and complementors play mirror-image roles. They see that the coopetition concept is based on this kind of value net structure (Brandenburger & Nalebuff, 1996/2011). There is some kind of coopetition relationship in each of these elements of value net with the main organization. On the whole, value net type of coopetition is based on macro- or meta-level coopetition structure. Coopetition is not restricted in one firm or organization—not even in one industry, but it covers cross-industry relationships, for example.

Cooperation-Based and Competition-Based Coopetition

In addition to different levels of coopetition, the dimension of coopetition between competition and cooperation has been emphasized in several studies. Here are some examples about these studies.

Eriksson (2008a, 2008b) finds two types of coopetition: competition-based and cooperation-based coopetition. Also, Kylänen and Rusko (2011) use the same concepts and emphasize the possibilities of competition-based strategy to turn on a practical level towards cooperation and vice versa. Thus, coopetition might exist in the form of unintentional coopetition without any planned coopetition process. Thus, in this sense, coopetition progress resembles the emerging coopetition (cf. Mariani, 2007).

Eriksson (2008a) notices in the branch of construction the importance of cooperation-based coopetition. He shows that due to high complexity and customization, long duration, and high uncertainty, construction transactions ought to be governed within relationships which have a high emphasis on cooperation and a lower emphasis on competition—that is to say, cooperation-based coopetition. Eriksson (2008a, 2008b) emphasizes in several studies the relevance to consider instead of competition, cooperation, or (pure) coopetition the competition-cooperation continuum. He classifies in this continuum three types of coopetition: competition-based coopetition, a state of symmetrical coopetition, and cooperation-based coopetition.

Rusko (2012) considers win-proposals and coopetition basing his outcomes also on the competition-cooperation continuum. Furthermore, he notices, for instance, that the study of Ritala (2010), which emphasizes value appropriation, can be placed in the category of competition-based coopetition which mainly follows win–win–lose logics among win–proposal perspective.

Chien (2016) considers cooperation-based and competition-based coopetition in the context of two dichotomies: operational level vs. strategic level and intentional vs. unintentional coopetition. Also, Rusko and colleagues (2018) study these two kinds of coopetition and introduce several managerial connections related to them. They see, for example, the connection between competition-based coopetition and following perspectives: incremental innovation, "dividing the pie," value appreciation, and "compete against partners" perspectives. Furthermore, radical innovation, "creating the pie," value creation, and "learning from partners" are linked with cooperation-based coopetition (Figure 5.4; Rusko et al., 2018; Rusko, 2019).

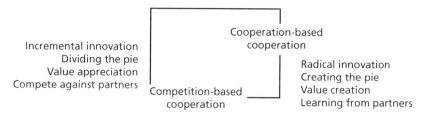

Figure 5.4 Competition-based and cooperation-based coopetition. *Source:* Rusko et al., 2018; Rusko, 2019.

Figure 5.4 shows the relevance of competition-cooperation continuum and dimension in coopetition discussions and multifaceted linkages of this with several management perspectives. Actually, dichotomy competition-coopetition is a robust tool to divide various management discussions.

CONTEMPORARY COOPETITION DISCUSSIONS ABOUT UNIVERSITIES

Direct Discussions of University Coopetition

Practically coopetition discussions about universities are nearly missing in the literature. Coopetition might be mentioned in the context of universities, but university coopetition is seldom the main focus of the study (Xiao-lin, 2010). This is an amazing situation due to the content of one of the most seminal books for coopetition: *Co-Opetition* written by Brandenburg and Nalebuff (1996/2011), which already introduced coopetition of universities. They even see university as an especially suitable example for better understanding some of the issues facing "our home institutions" (Brandenburger & Nalebuff, 1996/2011). Customers of value net in the context of university are students, parents of students, government (federal and/or state), companies, and donors. Competitors are other colleges, "freelancing instructors," private enterprise, hospitals, and museums. Competitors are competing for employees and financing, such as potential donors. Complementors are, according to Brandenburger and Nalebuff (1996/2011), other colleges and education, computers, housing, airlines, hotels, cultural activities, local employers, and copy shops. They name suppliers to be instructors, staff, administrators, and publishers.

One of the rare university coopetition studies is the article of Karwowska and Leja (2018). They see that the ability and willingness to perform coopetition in the modern university is an important factor of being socially responsible. Karwowska and Leja (2018) find coopetition suitable not only for the business community, but also in academic circles; hence, universities can create alliances and compete for resources while cooperating at the same time. The article of Karwowska and Leja (2018) is based on six case studies of socially responsible universities located in the United States, Turkey, New Zealand, Oman, Romania, and Poland and it closes with a remark that coopetition among universities may be the first step in the process of their consolidation which may be observed in Europe. Consequently, they might extend the definition of university social responsibility to include the advantages of coopetition.

Another study focused on university coopetition is the doctoral thesis of Übi (2014). He concentrates on the organizational level of university coopetition. Coopetition is measured by Übi on a social network analysis with two components: mandates (competition) and centers (cooperation). According to Übi a department of university has a mandate to teach its own students, which is its primary goal. This can be measured by the average grade of its graduates. The secondary goal of a department is measured by the social network analysis indicator: traditional conductance (Übi, 2014).

Furthermore, Mongkhonvanit (2014) considers coopetition in the context of universities in Thailand. He sees the connection between coopetition of universities and competitiveness of local industry and technology. Furthermore, he finds linkages with university clusters and coopetition among universities.

Dal-Soto and Monticelli (2017) study the coopetition strategies in the Brazilian HE. Their article establishes theoretical propositions about coopetition strategies based on the Consortium of Community Universities in the South of Brazil (called "Comung"). Dal-Soto and Monticelli (2017) create three theoretical propositions. The first proposition contains a new competitive scenario of higher education institutions (HEIs) to strengthen cooperative relationships in order to create mechanisms to protect the market. However, the interaction between competition and cooperation is not static, being susceptible to internal and external environmental factors which constantly create opportunities for value or threats. According to the second proposition, resources, such as knowledge, capabilities, and assets, are not homogeneous between institutions which compete for the same market. Third, for the coopetition strategy to provide better results, there must be a balance between competition and cooperation (Dal-Soto & Monticelli, 2017).

In addition to Mongkhonvanit (2014), Dal-Soto and Monticelli (2017), and Karwowska and Leja (2018), several studies focus on collaboration between universities without using the term "coopetition." Mostly, these universities also have a competition relationship, which means existing coopetition with each other. This chapter introduces some of these studies. Furthermore, in some studies the coopetition concept has been considered generally with the branch of education without focusing these studies exactly on universities. Also, this chapter shows some examples of them.

Indirect Discussions of University Coopetition

Management and marketing literature contains coopetition discussions, where university or universities are involved in these discussions, but not in the main role. That is, the coopetition perspective might be focused on a firm to firm relationship, for instance, but also university has some kind of role in this relationship. This section emphasizes these kinds of perspectives and discussions of literature.

According to Dagnino and Rocco (2009), coopetition discussions have mainly focused on inter-firm relationships and the role of inter-institutional relationships in these discussions has been minor. They notice blurring boundaries between firms and universities, which in fact enable coopetitive activities between these entities and provide new perspective to coopetition discussions. Especially, Dagnino and Rocco (2009) emphasize university–industry relationships in their study of coopetition. They see that universities and public organizations are the main source of entrepreneurship in biotechnology. Furthermore, they notice the crucial role of universities in boosting firms' learning processes via collaborative arrangements. Over 90% of the firms in biotechnology were involved in the middle of 1990s in some form of academic-industry relationship (Blumenthal et al., 1996; Dagnino & Rocco, 2009).

However, universities are not only a source for collaboration of firms, but they are also in the role of competitor related to industry and its' firms. Namely, there exists a new kind of rivalry in industries: competition with universities for IPRs (intellectual property rights; Dagnino & Rocco, 2009). Also Dagnino and Rocco (2009) find another type of coopetition between university–industry: coopetition for publications. Garcia and Velasco (2002) also noticed the wide coopetition activities in biotechnology, where the role of universities is also important. They do not emphasize as strongly as Dagnino and Rocco (2009) the linkage between coopetition and universities among biotechnology firms.

Discussions of Education and Coopetition

Muijs and Rumyantseva (2014) have noticed that collaboration persists in educational markets characterized by competition. They study the coopetition phenomenon and look at the applicability of this concept to education with a case study approach in a network of 11 sixth form colleges in England. Results, which were based on interviews of managers of each college, show that the collaborative network was perceived positively and the concept of coopetition was clearly applicable to this network, with collaboration and competition equally informing college strategies and policies, and many aspects of coopetition theory applying to the network. Muijs and Rumyantseva (2014) notice that competition continuously exists in these relationships in spite of the useful cooperation strategies and activities between the colleges.

According to Adnett and Davies (2003), Beacon schools, education action zones, and the specialist schools initiative seek to alter the mix of competition and cooperation within local schooling markets. They see that policy makers have been slow to recognize the need to promote coopetition activities in education. They claim that the English quasi-market processes reward schools inappropriately and discourage mutually beneficial cooperation between schools.

In Finland, the general trend among the institutions of research and HE is the collaboration between universities and polytechnics. According to Pelkonen and Nieminen (2015), public research institutes have more collaboration with universities than with polytechnics. The most common form of collaboration between HE institutions and research institutes is research projects. Furthermore, other common forms of collaboration are joint positions, infrastructure and data collaboration, joint units or premises, and collaboration in degree education (Pelkonen & Nieminen, 2015). This usual collaboration between Finnish universities and polytechnics has a coopetitive nature: In addition to cooperation, universities and polytechnics are competing for national and international students and public and private funding. That is, they have simultaneous activities of cooperation and competition.

Discussions of Higher Education and Competition-Based Coopetition

Watson and McGowan (2019) consider in their study competition-based entrepreneurship education in HE institutions. They have constructed effectuation-informed coopetition models in order to launch competition-based entrepreneurship education. Especially, start-up competitions stimulate and support nascent entrepreneurial behavior amongst students, graduates, and staff (Watson & McGowan, 2019).

According to Ferlie et al. (2008), coopetition is a newly emerging form of internationalization of HE. In coopetition, HE institutions simultaneously cooperate and compete in the same markets for the best students, academics, and resources. As a result, "selective networks of elite institutions (such as the Russell group in the United Kingdom) are no longer national, they tend to develop within a regional area (e.g., the League of European Research Universities, LERU, for instance) or at the international level (for instance Universitas 21 or the Worldwide Universities Network)" (Ferlie et al., 2008, p. 344). Thus, the perspective of Ferlie and colleagues (2008) about university coopetition covers meso-, macro-, and meta-level coopetition. They only mention once the term "coopetition" in this context, however. Furthermore, their perspective might be more synergic coopetition as competition-based or cooperation-based coopetition.

Discussions of Higher Education and Cooperation-Based Coopetition

Anderson and Maharasoa (2002) consider partnership between a university in South Africa and a university in the United States. They believe in their research that in combining efforts, universities can secure a more sustainable competitive advantage. They also consider it in their study coopetition. They see that coopetition between local and international universities is even gaining momentum in South Africa:

> Instead of engaging in futile attempts to fight foreign universities, collaborate with them in order to enhance the quality of their academic provision. In this way, universities are not just surviving, but are able to serve a broader and more diverse pool of customers. (Anderson & Maharasoa, 2002, p. 17)

However, the emphasis in the study of Anderson and Maharasoa (2002) is on partnership and cooperation. Cooperation of universities is a tool to compete against *other* universities and to achieve a sustainable competitive advantage. Thus, their study is focused on cooperation-based coopetition.

Walley and Custance (2010) introduce coopetition cases of a agri-food supply chain. One of the cases is focused on the "REEDNet case," which is one example of coopetition in the U.K. university sector, which has delivered education within the agri-food supply chain. Walley and Custance (2010) claim that "there are actually many examples of universities engaging in cooperative activity and this suggests that coopetitive intensity might vary across sectors with the conditions in the public sector being particularly favourable" (p. 190). Thus, Walley and Custance (2010) indirectly see university coopetition activities cover competition-based coopetition, symmetric coopetition, and cooperation-based coopetition based on the circumstances and features of the university. In Table 5.1 their work is placed in the field of synergic coopetition and macro-level due to inter-industry relationships.

TABLE 5.1 New Framework for Coopetition With the Case of Education and University Coopetiton Literature

	Micro-Level	Meso-Level	Macro-Level	Meta-Level
Competition-Based Coopetition	Watson & McGowan (2019); Watson (2019)	Muijs & Rumyantseva (2014)	Dal-Soto & Monticelli (2017)	
Synergic Coopetition	Übi (2014)	Ferlie et al. (2008)	Walley & Custance (2010); Ferlie et al. (2008); Garcia & Velasco (2002)	Ferlie et al. (2008); Adnett & Davies (2003); Karwowska & Leja (2018); Mongkhonvanit (2014)
Cooperation-Based Coopetition		Anderson & Maharasoa (2012)	Brandenburger & Nalebuff (2011)	Dagnino & Rocco (2009)

OUTCOMES

Contribution for Coopetition Discussions

Coopetition discussions cover two significant perspectives: levels of coopetition (micro, meso, macro, and meta) and dimension or continuum between competition-cooperation and especially in this perspective competition-based coopetition, symmetric coopetition, and cooperation-based coopetition. This chapter follows these perspectives in the context of university coopetition and develops a new framework, which combines two dimensions: levels of coopetition and competition-cooperation. This framework maps the contemporary coopetition discussions of HE and perceives the possibilities for future discussions of university coopetition. Thus, this study has two main contributions: new framework for coopetition discussions generally and the fresh perspectives to coopetition among universities.

University coopetition discussions are focused on meso-level, macro-level, and meta-level coopetitive activities. Micro-level coopetition is a less studied area of university coopetition. Only entrepreneurship education of universities with startup competition is focused on the micro level (Watson & McGowan (2019).

Generally, there is a lack of university coopetition research and discussions in the management and education literature. However, coopetition is in all of the noticed studies focused or linked with universities mentioned to be an important feature in the university relationships. This encourages the continuation and enlargement of the university coopetition studies among management and education discussions.

Coopetition seems to be a channel for competitive or even sustainable competitive advantage of universities. University coopetition has several implementations. It might be university–university coopetition, university–industry coopetition, or even international coopetition between universities and other actors. Generally, university coopetition does not follow the perspective of the seminal coopetition textbook written by Brandenburger and Nalebuff (1996/2011), where university coopetition leans on a multifaceted value net perspective.

A bit surprisingly, financing structures (public university, private university, or semi-public university) do not have any remarkable effects or importance on the content of coopetition according to coopetition literature. Perhaps, the financing and success criterions of universities are nearly the same despite the financing structure. In other words, each university aims to have several significant publications, high and effective levels of education, powerful projects and project financing, and high competence to attract students to the university, among others. These features have positive effects on both public and private financing of the universities.

COOPETITION IN THE INTERNATIONALIZATION OF HIGHER EDUCATION

The internationalization is a relevant part of everyday activities among universities. Furthermore, internationalization in universities is based on cooperation. These cooperative activities of internationalization in universities are coopetitive if competitive elements are also present in these activities. Universities have both national competition and international competition, which are distinct, but feed into each other (Marginson, 2006). In some studies, the main element in international competition between universities is the competition for graduate students (Luchilo & Albornoz, 2008; Marginson, 2006). According to Marginson (2006), relationships are structured by cooperation and competition and furthermore, individual institutions are operating at the same time locally, nationally, and globally. That is to say, on the meso, macro, and meta levels.

Marginson (2006) notices that the elite universities (so called Segment 1) with the highest reputation are winners in the international competition, but they are not actually competing in the international markets: foreign students do not increase their reputation, but these institutions are tempting foreign students. The high international reputation is based on research reputation and global power of degree. Nationally successful universities (Segment 2) run foreign degrees as a profit-making business.

Furthermore, Marginson (2006) named Segment 3 (operating commercially in the global market) and Segments 4 (small role internationally) and 5 (no role internationally). Actually, elite universities are winners of the competition in the international markets of universities, but this particular competition and coopetition resembles unintentional coopetition for them (Kylänen & Rusko, 2011).

Research literature contains several studies, which focus on competition actions and activities between universities, not only based on the cross-border movement of students. Reputation, or prestige, of the universities is a very important feature in these studies. The following themes, for example, are drivers for national and international competition and coopetition between universities:

1. National competition between individual researchers encourages them to international personal-level cooperation, such as joint research, in order to upgrade research outcomes and status (e.g., more high-level publications; Tirgar et al., 2019).
2. Universities are competing for foreign students and their tuition fees as a part of their business (Edwards, 2007; Marginson, 2006).
3. Competition among universities for the best doctoral students and researchers. In the background might be international rankings of the universities (Rust & Kim, 2012).
4. Competition between the networks or alliances of universities. In the university "market" is different local and international associations and groups, which might have competitive relationships between each other (Edwards, 2007).
5. National and international project proposals of universities compete for international financing, such financing of the European Union (Rust & Kim, 2012).

On the most official level, universities are allied together using official long-term agreements (Coelho & Braga, 2016). These agreements might be thematic, such as ICT-based and interchange of students, or based on the same or similar geographic area and conditions, among others (Ficarra et al., 2011).

CONCLUSION

Universities have an important role to invent, maintain, and direct new innovations of society. The contemporary innovation processes need more and more cooperation, critical mass of knowledge, and joint know-how, which is often based on international cooperation among universities. National and international financing of the universities is linked with the measured performance of the universities. Universities are competing with each other (e.g., in national financing), which encourages them to international cooperation in order to achieve measured results in the national and international comparisons. Thus, both cooperation and competition, and internationalization, are often present in the activities of universities. Universities have micro-level, meso-level, macro-level, and meso-level coopetition activities, and plenty of them also involve an international dimension.

However, university coopetition literature is not focused on the wide (enlarged) role of universities in society, business, and markets. All the PARTS of the value net, introduced by Brandenburger and Nalebuff (1996/2011), provide important research areas to the university coopetition discussions. That is, organization, competitors, customers, complementors, and suppliers. While basing university coopetition perspectives on these PARTS of value net, it is possible to find several new research themes for the discussions of university coopetition. However, the large perspective of Value Net might provide new ideas and unnoticed possibilities even to the practitioners of university coopetition in the field of internationalization, among others.

The marketizing tendency of universities has increased the importance of business perspectives of the universities. This tendency extends to the international markets of universities. For universities, the digital platforms will increase the intensity of cooperation and competition activities. In business, cooperation generally with other firms and even with the competitors are part of the everyday strategies and practices. The marketizing emphasis of universities will also increase the significance of cooperation among universities. This kind of university–university cooperation is also dyadic coopetition activity because of the existing competitive relationship of universities. Students are more and more internationally oriented and ready to have their university studies abroad and change the university. Furthermore, the role of distance learning and digitizing in HE has increased due to COVID-19. Digitizing has enlarged the amount of competing (MOOC) courses and training programs, which customers—that is to say students and education units—are able to consume. This challenges international university coopetition discussions.

The theme of this chapter—the internationalization in the context of university coopetition—provides possibilities for several further studies. Universities have several organizational levels, such as individual researcher and teacher, level of subject, level of instructors, and the level of university. Each of these levels have competition situations in one way or another, which encourages international cooperation with other individual teachers and researchers, units of subjects, faculties, and universities. The theme:

Coopetition in the Internationalization of Higher Education, contains various multifaceted possibilities for international networks, alliances, and ecosystems among universities. These manifestations will provide plenty of research themes in the field of coopetition.

CHAPTER 6

INTERNATIONALIZATION IN HIGHER EDUCATION IN THE CONFUCIAN HERITAGE CULTURE REGION

A Case Study of Japan

Bradley D. F. Colpitts

The interplay between higher education (HE) internationalization and neo-liberalization reforms has seen the massification, marketization, and commodification of HE sectors globally (Knight, 2013a; Marginson, 2013). The ensuing obsession with fomenting *world-class* institutions—world-leading entities with "abundant resources, concentration of talent, and favorable governance" (Yonezawa & Shimmi, 2015, p. 174)—and utilizing the associated global ranking systems as barometers to measure the success of this transition has compelled an overemphasis on research output over teaching globally. This approach has been criticized for contributing to homeostasis among the established world class stratum of higher education institutions

(HEIs) rather than disrupting it (Altbach & Reisburg, 2018; de Wit, 2018). The Confucian heritage culture (CHC) region has emerged as a potential challenger to traditional elite markets, especially those found in Western, English-speaking countries (Layne, 2012; Marginson, 2011). Japan is home to the first CHC HE sector to massify and embrace HE internationalization (Lee et al., 2020). As the country's population ages and traditional pools of students decline, the sustainability of Japan's current HE model is being challenged (Goodman & Oka, 2018; MEXT, 2013). The Japanese government has sought to reinvigorate the sector to regain its competitive edge over emerging markets in the CHC region and globally by investing heavily in substantial internationalization-driven reforms. To date, however, these objectives have failed to meet the quantitative-oriented standards the government has adopted as benchmarks of their success (Burgess et al., 2010; Pokarier, 2010; Rivers, 2010; Sanders, 2019; Yonezawa, 2020).

This chapter examines Japan's internationalization reforms by situating and contrasting them in relation to the CHC and global contexts. To this end, the chapter first provides a background on the history and idiosyncrasies of the Japanese HE sector. This is followed by an exploration of the shared characteristics of the countries which comprise the CHC region, and by situating Japan's HE sector within them. The chapter then turns to the history of HE internationalization in Japan and provides an overview of the unique challenges the country faces in achieving its reform-oriented internationalization objectives. It concludes by extrapolating possible avenues Japanese HEIs might take to bolster the international component of their campuses based on existing literature. Japan's HE internationalization efforts provide an interesting case study for stakeholders in HE, given its potential implications for emerging HE markets in this region, many of which are facing similar demographic trends and are likely to encounter the same challenges as their own HE markets mature.

THE JAPANESE HE SECTOR

Japan is home to a robust HE system, with a myriad of institutions serving differing communities of learners throughout the country. Japanese HEIs can be categorized into three primary types: (a) national public universities, (b) local public universities, and (c) private universities (Yonezawa et al., 2009). Whereas national public universities are administered by *national university corporations* with heavy government supervision, local public universities are overseen by municipal authorities within their region. The former are intended to serve as flagship universities driving global competitiveness in HE, whereas the latter are meant to attend to the needs of their respective local populations (Yonezawa et al., 2009). As of 2016,

Japan had 777 institutions, 86 of which were national public and 91 which were local public, and an additional 600 private institutions (Yonezawa, 2020). These private institutions account for 77.5% of universities in Japan (MEXT, 2016) and serve a comparable proportion of university students (Marginson, 2012). Of the three institutional typologies, national public institutions are the most likely to engage in internationalization practices, followed by private, then local public universities (Yonezawa et al., 2009). This reflects the demand placed on national public institutions to drive Japan's research agenda and the resultant need to attract global scholars to meet this objective.

The Japanese HE sector underwent a transformation in the early 2000s under then Prime Minister, Junichiro Koizumi, who initiated a wave of neo-liberal reforms aimed at making the sector more competitive through deregulation and corporatization, which saw all national public universities being incorporated (Yonezawa et al., 2012). These reforms allowed the number of institutions to grow by approximately 35% during a period in which the number of high school graduates declined by 39%, resulting in a significant oversupply of positions in universities (Goodman, 2010; MEXT, 2013). In other HE markets, such as the United States, institutions have remained fiscally sustainable by diversifying their program offerings to serve a more diverse range of students with differing needs (Bok, 2020). However, Japanese HEIs have continued to rely on high school graduates for 95% of new entrants and this pool of students declined by 39% in the 2 decades since 1990 before leveling off in 2010 (Yonezawa, 2020). With this demographic set to decrease again in the 2020s, it is likely that many institutions will not be able to remain financially sustainable, particularly as 48% are already below their intake capacity (Brown, 2017). This has precipitated the acquisition and takeover of smaller private institutions by larger HEIs with stronger name-value recognition (Goodman, 2010). The COVID-19 pandemic could apply additional pressure on the ability of Japanese HEIs to attract students both domestically and from overseas.

Historically, Japanese HEIs have subscribed to the Napoleonic model,[1] with universities largely subversive to, and therein reliant on, the state (Yokoyama, 2008). It has been suggested that throughout the 2000s, government oversight increased, disincentivizing more innovative or entrepreneurial practices among institutions (Ota, 2018; Saito & Kim, 2019; Yokoyama, 2006). HEIs in Japan have thus come to rely on government subsidies and tuition to ensure their financial sustainability, and this situation is becoming increasingly untenable as the traditional high school population which fills vacant positions at institutions continues to decline (Yonezawa, 2020). This propensity limits the ability or desire of institutions to pursue innovative means of growth, such as those offered through internationalization, and is intensified by employers' emphasis on the brand value of institutions over the quality of the education they provide (Yonezawa et al., 2012). Japan's private institutions are classified as nonprofit entities, receiving a 10% subsidy from the Japanese government, with the remainder of their income accrued by collecting tuition fees, even in the case of elite, research-driven private HEIs (Yonezawa et al., 2009). Take, for example, Waseda University—one of Japan's leading private institutions—which receives 64% of its funding from student tuition and a further 13% from government and organizational subsidies (Yokoyama, 2006). At present, virtually any student wishing to attain some form of postsecondary education is able to do so (Yonezawa, 2020) and in this environment, some scholars argue that the loss of traditional academic elitism in Japanese HEIs due to a push for egalitarianism and universal access has pushed the system into a pursuit of mediocrity, amid declining academic standards (Ishikawa, 2009; Rivers, 2010). Although other HE markets have turned to internationalization as a means of revitalizing their HE sectors and institutions (de Wit & Altbach, 2020; Marginson, 2018), Japan is continuing to grapple with the unique challenges its HE sector faces, particularly as regional rivals establish their own competitive HE systems.

DEFINING THE CHC REGION

Although the greatest beneficiaries of the internationalization of the HE market have historically been institutions located in Western, English-speaking countries (Aasen & Stensaker, 2007; Lumby & Foskett, 2015), institutions within the CHC region have emerged as the strongest challengers to this hegemony. This transition has occurred in concert with a gradual transfer of economic, social, and military power from West to East (Layne, 2012; Marginson, 2011). Across Asia, but with particular effect in the CHC region, the economic potential represented by the internationalization of HE markets has driven governments to launch a series of initiatives to make their own HEIs globally competitive (Hammond, 2016; Jon & Kim, 2011; Sanders, 2019) and many of these countries have adopted HEI ranking systems as proxy indicators of their success (Lee et al., 2020). In fact, Yonezawa et al. (2009) argue that "in East Asia, and as already seen in Japan, 'internationalization' tends to be regarded as an issue of 'global competitiveness' in research and human resource development" (p. 128). Although not a monolith, HE sectors in the region share some commonalities which suggest a similar approach to HE which Marginson (2011) has defined as characteristic of the Confucian-model. The lingering effect of centuries of contact among various actors within the region has left a (perhaps waning) influence of Confucianism on their approach to HE and HE internationalization specifically.

The countries which constitute the CHC region share a common historical Confucian influence which continues to exert itself both subtly and overtly (to varying degrees) on their cultures and economies. These seven unique countries and territories are: China, Japan, Korea, Taiwan, Hong Kong, Singapore, and Vietnam (Marginson, 2011). Although some scholars have argued that the Confucian influence has begun to recede in the wake of modernization and globalization (Park et al., 2019; Rowley et al., 2019), it continues to color many sectors of CHC societies, including education. The importance of this region to global HE is underscored by the massification of its HE sector and the potential ripple effects this will have across the globe, especially because China alone could produce an educated labor force 1.5 times the size of those in North America and Europe combined in the coming decade (Willekens, 2008). This will undoubtedly have ramifications for HE internationalization regionally and globally.

Despite a common Confucian influence, the countries which comprise the CHC region have clear differences in terms of both their modern and historical development, and the resultant economic and sociopolitical factors which underpin their respective societies. They do, however, share four key commonalities in their approach to HE: (a) strong government-centered policy making and control; (b) the sudden and rapid growth of participation in postsecondary education; (c) high stakes, one-chance national entrance examinations; and (d) high levels of government funding to develop national research capacities (Marginson, 2011).

Marginson (2011) notes that this approach to higher education offers several benefits: nation-state shaping of HE structures, funding, and priorities; universal tertiary participation; the standardization of entrance exams (although this can also be problematic); and accelerated, targeted public investment in research and world-class universities. Universities in this region have seen a rapid rise to become globally competitive, with Japanese institutions emerging first, followed by HEIs in Hong Kong and Singapore, and more recently China and South Korea (Lee et al., 2020; Sanders, 2019; Yonezawa et al., 2012). The expeditious rise of new HE players in the region is not without its problems, as some institutions, particularly in China, have struggled to maintain academic integrity in an environment which encourages competition centered in research output (Han & Appelbaum, 2018; Tang, 2019; Zeng & Resnik, 2010).

Japan is the most mature among the HE systems in the CHC region and its early transition towards universal tertiary education has allowed it to cultivate a robust research system (Lee et al., 2020; Sanders, 2019) and to develop several world-renowned institutions, such as Tokyo University and Kyoto University (Ota, 2018). These flagship institutions have been instrumental to Japan's HE internationalization drive, as they attract a steady influx of talent from East Asia and around the globe (Ota, 2018). However, as Japan's economy and HE sector stagnate, regional rivals have improved their HE competitiveness exponentially, slowly squeezing Japan's top HEIs out of the higher strata of global HE ranking systems (Yonezawa, 2010). These trends will pose a number of challenges to the internationalization of Japan's HE system going forward, as the sector's traditional reliance on international students from the CHC region is expected to be confronted by the greater capacity of institutions in other CHC countries to retain and educate their own (and other countries') students (Ota, 2018; Saito & Kim, 2019; Sanders, 2019). This might be further compounded by a continuing decline in Japan's own university student-age population and static views surrounding who attends university and how graduates are recruited into the labor force (Goodman, 2010; Yonezawa, 2020). The challenges posed to internationalizing Japan's HE sector need to be framed through the lens of the country's history with internationalization initiatives to better understand what has gone wrong and how these challenges can be solved going forward.

HISTORY OF JAPANESE HE INTERNATIONALIZATION

Japan's government has acknowledged the need to internationalize its HE system over the last 4 decades. This is evidenced by a series of initiatives in recent decades (Ota, 2018; Sanders, 2019; Yamamoto, 2018; Yonezawa, 2017). Just as its regional economic rivals in East Asia—namely, China, Korea, Hong Kong, Taiwan, and Singapore—enact projects to strengthen and internationalize their domestic HEI sectors, Japan has made substantial investments in keeping its HE sector competitive (Hammond, 2016; Jon & Kim, 2011; Sanders, 2019; Yonezawa, 2020). This large investment—the equivalent of USD$165.9m for the Top Global University Project (TGUP; 2014 exchange rates; Green, 2016)—reflects not only a need to attract more international students, but also a desire to infuse Japanese enterprises with global talent (Aleles, 2015; Brown, 2017). These initiatives began in 1983 with the formation of the National Council on Educational Reform under Prime Minister Yasuhiro Nakasone (Gibson, 2011) and have progressed into the most recent and perhaps most ambitious plan, the Top Global University Project (TGUP), which aims to build on the successes of its predecessors (Green, 2016; MEXT, 2014).

A program of *kokusaika* (which reflects a Japanese interpretation of internationalization), led by the Prime Minister Nakasone in 1983, had the dual aims to develop intercultural understanding between Japanese and non-Japanese, and "to promote Japanese values abroad" (Gibson, 2011, p. 104). The initial plan aspired to raise the number of international students studying in Japanese universities from a modest 10,000 students in 1983 to 100,000 by 2000 (Rivers, 2010). The plan met its target objective

3 years later than hoped, in 2003, but prompted substantial amendments within support networks for international students and to immigration law (Newby et al., 2009). This early initiative was criticized as a pretense for PM Nakasone's nationalistic agenda, including an ambition to rescind Article 9 of the Japanese constitution (which forbids the nation from having offensive military capabilities) and was said to be more concerned with economics, than a genuine desire to cultivate an international environment in Japanese HEIs (Gibson, 2011; Hammond, 2016). Nevertheless, this served as a catalyst for further internationalization initiatives in the HE sector.

Five years after Nakasone's plan achieved its key objective, Japan's Ministry of Education, Culture, Sports, Science and Technology (MEXT) established a far-reaching vision for internationalizing its HEIs with the Global 30 Project in 2008 (Aizawa & Rose, 2018; Aleles, 2015; Burgess et al., 2010). This initiative incentivized the internationalization of university campuses by offering an equivalent of USD$135.4m (2008 exchange rate) in grants to 30 public and private universities, encouraging them to become globally competitive by increasing the proportion of international instructors and students on campuses, sending more students abroad, and improving institutions' research records (Aizawa & Rose, 2018; Burgess et al., 2010). The initiative sought to increase the total number of international students studying in Japan from the earlier goal of 100,000 to 300,000 by the year 2020 (Rivers, 2010) and to provide programs for which Japanese proficiency was not an entry requirement. Japan had exceeded this goal by 2019 with a reported total of 312,213 international students—though this number is somewhat misleading given that more than a quarter of those included are in Japanese language institutes and not universities (Japan Student Services Organization, 2019). Global 30 showed some additional signs of success, as a year after its implementation a survey found 60.1% of Japan's HEIs had identified internationalization as a top priority. This prioritization was much more prevalent among national universities (at 89.6%) than private institutions (at 50%) which again complicates interpretations of the efficacy of this plan.

The Global 30 Project was subsequently bolstered by Go Global Japan in 2012, which placed a greater focus on improving the capacities of domestic students to compete in the global workforce (MEXT, 2014). The initiative aimed to instill the skills necessary for Japanese university graduates to compete in the global labor force; namely, by increasing the number of those with superior foreign language skills, strong communication abilities, and the varied compctencies necessary to succeed in the globalized economy (Rose & McKinley, 2018). These objectives were to be accomplished by developing overseas study programs, improving English language proficiency, and fostering internationalized HE campuses (West, 2015). The initiative identified two types of universities: (a) Type A (11 universities) which would target all students within the university, and (b) Type B (31 universities) where only specific departments were included (Rose & McKinley, 2018). The stated aims of this plan required an expansion of English as the medium of instruction programs to help improve the English ability of Japanese students, as well as to provide a greater number of English-language programs to attract students from overseas (Rose & McKinley, 2018).

The Global 30 Project and Go Global Japan laid the groundwork for the Top Global University Project—which was enacted in 2014—and Japan's current drive towards internationalizing its HE system is directed by this initiative. The plan aims to address many of the shortcomings which have impeded past efforts to cultivate an internationalized HE sector in Japan. The program again divided recipient universities into two categories: (a) 13 HEIs which aim to place among the top 100 universities in the world, and (b) 24 innovative HEIs which are tasked with promoting the internationalization of Japanese society vis-à-vis its graduates (MEXT, 2017). A few examples of this include Keio University's Enhancing Sustainability of Global Society Through Jitsugaku (Practical Science) and Ritsumeikan University's Bridging the World and Asia (MEXT, 2014). The key performance indicators (KPIs) identified by the government were: (a) internationalization, (b) governance, and (c) educational reform (MEXT, 2014). Notable under KPI-1 is the demand for a greater diversity of personnel and foreign language abilities among instructors and students, an increase in the ratio of instructors trained outside of Japan and students with study abroad experience, and more classes/syllabi offered in English and other languages (Brotherhood et al., 2020; MEXT, 2014). In terms of internationalization-focused components, KPI-2 additionally requires administrators who meet foreign language standards. KPI-3 promotes the admission of a greater number of students into HEIs based on external tests such as TOEFL as a means of moving away from central standardized tests to those which adhere to a global standard. To meet these KPIs and Japan's internationalization objectives holistically, however, there are still a number of obstacles the country's HEIs must overcome.

CHALLENGES TO CONTEMPORARY JAPANESE HE INTERNATIONALIZATION

Japan has a long tradition of insularity which still has ramifications for the internationalization of its HE sector today. The *sakoku* (locked country) period was forcibly ended by the American naval commander Matthew C. Perry in 1853 (Dudden, 2020). Following the opening of its borders to the global community, Japan recognized a need to rapidly industrialize its economy as a means of protecting itself and its interests, and it viewed education as a key component in this transition (Duke, 2009). In this respect, contemporary internationalization initiatives can be viewed as a continuation of a reactive (concerned with maintaining Japan's security and relative power) rather than a proactive approach to educational reform. This approach might explain the resistance to implementing substantive internationalization reforms and why—despite significant lip service given to the concept of internationalization—international instructors and students still feel neglected on campuses in the country (Brotherhood et al., 2020; Ishikawa, 2012; Whitsed & Volet, 2013). This orientation colors the challenges Japanese HEIs must overcome to compete both regionally and globally, perhaps the biggest of which is the lack of diversity within faculties in the country.

International instructors have been described as the "key to internationalization" (Postiglione & Altbach, 2017, p. 248), because they boost the capacity of HEIs to accommodate more international students; drive more and higher quality research output; and provide a more diverse, globalized set of perspectives which inform better quality decision-making (Sanders, 2019; Yonezawa, 2020). Japanese HEIs have struggled to cultivate a climate which accepts international instructors and students as little more than visitors (Brotherhood et al., 2020; Marginson, 2011). Given the aforementioned tendency of Japanese and CHC HEIs to benchmark their status regionally and globally against international HE ranking systems, it is notable that international staff and student ratios remain among the weakest criteria for Japanese universities in these rankings (Goodman, 2010; Yonezawa, 2010). Japan continues to lag considerably behind the OECD average proportion of 20% for international instructors and 7.8% for international students with ratios of 4% and 2.9%, respectively (Hofmeyr, 2021). By contrast, institutions in Singapore and Hong Kong aim to hire half of their instructors internationally (Altbach & Yudkevich, 2017). A small but growing body of literature on the perspectives of international instructors at Japanese HEIs suggests feelings of disempowerment and tokenism amongst many of these academics (Brotherhood et al., 2020; Rivers, 2010; Whitsed & Volet, 2013). This has a domino effect on the system as a whole, because there is evidence that without such instructors, institutions are less prepared to meet the demands of a more international student body (Bradford, 2016; Toh, 2014).

A more diverse body of instructors might be necessary to bolster the capacity of Japanese HEIs to deliver EMI programs. Despite criticisms that Anglicization—which encompasses the growth of said EMI programs, greater English usage in curricula, and the integration of English centered pedagogical models (Lanvers & Hultgren, 2018)—is increasingly encroaching into internationalization in HE, international students studying at Japanese HEIs have voiced a desire for the ability to study in English. A survey of international students at four of Japan's 13 TGUP grant-receiving "top type" HEIs found that 65.6% identified the ability to "study in English while living in Japan" was important (Aleles, 2015). The capacity of institutions to meet this demand has been questioned with existing faculties in the country lacking the English proficiency to deliver such courses and take on supervisory duties for graduate students who wish to complete their degrees in English (Bradford, 2016; Ota, 2018; Toh, 2014). The marginalization of foreign instructors is particularly concerning through this lens, since they could help accommodate a greater number of international students and offset the workloads of those current professors responsible for international students. More diverse instructors have also been found to engender the production of greater and more impactful research (Leydesdorff et al., 2019; National Science Board, 2016; Yonezawa, 2020), which could help reverse Japan's decline in HEI ranking systems. Furthermore, a lack of diversity is a comparative disadvantage for Japanese HEIs when competing with institutions in regions such as Singapore and Hong Kong, which have cultural and historical ties to the English-speaking world and more adaptive immigration systems to entice international instructors and students (Altbach, 2016; Jon & Kim, 2011).

A second issue EMI programs present on campuses in Japan is that they engender the segregation of campuses into two bodies: one composed of international, English-speaking instructors and students and another composed of local, Japanese-speaking instructors and students, with little opportunity for the two groups to intermingle. Japanese high school graduates often lack the language proficiency required to participate in EMI programs (Toh, 2014), despite the fact these programs are intended to serve the domestic student populace (Brown, 2017). A lack of opportunities to live and study abroad during university life for Japanese HE students compounds this problem, as increasing costs associated with overseas study and various levels of administrative bureaucracy complicate job hunting for students who do choose to study outside of the country (Brown, 2017). This might explain why Japanese students are becoming less internationally minded, with the number of them unwilling to work abroad after graduation more than doubling between 2001 and 2015, jumping from 29.2% to 63.7%. All of this begets the question as to whether EMI programs can help HEIs in Japan become more internationalized, and how this ethnic and linguistic segregation prevalent on campuses can be resolved (Bradford, 2016; Brotherhood et al., 2020; Rivers, 2010).

These challenges are not unknown to MEXT, which has overseen the implementation of the TGUP and its predecessors. The organization has released several white papers identifying these very issues impeding the internationalization of HE in the country (MEXT, 2013, 2014). These policy documents propose alleviating these problems by focusing resources into three keys area of the HE sector: internationalization, governance, and educational reform. There is considerable overlap with these three pillars though, with internationalization weighing heavily on the strategies underlying the other two components. As an example, one facet of educational reform in HEIs is expediting the usage of standardized, globally recognized English tests, such as IELTS and TOEFL, to address issues surrounding equivalency and to allow an easier transition for students looking to enter Japanese institutions from overseas (MEXT, 2014). However, the question of how committed institutions are to internationalization still remains, as well as the interrelated issues of what steps the government could take to incentivize them to do so and whether the criteria used to quantify the success of internationalization in Japanese HEIs actually measure what they purport to. The following section examines some of the strategies stakeholders in Japanese HE might employ to invigorate internationalization efforts.

CARVING A PATH FORWARD

Whether Japan can succeed in its drive towards achieving a robust internationalization of its HE sector will be based to some degree on its ability to diversify HE faculties. Similar to its contemporaries in the CHC region, Japan relies on global ranking systems to track the progress of its internationalization efforts and they figure heavily into government policy documents (Sanders, 2019). However, the investments made in internationalization initiatives have not succeeded according to these rankings (Yonezawa, 2010). As previously discussed, the TGUP is centered on the three tenets of governance, internationalization, and educational reform. Here, I suggest four overlapping sub-areas which could help HEIs achieve real growth in these areas: (a) attracting students from nontraditional markets, (b) emboldening HE leadership to build more diverse faculties, (c) promoting research on Japanese HE, and (d) improving the capacity of institutions to enact internationalization-focused activities. This section concludes by asking whether the present benchmarks are appropriate for provoking meaningful internationalization in the Japanese HE sector.

So far, this chapter has outlined many of the challenges facing Japanese HEIs. However, one of Japan's greatest strengths when appealing to international students is that unlike many institutions in the English-speaking West, Japanese universities do not charge international students higher tuition fees and often provide subsidies for these students (Marginson, 2012; Yonezawa, 2010). In fact, a study by Aleles (2015) found that in addition to the ability to study in English, the greatest pull factor for international students studying in Japanese universities was access to financial aid and loans. Nevertheless, 80% of international students at Japanese HEIs do not receive scholarship support (Yonezawa et al., 2012), suggesting that they can still bolster the fiscal sustainability of institutions unable to meet intake quotas from their traditional student pools. The affordability of studying abroad for potential international students might be even more poignant at present given the ripple effects of the pandemic on the economy, along with other fiscal realities impacting global markets, making more expensive Western universities less appealing destinations (Blankenberger & Williams, 2020; Choudaha, 2020; Friga, 2020). Furthermore, Japanese institutions ought to diversify where and how they attract international students, since the number of students from their three biggest overseas markets—China, Taiwan, and Korea—have been declining since 2010 as their HE sectors have developed from sender to receiver markets (Ota, 2018). Although this has been offset by an increase in students in language schools—mostly from Nepal, Vietnam, and Sri Lanka—these students face different economic realities and might require additional language supports due to a lack of familiarity with the Chinese characters used in China, Taiwan, and Japan (Ota, 2018). A greater number of international instructors will be required to meet these students' needs and this, in turn, will necessitate having skilled leaders capable of integrating them into the culture of these institutions.

To increase the number of talented international instructors and meet the needs of a more diverse student body, Japan ought to cultivate more effective HE leaders skillful in creating inclusive campus cultures. Leadership has been identified as a key deficit impeding reform in the Japanese HE system (Ito, 2014). This lack of leadership reflects a dearth in Japanese organizations more broadly, with Yonezawa (2020) noting that the "sense of crisis among Japanese enterprises has intensified, particularly because they face a shortage of globally active leaders" (p. 49). Such leaders are those who can use an international language (e.g., English), have sufficient intercultural competencies, and who hold other pertinent leadership skills. As part of the wider Japanese social and economic sphere, HEIs ought to be training current and future leaders to resolve this dilemma. Some scholars argue that remaining competitive in the knowledge economy requires leaders to move away from hierarchical systems of leadership, which are particularly pervasive in the Japan and the CHC region as a whole (Dimmock & Tan, 2013; Walker & Dimmock, 2002). While HE leadership research in the East Asian region is scant, there is some evidence of the efficacy of investing in bolstering leadership capacity. Nanyang Technological University (NTU) created a leadership training academy as part of its drive to improve its global competitiveness and capacity to attract and keep diverse talents. The results of this initiative are promising with NTU rising in the global rankings from 39th to 13th in 2016, placing it among the top young universities for 7 years running, resulting in it becoming one of the most diverse universities globally (Davie, 2020; Tonini et al., 2016). Japanese HEIs could benefit by instituting similar instructor-led, leadership training initiatives.

Although instructors might be the "'spearhead of internationalization,' a valuable resource with the potential to transform universities into more diverse, effective, and globally competitive institutions" (Brotherhood et al., 2020, p. 499), successful internationalization cannot be achieved by instructors alone. Japanese institutions ought to consider the full spectrum of options related to internationalizing their institutions. To encourage more innovative practices, MEXT ought to allow institutions more agency in determining their own agendas, as rigid, centralized control has been said to stifle institutional entrepreneurialism (Sanders, 2019; Yokoyama, 2006). Institutions ought to explore the full gambit of internationalization approaches, which includes "international partnerships and collaborations, international student and staff experience, international learning and research, and... to widen and integrate international activities across universities" (Soliman et al., 2019, p. 3). HE is a big business in Japan which ensures that many actors are invested in maintaining the status quo. However, were the government to reduce its coddling of HEIs in the country and allow for a more competitive playing field, it could compel institutions to attempt new or dynamic approaches which might make them more apt to embrace holistic internationalization of their institutional cultures in order to stay afloat. This could also expedite the exit of institutions on the periphery which act only as money-generating entities.

Lee et al. (2020) sought to address whether the "catch-up model"—which emphasizes large investments in STEM education and a strong focus on research output—and to which Japan subscribes, would succeed in boosting the profile of CHC regions globally. The authors note that in the decade spanning 2003 to 2013—although the number of Japanese universities in the top 500 of the Academic Ranking of World Universities (AWRU) index fell by nearly half—Korean universities increased by 3 (from 8 to 11) and Chinese institutions increased by more than threefold. However, very few of these institutions have been able to break through into the top 100, which corroborates the criticisms of these rankings systems as not being truly equitable (Lee et al., 2020). The use of quantitative metrics to benchmark the success of HE reforms might not be appropriate for arousing systemic internationalization in Japanese HEIs (Lumby & Foskett, 2016) and "recent research suggests that while internationalization might be occurring in Japanese higher education in quantitative terms... these metrics do not reflect the underlying realities of internationalization in practice" (Brotherhood et al., 2020, p. 498).

To better understand these issues, the Japanese HE research environment needs to open itself to the global HE research ecosphere; both to exert its influence on and be influenced by international HE research. At present, research on HE in Japan is largely being published in house and in Japanese, limiting the information exchange between it and the global scholastic body of research on this issue (Yonezawa, 2018). This insularity might contribute to the stagnation of Japanese-led research being published outside of the country over the last 3 decades; a trend which digresses from prevailing global trends (Postiglione & Altbach, 2017). Improving the capacity of Japanese institutions to publish in English ought to not diminish the importance of research conducted in the Japanese language. It ought to instead act as a bridge between domestic and international audiences. The promotion of collaborative research between Japanese and non-Japanese scholars of HE internationalization provides a chance not only to increase the inflow and outflow of information, but also enhance the impact of research conducted on attempts to internationalize the domestic HE market (Leydesdorff et al., 2019; National Science Board, 2016). A more diverse faculty within Japanese HEIs ought to embolden such ambitions. A greater body of research can provide scholars with a clearer picture of Japan's relative strengths and weaknesses in its internationalization push, and how it can be strengthened.

CONCLUSION

Japan's position as a global and regional HE force is likely to continue to decline without a significant and meaningful reform in the sector. This chapter has argued that traditional sources of students, both domestic and international, who once sustained many Japanese HEIs are declining due to new demographic realities in Japan and the ability of regional competitors to meet the needs of their brightest and most ambitious students. This makes Japan an interesting case study for other players in the CHC region as they face similar challenges in the near future (Yonezawa, 2020). Despite acknowledging this and paying lip service to implementing significant internationalization-oriented reforms (MEXT, 2014, 2017), these initiatives are not compelling the sector to take the appropriate steps necessary to meet its objectives. Japanese HEIs can be encouraged to make more meaningful progress towards comprehensive internationalization by changing the metrics by which these changes are measured. That is to say, they need to re-conceptualize what internationalization means in the Japanese HE context and how to best leverage this construct to improve both the qualitative and quantitative metrics underlying the transition. The comparative affordability of receiving an education in Japan is an advantage domestic HEIs can leverage to attract students. Additionally, cultivating skilled leadership is fundamental in attracting and retaining international instructors, who can contribute to enhancing the capacity of institutions to increase their output of globally impactful research—as well as their ability to attract and retain international students. Finally, affording institutions greater autonomy and agency in their own decision-making might allow more innovative practices to flourish and take root within Japanese HEIs. Ultimately, such measures can form the backbone of more comprehensive moves to ignite meaningful reform in the sector, however, more research on the subject is needed. Once the HE leader in the CHC region, the Japanese HE system needs to take serious measures if it means to create institutions at the vanguard of HE internationalization and innovation.

NOTE

1. Under Napoleon, the education system in France changed. Four grades of schooling were set up: primary, secondary, lycée (run by military units), and technical. Schools stressed the importance of obedience and military values, although primary education stayed almost as it had been prior to 1789.

CHAPTER 7

PROXIMITY IN INTERNATIONAL TEACHING COLLABORATIONS

The Case of INTENSE

Tine Lehmann
Veit Wohlgemuth
Aleksandar Erceg
Sunčica Oberman Peterka
Menno de Lind van Wijngaarden
Annette Ammeraal

The internationalization of higher education institutions (HEIs) has become an umbrella term referring to both internationalization at home (incorporating international and intercultural dimensions into curricula, research, and extracurricular activities) and internationalization abroad (distance learning, student and staff mobility, & credit and degree mobility; Altbach & Knight, 2007). Integrating both aspects seems therefore desirable, although quite challenging. Incorporating international and intercultural dimensions requires taking an outsider's perspective, which a local, non-diversified team might not have (Trompenaars, 1993). Internationalization abroad requires a lot of organizational effort, creativity, and perseverance to implement. Many academics, therefore, refrain from making the effort. Others may be willing, but might not know how to approach such internationalization efforts.

In order to design an international teaching module, five European HEIs joined forces in 2016 for the INTENSE project (INTernational ENtrepreneurship Skills Europe), aiming to build a teaching approach that develops the international, intercultural, innovative, and entrepreneurial skills of students. This project illustrates one specific approach of how to incorporate components of internationalization at home and abroad; while simultaneously being cost efficient, sustainable, and feasible for the HEIs. Other academics and administrative staff might consider this chapter helpful to inspire or launch similar projects.

In addition to presenting the INTENSE teaching concept, we engage in a CAGE distance analysis of the lessons learned in development and implementation of this international teaching approach. In essence, the CAGE model argues that cultural (C), administrative (A), geographic (G), and economic (E) proximity between countries improves cooperation (Ghemawat, 2001, 2007). We apply it to our case in order to discuss antecedents and consequences of our teaching approach and the role of distance/proximity in the internationalization of higher education. As a result, we provide the following additional contributions. Even though the CAGE framework was developed for a business setting, we review the usability of the framework in an academic setting. We also indicate that the CAGE model might be a helpful guide when selecting partner countries for successful international collaborations.

THE INTENSE PROJECT AND TEACHING APPROACH

In the following paragraphs, we illustrate the setup, structure, organization, and challenges of the INTENSE project (intense.efos.hr). It is a cross-border project initially set up by five HEIs from different EU countries. Later on, however, other HEIs joined this project. The founding members are the Hochschule für Technik und Wirtschaft Berlin (HTW, Germany), Hogeschool Utrecht (HU, the Netherlands), the University Colleges Leuven-Limburg (UCLL, Belgium), Turku University of Applied Sciences (TUAS) Finland, and the J. J. Strossmayer University of Osijek (EFOS, Croatia). The EU financed the project as an Erasmus+ strategic partnership.

INTENSE project had four main objectives. First, to promote the internationalization and the international competitiveness of small- and medium-sized enterprises (SMEs), students, and HEIs. Second, to strengthen the cooperation among SMEs, HEIs, and other stakeholders. Third, to advance interactive transnational teaching methods in the fields of entrepreneurship education and innovation pedagogy. Fourth, to enhance the employability of students and HEI staff.

Within the project, we developed and implemented a teaching module with 15 credits (European credit transfer system [ECTS]) in the field of international management, which is simultaneously taught at various HEIs across European countries. The international cooperation assures that perspectives of different cultures are integrated into the materials. Some components (the basics of international management and project management) are taught in regular national settings, with standardized content across all countries. The capstone of the module is a student consultancy project in which students guide small- and medium-sized enterprises (SMEs) in their internationalization process. The course components are also interlinked with each other—the international management component relies on case studies that were written by participants of the student consultancy in the previous semesters. Hence, one way of distributing the knowledge and experience the students gain within our transnational student consultancy is to have them write a case study about their project retrospectively. The best case studies are then edited by the lecturers and inserted as new teaching material for the international management component that is taught simultaneously across all countries. Therefore, we follow Apaydin's (2014) approach of creating a full circle of student experience and involvement. Figure 7.1 illustrates the cross-country collaboration within the student consultancy. Student Team A at a German HEI consults the German SME A wanting to internationalize to the Netherlands, by performing a market analysis of the Dutch market. Student Team B, from the Dutch HEI, supports Team A with relevant knowledge of

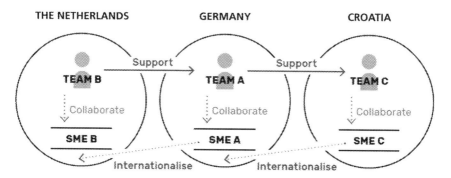

Figure 7.1 Transnational Student Consultancy. *Source:* Adapted from Lehmann et al. (2018).

the Dutch market, while at the same time having to consult a Dutch SME in their internationalization query. Simultaneously, Team A from Germany provides specific German market information to Team C from Croatia, to support the Croatian student team's task for their Croatian SME's market entry to Germany (Lehmann et al., 2018). This system of providing and receiving support to and from other student teams at different HEIs in different countries is the core collaboration component. Not only students and teaching staff benefit from these practical learning experiences, but so do the firms involved in these projects.

This system of mutual dependencies between student teams and the fact that there is something at stake for everyone, goes a long way. Lecturers often used personal connections to recruit SMEs for the projects and therefore did not want to disappoint these connections; whereas, students often hoped to land internships or jobs at these SMEs. This interconnected approach created a lot of potential for friction and a high demand for cooperation between the HEIs.

Depending on the funding and pandemic situation, we executed the consultancy in different ways. Some instances relied completely on virtual communication across countries, whilst others involved occasional student mobility.

Other outputs of the project requiring cross-country collaborations were the development of teaching materials, an SME toolkit to support the internationalization of partner companies, joint training programs, and policy recommendations for stakeholders involved in business development and curriculum development.

THE CAGE FRAMEWORK IN CROSS-COUNTRY TEACHING COLLABORATIONS

The HEIs and the lecturers involved need to constantly work together to make this system of mutual support work. Collaborations between HEIs from some countries could possibly have a higher likelihood for success than others. This is also a central question in the field of international management: "How do you select appropriate host or partner countries, if we have a choice?" Furthermore, "What challenges are likely to be present in specific countries, if we cannot choose them freely?" Many international management scholars address these questions in a business context, for example in the Uppsala model of internationalization (Johanson & Vahlne, 1977). It postulates that it is easier to engage in host countries that are in close proximity to the home country.

Ghemawat (2001, 2007) developed this distance-related framework further by specifying proximity within the CAGE framework. Distances can be of a cultural (C), administrative (A), geographic (G), and economic (E) nature. Depending on the industry and type of internationalization, some distances have more impact (Beugelsdijk et al., 2018). While the framework was developed for use in a business context, it might also be helpful to assess the likelihood of successful HEI collaborations between countries. Ghemawat (2008) himself applies the CAGE framework to discuss globalization in business education. Thomas and Ghemawat (2008) use the CAGE framework to analyze the potential to include globalization and semi-globalization in curricula, but do not discuss HEI collaborations. In the following, we present the CAGE dimensions in short.

Cultural Distance

Attributes which create cultural distance are different languages, ethnicities, religions, social networks, and social norms. These create different interpretations on how to structure relationships. While some cultural differences like languages are easily perceived, others are more subtle. As an example, social norms are often intangible, but may create conflicts if not followed.

From a business perspective, industries that rely on high linguistic content, national identity, or country-specific quality associations appear to be highly affected by this dimension (Ghemawat, 2001, 2007). In education, most content is of a linguistic nature. Therefore, this factor appears to be important for HEIs. Furthermore, teaching practices and tools may strongly differ as cultural preferences might diverge. An example might be an open debate within the opinions in the classroom versus those of the instructor.

Administrative Distance

The reasons for administrative distances are the absence of colonial ties, the absence of shared monetary or political associations, political hostility, and institutional weakness. In a business context, industries that are a source of national reputation—vital to national security or seen as an entitlement which requires certain standards—appear to be affected the most by this distance. This dimension is at times also referred to as political distance or political support and a certain friendliness between partners can overcome these challenges. For example, the EU is in essence a political attempt to reduce this distance (Ghemawat, 2001, 2007).

Although HEIs are not related to national security, they may be a source of national reputation. Furthermore, education is highly important for the future economic and societal development of nations. Usually, certain quality standards are enforced, for example, through accreditation processes. These standards in education can differ strongly across countries. Moreover, educational values and norms are highly path-dependent and hence will vary across countries.

Geographic Distance

Geographic distance between countries is impacted by the lack of a common border, physical remoteness, as well as weak transportation and communication links. This distance becomes particularly important with the need to communicate often and with the requirement for local supervision. Industries with products that are fragile, perishable, or with a low value-to-weight ratio appear the most affected. In addition, industries in which communication is vital are also affected. In essence, this distance refers to the costs of transportation and communication infrastructure (Ghemawat, 2001).

For HEIs and collaborative projects, communication is indispensable. Furthermore, this distance becomes important when scheduling physical meetings. However, it ought to be noted that the advances in communication and transportation technology since Ghemawat's (2001) foundational outline have been strong. Although we still cannot "email the handshake," overall, infrastructure developments have reduced such distances—at least in developed countries.

Economic Distance

Economic distance between countries refers to differences in income as well as differences in the costs and quality of inputs and infrastructure. This distance is the most important attribute for the majority of businesses; particularly if the demand for provided products and services depends on income, or if production costs are high? (Ghemawat, 2001).

For HEI collaborations, demand problems might apply if student fees differ strongly across countries involved in the project. From a cost perspective, there might be differences that allow for arbitrage considerations; but also for frustration, if the same effort does not result in the same positive cash flow.

THE CAGE DISTANCES WITHIN THE INTENSE PROJECT

The collected observations during this project have enabled the authors to make the following qualitative conclusions with respect to CAGE distances.

Cultural Distance

Within the INTENSE project, cultural distances did not have such a strong impact on the collaborations for several possible reasons. Firstly, students and staff specialize in the field of international management, which directly addressed these challenges and thus probably prevented some. Most participants even attended intercultural training beforehand. Secondly, although English was not the participants' native language, all participants were fluent in English and it served as an intermediary language—if none of the partners could speak the other's main language.

The cultural aspects of education are still within a setting of highly developed industrialized countries with many similarities in higher education. Some of the HEI partners already have a highly diverse student and teaching body with many nationalities and international experiences. This makes the participants' communication already cross-cultural to a large extent. International business schools aim to transfer knowledge, skills, values, and attitudes of acculturation and globalization.

However, the existing diversity in international experiences among students and staff varied between the HEI partners. We did observe that students from less internationally diverse HEIs tend to stick together. This was especially obvious in face-to-face meeting situations, where we relied on mobilities to bring the teams from all the involved countries together. In such situations, the students from less culturally diverse countries would mainly sit together and only mingle with their cooperating teams from other countries when facilitated by the lecturers. Hence, it could be that, besides cultural proximity between different HEIs, the degree of international diversity within an HEI is also worth considering.

This does not mean there are no cultural differences and complexities in aligning the curriculum and project. We did encounter the standard intercultural challenges such as miscommunication and different approaches to schedules and deadlines (Hall, 1989). A further cultural distance we could identify was the general connection between HEIs and SMEs. In some countries, strong ties between HEIs and the business community are the norm. Whereas other countries struggled to convince SMEs of the fruitful relationship, especially because the lecturers had little experience with working in a real-life consulting project.

Within learning, individualism and collectivism can have an effect (Hofstede et al., 2010). Individualistic cultures tend to emphasize independent thinking and focus on individual needs and assertiveness. The collectivistic cultures tend not to speak up in public too much and are more concerned with what the lecturer might think. In the INTENSE project, the cultural difference of this dimension could be noted as well. However, by encouraging students to actively participate and to formulate their advice to businesses in the project, the students were able to bridge the differences.

With respect to the Hofstede dimension of power distance, countries with the small power distance tend to have student-centered education; whereas high power distance countries have lecturer-centered education. This tendency manifested itself in the project when students sometimes remained passive and awaited instruction or approval to undertake the next steps. However, because of the aforementioned multi-cultural teams of the HEI, the effects were not strong.

We felt the overall impact of cultural distances was smaller than expected, given the dominance of cultural studies in the international management curriculum? (Taras et al., 2010).

Administrative Distance

Since all partner countries of INTENSE are EU members, we initially assumed that administrative distances would not be an important factor, as all HEIs were reformed within the Bologna process, which aims to harmonize higher education systems across the EU. However, according to our experience, administrative distance turned out to be the most crucial type to be considered before setting up relationships.

As with other teaching staff (Minett-Smith & Davis, 2019), we had to realize that the often-assumed intrinsic motivation and like-mindedness of the instructors is not found everywhere. Some lecturers minimized collaboration as it was perceived as too time demanding and difficult. We attribute this mainly to administrative distances, as incentives for lecturers to participate in cross-country collaborations varied. Some lecturers did not receive any time or financial compensation for their involvement in the project, while others did. Additionally, not all partners were in the same positions within their HEIs. Some HEIs had formalized their EU project involvement in such a way that the contact person was a project management professional and not a lecturer. Hence, the inputs for the teaching approach came mainly from this project management professional. Only when the material was finalized, did the actual lecturer join the project team. While this brought valuable insights to project management discussions, this differing perspective created quite a bit of tension among the long-term lecturers. In other partner HEIs, lecturers came and went as they had only fixed-term contracts. To sum up, it is essential to understand each person's position within their home HEI, as well as to understand their incentive system and boundaries. These details ought to be clearly and openly discussed in a kick-off workshop.

Furthermore, academic calendars and course requirements across universities varied greatly, which made the scheduling of work phases and team meetings difficult. The academic calendars varied so greatly that a cooperation in the spring/summer term between all five partners was nearly impossible. Some HEIs would have a spring term, while others had a summer term. Hence, for some HEIs, the term was already over and they went into early summer vacations, while other HEIs were just starting their term. This made the planned student collaborations across countries (see Figure 7.1) impossible. Whilst the overlap in the winter/fall term was larger—due to other constraints such as exam periods, and so on—we sometimes had only one specific week of overlap where we could organize face-to face meetings.

Another challenge we faced was steering the enrollment for the consultancy project. In Germany, for instance, lecturers did not know how many students would participate in the course and what their background knowledge was until the first class meeting. Furthermore, students were allowed to withdraw from the course throughout the first 3 weeks of the course, which is difficult for a real-life consulting project. In the Netherlands, the project was also open to incoming exchange students, meaning that an Irish student, for example, was working on the project and had to interview Dutch wholesalers. For students not able to speak the native language, this was quite a challenge. In Croatia, it was not possible to adapt the curricula; hence, the student consultancy was a volunteer course for the students.

Although the European credit transfer system (ECTS) aims to ensure a comparable workload for students, the workload expectations differed substantially across countries. Additionally, the course design and execution of the curriculum varied substantially. In Croatia, the student consultancy was offered as an extra-curricular activity. In the Netherlands, the entire teaching approach of 15 ECTS was included in a large 30 ECTS module. By contrast, in Germany, the 15 ECTS teaching approach was split across three courses of five ECTS each. While a curriculum change in Croatia was not possible, the German curricula took 5 years to be effectively adapted. Resolving these situations early on—as well as discussing the progress of both teams and the quality of their work regularly—is crucial to avoid misunderstandings (Wohlgemuth et al., 2019). Nevertheless, the inflexibility of HEI systems and courses of study created challenges in times of highly volatile environments.

Administrative distances seem to be the most crucial challenge in setting up collaborations. Since the EU Bologna process aims to harmonize higher education across the EU, we assume that this distance has an even stronger impact on collaborations between countries that are not part of a political or economic union.

Geographic Distance

All partners of the INTENSE project are EU countries and thus geographical distances between them are not large on average, but some of them are closer to each other than others. Consequently, traveling to the project meetings was, for some partners, time and money consuming. The geographic distance also implies the average distance of some cities to national borders, the condition of roads, access of transportation, and overall communication infrastructure (Miloloža, 2015). Only one partner was from a capital city, which made transportation for the remaining partners a little more difficult. Many of them needed to travel long distances to an airport (sometimes several hundred kilometers) and then to the city of the partner, which for some, resulted in an entire day of traveling. Three partners had a rather small distance with joint borders, whereas two partners had a larger geographic distance. As a result, we did see a greater number of face-to-face meetings between partners who were geographically closer.

Hence, the distances between countries of the INTENSE project did not allow for much face-to-face communication, due to reasons of cost and environmental concerns which result from traveling. Therefore, cross-country team communication relied mainly on virtual tools. Various channels, such as e-mails, text messenger services, video-conferencing, phones, file sharing services, and so on, were utilized. No specific medium was found superior in all cases, but the diversity of means created additional value (Tenzer & Pudelko, 2016). Nevertheless, we tried to ensure scheduled face-to-face meetings at least twice per year in the form of 2- or 3-day project meetings. Geographic distance was not a total barrier to working together, meeting each other, and learning from each other in this project. Yet, this must be taken into consideration when planning a project, because it sometimes can cause problems in the realization of some activities (e.g., student and/or instructor exchange in a cost sense and ease of implementation).

Overall, our experiences show that a combination of virtual communication and face-to-face contact is beneficial. Less distance would allow for more personal contact which would probably be better. However, while virtual communication is not perfect, it was sufficient for our purposes. The COVID-19 pandemic revealed that we can efficiently move many activities online (and save money and time); but, at the same time, virtual interaction cannot replace human contact, we can simply plan it much better and use money and time in more efficient ways.

We conclude, therefore, that geographic proximity is beneficial, but not crucial in this setting. Students and instructors are familiar with and become used to combining these means of communication. Additionally, the nature of the HEI's business allows for effective use of multiple methods of communication.

We did realize—as discussed by Johanson and Vahlne (1977) and Ghemawat (2001)—that geographic distance did play a role for our internationalizing SMEs. Most SMEs internationalized to a neighboring country, not only for reasons of geographic proximity, but because neighboring countries are usually closer regarding other elements of the CAGE framework (cultural, administrative, economic factors, or all of them). This project also showed more interest from SMEs to internationalize toward economically stronger or stable countries, because they saw it as an opportunity (market size, possibility to grow, etc.). Sometimes, certain foreign markets could be geographically further away, but economically closer, thereby becoming good targets for internationalization. The fact that all partners are EU members makes them closer and more desirable destinations for internationalization. At the same time, SMEs are lacking the knowledge and experience in the process of internationalization, and projects such as INTENSE can help SMEs understand the nature of internationalization, their possibilities, as well as the chances to succeed in foreign markets.

Economic Distance

All INTENSE project partners come from the EU, and thus the distances between them are not too big. One of our project partner countries, Croatia has the lowest GDP per capita and therefore the highest economic distance from other project partners (Miloloža, 2015). Thus, the Croatian project partner received the lowest financial compensation in absolute EUR values for its project participation. Although EU funding tends to create similar relative compensation (based on the country's income levels), this occasionally created problems for the local lecturers. In our project, we had three groups on which we can evaluate the effect of the economic distance—students and lecturers who are project partners, SMEs who were consulted during the project, and the HEIs themselves.

For the first group, the economic distance was evident in the aforementioned financial compensation for the project partners, researchers, and the infrastructure needed to travel between countries. Due to the slightly worse infrastructure, the most challenging item to plan for project partners was organizing the trips (students and lecturers) from and to Osijek, Croatia. The difficulty was primarily experienced in air transport, since the Osijek airport does not have any international connections. It was necessary to go to Zagreb or Budapest in order to fly to the other project partners' countries. Although both cities are close to Osijek (approx. 250 km), it meant additional time and resources to get there before flying. As Miloloža (2015) states, economic distance is related to the relative purchase power. Partners from Croatia solved these challenges regarding travel issues and additional time and resources by using low-cost airlines which offered lower prices for transport from Croatia. This enabled project partner lecturers and students to attend all meetings and training during the project. Other project partners also found it challenging to arrive in Osijek, due to the previously mentioned problems in infrastructure; however, this was solved with planning and some additional resources (time and money).

The second group were SMEs who wanted to expand their markets. SMEs consulted during the project were primarily interested in entering the German market, which is both economically and geographically the largest among all project partners' markets. This resulted in an imbalance between companies which wanted to enter the German market and German companies which wanted to enter other project partners' markets. As shown in Figure 7.1, balance between outgoing and incoming to and from the same market is more than desirable for the organization of the consultation process. Ghemawat (2001) states that companies usually choose the target country based on the smallest economic distance between their home and host countries. In our project, we saw that this was not the case since most Croatian companies decided to expand their market into Germany, based on the economic strength of the target country. This was happening due to the ties Croatia has with Germany, not only economically, but in all other aspects. Dutch SMEs chose the German market, which is also the closest and strongest from an economic perspective. One other SME example from Croatia wanted to expand to the Finish market, which has the biggest economic distance, based on the products it was producing. According to Shaheer and Li (2020) a consequence ought to be increased information stickiness, that is, the demands and needs of the Finish customers are costly or complicated to transfer to the Croatian producers. The project partners (lecturers and students) worked together with SMEs to resolve this issue. Students' reports contained information about foreign market-entry mode commensurate with the potential SME's target investment, which was essential (Tsang & Yip, 2007).

Finally, the third group consisted of the HEIs themselves. All HEI project partners were state-owned and non-profit organizations. Due to this fact, they were not influenced by the same mechanisms as businesses, so the economic distance between project partners did not have any significant impact. On the other hand, if the project partners were private-owned HEIs, the economic distance could substantially affect their operations. This is also evident in the research of Meschi and Riccio (2008) who suggest that organizations from wealthy countries will work more often with organizations from similarly wealthy countries than from less wealthy countries.

DISCUSSION AND CONCLUSION

Our chapter contributes to internationalization in higher education in several ways. First, teaching and administrative staff can learn how to execute similar university collaborations with virtual or physical interaction. We outlined one specific approach to facilitate the transfer of host and home country knowledge and to create networks with international HEIs and SMEs. Our transnational student consultancy, while coming with administrative challenges, has enriched our curricula and positively influenced our teaching. We encourage other scholars to set up similar projects or join the network.

Second, the CAGE framework was developed for a business setting. We review the usability of the CAGE framework in an academic setting and therefore support theory development in higher education settings. The CAGE framework appears as a suitable tool to structure distance-related challenges one might encounter in international collaborations of HEIs. This supports its applicability in other settings than initially intended.

Third, we illustrate how to select partner countries for successful international collaborations, based on the CAGE model. We demonstrate in which ways the different types of distances might influence the collaboration between HEIs and which issues ought to be considered when assembling a transnational HEI network. The CAGE model helps in making differences explicit, enabling HEIs to take appropriate measures to overcome them. We can show that even though all our partner HEIs function under a joint administrative framework (the EU Bologna Process), we still perceived the administrative distance as the biggest challenge. Hence, we can only assume how impactful this factor will be in collaborations with a much larger administrative distance. We can furthermore show that the cultural distance challenge might be relatively small, especially if staff and students of the HEI itself are already culturally similar.

Mitigating the administrative challenges is a difficult task, as most HEI systems and curricula are rather rigid and do not allow for much flexibility. We recommend facilitated workshops with all HEI staff at the beginning of the cooperation, in which incentive structures and barriers are made clear and transparent. Furthermore, we suggest the cooperating partners develop joint processes and structures that align with their national HEI structures as much as possible. These processes might include a joint grading approach, clear structures of communication, and roles of responsibilities within the transnational lecture team. While we were aware of such issues at the beginning of our project, we underestimated the necessary degree of detail. Many of our structures and processes were rather general. More clear and detailed structures and processes would have potentially mitigated some of the challenges we encountered along the way.

When implementing a similar project, other scholars might bear in mind some specifics of which might not apply to other projects. All founding members are from EU countries and there was a strong political will and support for such projects, including Erasmus+ funding. As a result, our administrative challenges might have been smaller in comparison to other settings, although we perceived them as the most important aspect. Therefore, we recommend placing a particular focus on the administrative type of distance.

CHAPTER 8

A CRITICAL REVIEW OF TRANSNATIONAL EDUCATION PARTNERSHIPS IN U.K. HIGHER EDUCATION INSTITUTIONS

Eun Sun Godwin
Jenni Jones
Joshua Whale
Tanya Mpofu

This chapter aims to encourage "re-thinking of the transnational education (TNE) partnership" by critically reviewing the current UK TNE partnership approach around three core elements of internationalization in higher education (HE): institutions, people, and knowledge (Kehm & Teichler, 2007). TNE has become increasingly popular and important in the United Kingdom as internationalization has become key to HE sustainability and growth (Naidoo, 2009; HE Global, 2016; Hills, 2017). There can be confusion between various similar terms such as "TNE," "offshore education," and "borderless education" (Knight, 2005). In the U.K. context, Universities UK International (Universities UK, 2018) defines *TNE* as "the delivery of an educational award in a country other than that in which the awarding body is based... (such as)... branch campuses, distance learning, joint and dual degree programs, fly-in instructors, or a mix of these, often referred to as blended learning" (p. 2). The Higher Education Statistics Agency ([HESA]; 2021b), which collects U.K. HE data, defines a TNE student as one who studies "for awards or courses of U.K. universities, but studies overseas without coming to the U.K." (para. 1). These definitions agree with that of the Council of Europe and UNESCO (2007), highlighting the separate national space between an awarding institution and the institutions delivering the educational award.

Effective partnerships require a "dynamic collaborative process between educational institutions which brings mutual thoughts" involving "share[d] ownership of the project" and "decisions... taken jointly" (British Council, 2015, p. 8) by both partners. However, neoliberal globalization in the HE sector, promoting the key virtues of the market such as efficiency or competition, has driven "knowledge economy/capitalism" where "knowledge" is commoditized, priced, and sold (Robertson et al., 2002; Olssen & Peters 2005; Sakhiyya & Rata 2019). Indeed, education has been included as a "tradable" product in the World Trade Organization's (WTO) General Agreement on Trade in Services (GATS) in 1995 (Robertson et al., 2002). GATS, in turn, opened a door for universities to sell their "education product" to a global marketplace (Campbell et al., 2000) where mostly Western universities in English-speaking countries—including Australia, the United Kingdom, and the United States—are dominant as providers or sellers (Naidoo, 2009; Chen, 2015). The potential pitfall of TNE partnerships in the neoliberal HE sector is "institutionalized" partnerships where the actual interaction between the involved people (instructors and students) and ideas/knowledge flow is limited within a rigid institutional framework. Indeed, the majority of the relevant research has had "a leaning toward a focus on the home institution rather than the trans nationalization host" (Branch, 2017, p. 65)[1] leaving a gap in the literature with a dearth of studies on local stakeholders (instructors and students). This chapter aims to address the gap.

This chapter will firstly discuss the globalization of HE, with an emphasis on the debates around the neoliberal, unidirectional approach towards TNE partnership and the institutional level quality assurance challenges with a focus on the U.K. context review. The review will be followed by an investigation on the perspectives of instructors and students (key people/stakeholders) within two TNE-partner institutions in South Asia through sharing preliminary findings from an ongoing research project on TNE partnership led by a business school in a U.K. university.

REVIEW OF THE CURRENT U.K. TRANSNATIONAL EDUCATION PARTNERSHIP APPROACH

This section intends to provide a critical review on the implications of neo-liberalism to TNE partnership under GATS agreement within the WTO, using the United Kingdom as an example. Under GATS, there can be four main categories of "trade" in education:

1. Cross-border supply (any type of course provision across borders including distance learning)
2. Consumption abroad (international student flows)
3. Commercial presence (foreign universities' setting up branch campuses or establishing other partnerships with local institutions in the host)
4. Presence of natural persons (teachers' or researchers' travlling to another country to provide education services; Naidoo, 2009; Robertson et al., 2002).

Among these categories, TNE partnership is established through either the first mode (virtual/distance learning) or through the third mode which in various ways, including franchising, branch programs at foreign campuses, and twinning agreements (Naidoo, 2009).

At "Institutions" Level

Here, the discussion will be based on the notion of "transnationality of HE." Thus, the globalization theory of Robertson et al. (2002) incorporating concepts of spacing, scaling, and territorialization will render a useful framework for the discussion. Firstly, globalization involves "integration" of the world and thus, redefines spaces with "increased pressure of motion on fixity" (p. 475) with, for example, trade agreements intended to lower any barriers of market entry. In the HE sector under GATS, this means that any education-related/socio-cultural policies ("fixity" in the quote above) can be challenged if they are considered as "barriers" to "international" movements of educational service product and consumers (motion). Moreover, GATS and its influence on internationalization of HE has intensified marketization of the education sector. TNE partnership under GATS takes the form whereby provider universities use the partnership as their vehicle for international market entry taking a business approach. TNE has been described as a new revenue creating opportunity (Garrett & Verbik, 2004b) and a lucrative income source (Haslet, 2020; Kernohan, 2019; Lawton, 2018). Several studies on HE internationalization address the topic from the business angle (students as informed customer [Baldwin & James, 2000]; market entry strategy of universities [Tayar & Jack, 2013]; innovations in marketing of HE [Naidoo & Wu, 2014]. As a result, there is an increasing competition in the HE market (Lowrie & Hemsley-Brown, 2011) which further encourages standardization of strategy (Hayes, 2019) and program (Teichler, 1996) among HE institutions. For example, Branch (2017) notes that TNE most commonly occurs in subjects like "business and information technology which are easiest to sell" (p. 28). Success of TNE provision is also often measured by market data such as the percentage of overseas income to the total income of the university, or market share (Ayoubi & Massoud, 2007).

Consequently, these changes in spaces ("respacing") between national versus global/international dimensions involves "rescaling" of governance in education. In many countries, the focus of national education policy is on human development (Campbell, 2012) and often designed to meet wider socio-cultural and economic goals of the country. However, neoliberalism shifts the governance power and control from national government to either supra-national governance organizations such as WTO or sub-national units such as business (Robertson et al., 2002). Hence, rescaling of governance in education implies a weakening of national governments' role in the sector. For example, "tertiary education falls very largely within the ambit of GATS...[which excludes]...services provided under government authority and without commercial purpose" (Robertson et al., 2022, p. 483). This implies that the role of national government in HE is limited whilst assuming "commercial purpose" of the sector which further contributes to its marketization. The United Kingdom's major quality control authority in the HE sector, the Quality Assurance Agency (QAA, 2021a), adds: "Such programmes [TNE] may belong to the education system of a State different from the State in which it operates, or may operate independently of any national education system" (p. 7). This additional factor implies the rescaling of governance as it recognizes the potential that a U.K. TNE program might run independently from the host country's education system.

Moreover, rescaling in governance involves *reterritorialization*—"active construction and reconstruction of territories for the purposes of governing" (Robertson et al., 2002, p. 476). Within TNE partnership under GATS, Western universities have been the major provider[2] and non-Western/developing countries, mainly the host countries. Thus, transnationality of HE implies that the Western (neoliberal) approach towards HE can be transferred to their TNE partnership in the non-Western host country. Many Western governments have increasingly seen HE as private goods (emphasis on individual/private benefit rather than social benefit; Altbach & Davis, 1999) and thus, HE policy in these countries also focuses on maintaining a well-functioning market. Competition and Markets Authority (CMA) regulating consumer protection and competition in the U.K. HE sector can be an example (Competition & Markets Authority, 2015). Together with rescaling in governance to supra- (GATS) and/or sub-government (Western TNE provider universities), transnational education provision expands the providers' "horizons of operation" (Robertson et al., 2002, p. 479) under a familiar market framework (reterritorialization) to the host country, where these approaches potentially conflict with other priorities in HE education polices in the countries (CHEA, 2005; Rutherford, 2001). Concerns over universalism/convergence in HE as a result of globalization particularly regarding the dominance of English (Huang, 2003) as the *lingua franca* (Altbach, 2003a) and cultural hegemony/imperialism (Alderman, 2001; Ordorika & Lloyd, 2015) are in line with this potential reterritorialization through TNE. However, discussing each of these topics in detail are beyond the scope of this chapter. Instead, reterritorialization in TNE partnership will be discussed with a focus on quality assurance related issues in the U.K. context. As TNE has opened new market opportunities for universities and contributed to fast growing global/international consumers, quality control has also been raised as an important issue (Alderman, 2001; Yang, 2008)—including challenges in quality assurance in staffing in twinning/branch campuses (Altbach, 2007) or whether the students in host countries are appropriately informed about their choices (Baldwin & James, 2000).

Discussion on who is responsible for quality assurance also seems to be between international agencies (e.g., Global Alliance for Transnational Education [Pease, 2001]; the International Network of Quality Assurance Agencies in Higher Education [Cheung, 2006]) versus quality assurance agencies in the providers' home country (Coleman, 2003; Eaton, 2012) without much discussion about the host country/institutions' involvement. This reflects rescaling of governance in HE from national government to supra- or sub-national agencies. Moreover, leaving the governance on quality assurance to the providers' home country government/regulatory body regarding who is setting the standard for whom and for what purpose, raises questions about reterritorialization of providers' operation in the host. In the following sub-section, this chapter develops this discussion further by focusing on the United Kingdom's TNE partnership case.

Since 2010, there has been a continuous increase in U.K. revenue from education-related exports and TNE activities (HM Government, 2019, Figure 8.1, p. 8). Exploiting the first mover advantage, over 80% of U.K. HE institutions were delivering degree programs overseas in 2015/2016, with substantially growing TNEs (Hiles, 2016b). More recently, in the year of 2019/2020, a total of 432,500 TNE students studied post- and undergraduate programs with U.K. HE providers (HESA, 2021a). Compared to the number in 2007/2008 (195,770 students [Universities UK, 2020]), the figure has more than doubled within a decade. The U.K. Department for

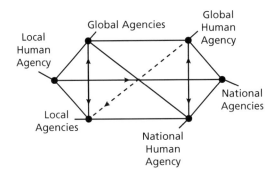

Figure 8.1 Glonacal agency heuristics. *Source:* Marginson & Rhodes, 2002.

Education estimated TNE activity to be valued at £2.1 billion in 2018, a growth of 92.3% since 2010 with only a 0.8% dip in the figure between 2017 and 2018 (HM Government, 2019).

Despite this continuous growth in recent years, calculation of TNE value remains a challenge partly due to its low priority in the list of core interests in the relevant policy discourse (Kernohan, 2019). A lack of, or poor quality of, available data, complexity in terminology, and difficulties in defining the scope/scale of TNE-related activity (Garrett et al., 2017; Garrett & Verbik, 2004b) have added further challenges (Hiles, 2015; Hiles, 2016a). Although the U.K. revenue from education-related exports and TNE activity has increased steadily, the latter contributes insignificantly towards the total revenue without affecting the overall trend (HM Government, 2019). Hence, this chapter will focus on the understanding and perception of TNE partnership reflected in the relevant regulations and guidelines rather than figures in evaluating the significance of TNE partnership in the U.K. context.

With a growing market size of TNE, ensuring quality across borders has become important in the discussion of the relevant strategy and policy in the United Kingdom. The U.K. debate on who has the ultimate responsibility for quality of TNE is largely between whether this responsibility ought to be under the centralized quality regulatory body such as QAA audit (the U.K. regulatory) or should be left to individual provider universities. Others suggest global or international quality assurance schemes as an alternative (Garrett & Verbik, 2004b). However, in this debate, there is not much consideration towards host country or institutions where the actual delivery is happening.

Moreover, "despite the apparent scale of activity, there would appear to be no U.K. professional or institutional association dedicated to transnational higher education" (Garrett & Verbik, 2004b, p. 8). As the sole official body to carry out assessments and evaluations of U.K. HE regulations, the role of the QAA in U.K. TNE has been limited to provision of the U.K.

Quality Code for Higher Education (2018) on behalf of the U.K. Standing Committee for Quality Assessment (UKSCQA). Although this code is used as a key reference point for TNE providers, the expectations for standards and quality it sets are for U.K. HE providers in general rather than those specific for TNE partnership. Judgment of good quality or a successful TNE partnership also very much relies on the transnationality of the program. For example, a recent report from the British Council (2021) on TNE partnerships in 12 European countries introduced several success stories highlighting the benefits TNE brought to the host countries and institutions. One of the cases was that of Lancaster University Leipzig (a branch campus of the U.K.'s Lancaster University) and its ambitious growth plans for a "one campus culture" with a commitment to provide "the same academic quality and student experience" (British Council, 2021) to its students as that of its U.K.-based students. However, although the benefits from these successful cases are apparent, it is also clear that the emphasis is very much on transnationality of the same service and experience in the U.K. providers to the host country with a lack of locality of the host institutions/countries in measuring such success.

Nonetheless, there is a growing awareness and efforts to include the host country in the TNE partnership discourse. Recently, the QAA (2021) suggested Quality Evaluation and Enhancement of the U.K. TNE (QE-TNE) focusing on four core purposes and outcomes: strengthening the reputation of the U.K. TNE, provision of valued information and insights, building mutual trust, and delivering benefit for TNE stakeholders. Although this is still a voluntary service, the shift in the focus to "greater local understanding of U.K. HE and detailed insights into host country operating environments for the U.K." (QAA, 2021, p. 4) is clear. Indeed, more recent QAA reviews of U.K. TNE provision across a range of countries beyond Europe—including Hong Kong (SAR), China, and India—highlighted areas of good practice in how providers responded to the host institutions' needs. Consider Oxford Brookes University's provision of academic and professional advice in China's context (QAA, 2012), Staffordshire University's provision of diverse progression routes, and the University of Wales' assessment management in a foreign language (QAA, 2018). Healey (2015) also noted that U.K. TNE partnerships are becoming multidimensional and collaborations between partners are much more than just a non-U.K. education institution offering a course developed by a U.K. HE institution. In a comprehensive survey conducted by the Observatory on Borderless Higher Education and Joint Information Systems Committee on U.K. TNE, nearly 40% of respondent institutions rely on host country's local lecturers in their program delivery whilst around 70% of respondents are considering joint operation of TNE programs compared to full online provision (e.g., distance learning; Lawton & Jensen, 2015). Hence, including local aspects (e.g., cultural, legal, and environmental) of the host countries in quality assurance is becoming strategically important to the provider institutions as well as to the host institutions (Kernohan, 2019). In the following section, the analysis proceeds on to the people level (Kehm & Teichler, 2007) to incorporate host aspects which have been neglected in the institutional level of discourses on TNE partnership.

At People Level

This section shifts the focus of analysis of TNE partnership to the local and people level. Instructors and students in partner institutions are important internal stakeholders in TNE partnership delivery and in engaging with the day-to-day learning and teaching of programs from the provider institutions. Local instructors play an important role in TNE partnership by delivering the program to their own students and are concerned with the quality of the teaching, learning, assessment, and student support provided. Studies found staff engagement is key to a successful partnership with its progression and value creation (Bordogna, 2018; Helms, 2015). Similarly, students' perception of their TNE partnership will determine their sense of belonging/community. However, despite the significance of these stakeholders' role in the success of partnerships, there is a dearth of research on the analysis of instructors' experiences (Bordogna, 2018) or students' experience (Hills, 2017) in TNE partnership. This section attempts to address this gap in the relevant research. This approach will also be a response to the calls for an encompassing framework of TNE partnership taking a more local-global axis to TNE research (Deem, 2001) by paying attention to the perception/understanding of instructors and students in host institutions towards TNE partnership.

For this, the Marginson and Rhoades's (2002) glonacal agency heuristics (GAH) model (Figure 8.1) will be revisited. In this model, TNE partnership is understood to comprise of two main aspects, *level* (global, national, and local) and *domain* (human and institution agencies). In contrast to the emphasis on the global and home country national level of institutions in conventional TNE discussions, this model provides a framework to demonstrate how TNE partnership as a multidimensional phenomenon is exposed to compounded communications, complex information flows, and interconnected social relationships across borders (Marginson, 2004). The model recommends reciprocal and simultaneous flows of ideas, activities, and influences among these global, national, and local agencies. Hence, it provides a useful benchmark to evaluate TNE partnership and the interactions amongst different stakeholders in the partnership at various levels.

This section highlights the role and perception of human agencies who are important stakeholders in this partnership. There are a variety of internal and external stakeholders involved within TNE partnership with differing priorities, interest, influence, and power (Shams, 2016). Stakeholder theory provides an additional useful insight in this section's analysis. Stakeholder theory focuses on the mutually beneficial relationships and multiple reciprocal exchanges that are crucial to an organization's operation and ultimate value creation (Freeman, 1984). Here, the theory suggests that "value should be created both with and for different stakeholders" (Freudenreich et al., 2020, p. 5). From this view, students as customers and module instructors as both business partners and employees are seen as not just receiving value but also contributing to value as active participants. The focus of this section will be on the viewpoints of these internal stakeholders amongst agencies in the GAH model notwithstanding the influence of external stakeholders (government and society).

PERCEPTIONS OF HOST INSTITUTIONS' PEOPLE: INSTRUCTORS AND STUDENTS

In this section, findings will be shared from an ongoing research project exploring host institution instructors' perceptions of their TNE partnership with the provider institution in the United Kingdom, and their full-time, final year undergraduate students' sense of belonging/community. The findings were gathered from two TNE partner colleges (both in South Asia) connected to a business school in the United Kingdom. It is important to note that both TNE partners in this study have long-standing and mature relationships with the university. The words students used when they were asked to summarize their student journey include "rollercoaster," "enlightening," "positive," "memorable," "marvelous," "unique journey," "learning with fun," "lifetime learning," and "exhilarating experience." This demonstrates that the findings discussed next are set against a backdrop of mostly highly satisfied students and instructors (module instructors).

Six semi-structured interviews were carried out virtually using Microsoft Teams, with module instructors of two different TNE partner colleges—both from the same South Asian country—connected to the same U.K. business school. Questions were asked about the use of university teaching material, the degree of autonomy the instructors felt over their delivery and the assessments, their experience of blended learning during the COVID-19 times, together with their views about the communication and their sense of belonging. In addition, a focus group was carried out, again through Microsoft Teams, totaling 58 students from the same two TNE partners. Ten students made the majority of the contributions verbally and through the "chat" function sharing photos and comments throughout the discussion. Questions asked in the focus group included those on the key skills they felt they had learned from the provider institution's program, the teaching and the overall student experience including positive versus negative factors having impacted their sense of belonging and feeling of being part of the wider U.K. university community.

There were a number of similar and emerging themes from both the interviews and the focus group and these centered around autonomy, communication, interaction in the classroom, and teaching style, as well as a clear focus on their sense of belonging.

Autonomy

All six instructors expressed their mixed feelings about autonomy:

> I would say that the university has given us autonomy to deliver the subject, but they always expect us to adhere to the main content (and guidelines) given by the university. (Instructor 2)

The instructors overall were not negative about the restrictions and the guidelines imposed on them by the provider university regarding teaching material and the assessment. At the same time, they felt they had some control over the material (e.g., adding materials) and how they teach the lessons:

> The university has given very good and rich resources... that covers almost all the area, but as far as the question of making things clear, the teacher always has the liberty to explain in different ways. (Instructor 1)

The additional materials usually involved localized materials such as "local case studies," "examples in the local context," "extra materials... in our localized context," and "local videos, local journals" to make it easy for the students "to relate to that topic" (quotes from Instructor 6). Some instructors felt the autonomy with respect to choosing materials, to the extent that they do not need to consult with the provider agencies (e.g., the module leaders).

The question about virtual learning environment (VLE) use shows similar responses. Several instructors mentioned that a different VLE was used to offer a more easily accessible platform to house additional teaching material for students and to avoid technical issues for some students struggling to connect to the provider university's VLE:

> We have a Google platform, Google Classroom, we are using for our internal purposes, so we are also posting important readings. Sometimes students just

do not open canvas...or...the student faces issues, logging into the canvas. (Instructor 5)

These examples show how a local voice is incorporated into daily practice at the host institutions by instructors although it is mainly done informally.

At the formal level, the local instructors' role seems to be more limited. Two instructors felt that they would like greater autonomy over the type of assessment offered—preferring exams (as this is more typical in academic intuitions in their country)—and more control over the marking, with a desire to credit the students for additional contribution which the U.K. module leaders—external to the teaching—might not have observed. They mentioned that this would give them a greater feeling of ownership towards the module:

> But our faculty is always limited by the module inspection by the learning outcomes that faculty must ensure the students have safety by other evaluation guidelines. (Instructor 1)

> (I wish)...if I could have the autonomy of a certain...degree...in the assessment. For example, there is the assessment of supposing 100 marks, so if the module leader would allow me to have at least forty percent from my side. Then...we will not have to depend on all the assessment on them to get the mark. (Instructor 4)

As discussed earlier, there have been many criticisms directed towards a lack of debate about adaptation of learning/teaching content, delivery, and assessment within TNE partnerships from a local context. However, as Yang (2008) noted, "The global–local nexus is a twofold process of give and take, an exchange by which global trends are reshaped to local ends, and a dynamic interaction between global trends and local responses" (p. 282). Hence, instructors ought to be able to exercise a direct influence within TNE partnerships (Bordogna, 2018) for the student's learning experience to be the most effective, and the curriculum must be adapted and tailored to the local context and needs, while the local instructors are the best agencies to do this (Shams & Huisman, 2012). Dunn and Wallace (2004) also state that students expect and want to have the local context addressed in their course through culturally specific case studies whilst being critical of references only from developed countries' perspectives. Deem (2001) also stated that institutions in partnerships ought to take advantage of distributed knowledge systems locally rather than globally. In these two TNE partnership cases, instructors had opportunities for flexibility, particularly in an informal way such as additional teaching content for workshops and the teaching style, which provided students with opportunities to apply their new knowledge and skills in the local context and beyond. However, at the same time, they didn't have the flexibility in the formal domain, for example, assessments and marking due to local or host restrictions.

Hence this dynamic brings a major dilemma in TNE partnerships: the level of emphasis and balance between standardization and local adaptation (Shams & Huisman, 2012). The centralized-standardized model has been heavily criticized with the suggestion that it restricts academic autonomy and ultimately the quality of the educational experience at the receiving end (Shams & Huisman, 2012). At the same time, a certain form of quality assurance and control in the host institutions comparable to those of the provider is required (Coleman, 2003; Eaton, 2012) for the students' satisfactory learning and the provider institutions' reputation (Kernohan, 2019). Moreover, in this study, although the local instructors (local agencies in host institutions) might have felt autonomy within their own VLE space, this does not help to reciprocate the contextual knowledge back to the United Kingdom, and thus the flow of information is still not reciprocal as the GAH model suggests. Local instructors' putting their own materials on a separate VLE meant that the U.K.-based module leaders/instructors potentially do not have access to these resources. This can create a reverse brain-drain (British Council, 2021) scenario whereby local knowledge is not being shared back into the provider institution, not influencing and/or improving the knowledge base back there, and in turn, not feeding into future learning or future partnerships going forward. Thus, the balance between standardization and local adaptation is important so that students gain both local and global knowledge whilst one does not overshadow or dominate the other within these TNE partnerships.

Communication

Heffernan and Poole (2004)—through examining the relationships between Australian universities and their offshore partners—cited communication, trust, and a shared vision as critical to the prevention of relationship deterioration and termination. Bordogna (2018) also agrees that "fundamental to the success of a TNE partnership are the social relationships which establish between these awarding and host operational faculty members" (p. 4). The majority of the instructors in this study mentioned positive communications and interaction between module instructors in the host and module leaders in the provider institution—such as regular email updates and virtual meetings, and quick turnaround and resolution for queries—as key in successful partnership in decision-making and sharing experiences:

> Some of my colleagues have said that they have not got a prompt response and as a result, there has been a delay in decision-making. So... there should

be feedback sessions or module review sessions...which helps the module lecturers like us to reflect on our teaching and teaching methods, pedagogies to share our experience. That is important. (Instructor 5)

Students' comments were only on the communication within their own college with their module instructors. Nonetheless, they made positive comments on the helpful module instructors and the supportive student support services in their institutions.

Little was mentioned about two-way communication or collaboration, suggesting that the communication is generally one way, module leader to module instructor and module instructor to student. This unidirectional flow of communication implies that decisions are made by the providers' module leaders and the host instructors receive the decision suggesting a greater control given to the former than the latter. Regardless of the positive perceptions of responsiveness of the module leaders to the instructors towards their queries/requests, this is still distant from what the GAH model encourages—reciprocal and simultaneous flows of ideas and activities amongst agencies at different levels. Moreover, this unidirectional way of communication reflects the consequence of reterritorialization (the provider's agencies have dominance over decisions) which some critics have noted as it can potentially result in "harmful consequences of neo-colonialism" of "othering" in HE whereby human agencies in non-Western host countries can be reduced to objects of knowledge (objectification) under sweeping generalization and characterization with negativity (Rhee & Sagaria, 2004, p. 81).

Interaction in the Classroom and Teaching Style

Although differences in teaching style was queried only in the instructor interviews, this was a subject that came to the fore regularly by both instructors and students. The perception seemed to be that the TNE partner's teaching style was quite different than the typical South Asian culture would normally offer, suggesting the potential influence of the U.K. provider university. For example, students perceived that typical South Asian teaching tends to be more theoretically than practically oriented, and as a result, endpoint exams rather than ongoing practical projects are more common as assessments. Students seemed to regard this more applied "U.K. style" of learning highly positive, distinguishing themselves from other students in the country using languages such as "our university" or "we" as the provider university students:

Here colleges are usually focused at providing a theoretical knowledge but our university endows us the right values at an early age...critical thinking style, leadership style...those formative assessments improved our understanding level and made lessons quite interesting throughout the journey. (Student)

It was a really very different experience for all of us because in typical X style of learning, we are... focused on theoretical and exams but in the university, we are mostly focused on the assignments which has really helped us to enhance our speaking skills, presentation skills, and research skills. (Student)

The students expressed several other positive experiences including participating in different on- and off-campus projects and trips, hence they felt they could apply the skills they learned from the course (mostly citing time management, presentation, and research skills as their key learning), sharing photographs and success stories:

We organized a business idea pitching competition by inviting millionaires of the city to be jury members. This was televised and will soon be aired all through X. (Student)

An interesting observation is that although students perceived the skills they learned and applied to such projects/competitions were from the provider university, the projects/trips were not organized by the latter but either by the host institution or other local (or national) agencies in the host country. This highlights the importance of the local agency's role as suggested in the GAH model in enhancing students' experience and satisfaction.

Another intriguing finding is that the instructors' perspective towards the United Kingdom versus their own teaching seemed to be the opposite to that of students. For example, the interviewees/instructors thought they were more accommodating, offering more local/topical material, providing more interaction in the classroom, and more opportunities to explore the topics than their U.K. partners. This is a potential misconception towards the U.K. HE approach of teaching, perhaps because their assumption is based on the material offered for them to teach from rather than from actual observations:

There are some differences like we instruct students in a more descriptive way of analysis... [L]looking at the content of the slides we found the teaching at the university was more research based. I think that is the biggest difference. (Instructor 5)

The instructors' perception of differences in teaching style also contrasts with conventional findings in research by which Western education is more experiential and Eastern education takes a more formal approach (Dunn & Wallace, 2004). This might reflect different understandings of what a practical or interactive approach in teaching is in different cultures. However, combined with students' perceptions, important implications suggested from these findings are (a) a degree of freedom afforded to the instructors to teach how they wish; and (b) the instructors' constructive mediating role in conveying to the students what the provider institution intended. For example, an instructor made a comment about their smaller classes and the advantage of providing an opportunity for deeper discussion, pointing it out as one of the differences from U.K. HEIs:

> (Because of a smaller classroom)...we know the students more closely. There's a lot more interaction, which also...spills over in the teaching, so it's more detailed, getting into deeper...And that is primarily different by the colleges. (Instructor 3)

Studies argue that variation in teaching methods and staffing within external partnerships is inevitable (Coleman, 2003); as such, students cannot expect to receive the same teaching and learning experience as those studying at the main campus (Altbach, 2010). However, this does not seem to be the case for these TNE students based on the findings above. Factors negatively affecting their learning experience are mainly time-management issues between job and study, which resembles those of students in the provider university. On the contrary, positive experiences of students in the partner institutions seem to have been enhanced thanks to smaller groups, greater flexibility with the material, as well as extra-curricular activities such as external competitions and study trips. These are examples highlighting the importance of the local agency's (both institutional and human) role in TNE partnership for the quality and student satisfaction assurance.

Sense of Belonging

Belonging is about feeling that you are connected to and feel accepted as a member of a group or community (Humphrey & Lowe, 2017) and is closely aligned with the concepts of academic and social engagement (L. Thomas, 2012). Belonging in education is found at multiple levels: relationships within the educational microsystem (with friends and a peer group), mesosystem (between the student, her/his peers, and her/his teachers), and macrosystem (the student and the educational establishment; Cureton & Gravestock, 2019). Both instructors and students were given a direct question about their sense of belonging (how much they felt part of a university community) in this study and both parties made comments in respect of the micro, meso, and macro systems using terms including ownership, partnership, pride, and identity. Students were asked to rate their sense of belonging and the results ranged from 7–10 out of 10 (10 being a high sense of belonging).

Ownership was reflected in answers from instructors regarding their own mode of teaching, and from students in regards to their ability to get involved with peers in practical projects and assessments (microsystem) as discussed in the previous sections. Partnership was also mentioned by both parties (mesosystem). Instructors perceived that partnership mainly comes from the support given by the U.K. module leaders through induction/ orientation exercises, providing the teaching material, using the same systems, supporting/doing the assessment moderation, and resolving the queries quickly:

> I feel the partnership is very strong... The main reason is the support the university provides to the local partner here... I am a visiting lecturer for some other institutes, but I have not seen such strong partnerships because always something is lacking in communication and support from the university side. (Instructor 2)

One thing to note here is the link made amongst local instructors' perception on partnership, support from the provider institution, and quality assurance:

> But here, they (the U.K. business school) give fuller support and they are very much conscious about what we do, and how we maintain the quality. And with our assessments we are aligned with... the quality. So, in that case the partnership is strong. (Instructor 2)

In other words, the local instructors care about the quality in their delivery (another example of their sense of ownership), and thus, they consider interest and support from the provider institution regarding quality assurance as "partnership." This in turn seems to be related to "pride" which enhances "sense of belonging" in both instructors and students. For example, one of the instructors commented that the students have a significant sense of pride being part of a larger U.K. university:

> I feel that... there's a great degree of... (student)... belonging... (to the University)... and identification because to a great extent there's a lot of pride... with being associated with the university. (Instructor 3).

Indeed, in the focus group, the students proudly shared photographs of their group activities representing the university, wearing university branded matching t-shirts in external events (macrosystem) and of others standing in front of the U.K. university buildings when they visited the campus. These photographs as well as terms they used such as "we," "us," and "our university" demonstrate how they had identified themselves with the wider university. Pride and identity were also mentioned in respect of the access given to university materials and support offered, potentially because they felt that this was equal to the support given to those physically at the U.K. university:

> The course work and all the materials we have been getting for the university, makes us feel like we are part of the university. (Student)
>
> Module leaders to organize...(and)...conduct the orientation sessions make them (students) understand more of modules...This type of sessions let them know that they are also a part of the university, just like students, who are studying there on the physical campus. (Instructor 2)

Two instructors also mentioned "lack of training for module instructors" and "one-way communication" as factors which contributed to a lack of belonging. This emphasizes that the providers' support to maintain the same quality in the host institutions, particularly through interaction between human agencies (the module leaders and the module instructors/students), is key in enhancing the sense of belonging in the host institution. Recent work has linked belongingness with student retention and student success (Cousin & Cureton, 2012; L. Thomas, 2012), so this is a crucial component for both key stakeholders, with and for each other.

This finding also implies that it is still possible to facilitate a sense of belonging in the students of the host institutions without reterritorialization (the providers' close control in delivery of the program to replicate it), and in the process, the local agency's role (particularly the instructors') is critical. For example, students seem to link supportive interactions with their module instructors and host institutions' buddying programs to their perception on partnership:

> Even our module lecturers make us feel part of the university—they are very skillful; they have been delivering it in a very perfect way. (Student)
>
> We have a very good environment in our college to interact with our junior batches and as well as with the senior batches. This allows us to share our knowledge with each other. (Student)

This is closely in line with the findings of Heffernan and Poole (2004) that internal commitment of the provider institution—identifying the key roles and responsibilities of the partner—maintain a win–win relationship whilst sustaining key personnel (human agency) are key factors determining success or failure of TNE partnership.

IMPLICATIONS FOR "KNOWLEDGE" LEVEL AND CONCLUSION

The aims of this chapter were to encourage re-thinking of the U.K. TNE partnership approach with a review of the topic at institution and people level. The relationship between the global and local level is a complicated one (Marginson, 2006), yet effective partnerships require a "dynamic collaborative process between educational institutions that brings mutual thoughts" which involves "share[d] ownership of the project" and "decisions...taken jointly" by both partners (British Council, 2015, p. 8). Unlike discourses at the institution level, the preliminary findings from an ongoing project exploring instructors' and student's perceptions of their TNE partnership (review at people level) suggest that relationships are not only important for direct practices involved in the partnership (e.g., sharing knowledge and decision-making) but are also associated with quality issues. These findings also suggest that the local instructors' role is critical in enhancing the quality of program delivery and positive perception towards TNE partnership from other stakeholders such as students in the host institutions. This is in line with findings by AQUA (2003) that there is a perceivable connection between the (quality) standards of the program and the relationships built with each other in the partnership. A successful TNE partnership is one in which instructors interact with, share, and negotiate tasks and outcomes which suit the requirements of a multitude of stakeholders (Bolton & Nie, 2010) and hence, what matters is the relationships which are built between instructors, students, and institutions to sustain for the long term (Marginson, 2004).

The discussions on TNE partnership at the institution and people level have implications for the partnership at the knowledge level. There have been concerns over cultural imperialism or hegemony (Ordorika & Lloyd, 2015; Westwood & Jack, 2007) by market-driven and institutionalized TNE partnership in U.K. HE institutions, which can result in mere replication of Western knowledge product in many non-Western/developing countries' partners (reterritorialization of HE). However, the vision for TNE partnership ought to be that such a partnership is for the benefit of all and, more importantly, "broader public interest is not sacrificed to commercial interests" (Garrett & Verbik, 2004b). Considering that the ultimate purpose of education ought to be developmental, the goals of international education partnership should also broaden their scope such as capacity development of the host country and the stakeholders in the country at various levels (OECD & World Bank, 2007).

To achieve these goals, the discourse about ownership and other entailing issues such as quality assurance in the educational partnership should involve a wider scope of stakeholders. In fact, the trend of international educational partnership seems to be shifting from trans-national to multi-national (Healey & Bordogna, 2014). In global business, the distinction between the former and the latter lies in where the "center of gravity" in the business is located (Healey & Bordogna, 2014, p. 47). It seems that—in international education partnership also—there is a growing trend towards a similar shift of center of gravity from the provider university to local partners and other related stakeholders in terms of provision of facilities and adjustment of curriculum/program contents to localized context. This can be seen in several case studies reviewed in Healey and Bordogna (2014) and in the study introduced in this chapter.

This shift brings implications to the educational partnership at knowledge level. Following Lehmann's (2010) categorization of multinational firms' architecture/strategy of information systems (Figure 2.1 on p. 12), although local autonomy and responsiveness can be high in both transnational and multinational models, centralized/global control is lower in the latter model. As the trend of educational partnership is shifting from transnational to multinational, the manner in which the knowledge ought to be managed in such partnerships might also be informed by multinational information management reflecting the elements of high local autonomy/responsiveness and low global/centralized control.

Based on the arguments so far, this chapter proposes a new model of multinational education partnership adapting the key concepts from TNE partnership that this chapter has addressed so far (i.e., three elements of TNE: institutions, people, and knowledge [Kehm & Teichler, 2007]; GAH model [Marginson & Rhodes, 2002]). Figure 8.2 describes how current

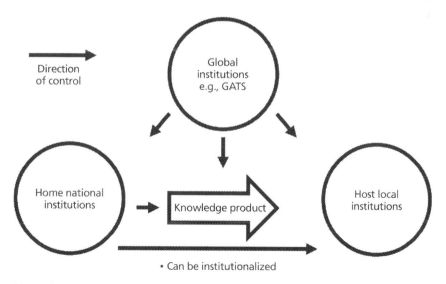

Figure 8.2 Transnational education partnership.

TNE partnership is often shaped. The major agencies at global, national, and host local/national are institutional ones and the direction of control is unidirectional from global and/or providers' home to host institutions. This framework highlights that TNE partnership can often be institutionalized, and the knowledge is often considered as a product to be sold to host countries whilst raising concerns over rescaling and reterritorialization.

This chapter proposes a new model of MNE partnership as demonstrated in Figure 8.3. In this figure, the main differences are:

1. Human agencies (people) are visible and interact with the partnership.
2. The direction of ownership and influence is two-directional whilst the interaction between different levels of agencies including both institutional and human are more dynamic and fluid.

In this partnership, knowledge flows in both directions not only between institutions but also reaches people involved in the partnership.

It is encouraging to see QAA's (2021) recent recognition that "the interest of U.K. TNE is best served by a program of country-specific quality enhancement activity" and its recommendation that "U.K. degree-awarding bodies...might delegate aspects of...(how the awards are delivered)...to partners" (p. 3). MNE model of partnership supports such changes further responding to the call from Deem (2001) that the focus in international partnership ought to be switched from knowledge production at the global

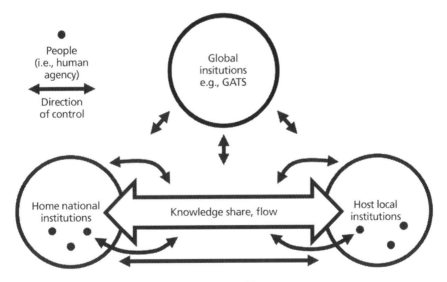

Figure 8.3 Multinational education partnership.

level to knowledge innovation. Proposing a new MNE module, this chapter recommends a rethinking of the TNE partnership—a move away from a unidirectional to a multi-directional approach, whilst being sensitive to multiple contexts and agencies involved in the partnership.

NOTES

1. Host institution/country refers to where the TNE partners deliver the program which is provided by the provider universities.
2. From here onward "providers" refer to "provider university" throughout the remaining chapter.

CHAPTER 9

INCREASING THE INTERNATIONALIZATION OF BUSINESS EDUCATION BY UTILIZING VISITING INSTRUCTORS

Joan Lofgren
Oleg V. Pavlov

Higher education has undergone significant internationalization (Knight, 2008b; Knight & Altbach, 2007; Lofgren & Leigh, 2017), which can be seen in the recruitment of international instructors, students, and staff members. Studies of the internationalization of business education have often highlighted the recruitment of foreign students and exchange student experiences. However, instructors also represent an important internationalizing element in business schools when recruited from a global pool of academic talent. Instructors who are successfully teaching internationally often possess competences, skills, and attitudes that are distinctly different from those utilized in domestic teaching, as they have to adjust domestic teaching practices to different cultural settings.

Internationally recruited instructors bring a diverse array of institutional and cultural practices to the foreign classrooms. Such instructors have been sometimes referred to as "flying faculty" (flown in for brief periods) when their teaching stints are short and often arranged alongside their full-time affiliations with home universities. The phenomenon has also been called "educators *sans frontières*" (see Leung & Waters, 2017). The global COVID-19 pandemic might have challenged the "flying in" part of these stints, since during that period many visiting instructors were only able to visit foreign campuses virtually, teaching via video conferencing software such as Zoom. However, short teaching assignments in foreign programs, whether carried out virtually or in person, are still part of the flying faculty model.

This growing phenomenon of short-term visiting instructors in business education is largely under-researched. This chapter addresses the lack of research on the flying faculty model by focusing on two main questions:

- What are the benefits and drawbacks of employing international instructors on short-term contracts?
- How can theoretical concepts used in international business (IB) theory, such as adaptation versus standardization, help to better understand the prospects for success of visiting instructors teaching abroad?

We focus the discussion on a case study of the Aalto University School of Business bachelor's program in international business located on a satellite campus in the city of Mikkeli, Finland. This unique program—we shall call it the Mikkeli program—relies almost exclusively on visiting instructors from around the world to teach 3-week courses in English. The instructors are recruited individually and sign a contract for a given course. The case provides fertile ground for considering the benefits and drawbacks of the flying faculty model and the lessons to be learned from the experience. The Mikkeli program reflects an array of issues relevant to the internationalization of higher education through instructor recruitment. The authors of this chapter have first-hand knowledge of the case: Joan Lofgren has served as program director for 12 years, and she taught in the program prior to becoming the director; Oleg Pavlov has taught in the program for 7 years as a visiting instructor.

THE FLYING FACULTY PHENOMENON

In this section, we address general trends as well as dominant approaches to international instructor recruitment, identify benefits and drawbacks of the flying faculty model, and link the discussion to a theoretical approach from the field of international business (IB) strategy.

Recruitment

The recruitment of instructors on short-term contracts reflects several trends in higher education. First, universities have been steadily moving away from a tenure-based employment model by hiring more contingent instructors than in the past (Bess & Dee, 2007; Cross & Goldenberg, 2009; Vedder, 2019). In response to changing demand for courses, universities hire *adjunct instructors* who are often academics without tenure-track appointments, pursuing teaching opportunities in an entrepreneurial manner. Even though most adjunct instructors teach locally, their career trajectories might take place in an international context, comprising short-term contracts in various countries.

Second, tenured instructors might be seconded to teach abroad on an additional or extended contract from their home university. This model of *seconded instructors* is popular with Western universities that offer offshore academic programs. Larsen and Vicent-Lacrin (2002) point out that international trade in educational services has increased substantially in the OECD area, including services offered by educational institutions operating abroad. Smith (2014) as well as Almond and Mangione (2015) describe examples of educational programs developed by U.K. universities and taught in the Middle East by instructors from those U.K. universities. These instructors deliver face-to-face courses in short modules, such as 10 days in the case of a geography program set up by a U.K. university in China (Szkornik, 2017). The students of seconded instructors might be "locals" who study at a foreign campus of the home university, or the students might be from the home campus who are part of a study-abroad tour. In either case, instructors are recruited from the pool of existing instructors at the home university, so only internal recruitment is needed.

A third approach to the flying faculty model is common in executive education programs, which might fly in an experienced instructor to deliver a course over a short period, such as a week. Such instructors typically have secure tenured positions at well-respected universities differentiating them from adjunct instructors who do not have tenured appointments. Because contracts are signed by individual professors and are independent of their home universities, such instructors are *part-time freelancers* contracting to teach in short stints.

The three sources of international instructors are summarized in Table 9.1. Relying on flying instructors has several benefits and drawbacks, which are discussed in the following section.

TABLE 9.1 Flying Instructor Recruitment	
Type	Definition
Adjunct	Instructors without tenured appointments hired based on changing demand for courses. External recruitment.
Seconded	Instructors who teach abroad for their home universities. Internal recruitment.
Part-Time Freelancers	Established tenured instructors who contract individually with academic programs. External recruitment.

Benefits and Drawbacks

Among the many benefits of the flying faculty model for destination programs is the opportunity for the talented instructors to share their expertise, bring new approaches to teaching and learning, and expose students to interesting cultural differences. Instructors also appreciate the opportunity to experience a foreign culture and form new contacts, which can be both professionally and personally beneficial (Almond & Mangione, 2015; Smith, 2014). Some education managers also see international teaching as professional development, which promotes instructors' careers (Smith, 2014).

The drawbacks might include perceptions in one's home university or department of divided loyalties—"Why would an instructor "disappear" in the middle of the semester to go and work elsewhere, why not focus on the home front?" While flying faculty arrangements are highly flexible and maximize the use of a global academic talent pool, governance issues can complicate operations. It might be difficult to agree on and enforce teaching quality standards, and the communication and coordination required between the institutions and the instructor are considerable. The program director must spend significant time onboarding new instructors and following up on course feedback. Still, many universities consider the flying faculty model to be worth the effort.

Similar to how IB theories distinguish between the home country (where the headquarters of a company are located) and the host country (the target of the investment), Table 9.2 summarizes benefits and drawbacks of employing international instructors from the point of view of the instructors, their home university, and the host university abroad. We now move to analyzing the way in which instructors crossing borders export educational services, and if necessary, adapt them to the host country context.

INTERNATIONALIZATION OF EDUCATIONAL SERVICES

To understand how internationally recruited instructors on short-term contracts operate in their temporary positions, we frame their teaching as a service

TABLE 9.2 Benefits and Drawbacks of Flying Instructors

Perspective	Benefits	Drawbacks
Instructor	• Expanding teaching competencies • Exposure to new teaching methods and practices • Experiencing new cultures • Professional development which promotes careers • Ability to earn extra income	• Disruption in teaching at home university • Greater workload • Jetlag • Culture shock • Loneliness
Home University	• Building international partnerships • Bringing back best practices • Sharing cultural experiences with students at home • Opportunities for cooperation, (e.g., in research with other instructors and/or arranging joint student projects)	• Perceived neglect by instructors of duties at home institution • Students at home institutions temporarily lose access to their instructors • Suspicions of divided loyalties by administration at home institution • Potential conflict of interest
Host University	• Access to global talent pool; talented academics share their expertise • Bringing in best practices from abroad • Cultural diversity in academic community; instructors expose students to cultural differences	• Extra management efforts needed to manage instructor's network • Disruptions due to cancellations, especially last-minute • Governance issues • Difficulty enforcing teaching quality standards • Need for extensive communication and coordination (e.g., around teaching methods and assessment practices)

that is exported to another context. A service is defined as a transaction in which no physical goods are transferred from buyer to seller—involving intangible goods (see www.corporatefinanceinstitute.com). When instructors are recruited to teach abroad, they engage in the export of educational services.

Education Service Provision

The literature on service science (Grönroos & Ravald, 2011; Spohrer et al., 2007) casts higher education as an ecology of service systems which deliver value by generating and transferring knowledge (Lofgren et al., 2019; Pavlov & Hoy, 2019). In providing educational services, value is created by the collaboration of students, instructors, staff, and other stakeholders.

Instructors who are recruited to teach abroad are expected to engage in the co-creation of value—however short their teaching stint might be. In a sense, they are exporting educational services from one market, culture, or institution to another.

In higher education, the roles of a seller and a consumer are blurred. Carneiro et al. (2008, p. 88) point out that services tend to be inseparable from their delivery and consumption, which is particularly true of the delivery of educational services. If we consider the component of learning, the teacher's delivery of their service is inseparable from the students' "consumption" of that service and its co-creation. Because of this inextricable relationship, the pressure to adapt to local contexts can be strong.

Trade in Services

Placing education in a broader context, Larsen et al. (2002) pointed out that education had been largely absent from the debate on globalization since it was considered to be a non-traded service. The global expansion of the knowledge economies led to more cross-border trade in services and greater international competition for expertise, which, in turn, stimulated research interest in the internationalization of education services (Kubota, 2009, p. 613). Educational services have been a major business in economies such as Australia, Canada, New Zealand, the United Kingdom, and the United States (Larsen et al., 2002).

The general agreement on trade in services (GATS) framework identifies four categories of traded services: cross-border supply, consumption abroad, commercial presence abroad, and presence of individual service-providers abroad. The traveling instructors fall in the last category on this list (Larsen et al., 2002, p. 851). However, researchers have noted that it might be difficult to estimate the volume of this kind of trade in services (Larsen et al., 2002, p. 852) due to the lack of reliable figures on the amount of money spent on international instructors.

BUSINESS STRATEGY IN EDUCATIONAL EXPORTS

Studies of international business strategy often stress the choice firms face when going abroad—adapt the product or service to the local market or maintain and sell the same product globally (Ryans et al., 2003; Venaik & Midgley, 2019). As internationalizing service providers, visiting instructors face that same choice. Their service being course delivery, they make decisions on the extent to which they will adapt the course content to the foreign context (given the leeway to do so), adjust their teaching methods in the classroom, and adjust their linguistic and cultural practices.

Standardization versus Adaptation

Standardization of higher education can be seen in the plethora of accrediting bodies at national and international levels. For example, in business education, the Aalto University School of Business enjoys triple crown accreditation: AACSB (Association to Advance Collegiate Schools of Business), EQUIS (EFMD Quality Improvement System), and AMBA (Association of MBAs). While each accredited program is held accountable mainly for following its own strategy and continuous improvement goals, standard criteria are explicit and implicit in accreditation practices. These accreditation credentials ensure a certain accepted standard of education worldwide.

At the European level, standardization in higher education is seen as a key element of European integration. For instance, Finland has been a member of the EU since 1995, and it has been influenced by the European standards-based governance (Elken, 2017). The country follows the Bologna Process established in 1999 and applies the European Credit Transfer System (ECTS) in negotiating exchange partnerships within the Erasmus framework. These educational standards provide order and common thresholds, contributing to efficiency in interaction, and enhancing coordination (Elken, 2017). When recruiting international instructors from a large pool of potential candidates, such standards ease the administrative and talent management burden.

The standardization of quality criteria in business education can be seen as a facilitating factor in promoting the flying faculty model—the idea being that instructors from an accredited institution have already been significantly vetted for quality. If a promising candidate for a course to be taught abroad has written their curriculum vitae (CV) according to the AACSB criteria, it clearly demonstrates to the prospective employer that they qualify as a scholarly academic. This kind of standardization does not necessarily mean, however, that scholarly academics would teach in the same way wherever they are hired in the network of AACSB business schools—or, that they ought to. In that sense these standards might serve as a screening tool, rather than as a strict regulation for teaching.

Standardization in the Classroom

Depending on their compensation, instructors might face pressures to standardize their teaching to save time. However, even if the instructor uses the same material as in the home institution, teaching in an intensive course might require changes to the instructional format (Whieldon, 2019, p. 64). This is true whether the instructor is moving to a new educational institution in the home country or teaching abroad. International instructors might indeed feel pressure to adapt to local contexts in order to succeed; after all, communicating with students in the classroom demands emotional intelligence and "reading the room." This mirrors what we have learned in IB research about internationalizing firms. As Ang and Massingham (2007) explain, multinational corporations often face a decision whether to standardize or adapt their operations. And that, in turn, is affected by national culture, through human resources, marketing, or other operations. Higher education can be placed in the realm of knowledge management, which faces similar issues even if not dealing with traditional product management. Instructors create a product (design a course) and deliver a service (face-to-face teaching in another country), and thus manage knowledge transfer as experts in their fields.

A teacher moving to a foreign setting is likely to face different institutional practices. For example, it is common in the United Kingdom to arrange moderation, meaning that grading is a multistep process in which the original instructor's summative marks are reviewed by other instructors (Institute for Academic Development, 2020). Other norms might include privacy practices, scheduling practices, how students address instructors, openness to sharing opinions in class, and the ability of the instructor to randomly ask students to speak in class (also known as "cold calling"). Such practices cannot be separated from cultural contexts (Hofstede, 2001).

Concerning cultural differences in the classroom, instructors who are successful in teaching internationally possess competencies, skills, and attitudes that are distinct from those in domestic teaching (Dunn & Wallace, 2006). Instructors must be aware of the cultural biases and be competent intercultural communicators (Dunn & Wallace, 2006; Teekens 2003). They ought to be willing to adjust their course content to include country-relevant material (Dunn & Wallace, 2006). They also might need to adjust their classroom practices to cultures that do not share Western notions of academic codes of conduct (Dunn & Wallace, 2006).

The following section outlines three major types of approaches instructors might take when teaching abroad.

Instructor Approaches to Standardization

Keeping the discussion of standardization versus adaptation in mind and based on our experience, we propose the following classification on how instructors adapt to the standardization trade-off in their international teaching. Imagining adaptation of teaching practices as a continuum, we place no adaptation at all (i.e., standardization) at one end and a complete adaptation at the other end.

> *Universalists*: Universalists do not adapt their courses. Such instructors think that whatever works at home, works abroad. They have achieved success in their home universities, and that speaks to their ability to teach well in other settings. Business students are business students throughout the world. Universalists embrace standardization of teaching.
> *Acclimators*: Instructors in this category are highly attuned to design and deliver courses which fit the mission, strategy, and culture of the programs in which they teach abroad. They embrace complete adaptation to the local context.
> *Pragmatists*: Pragmatists fall between universalists and acclimators on our scale. These instructors feel the need to maintain their academic identities, shaped in their home countries, but choose to adapt to local contexts when they perceive the need to do so.

The latter two categories might choose to bring lessons learned during their short teaching trips back to their home universities. Below, we discuss these three approaches to international teaching in light of the Mikkeli IB program, but first give an overview of the program's operations.

THE MIKKELI INTERNATIONAL BUSINESS PROGRAM

This section outlines the features of the Mikkeli international business program.

Program Overview

The bachelor's program in international business located at the Mikkeli campus of the Aalto University School of Business (formerly Helsinki School of Economics, HSE) is an English-language program taught almost entirely by visiting instructors from around the world. Instruction relies on international instructors traveling to Mikkeli for 3-week courses (for an overview, see Lofgren & Leigh, 2017; Lofgren et al., 2019). The international aspects of the Mikkeli program are an example of the increasing globalization trend in higher education as a whole, not least in business studies. When it was founded in 1989 however, the international nature of the Mikkeli program was unique in Finland and Scandinavian countries. As a program in the School of Business, the Mikkeli program is a member of the global family of accredited undergraduate business programs, as recognized by the school's accreditation from AACSB and EQUIS, as well as indirectly from AMBA. Other key elements of the program are:

- *Degree awarded*: Bachelor of Science in economics and business administration
- *Accreditations of the School of Business*: AACSB, EQUIS, AMBA
- *Enrollment*: approximately 250 (2/3 of degree students from Finland, 1/3 from abroad; approximately 70 exchange students)
- *Applications*: 1,000+ for approximately 80 study places
- *Graduation rate*: approximately 95% on-time graduation rates (within 3 years)
- *Visiting instructors*: 60 per year
- *Full-time staff*: 10
- *Course calendar*: 80 courses a year, in 15 three-week modules, run year round
- *Mandatory exchange*: at one of 50 partner universities
- *Tuition charges for non-Finnish or foreign degree students*: EUR 12,000, but waivers offered to top candidates.

The Mikkeli program relies on the flying faculty model, that is, visiting instructors are contracted on a temporary basis, which is highly unusual for an undergraduate program. Unlike a traditional instructor recruitment model, in which the tenure system guarantees that the university has access to continually employed instructors, this program provides a vivid example of extremely flexible instructor resourcing.

Recruitment and Onboarding Processes

The Mikkeli program challenges traditional thinking about access to instructional talent. The virtual network of instructors is a unique aspect of the Mikkeli program, comprising over 120 instructors, mostly from North American and European universities. Teaching contracts are negotiated annually. The program director engages in recruitment year round—at conferences, when visiting partner universities, or where existing instructors are located. The director builds the instructor roster each year, starting with a "blank slate." For such a program to work, the program director needs to have access to an extensive pool of instructors who are potentially interested in teaching.

The program director communicates with instructors in the instructor network several times a year. The recruitment and orientation processes help integrate new instructors into the "Mikkeli way of doing things." While the flexibility to not invite an instructor to return is always in the background, there is a core of veteran instructors teaching the same courses each year; they are a source of expertise for student projects and might supervise postgraduate students. These veteran instructors also help to recruit new instructors to the program, using their own networks at their home universities—nationally or internationally—on behalf of the program.

It might seem highly risky not to have teaching resources guaranteed through permanent or at least long-term contracts, but the breadth of the instructor network has helped to ensure that no courses are canceled in cases when an instructor needs to cancel. The network is rather stable, with approximately 80% of the instructors returning year to year. There are various reasons for instructors to teach in the Mikkeli program. Short-term teaching trips provide academics with experiences which stimulate transformational learning, new research, and encourage them to try different teaching methods (Smith, 2014). Foreign teaching is a good CV booster and might provide a break from the routine and committees at their home institutions. Instructors have commented, however, that due to remote meetings becoming more common, they continue to be well-connected to their home universities during the module in Mikkeli.

It is often pointed out that contingent instructors have very little bargaining power when negotiating their contracts (Childress, 2019). The international instructors who come to Mikkeli possess some bargaining power because they often have tenured or permanent positions at their home institutions. Instructors recruited to the Mikkeli program cannot affect the salary packages available—which depend on one's degree—but the decision whether to teach abroad in another program is made easier by having a firm foundation at home. Visiting instructors who have taught successfully in the program can sometimes negotiate an assignment in one of the more popular modules, for example, in the summer. Highly successful professors might try to "call the shots" by limiting their availability to certain prime modules. However, the needs of the program are prioritized over instructor preferences when they collide. Instructors might also be interested in just one round of teaching to boost their CV or might simply want a change of pace without being interested in returning. The program director does try to avoid hiring "academic tourists" who are uninterested in establishing a relationship with the program. Moreover, since performance is evaluated at the end of each teaching visit, the basis for negotiation is very different from the tenure-track systems in which most Mikkeli visiting instructors operate at home.

Governance and Quality Processes

Mikkeli is a city 3 hours north of Helsinki. The geographic distance from the main campus of Aalto University in the Helsinki region has encouraged autonomy in running the program. Several years ago, however, Aalto University switched to a matrix governance structure, which led to a tighter integration of the program with the School of Business and Aalto University as a whole. Some governance structures have persisted throughout the changes. For example, the program director and manager of academic operations prepare an annual curriculum proposal—including all courses and instructors—for review by the Mikkeli Program Committee, which is comprised mainly of instructors at the main campus in Espoo (near Helsinki). It then goes to the School of Business Committee on Academic Affairs for formal approval. The program, however, has still maintained significant autonomy due to its special position within the university. The visiting instructors are not involved in the formal academic governance structure but might participate in special projects on an ad hoc basis, such as accreditation site visits.

One of the common concerns about the contingent instructor model is that it lowers the quality of instruction when compared to the tenured instructor model (Manning, 2018). However, the program director in Mikkeli works closely with the instructors to ensure consistent quality across the program. University programs, like other service organizations, must focus on the quality of services provided in order to maintain a competitive advantage and attract and retain students and instructors (Ali et al., 2016). The Mikkeli program demonstrates that having a permanent employment relationship with instructors is not a necessary condition for quality teaching as long as robust quality assurance mechanisms are introduced and followed.

The Mikkeli program has extreme flexibility in teaching resources and more leverage for maintaining teaching quality than traditional academic departments. Quality monitoring is also applied to instructors' performance using course feedback from the students—reviewed alongside feedback from the instructors on their own performance, the performance of the students, and the services provided, such as academic advising, housing, and so on. Thus, quality standards serve as a filter through which invitations to come back to teach again are negotiated. The assumption is that all instructors in the program must perform and engage in continuous improvement of their courses.

The program quality committee, comprising the program director and two other senior staff members, reviews course feedback reports—in particular regarding instructor performance—and identifies any necessary follow-up, which the program director usually implements. In addition, at several points in the annual cycle, a student quality committee advises the program director and manager of academic operations on various development issues emerging within the program. At the School of Business level, the Mikkeli Program Committee includes representatives from various master's programs and other instructors, as well as alumni and a representative from industry.

Instructors who have performed well in Mikkeli demonstrate qualities such as the ability to cope with a fast-paced, intensive learning environment; responsiveness to student feedback; creativity in teaching methods; and a willingness to change direction if needed.

Standardization Versus Adaptation in Mikkeli

The Mikkeli program expects some degree of standardization of its instructors, especially concerning basic courses which use globally accepted textbooks and cases. Instructors' credentials are included in school-level reporting on sufficiency. Returning to instructor standardization approaches outlined above, the instructor types can be seen in the Mikkeli Program in Figure 9.1.

Universalists: These instructors take the approach that what works at home, works in Mikkeli. They might use the same textbook and use the same teaching style, as well as language (English). Instructors who teach in a different language than English at their home universities face a clear challenge of localization in terms of language. The course assessments might also be the same, or perhaps only minimal changes are made given the 3-week module system. A rough estimate would be that approximately 25% of the Mikkeli instructors maintain this position, based on the Program director's experience.

Pragmatists: These instructors make conscious, calculated decisions to adapt to Mikkeli and Finland when needed. They might have ex-

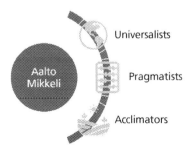

Figure 9.1 Approaches to standardization by visiting instructors in Mikkeli.

perienced failure with the universalist approach and are now more open to adaptation. Approximately 50% of the Mikkeli instructors can be observed as using this approach, based on the program director's experience.

Acclimators: These instructors seek to discuss their course plans with the program director and receive guidance on how to "fit in" and do things in the "Mikkeli way." They are very responsive to suggestions and make few assumptions about what might work in Mikkeli versus what usually works at home. Approximately a quarter of the Mikkeli instructors can be said to be acclimators, based on the program director's observations.

All three approaches have been successful in Mikkeli but further study would be required to more accurately estimate the percentages.

CONCLUSION

Employment of international visiting instructors on short-term contracts increases internationalization of business education. This chapter first defines the term, flying faculty, and then, following the international business framework, discusses associated benefits and drawbacks from three perspectives: instructors, the home institution, and the host institution. By viewing international teaching as cross-border trade in educational services, we ask if theoretical concepts from international business theory, such as adaptation and standardization, can help us understand the prospects for success of international visiting instructors. We differentiate three instructor approaches to teaching based on the degree of standardization: universalists, pragmatists, and acclimators.

The analysis identifies several factors which contribute to the successful operation of the bachelor's international business program over the years, such as:

- Establish and maintain a network of qualified instructors who are willing to travel to teach.
- Implement and communicate clear expectations regarding teaching quality and invite back only instructors who satisfy these requirements.
- Provide sufficient staff support to instructors.
- Recognize that visiting instructors might adopt varying teaching approaches.

Because recruiting contingent instructors drawn from a global pool of academic talent is likely to stay, it is important to continue the research on international short-term teaching. Future research might collect additional data on adaptations that instructors employ when teaching abroad. These data might answer such questions as: "To what extent do content and course delivery vary when instructors teach at home and at host institutions?"; "How much do instructors adapt their teaching-abroad styles over time?"; and "Is any approach to teaching abroad more successful than another?" Addressing such questions will further contribute to understanding the internationalization of higher education.

CHAPTER 10

INTERNATIONALIZATION AT THE SEMI-PERIPHERY

Alternative Forms of Practice and the Determinants of Adoption

Başak Topaler

The growth of internationalization in higher education in the last few decades brought about a significant increase in the volume of research, which specifically focused on this topic (Bedenlier et al., 2018; Kehm & Teichler, 2007; Yemini & Sagie, 2016). Yet studies have so far been largely Anglo-Saxon and Western European driven, which constitute central destinations of the international student network. Despite some recent exceptions (see Jumakulov et al., 2019; Komotar, 2019; Tamrat & Teferra, 2018), there is a limited understanding of how internationalization is interpreted and practiced outside this center.

Research suggests that internationalization of higher education evolving under different contextual conditions might take different shapes and meanings (Maringe et al., 2013; Tight, 2021). A useful framework to understand patterns of internationalization at the global level is the center-periphery model (adopted from the world system theory; Wallerstein, 1974). The framework is applied by empirical research to study the flow of international students and the societal outcomes of the flow (see Altbach, 2003a; Chen & Barnett, 2000; J. Lee, 2008.). Economically developed Anglophone countries such as the United States, the United Kingdom, and Australia constitute the core destinations of internationalization, which get the greatest share of students from the global higher education market. Universities in clearly peripheral destinations such as Malaysia and Vietnam receive almost no international students—not least due to their limited academic resources and capabilities (Barnett et al., 2016; Shields, 2013). In between the center and periphery exists the semi-periphery, composed of economically developing countries with some participation in the international network (Schott, 1988; Shils, 1988; Üsdiken, 2014). Some countries of this intermediate strata (e.g., Mexico, Singapore, Hong Kong, & Turkey) are indeed recognized as regional hubs due to their significant mobilization of international students from neighboring countries (Cantwell et al., 2009; Chan & Ng, 2008; Kondakci, 2011; Kondakci et al., 2018).

Institutions of higher education in such contexts of the semi-periphery might form partnerships with countries of the center as well as the periphery. Affiliations with the center are likely to be formed with academic motivations such as improving teaching and research quality, or social motivations such as building up reputation and prestige (Altbach & Knight, 2007; Kondakci, 2011; Maringe et al., 2013; Rose & Kinley, 2018). Affiliations with peripheral countries, however, are mostly facilitated by cultural, political, historical, or geographical proximity (Barnett et al., 2016; Kondakci, 2011). The processes through which these alternative forms of internationalization (center- and periphery-focused) diffuse and are adopted by universities is both a theoretically and empirically interesting, yet understudied, phenomenon.

This chapter investigates this phenomenon in the context of Turkish higher education, which has significant international networking with a wide range of countries from both the center and the periphery. Interestingly, practices of internationalization targeting peripheral and central countries have come to be distinct and have diffused concurrently over time. The theoretical framework of the chapter proposes organizational characteristics of universities that affect the adoption of these practices—separately and in combination. Study hypotheses are tested with longitudinal data on Turkish universities, and the findings provide important insights into how internationalization is practiced outside well-studied higher education contexts.

The following section describes the context of the study. The hypotheses development is presented first, and methods and the empirical results follows. This is concluded by a discussion of the principal findings, contributions, and implications of the study.

EMPIRICAL CONTEXT

University Models in Turkish Higher Education

As in many other parts of the developing world, the formation and structuring of the university in Turkish higher education was directly influenced by the Western Universities. In the young Turkish Republic (through the 1930s and 1940s), universities were modeled on the continental European "classical" university (Öncü, 1993). Initially comprised of faculties of sciences, letters, theology, law, and medicine, the classical universities became more comprehensive over time as faculties from a wider range of disciplines were added. Instruction in these universities was entirely in Turkish, whereas a separate school of foreign languages was responsible for providing the students with proficiency in foreign languages.

Turkey experienced the influence of the United States along with the political rapprochement between the two countries in the aftermath of World War II (Üsdiken, 2011). A spillover of this rapprochement to the higher education field was the establishment of Middle East Technical University (METU) in 1956, which became the first instance of an "American" model university characterized by a narrow range of professional faculties (Üsdiken et al., 2013). The premise that METU was to extend its reach to students from the Middle East (Okyar, 1968) also served to justify English-medium instruction for the first time in Turkish higher education. The American influence in METU, and its successor Boğaziçi University[1] (1971), is also evident from their stronger focus on producing international research and publications (Inelmen et al., 2017; Üsdiken & Wasti, 2009).

In summary, the classical and American university models represent distinct identities in terms of their instructor composition (wide vs. narrow disciplinary range) and language of instruction (Turkish vs. English). The research-oriented identity of the American-modeled university is also in contrast with the classical university identity, which accommodates greater numbers of students and relatively more teaching loads (Inelmen et al., 2017; Üsdiken & Wasti, 2009).

Internationalization in Turkish Higher Education

Internationalization in the context of Turkish higher education has traditionally been periphery-focused—oriented towards neighboring and less developed countries. The earliest attempt of internationalization was the establishment of the above-mentioned Middle East Technical University, where instruction was entirely in English. Despite some achievements in its first few years, the university's international student population declined speedily as funded bursaries were drained (Okyar, 1968; Üsdiken, 2011). Soon it had become a university catering almost entirely to Turkish students.

Concern with internationalization in the sense of targeting foreign students began to surface in the early 1990s. These initial proactive steps were politically motivated. They were geared towards the Turkic republics which had gained independence after the demise of the USSR—extending later to some Balkan countries as well (KAM, 2015). As this path developed over time, Turkey has become a regional hub that attracts significant numbers of international students from the Balkans, the Middle East, and Central Asia (Kondakci, 2011). The number of full-time international students in the field increased from 7,600 in 1990 to 16,650 in 2000, reaching 185,000 in 2019.

The 2000s marked a significant shift in the focus of internationalization towards the center. This started with aspirations for rapprochement with the European Union, as Turkey became a part of the Bologna Process in 2001 and of the Erasmus+ project in 2004. Student exchanges under the Erasmus+ program increased from 1,440 in 2004 to 7,650 in 2019. Another initiative in the mid-2000s was the establishment of international joint (or dual) degree programs with The State University of New York. Students enrolled in these programs receive 2 years of tuition in the United States and the remaining two in Turkey.

Notably, these center-focused practices of internationalization are motivated by status aspirations and gaining recognition in the global context (Aydinli & Mathews, 2021). A report by the Ministry of Development in 2015 identified center-focused internationalization as a strategic area because of the "contributions that it could make to the development of the country and cooperation with other countries" (KAM, 2015, p. 2). The report also recommended that universities expand degree programs taught in English, which had been the case in other countries where English is not the native language (Kirkpatrick, 2011; Soler, 2019). Internationalization with a focus on the center was also recognized as one of the three major aims in a 2014 report by the president of the Higher Education Council (YÖK), which was identified as a way to improve the quality of Turkish higher education (Çetinsaya, 2014).

Despite this turn towards the center, the periphery-focused internationalization has also continued to be significant over time in student volumes (Higher Education Management Information System of Turkey, 2020; UNESCO Institute for Statistics, 2020). Furthermore, the periphery- and center-focused variants of internationalization have remained distinct in the way they are practiced and the organizational context in which they are adopted. The former is characterized by full-time foreign students received from peripheral countries, which usually leads to growth in the student population of the university and an associated increase in teaching loads.[2] Because incoming students usually lack proficiency in English, the periphery-focused internationalization does not trigger an increase in courses (or degree programs) taught in English. The center-focused internationalization, which involves student exchanges with European countries and joint degree programs with the United States, does not necessarily increase the student population as the periphery-focused variant. It is also perceived as more prestigious due to affiliations with prominent contexts of higher education. Another source of prestige for the center-focused internationalization is its association with English-medium instruction, which is by itself a status conferring practice in the context of Turkish higher education (Selvi, 2014; Topaler & Üsdiken, 2021).

THEORY AND HYPOTHESES DEVELOPMENT

The diffusion of practices has long been one of the central concerns of organization theory. This research provides important insights on the processes through which practices diffuse in organizational contexts and the conditions under which they are adopted (Kennedy & Fiss, 2009; Strang & Soule, 1998). Studies also recognize that organizational contexts are characterized by multiple forms of rationality that lead to the emergence and concurrent diffusion of distinct or alternative forms of a practice (Naumovska et al., 2021; Raffaelli & Glynn, 2014; Topaler & Üsdiken, 2021).

As discussed in the "Empirical Context" section, the periphery- and center-focused variants of internationalization in the context of Turkish higher education is a clear instance of such practice variation. The factors that might shape universities' orientation towards these alternative practice forms—separately and in combination—are shown below. In order to predict this behavior, insights from the research on organization theory—since universities are just like other organizational forms operating in various contexts—are then applied. Accordingly, the focus is on the factors proposed in this literature to shape organizational behavior: organizational *identity, ownership and governance*, and *status* (Greenwood et al., 2011; Naumovska et al., 2021).

Referring to organizational members' shared beliefs about "who we are," organizational *identity* also has implications for what activities constitute appropriate action (Anthony & Tripsas, 2016; Georgallis & Lee, 2020). Organizations perceive practices that align with their identity as more appealing and legitimate; and, therefore, are more likely to adopt them (Gioia et al., 2013). External stakeholders also evaluate organizations more favorably when they engage in activities consistent with their identity claims (Zuckerman, 1999).

Given these dynamics, a university's identity ought to be influential on the extent to which it adopts the periphery- or center-focused variant of internationalization in the context of Turkish higher education. As noted in the "Empirical Context" section, the *classical* university identity in this context is characterized by a wide range of faculties and a greater focus on the teaching function, whereas the *American-modeled* university is characterized by instruction in English and a greater emphasis on international research and publications.[3] The periphery-focused variant of internationalization, which is in the form of incoming full-time students, will likely be more extensively adopted by universities pursuing a classical identity that is congruent with higher student intakes and teaching loads. However, the center-focused variant—which targets countries of the center—fits better with the American-modeled identity and a stronger concentration in the research function. Hence, it may be hypothesized:

Hypothesis 1: *Universities which pursue the classical identity (characterized by a wide range of faculties and teaching orientation) will adopt the periphery-focused variant of internationalization to a greater extent than the center-focused variant.*

Hypothesis 2: *Universities which pursue the American-modeled identity (characterized by instruction in English and research orientation) will adopt the center-focused variant of internationalization to a greater extent than the periphery-focused variant.*

It is also possible that a university adopts the periphery- and center-focused variants of internationalization in combination. Hybrid practice forms are widespread in contexts where multiple forms of a practice diffuse concurrently (Naumovska et al., 2021; Raffaelli & Glynn, 2014; Topaler & Üsdiken, 2021). Hybridity might provide the organization with the ability to meet a wider range of expectations and demands as well as greater adaptability to the environment (Battilana et al., 2017; Greenwood et al., 2011). Organizations thus adopt hybrid arrangements to create and pursue market opportunities and gain competitive advantage (Battilana et al., 2017; Dalpiaz et al., 2016; Tracey et al., 2011).

Members of an organizational context might vary in the extent to which they seek these benefits, depending on how sensitive they are to competitive pressures. A critical organizational factor in this respect is the *ownership* (and *governance*) structure. As prior research shows, organizations with private ownership are more heavily influenced by market logic compared to their public counterparts (Edelman, 1992; Goodrick & Salancik, 1996). Studies in higher education contexts also identify a fundamental difference in the goals of private and public institutions, the former prioritizing an economic rationale over others (Kraatz et al., 2010; Seeber et al., 2016). Universities with private ownership might thus be more oriented towards hybrid practice forms, which facilitate greater market benefits.

Following these insights, the hybrid practice of internationalization in the context of Turkish higher education will be more likely for private universities (relative to public universities).[4] Hybridity in this context can provide market advantages such as accessing a broader population of students both from the center and periphery. It might also serve as a way of signaling a greater commitment to internationalization in its "ideal" state, which targets enhanced intercultural interaction (Tight, 2021). Hence:

Hypothesis 3a: *The hybrid practice of internationalization (the periphery- and center-focused variants in combination) is more likely to be adopted by private universities than by public universities.*

Notwithstanding the benefits mentioned above, studies also document various organizational challenges of hybridity, such as conflict among members about the appropriate way to organize (M. Dunn & Jones, 2010; Kim et al., 2016) and difficulties in strategic decision-making and implementation (Glynn, 2000). Furthermore, organizations adopting hybrid practices may be perceived by their key stakeholders as making conflicting claims and multiple binding commitments—consequently facing problems of legitimacy (Glynn, 2000; Kraatz & Block, 2008).

Given these challenges, the pursuit of competitive advantage might not be realized unless hybridity is effectively managed. Critical managerial capabilities are required to balance disparate demands of the distinct practices adopted or to find cooperative solutions to the tensions they generate (Battilana & Lee, 2014; Kraatz & Block, 2008; Pratt & Foreman, 2000). High-status actors who have a greater stock of these capabilities (Podolny, 1993; Sauder et al., 2012) will be more likely to overcome these challenges.

The hybrid practice of internationalization in Turkish higher education (adoption of the periphery- and center-focused variants in combination) is challenging as it requires managing a high level of cultural diversity in the student population, the configuration of a common curriculum, and issues with the language of instruction. These challenges can be better managed by high-status universities that have more advanced tangible and intangible resources (Merton, 1968; Siegel & Leih, 2018). Besides these managerial issues, the hybrid practice of internationalization might be penalized by internal and external stakeholders of a university due to the confusion that co-existing affiliations with high- and low-status partners generate (Podolny, 1993). Yet, research also suggests that this penalty is not so strong (or might even be absent) for organizations who already have established social standing in their field (Phillips & Zuckerman, 2001). Given these dynamics, high-status universities will be less likely to experience the "costs" of hybrid internationalization.

Due to the inherent advantages held by high-status universities in managing the challenges of hybridity, these universities will be more likely to realize the market advantages that the hybrid practice of internationalization can potentially provide. Hence,

Hypothesis 3b: *The hybrid practice of internationalization (the periphery- and center-focused variants in combination) is more likely to be adopted by high-status universities than by low-status universities.*

METHODS

The data of this study were coded annually (between the years 2013 and 2019) for all universities in Turkish higher education (124 public and 83 private). They were recorded from the yearly manuals for the central university entrance examination, higher education statistics published by the Higher Education Council (YÖK), and relevant legal documents. Government intervention after the coup attempt in July 2016 led to the closure of 15 private universities, whose data is not available after this date. Two public universities are established with intergovernmental agreements (Galatasaray University with France and Türk-Alman University with Germany) and have special arrangements for the recruitment of international students (or academic staff). Due to the lack of initiative from the universities themselves, these two universities were excluded from empirical analyses. The total number of universities in the study sampled over time is presented in Figure 10.1.

Dependent Variables

The *periphery-focused variant of internationalization* was measured as the ratio of the total number of full-time foreign students to the total number of students enrolled by the university. To measure the *center-focused variant of internationalization*, the ratio of the sum of the European Erasmus+ and the United States joint degree programs to the total number of bachelor's programs was calculated.

The hybrid practice of internationalization refers to the adoption of the periphery- and center-focused variants in combination. A university practice was regarded as a hybrid when each form of internationalization was adopted more extensively than the 75th percentile across all universities (Greckhamer et al., 2018). Robustness analyses were conducted where hybridity was measured using the threshold of the 50th percentile rather than the 75th (reported below).

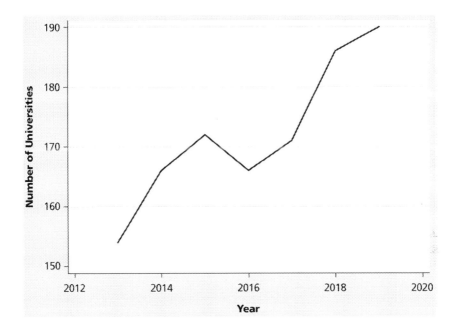

Figure 10.1 Number of universities in Turkish higher education, 2013–2019.

Independent Variables

As mentioned above, the classical university identity is characterized by a wide range of faculties and teaching orientation. The measurement for the *range of faculties* is based on the twelve main areas of research and teaching specified by the inter-university assembly (such as education, natural sciences and mathematics, social sciences, etc.). A Herfindahl/Simpson index was calculated (Simpson, 1949) based on the proportion of incoming students in each of these existing areas to the total intake of a university. This score was then subtracted from 1 so that a higher score indicates a wider disciplinary range. *Teaching orientation* was measured with the ratio of the total number of students enrolled by the university to the total number of full-time academic staff.

Again, as noted above, the university features which characterize the American-modeled identity are instruction in English and a greater focus on international research and publications. A university's involvement with *instruction in English* was measured as the ratio of the total number of programs with English-medium instruction to the total number of programs. *Research orientation* was measured as the ratio of the total number of academic publications indexed by the web of science database to the total number of full-time academic staff.

The *status* of universities as selectivity in admissions, which is recognized in prior research as a good proxy for prestige in higher education (Alon, 2009; Askin & Bothner, 2016; Davies & Zarifa, 2012) was measured. Universities in Turkish higher education admit students through a state-run, centralized examination. Entrance scores in this exam provide a reliable basis on which universities can be compared in terms of selectivity. To determine universities' relative position, the entire set of scores in a particular score type were z-standardized (verbal, quantitative, language, and equally weighted) in each year, and then each university's selectivity score (relative to other universities) in each year was calculated as the mean z-score of its programs.

Finally, a dummy variable was used to designate the ownership structure of universities, coded 1 for private universities and 0 for public universities.

Control Variables

The *internationalization of academic staff*, which is not directly involved in the theoretical framework of this research yet provides another key element of internationalization in higher education. This variable was measured as the ratio of foreign academic staff to the total number of academic staff.

Research shows that organizations are concerned about the extent to which they have critical resources for practice implementation (Ansari et al., 2010; Greenwood et al., 2011; Raffaelli & Glynn, 2014). Although a direct effect of organizational infrastructure was not included, several other control variables that indicate the organization's capability and readiness to implement a practice were.

The first of these is the university's embedded-ness in the global institutional environment of higher education, which provides an important basis for internationalization. Memberships in university associations establish cognitive and normative linkages to the global discourse and signal a university's openness to international instructors, student population, and curriculum (Zapp & Lerch, 2020). Two variables to account for such memberships. Membership in the European University Association (EUA) was coded as 2 if the university is a full member, 1 if an associate member, and 0 for non-members. Membership in the International Association of Universities (IUA) was measured with a dummy variable taking 1 for members and 0 for non-members.

As a final infrastructural variable, the disciplinary profile of the university was added, which might also influence the extent of internationalization (Seeber et al., 2016). Following UNESCO's International Standard Classification of Education, three control variables were added to measure the proportion of programs in health, STEM (Science, Engineering, and Agriculture), and social sciences. A list of the program types placed under each category is available in Table 10.1a).

Internationalization at the Semi-Periphery • **167**

TABLE 10.1a   Descriptive Statistics

	Mean	St. Dev	min	max
Range of faculties	.44	.12	0	0.59
Teaching orientation	.02	.01	0	0.09
Instruction in English	.28	.32	0	1.00
Research orientation	.04	.03	0	0.53
Private university	.37	.48	0	1.00
Status of the university	.45	.26	0	1.00
Int. of academic staff	.03	.05	0	0.35
EUA member	.56	.84	0	2.00
IUA member	.06	.24	0	1.00
Ratio of programs in health	.16	.19	0	1.00
Ratio of programs in STEM	.30	.16	0	1.00
Ratio of programs in SOSC	.18	.11	0	1.00
Year	2016.1	2.01	2013	2019

Estimation Method

The effects on the adoption of the periphery- and center-focused variants, using random effect regression analysis ("xtreg" command in Stata 15.0) which controls for unobserved differences across universities were also tested. In models tested for the adoption of the periphery- and center-focused variants in combination (the hybrid practice of internationalization), logistic regression analysis was applied ("xtlogit" command in Stata 15.0) due to the binary nature of the dependent variable (Baltagi, 2013).

Analysis of longitudinal data requires special consideration of de-trending. To account for those variables that have a trend over time, *year* was used as a control variable (Curran et al., 2012). All independent and control variables were included in the models with a 1 year lag to mitigate the possibility of simultaneity. The final data set was based on 1,001 university-year observations belonging to 199 universities.

FINDINGS

Table 10.1 displays the descriptive statistics (Table 10.1a) and pairwise correlations (Table 10.1b) of the study variables for the panel data. To obtain more easily interpretable coefficient estimates, the variables teaching orientation and research orientation were rescaled—divided by 1,000 and 10, respectively.

TABLE 10.1b Pairwise Correlations

Variables	(1)	(2)	(3)	(4)	(5)	(6)	(7)	(8)	(9)	(10)	(11)	(12)	(13)
(1) Range of faculties	1.00												
(2) Teaching orientation	0.24*	1.00											
(3) Instruction in English	-0.13*	-0.32*	1.00										
(4) Research orientation	-0.10*	-0.20*	0.34*	1.00									
(5) Private university	-0.15*	-0.13*	0.50*	0.04	1.00								
(6) Status of the university	-0.33*	-0.48*	0.52*	0.39*	0.37*	1.00							
(7) Int. of academic staff	-0.07	-0.25*	0.51*	0.16*	0.49*	0.44*	1.00						
(8) EUA member	0.18*	0.04	0.14*	0.24*	-0.18*	0.09*	-0.02	1.00					
(9) IUA member	0.10*	0.10*	0.07	-0.07	0.17*	0.03	0.02	0.13*	1.00				
(10) Ratio of programs in health	-0.21*	-0.16*	-0.26*	0.10*	0.01	0.06	-0.20*	0.08*	-0.03	1.00			
(11) Ratio of programs is STEM	-0.28*	0.05	0.27*	0.15*	0.01	0.10*	0.03	-0.02	-0.04	-0.52*	1.00		
(12) Ratio of programs in SOSC	0.07	0.02	0.33*	-0.00	0.21*	0.07	0.24*	-0.00	0.01	-0.39*	0.02	1.00	
(13) Year	-0.10*	0.12*	-0.01	0.03	-0.02	0.25*	-0.05	-0.03	-0.01	0.09*	-0.03	-0.03	1.00

* Shows significance at the .01 level

As can be seen in Table 10.1b, pairwise correlations between the study variables are not very high. Further, the features which characterize a particular university identity are positively correlated (range of faculties and teaching orientation for the classical identity, 0.24, $p < .01$; instruction in English and research orientation for the American-modeled identity, 0.34, $p < .01$).

Table 10.2 shows the results of the regression models, with the estimated effects and standard errors. The results for the periphery-focused variant

TABLE 10.2 Regression Results

	DV: periphery-focused		DV: center-focused		DV: hybrid	
	Model (1)	Model (2)	Model (3)	Model (4)	Model (5)	Model (6)
Int. of academic staff (l)	4.25** (1.07)	6.22** (2.01)	9.72** (4.09)	3.04 (4.67)	0.49* (0.25)	0.14 (0.31)
EUA member (l)	0.65** (0.21)	0.58** (0.18)	1.19*** (0.36)	1.10*** (0.37)	0.10*** (0.02)	0.10*** (0.02)
IUA member (l)	−0.84 (0.60)	−0.67 (0.60)	−0.55 (1.31)	−0.48 (1.27)	0.01 (0.07)	−0.01 (0.07)
Ratio of programs in health (l)	0.38 (0.62)	0.81 (0.71)	−0.74 (1.30)	−1.33 (1.58)	0.04 (0.07)	0.02 (0.10)
Ratio of programs in STEM (l)	−0.70 (0.62)	−0.62 (0.75)	0.88 (1.36)	−0.32 (1.64)	0.09 (0.08)	0.04 (0.10)
Ratio of programs in SOSC (l)	0.21 (0.74)	0.76 (0.83)	2.51 (1.60)	1.88 (1.81)	0.15 (0.12)	0.12 (0.13)
Year	0.32*** (0.02)	0.30*** (0.03)	0.13*** (0.05)	0.18*** (0.06)	0.01 (0.00)	−0.01 (0.00)
Range of faculties (l)		0.26+ (0.13)		−1.92 (1.93)		−0.03 (0.12)
Teaching orientation (l)		21.54** (10.01)		−30.61 (20.35)		0.22+ (1.39)
Instruction in English (l)		0.08 (0.55)		2.47** (1.02)		0.04 (0.07)
Research orientation (l)		1.57 (2.06)		10.03** (4.50)		0.21 (0.35)
Private university		−0.03 (0.32)		0.30 (0.69)		0.11* (0.04)
Status of the university (l)		−0.16 (0.48)		−1.28 (0.92)		0.19*** (0.07)
Constant	0.55 (0.36)	0.07 (0.65)	−0.51 (0.79)	1.11 (1.61)	−0.05 (0.05)	−0.12 (0.10)

Note: Standard errors are in parenthesis, l: lagged, $N = 1{,}001$ (199 universities); ***$p < 0.01$, **$p < 0.05$, *$p < 0.1$, +$p < 0.5$

are presented in Model 1 and 2, the center-focused variant in Model 3 and 4, and the hybrid practice in Model 5 and 6.

The estimated effects of the control variables presented in Model 1, 3, and 5 of Table 10.2 show that the adoption of the periphery- and center-focused internationalization (both separately and in combination) is positively influenced by the internationalization of academic staff and membership in the European University Association. The likelihood of adoption increases over time for both practice forms, but not in the case of the hybrid practice.

Model 2 of Table 10.2 shows support for Hypothesis 1, as the two characteristics of the classical identity (wide range of faculties and teaching orientation) have a positive effect on the extent to which a university adopts periphery-focused internationalization. The primary factor yet seems to be the teaching orientation ($\beta = 22.73$, $p < 0.05$), while the effect of the range of faculties is only marginal ($\beta = 0.24$, $p < 0.5$).

Hypothesis 2 is also supported as the features which characterize the American-modeled identity (instruction in English and research orientation) both have highly significant effects on the extent to which a university adopts the center-focused internationalization (Model 4 of Table 10.2; $\beta = 2.47$ and $\beta = 10.03$, $p < 0.05$).

Model 6 of Table 10.2 shows that the hybrid practice of internationalization is more likely for private universities ($\beta = 0.12$, $p < 0.1$) as well as those with high-status ($\beta = 0.18$, $p < 0.01$), which yields support for Hypothesis 3a and 3b.

To increase confidence in the findings, additional analyses (available in the Appendix) were perfomed. To this end, the hypothesis testing models were estimated (Table 10.2, Model 2 and 4) using fixed-effects instead of random-effects regression analysis. The variables *private university*, *EUA membership*, and *IUA membership* dropped out of these analyses since they do not vary within universities. These analyses yield the same pattern of results as the main analyses reported above.

Further analyses to check for the robustness of the support for Hypothesis 3a and 3b was conducted. In the main analyses reported above, the 75th percentile threshold was used for marking significant engagement with a particular variant of internationalization. Supplemental analyses, where the 50th percentile threshold was applied, yield the same pattern of results, showing that the hybrid practice of internationalization is more likely for high-status universities and private universities relative to public ones.

Finally, a check for the robustness of the findings supporting Hypotheses 2 by conducting separate analyses for the two practice types involved in the center-focused internationalization (student exchanges under the European Erasmus+ program and joint degree programs with the United States). As in the main analyses reported above, both instruction in English and research orientation have the predicted positive effects on the extent to which a university adopts the Erasmus+ program and the joint degree programs with the United States. As the only deviation from the hypothesis, the effect of research orientation on the adoption of the Erasmus+ program is marginal rather than fully significant.

DISCUSSION AND CONCLUSIONS

Increasing evidence suggests that the internationalization of higher education is not merely a Western phenomenon. Various economic, political, cultural, geographical, and historical factors led to the emergence of regional hubs outside the traditional destinations (Bedenlier et al., 2018; Kondakci et al., 2018). Case studies of increasingly diverse locations around the globe provide a better understanding of how the internationalization of higher education is understood and practiced outside the Western context. These studies provide important insights on patterns of student mobility across countries (e.g., Kondakci et al., 2018) and the intentions and impacts of specific government policies (e.g., Chan & Ng, 2008). What is missing is a micro-level investigation of the ways in which internationalization is practiced by universities. This chapter fills this gap by introducing an organization theory perspective to understand practice variation in internationalization.

In this chapter, I studied the context of Turkish higher education, which constitutes a central hub in Western and Central Asia (Kondakci et al., 2018). This context presents an interesting case of practice variation in internationalization, where periphery- and center-focused variants have diffused concurrently over time and remained distinct in the way they are practiced. The former variant of internationalization—which is practiced as admitting full-time students from peripheral countries—is more extensively adopted by Turkish universities with a classical identity (characterized by a wide range of faculties and a focus on the teaching mission). The center-focused variant of internationalization, which involves Erasmus+ exchange and joint degree programs with higher education institutions of the developed world, is more likely to be adopted by American-modeled universities (characterized by greater research orientation and English-medium instruction). Notably, the spread of instruction in English in the Turkish higher education field occurred way before the emergence of an internationalization discourse in this context, mainly with the influence of the prestigious universities which pioneered this practice (Boğaziçi & METU; Barblan et al., 2008; Mızıkacı, 2010). Thus, it has not been a case where internationalization led to "Englishization" (Kirkpatrcik, 2011).

The adoption of the periphery- and center-focused internationalization in combination (the hybrid practice of internationalization) appears to be more likely for higher-status universities and private universities relative to public ones. This hybrid practice produces greater cultural diversity since students from the periphery, semi-periphery, and the center study together. Graduates of such universities are likely to be more internationally knowledgeable and inter-culturally skilled, which is recognized as a desirable end of internationalization (Altbach & Knight, 2007; Delgado-Márquez et al., 2013; van der Wende, 2007). It might thus be the most productive way of internationalization, especially when the university is successful in managing its challenges of hybridity. Indeed, there is room for hybridization in any context where multiple practice variants emerge and diffuse (Battilana et al., 2017). Studies of practice variation in internationalization, therefore, ought to consider different forms of hybrid arrangements and their implications.

This chapter extends the mainstream literature on the internationalization of higher education by demonstrating alternative practice forms and adoption mechanisms outside the well-studied contexts (Bedenlier et al., 2018; Tight, 2021). Although these findings are based on data from a single country, they are informative for understanding how internationalization is experienced in contexts with similar characteristics. Countries such as Mexico, Hong Kong, and Singapore are recognized as regional hubs (like Turkey) due to their significant international student intake from neighboring countries (Cantwell et al., 2009; Chan & Ng, 2008; Kondakci et al., 2018). The duality in the practice of internationalization observed in the context of Turkish higher education is likely to be present in these contexts, perhaps in different forms and with other possible determinants. A fruitful direction for future research might be to examine how countries of different "types" experience internationalization (Aydinli & Mathews, 2021; Marginson & Rhoades, 2002).

The perspective of practice variation in internationalization developed in this chapter might be extended to provide a deeper understanding of already well-studied, central higher education contexts. Although internationalization is widely "theorized" as a desirable practice in higher education (Altbach & de Wit, 2015; King et al., 2011), a commercial approach to internationalization has received criticism (Bedenlier et al., 2018; Seeber et al., 2016; Tight, 2021). This is the case, for instance, when universities admit more and more international students to generate income (Altbach & Knight, 2007; Maringe et al., 2013). Prestigious research universities try to avoid this stigma by concentrating their international population at educational levels that support their research activities (Delgado-Márquez et al., 2013). Universities thus need to strategically manage the portfolio of their internationalization practices at different levels and under the constraints of their organizational resources (Siegel & Leih, 2018).

The findings of this chapter, overall, confirm the observation that the immediate organizational context of universities is very relevant to understanding their rationales for internationalization (Seeber et al., 2016). Going a step further, the specific ways in which organizational identity, ownership structure, and status position affect universities' adoption of different types of internationalization practices was established. Internationalization of higher education is perhaps an even more complex process, subject to the simultaneous influence of historical, geographic, cultural, and linguistic aspects of the national context—as well as regional and local elements (Aydinli & Mathews, 2021; Bedenlier et al., 2018; Marginson & Rhoades, 2002; Rose & McKinley, 2018; Seeber et al., 2016).

Future studies might thus benefit from applying set-theoretic methodologies (e.g., qualitative comparative analysis) in exploration of the effects of these factors in combination (Fiss et al., 2013; Greckhamer et al., 2018) to shed light on the many different paths to internationalization.

NOTES

1. The American high school Robert College in İstanbul was transformed into a public university in 1971 under the name of Boğaziçi University.
2. The most recent initiative of internationalization in Turkish higher education has been the Mevlana exchange program, launched by Turkey's Council of Higher Education (YÖK) in 2011 and started to be implemented in 2013. The program has a comprehensive focus, targeting countries worldwide (except the Erasmus+ area), without imposing any geographical limits. It is not included as an additional practice type in this chapter, not only because of the lack of a clear focus on the periphery or center, but also since student exchanges under the program are yet very small.
3. A similar distinction is made between the traditional Grand Ecole identity and the later introduced U.S. model in French higher education—the latter leading to the creation of international programs and partnerships with foreign institutions (Kodeih & Greenwood, 2014).
4. Despite being not-for-profit, private universities in Turkish higher education depend mainly on student tuition fees to survive (Barblan et al., 2008). They are thus more like market organizations relative to public universities funded by the state.

CHAPTER 11

MANAGEMENT EDUCATION

Internationalization, Accreditation, and the Pandemic

Michael Osbaldeston
Adriana Kudrnová Lovera

The internationalization of higher education has been on the agendas of national governments and university leaders around the world for decades, but the topic has achieved greater prominence in recent years due to the increasing realization that universities have a responsibility to prepare students for leadership roles in a global world. There are different reasons for this: The issues faced by employers are increasingly global; companies and NGOs are increasingly organized internationally with a global focus; and students have increasingly been taking an international perspective when choosing where to study, often deliberately choosing to go abroad to widen their experience.

Greater international awareness of issues such as climate change, geopolitics, poverty, inequality, and radicalization has enhanced the international debate within the academic community and led to a re-examination of the ways in which internationalization is conceptualized, systematized, and operationalized within the strategic development of most universities. While the coronavirus pandemic has been a profound shock to many of these strategies, traditional approaches to international education already faced considerable challenges due to concerns about sustainability, environmental impact, elitism, and other ethical considerations.

Nowhere in the higher education sector have these topics been more hotly debated than in the field of management development, where quality assurance, differentiation, and collaboration have been critical to the rapid growth of business schools across the world. In this chapter, the authors draw on their considerable experience in the European Foundation for Management Development (EFMD) to describe the development of accreditation of international management education over the past 20 years, discuss some of the ongoing challenges, and identify the changes that are likely to emerge from the current pandemic.

INTERNATIONALIZATION OF HIGHER EDUCATION AND MANAGEMENT EDUCATION

Knight's 2003 definition of internationalization as "the process of integrating an international, intercultural, or global dimension into the purpose, functions, and delivery of post-secondary education" has been widely accepted (Knight, 2004). More recently, however, Knight (2014) acknowledged that her original definition has the weakness that "traditional values associated with internationalization such as partnerships, collaboration, mutual benefit, and exchange are not articulated—only assumed" (p. 17). The description was thus expanded with the addition of: "...in order to enhance the quality of education and research for all students and staff and to make a meaningful contribution to society" (de Wit & Deca, 2020, p. 23). There is an increasing focus on how internationalization contributes to outreach, social responsibility, and engagement, as a recent European report (TEFCE) notes, "In the absence of prioritizing engagement over research excellence..., some universities have failed to develop the appropriate infrastructures to translate the knowledge they produce into the range of contexts..." (Benneworth et al., 2018, p. 51). Assessments of internationalization have generally focused on structural issues such as relevant research and publications, student and instructor diversity, international partners and networks, and international corporate connections. Yet there is a strong argument for rebalancing attention toward processes which are more outcome-related, with greater focus on the development of international relevance and outreach.

Although university-based business schools have existed for over a century, it is only in the last 50 years that they have become one of the major success stories in higher education, both from an academic perspective—instructors, research, and publications—and from a business focus—customers, revenue, and profitability. In recent decades, business schools have spread rapidly from North America through Europe to Asia and beyond, currently numbering over 16,000 worldwide with new additions being launched almost daily, particularly in emerging economies. Yet despite this success, there has also been increasing criticism in recent years, fueled in part by the frustrations of global economic recessions. Business schools have been charged with being too analytical, insular, and theoretical; insufficiently global, integrative, and collaborative; and lacking in values, ethics, and social responsibility (Naudé, 2021). It is hardly surprising, then, that many leading schools have increasingly turned their attention to internationalization to expand their reach and demonstrate their worth. In addition to the global issues which affect higher education generally, instructors and students in management education tend to be more mobile internationally, and while they accept higher costs, they also expect higher benefits (e.g., some MBAs are the highest-priced but also the most sought-after master's degrees in the world; Engwall et al., 2016). As management education has become increasingly competitive, it has become crucial to use internationalization to enhance differentiation, with an array of different international strategies being employed. At the same time, management research disseminated through journal publications, books, cases and learning materials, has become increasingly cross-cultural.

INTERNATIONALIZATION AND ACCREDITATION

The accreditation of management education originated over a century ago with a focus on North American business schools, followed by other program accreditation systems confined to specific countries. It was not until the 1990s that the growing demand for a European approach to accreditation led the European Foundation for Management Development (EFMD, originally founded in 1971) to seize the initiative and work towards the launch of the European Quality Improvement System (EQUIS) in 1997. EQUIS was designed to provide business schools in Europe—and subsequently worldwide—with a rigorous tool to assess and improve quality in all aspects of their operations. Over a relatively short period of time, EQUIS has enabled an elite group of institutions (currently 204 schools in 45 countries) to state with confidence that they are part of the "top 1% of leading business schools" worldwide. It was not long before EFMD also launched a Program Accreditation System—formerly known as EPAS and recently rebranded as EFMD Accredited—in 2005 with 131 programs currently accredited at 100 institutions across 39 countries. After more than 20 years of continuous development, the Financial Times stated that 5-year accreditation from EQUIS is now regarded as "the gold standard" for international business school accreditation.

EQUIS aims to recognize quality and quality assessment in the world's best business schools—through the award of a quality label which is valued worldwide by students, instructors, employers, and the media (having now become a prerequisite for entry into some prestigious rankings)—and also to recognize improvement through the need to meet and continue to achieve internationally agreed quality standards. From the start, EQUIS was conceived as an accreditation system rooted in respect for diversity of institutional and cultural contexts. It does not promote any "one best model" of a business school, but rather embraces higher management education at all levels without imposing standardization of program design, course content, or delivery mode. However, it is also firmly grounded on several transversal issues, one of which is looking for an international dimension throughout a school's activities. Although EQUIS was originally designed within a European context, it has also recognized the dilemmas which result from applying universal standards in widely differing international contexts and the system has thus evolved to ensure that it can be applied in all regions of the world, especially in rapidly emerging economies.

The criterion of "respect for diversity" is a particular case in point. While EQUIS is designed to promote diversity of all types, it also inevitably reflects the nature of diversity encountered within a school's original geographical region. Assessment of quality begins with an understanding of the particularities of the local context before progressing to assess international application across all dimensions and thus ensuring it is possible to recognize top-level business schools in Europe, Asia, and the Americas. However, this inherent flexibility in assessment does not imply any lowering of expectations regarding quality standards because of local constraints. Rather it is a feature of an assessment process capable of accepting wide differences in the organization and delivery of management education across the world.

At the heart of the EQUIS accreditation process is an issue which has engendered continuous debate since the organization's foundation: "Exactly what is meant by the term 'internationalization' and how best can it be assessed?" Internationalization has generally been perceived as being reflected in the mix of nationalities amongst students and instructors, together with advisory board members, partner schools, and recruiting organizations. While a school's cultural diversity, measured by nationality, is of course important, a much deeper understanding of internationalization results from an assessment of how a school has adapted its education and research to an increasingly global managerial world and (an issue which we will return to later), how a school responds to unexpected international shocks such as the global pandemic. Further, deeper evidence of the degree of internationalization can be reflected, for instance, by research that explores international challenges, education (which incorporates an international curriculum and is accessible across the world), and exposure (which encourages international mobility and employment). In a broader context, other more recent developments such as the growth of joint programs between business schools, the dissemination of online learning methodologies, the establishment of satellite campuses, increasing institutional collaboration and partnerships, and the emergence of mergers and other forms of restructuring (many of which have taken place across international boundaries) all need to be considered if we wish to understand and assess this complex and multi-faceted concept.

In order to assist academic leaders and accreditation reviewers alike in assessing the degree of internationalization of a business school, EQUIS developed a model (first launched in 2018) which encourages thinking beyond nationality mix and incorporates a wider range of international measures, grouped into four broad categories:

- *policy* issues influencing the development of the whole school;
- *content* aspects of the learning and development process;
- *context* issues resulting from the experience of the various stakeholders; and
- elements of the wider *network* in which the school participates.

Each category encompasses three further dimensions (all assessed within the EQUIS Quality Profile, a tool used by EQUIS Peer Review Teams). When evaluated on a simple low/medium/high scale, these 12 dimensions produce an overall profile of the extent of a school's internationalization, together with its relative strengths and areas for further improvement. This model (which has become colloquially known as the "internationalization spider diagram"; see Figure 11.1) also enables a school to demonstrate its international quality improvement journey over time with past versus present profiles, or to illustrate its future international strategic objectives with present versus planned future profiles.

Policy

1. *Strategy*—Does the school have a well-defined strategy for internationalization together with plans and resources for its implementation?
2. *Recognition/Reputation*—What are the competitiveness, recognition, and ranking of the school in international markets?
3. *Governance/Advisory Board*—Is there an international dimension in the school's governance and advisory system?

180 ▪ M. OSBALDESTON and A. K. LOVERA

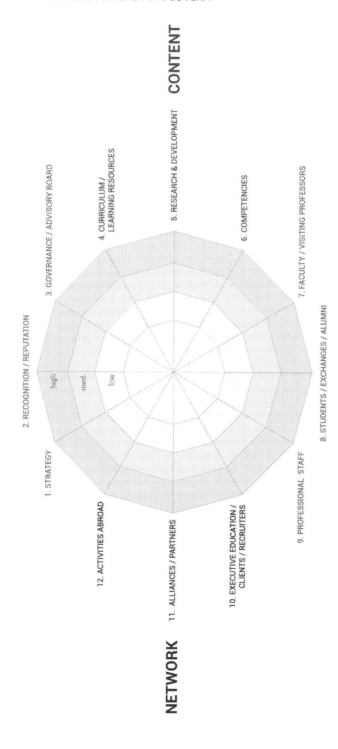

Figure 11.1 The internationalization spider diagram.

Content

1. *Curriculum/Learning Resources*—What are the international perspectives, content, and resources of the school's qualifications and executive education programs, and how is the learning made accessible/disseminated internationally?
2. *Research and Development*—What are the international scope, dissemination, and recognition of the school's R&D?
3. *Competencies*—Is global-mindedness developed, is language learning provided, and is English widely used for learning materials, teaching, and publication?

Context

1. *Instructors/Visiting Instructors*—What is the intercultural and experience mix of core, adjunct, and visiting instructors?
2. *Students/Exchanges/Alumni*—What is the intercultural mix of degree-seeking and exchange students and the international spread of alumni?
3. *Professional Staff*—Is there an international/partnerships/exchanges office with an intercultural mix of professional staff?

Network

1. *Executive Education/Clients/Recruiters*—Does the school have international corporate links with clients and employers, including international companies with domestic offices?
2. *Alliances/Partners*—What is the quality of the school's international academic partners, strategic alliances, and professional networks?
3. *Activities Abroad*—What is the school's level and quality of internationalization outside its home country, such as satellite campuses, joint programs, and franchised provisioning (where applicable)?

Although participating schools have generally welcomed this broader interpretation of internationalization within the EQUIS (and EFMD Accredited) accreditation system, there continue to be ongoing pressures to redefine standards, introduce new areas of assessment, and continuously evolve processes to reflect and even anticipate developments in management education—none more so than in the context of the current coronavirus pandemic.

The EFMD Quality Services team is currently using external sources and EQUIS data to further research and publicize the benefits and challenges of internationalization. Some of these relate to schools aiming to become more international; the intersection of internationalization and the ethics, responsibility, and sustainability (ERS) transversal standards; and the diverse strategies that schools are adopting to increase their internationalization in widely different national contexts and regions. This ongoing research will be used to identify new opportunities and strengthen current dimensions of internationalization, to raise awareness of the challenges and potential pitfalls of becoming more international, to highlight successful strategies to internationalize despite local limitations, and to disseminate illustrative case studies drawn from schools around the world.

APPROACHES TO INTERNATIONALIZATION

More than 20 years of accreditation experience by the authors drawn from across the world has clearly demonstrated that there is no single best model for internationalizing a business school. Rather, there are a variety of successful strategies, depending upon the scope, size, resources, and location of a school (as illustrated by the brief case examples in the next section). However, some of these strategies might be more affected than others by the constraints imposed by the current pandemic, especially those approaches which rely heavily on international recruitment and exchange of students and instructors across borders. Whilst it is premature to assess whether these will become permanent barriers, some schools are responding to the current context by re-evaluating the long-term viability of their internationalization strategies and searching for new opportunities resulting from the rapid growth of online learning.

Some large graduate business schools have focused on developing programs delivered in a single location but where everything is designed from an international perspective—curriculum, instructors, students, research agenda, and so on—such that the national base is largely irrelevant to their operations. These relatively few schools have developed a truly international community where no single nationality predominates. Others, perhaps originally based in a single European location, have chosen a different path, by establishing a subsequent "sister" school in a different geographical region. Here, students and instructors can be recruited initially to either site and then enabled to move seamlessly between the dual locations to experience the contrasting cultural settings. Another option is schools that have invested in supporting fledgling institutions, often located in developing countries, with financial, human, and managerial resources, and then withdrawing their active involvement at a later stage once the new school has gained sufficient strength and independence. Such "founding" schools often retain an informal relationship with the new institutions long into the future. A variation on this latter model is the formation of an international joint venture where an established school or educational foundation in one region of the world initiates a joint project with one or more other partners, working together to build a new institution from scratch in another region in order to enhance management education provision globally.

A more complex multi-campus strategy involves establishing a global network of interlinked campuses, either on a stand-alone basis or in partnership with other schools in each region, where students can be globally mobile, transferring from one location to another to complete their studies on the basis of international credit accumulation. Instructors might contribute to research and teaching in any or all of the locations or choose to develop their careers by periodically moving between locations. A somewhat less complex model involves selected partnerships, where an independent school chooses to work with a variety of international partners (often using their accreditation status for selection) to develop a variety of activities such as research networks/centers or joint programs or student exchange facilities. Some of these partnership programs are now so well-established that they are assessed as delivering a higher quality of education or research than any one of the partner schools could provide alone. A further option involves independent schools that might choose to be nationally based, but internationally open, by encouraging an influx of international exchange students and visiting instructors, and promoting overseas instructor secondments to build an ever-changing international learning community. The growth in demand from Chinese and Indian students in particular to study abroad, especially at the postgraduate level, has encouraged many schools in Europe and Australasia to expand internationally on this basis.

Table 11.1 outlines a range of distinct strategies undertaken by business schools today (EQUIS/EFMD accredited), including some which have emerged within the limits of a global pandemic. The wide variety of internationalization strategies are illustrated by the following business school mini-cases (summarized from the schools' promotional material). In each example, an internationalization strategy is illustrated.

Internationalization at Home—Maastricht University (The Netherlands)

> Mission: To help students develop the competencies and character strengths to serve as ethical leaders, innovative researchers, or empathic professionals who can help create conditions which mitigate some of the world's many problems including inequality, poverty, migration, and the climate crisis.

TABLE 11.1 Business School Internationalization Strategies

Strategy	Structure	Some Examples
Full Internationalization at Home	Single School	London Business School; International Institute for Management Development (IMD); Maastricht University
"Sister" Schools	Dual Schools	INSEAD
"Founding" > "Fledgling" Schools	New School in a Developing Country/Region	IESE Business School, University of Navarra & IPADE Business School
Joint Venture	New School Formed by Two or More Partners	EFMD & China Europe International Business School (CEIBS)
Multi-Campus/Global Network	Multiple/Interlinked Schools	SKEMA; Hult International Business School
Selected Partnerships/Global Alliance	Multiple/Network of Schools	Global Alliance in Management Education (CEMS); Global Network for Advanced Management (GNAM)
Students/Instructors Exchange Partners	Multiple Schools	University of St. Gallen; WHU-Otto Beisheim School of Management
Technology Enhanced	Virtual Campus	IE Business School
Online Dual Degrees	Online Consortium of Schools	European Common Online Learning (Ecol) Initiative
Virtual Exchanges	Virtual Partnerships/Network	Smith School of Business, Queen's University; EM Strasbourg

The university, which brands itself as the "European University of the Netherlands," aims to move beyond the assumption that merely bringing together people from different countries and cultures will make students into global citizens. Rather, the university has chosen a more intentional approach to ensure that education in an international classroom purposefully promotes meaningful interaction. Supported by a grant from the Dutch government, Maastricht students and teachers identified an "evolving" framework structured around three pillars: global literacy (systems thinking), social responsibility (normative competence), and transformative engagement. Each pillar includes knowledge elements, skills, and attitudes/characteristics. The university seeks to integrate into the curriculum its hallmarks of problem-based learning, work-integrated experiential learning, and students engaging with stakeholders on internal and community projects. Students also benefit from teaching tools for individual competencies, as well as support for student-led initiatives via grants and coaching ("Global Citizenship Education," n.d.).

"Sister" Schools—INSEAD (France and Singapore)

Mission: INSEAD brings together people, cultures, and ideas to develop responsible leaders who transform business and society.

With over 80% of its student intake coming from European countries, French-based INSEAD was already an international school by the mid-1970s. 20 years later, a rise in global business activities and a desire to internationalize the school's reach outside Europe spurred the creation of a second campus. Singapore was selected as the new location for several reasons. INSEAD had proven expertise in Asia thanks to its Euro-Asia Centre; there was an alignment between Singapore's vision of developing an international educational hub and the school's strategy of building local knowledge and a learning network; and finally, Singapore offered an attractive quality of life. The school took important steps to ensure that the new campus was positioned on an equal level with the original campus in France. They did this by sending instructors and staff with regional expertise from their Euro-Asia Centre alongside some of their other outstanding instructors and staff to set up the new campus. INSEAD also committed significant investments to help the campus achieve scale and quickly become self-sufficient. The new model of "one school, two campuses" allowed students to pursue their programs seamlessly across the two campuses. With evaluation and promotion standards perfectly aligned, instructors could also easily move between both campuses. In addition, the two campuses had predominantly international student bodies rather than largely French or Singaporean students. Since then, INSEAD has also opened locations in the Middle East and North America, and now markets itself as "the Business School for the World" (Hawawini, 2017).

Multi-Campus Structure—SKEMA (France, etc.)

Mission: To offer students a truly global and multicultural experience by combining academic life with international professional experience.

SKEMA was founded in 2009 following a merger between two French institutions in the face of government reforms and increasing financial pressure. Given the increasing competition for local and international students, a merger might enable the schools to thrive and pursue their shared dream of becoming a truly global business school. The schools had to navigate the challenges of forming a single school: losing their unique brands and having to establish shared governance and standards, and a single identity and strategy in pursuit of a global multi-campus school. Working together, the schools leveraged their respective competencies and developed new synergies: they now had a larger pool of resources, partnerships abroad, and were able to eliminate duplicate costs in terms of HR, marketing, and so on. The school boasts multi-site programs that offer mobility, professional expertise, and interdisciplinary programs (technology-management). SKEMA has set up additional campuses in "scientific hubs" and is continuously looking for synergy with the school's local environments in terms of research and business partnerships. The school proactively involves global companies in its governance, programs, research, incubators, and so on. With seven campuses in Brazil, China, France, South Africa, and the United States, SKEMA offers more than 50 programs and boasts over 8,500 students of 120 different nationalities (Guilhon, 2015).

Technology Enhanced—IE (Spain)

Slogan: To Reinvent Higher Education

Over the last 25 years, Madrid-based IE has heavily invested in technological innovation. The school is modeled around four pillars: technological immersion and a culture of innovation; an entrepreneurial mindset; humanities to understand the world; and a diversity of nationalities, cultures, and ideas. With a largely international student body, the school has had to adapt quickly to travel restrictions during the COVID-19 crisis. IE announced a new fluid learning model, in which students have the option to attend class either in person or online. Classrooms have been equipped to become "hybrid," with cameras, microphones, and even large screens which help "bring in" students who connect online. Prior to the pandemic, the school had already developed a highly interactive classroom: the *Window on the World* (WoW) room—a virtual classroom consisting of a 45 square meter video wall made up of 48 monitors arranged in a U-shape. The WoW room allows students to connect and collaborate no matter where they are. The school's pioneering spirit today makes it an outstanding leader of innovative learning models. Since 2002, over 3,000 undergraduate and postgraduate students have participated in online modules every year ("WOW Room Takes IE's Commitment to Technology Immersion in Learning Environments to the Next Level," 2016).

Joint Venture—CEIBS (China)

> Vision: To become the most respected international business school by linking East and West in teaching, research, and business practice and by promot-

ing China's social and economic development through high-impact knowledge creation and dissemination.

China Europe International Business School (CEIBS), a joint venture for management education, was co-founded by the Chinese government and European Union (EU) in 1994, with Shanghai Jiao Tong University and the EFMD serving as its executive partners. In this way, CEIBS was uniquely positioned to benefit from both European and Chinese know-how. It was the first business school in mainland China with its own campus when it established a facility in Shanghai. Although the school's "China Depth, Global Breadth" motto was adopted less than 10 years ago, it has been long evident in many facets of the school, including its governance—composed of 50% Chinese and 50% non-Chinese. CEIBS has become an attractive option for students who want to understand China in the context of a global economy; noteworthy is its requirement for foreign MBA students to learn Chinese. The school also has a campus in Accra, Ghana. Dean Ding Yuan (Bentil, 2019) says, "CEIBS is the only top business school from an emerging market which can provide Africans with substantial insight into how to do business in another emerging market" (para. 20). In addition to Africa, CEIBS is focused on strengthening its ties in the United States and Europe. In 2019, the school celebrated its 25th anniversary by breaking ground on its new European gateway campus in Zurich. As of December 2019, CEIBS had more than 24,000 alumni, with 64 regional chapters of the CEIBS Alumni Association around the world (Bickerstaff & Wood, 2012).

Multi-Campus Structure—Hult International Business School (United States)

Motto: Get Plugged Into the World

Education First (EF)—a global company offering language and cultural immersion programs—already held an international outlook and its own paradigm of learning theory when it acquired the Arthur D. Little School of Management and rebranded it as Hult IBS in 2003. The school has successfully leveraged its parent company's international business experience and education ideals of experiential learning. The school has expanded remarkably, from 26 students in one Boston campus to campuses in Shanghai, Dubai, London, and San Francisco; and additional "rotation centers" abroad, all within its first decade. Students are from 140 nationalities. Nevertheless, the campuses are considered to constitute branches of one school. Management is centralized, while branch operation is decentralized. Campus-specific activities are complemented with online activities for the wider school community and through individual mobility and travel. The Global Rotation Program allows students to easily move across campuses for 6 months or a year at a time. Thus, the school seeks to have a diverse student body, which will be "transformed into a body of 'global citizens'" (Forstorp & Mellström, 2018, p. 264). The school seeks to instill cross-cultural skills which would function anywhere in the global market, among them: mobility, adaptability, and the ability to overcome the barriers of diversity.

Global Alliance/Virtual Exchanges—Global Network for Advanced Management (Global)

Mission: To drive innovation and create value by connecting leading global business schools, their resources, and their stakeholders.

The Global Network for Advanced Management brings together schools from around the world to develop innovative initiatives that leverage the schools' comparative advantages. One successful program is the Global Network Courses, through which member schools can offer for-credit virtual courses open to MBA students from throughout the network. Students thus join other students abroad during online lectures, discussions, and team projects. Whilst in a typical term a student could find a few Global Network Courses to choose from, in 2020 the number of courses saw a steep increase, revealing the growing interest from schools in the model. Student interest might have also peaked due to the increased range of topics available and a desire to interact with students in other countries.

The network also offers students the opportunity to participate in Global Virtual Teams, where they team up to work virtually on an assignment with students in other countries. The virtual teams experience is preceded by a series of lectures on the theory and practice of leading, managing, and functioning in worldwide teams. Students gain hands-on experience working within an international team and can develop their effectiveness and leadership. In the Spring of 2016, EGADE, HEC, and Yale SOM participated in the first collaboration, made up of 108 cross-school teams and a total of 515 students. This model of collaboration certainly gained more popularity during the COVID-19 pandemic and beyond ("Video: Global Virtual Teams Course," 2019).

INTERNATIONALIZATION: CURRENT AND ANTICIPATED EFFECTS OF THE PANDEMIC

The onset of the COVID-19 pandemic raised new and significant questions about current approaches to internationalization. Efforts to contain the spread of infection, including domestic lockdowns, international travel restrictions, and campus closures, left many international students in limbo, whilst many institutions have adapted quickly to continue their activities online. This rapid transition to virtual learning, which can then be disseminated worldwide, accompanied by pedagogical training for instructors to support the revision of their teaching methodologies, deserves applause. Yet, at the same time, many international and exchange students sought greater safety and security by returning to their home countries wherever possible. In tandem, accreditation bodies, ranking agencies, and business school associations have shared experience and best practices in response to this severe educational disruption in order to provide a collaborative platform of knowledge and solidarity. Beyond these immediate short-term impacts, institutions are now grappling with the implications for some of their internationalization strategies—in particular, those which have focused on the international mobility of students and instructors.

Prior to the pandemic, many universities—particularly those in Australia, North America, and the United Kingdom—were becoming increasingly dependent on income from international students, who in many cases are required to pay higher tuition fees than their local counterparts. For example, figures published in 2020 show that in 2017–2018, Chinese student fees provided £1.7 billion to U.K. higher education institutions, comprising around 5% of total income, which can only have grown in more recent years (Baker, 2020). Institutions with a large percentage of international students suffered a major loss in tuition fee income due to the pandemic, from a decrease in international student enrollment. Some of these schools have invested so heavily in international recruitment that the majority of their student bodies now consist of international students. They stand to lose a substantial proportion of their fee income if such enrollments do not recover rapidly.

An early 2020 survey from Studyportals found that a majority of prospective students (73%) who had planned to enroll in courses abroad in the following 6 months were continuing with the same study plans, whilst the remaining students (27%) were considering postponing their studies or enrolling in online courses (Bothwell, 2020). A later survey in 2020 reported by *University World News* found that over 50% of prospective international students were considering changing their plans and wished to postpone their studies or study in a different country ("53% of International Students Pondering Delay or Switch," 2020). More than half of students surveyed were not interested in studying wholly online, and 53% still hoped to travel abroad for their studies in the near future.

The findings of a 2021 survey by Cialfo of 3,800 high school students from more than 100 countries indicated that a majority with international education aspirations will not be changing their plans as a result of the pandemic—with a minority stating that the crisis has made them more hesitant to study abroad. Whilst the emergence of the pandemic might be having only a modest influence on their international study plans, access to financial support and job uncertainty in foreign countries after graduation are their primary concerns. These results mirror the findings of the Institute of International Education—that the number of U.S. educational institutions attracting international student applications in 2021 exceeded those experiencing declines, in stark contrast to what was occurring only a year prior, in 2020.

Whether prospective international students will be more likely to study locally in the future remains uncertain. However, it is possible that the pandemic, together with other travel related factors, might indeed create permanent changes in the flow of students to and from different countries. In addition to the sudden restrictions of movement across borders imposed by the pandemic, students intending to study abroad could be deterred by ever tighter visa requirements, a backlog of visas to be processed, strict quarantine requirements, and "unwelcoming" or even discriminatory experiences reported by foreign students already studying in some countries. Furthermore, the perception that some countries have better managed the pandemic might also sway student plans. Anglophone countries such as Canada and the United Kingdom may benefit from their more liberal immigration and post-study regulations together with the relative success of their vaccination programs.

Just as schools have adapted their practices to the changing environment, EQUIS is also responding to the changing realities of business and management schools. In 2019, EQUIS created a Digitalization Task Force to draw on the experiences of deans of EQUIS-accredited schools from across the world in relation to the benefits of digitalization for international management research and education. Evidently, the rapid transition seen in many business schools from a classroom to a virtual (or hybrid) learning environment necessitated by the pandemic further amplified the need for EQUIS to reflect on this topic.

Digitalization has rapidly shifted from a marginal activity in business schools to a key feature of higher education. However, it remains unclear to what extent digital activities are truly engrained in broader school strategies to meet key institutional goals. Whilst an increasing number of activities takes place online, the question still remains about the quality and impact of such interactions. Yet we are experiencing an exciting moment in which schools are developing innovative ways to create new learning and collaborative spaces for their students and staff. Some commentators expect digitalization to expand accessibility to meaningful international experiences and to quality education provision in some parts of the world (Rampelt et al., 2019).

A broader conception of internationalization inclusive of digital experiences could perhaps lead to an evolution in the language of internationalization towards "participation and experience" and away from "enrollment and exchange." This type of shift could potentially spur new schools to consider international accreditations when in the past they would have not done so.

Virtual student exchange models (also known as collaborative online international learning) have existed for many years and are particularly attractive to poorer and more risk-averse students who are keen to access the reputational resources and networking assets of an overseas institution on a short-term basis or to study for a wholly online degree. However, critics point to the inability to replicate the deeply immersive and often transformational nature of traditional study abroad, which takes students out of their comfort zone and embeds them in a different cultural and linguistic context. Whilst taught content can be reproduced online for many subjects, the out-of-classroom wider experiences are much harder to replicate. In any case, it is still early in our shared journey to discover the full potential of technology to provide meaningful experiences and enrichment across borders.

CONCLUSION

Whatever the short-term challenges, some commentators have suggested that a significant "silver lining" might emerge for business schools from the current "black swan" crisis. The business education ecosystem might develop its own immune system, with more flexible, innovative, and collaborative international strategies involving greater integration of virtual connections. Schools might become more resilient, more relevant, and better prepared for future disruption, while students might be more open, more selective, and increasingly flexible in how they plan for their international management education. International accreditation systems will certainly need to continue to evolve in response to this ever-changing context of management education.

CHAPTER 12

CRITICAL SUCCESS FACTORS OF INTERNATIONAL EDUCATION PROGRAMS

Laura Colm
Brandi DeMont
Amanda Swain

Travel as an opportunity for instruction and as a pedagogical concept emerged in the Anglophone context in the 17th century, when young men from upper-class British families began "completing their education" after boarding school by traveling across Europe (Prebys & Ricciardelli, 2017). As that experience became accessible to a larger number of students, study abroad started being recognized as a necessity for preparing young adults to face a globalized and increasingly interconnected world. The global education industry is now not only among the largest but also one of the fastest developing sectors worldwide. The higher education market therefore plays a significant role globally, with the number of tertiary students having more than doubled between 2000 and 2014, reaching 207 million (OECD, 2017a).

Though these figures reflect the pre-COVID-19 pandemic situation, experiential programs are primed to recover rapidly and might grow even further with the return of in-person instruction (Basiri, 2021). Such programs not only offer valuable opportunities for students to improve their professional skills and intercultural competences, but also are/represent fundamental milestones for personal growth, because they allow students to become more autonomous and familiar with other cultures, to experience different types of learning and lifestyles, and to leave the "comfort zone" of their home institution. Moreover, according to Alonderiene and Klimavičiene (2013), a university's international experiential partnerships and their offerings influence the decision-making processes of students as they choose among institutions. This is particularly relevant in the U.S. context, where a highly segmented and competitive higher education market requires attention to the needs of students to ensure enrollment. In this light, it is fundamental that international experiential education providers gain a thorough understanding of students' needs and drivers when they are selecting programs.

This chapter aims to illuminate the critical success factors of international education programs that providers can obtain by offering high level experiences to their students, in order to improve their market positioning. To this end, the chapter first offers an overview of the international study abroad experiences phenomenon, highlighting the characteristics of both the demand side (student expectations from such experiences) and the supply side (providers of these programs). Then follows a brief review of relevant literature regarding the concept of "experiences" in business and especially the characteristics of "service experiences" in the education sector. This section helps underpin the theoretical foundations of experiential learning and outlines the relevance of experiences for a service provider and its customers, particularly in the dynamic context of higher education.

This research is based on a case study of a leading American third-party study abroad provider for college-aged students. This case study was developed using a qualitative method of data collection and analysis. The main findings of the case study are outlined as four critical success factors and discussed in terms of their deployment and management as the study implies.

STUDY ABROAD: AN OVERVIEW OF THE PHENOMENON

Study abroad entails the pursuit of educational opportunities in a country other than one's own. This broad definition allows for a variety of study abroad types and lengths, which is described below. The Association of International Educators ("Trends in U.S. Study Abroad," n.d.) reports that in the 2018–2019 academic year, U.S. higher education institutions saw close to 350,000 students enrolled in a study program outside the country—a number which corresponds to 1.8% of students enrolled in American higher education institutions. Study abroad also constitutes a considerable part of the experience economy, with international students contributing $300 billion to the global economy in 2016 according to ICEF Monitor ("International Students Generate Global Economic Impact," 2019). This impact does not include the intangible benefits for international students, such as increased intercultural competence, global connectedness, and personal growth (Mohajeri Norris & Gillespie, 2009).

Cultural intelligence, or CQ (Earley & Ang, 2003; Ang et al., 2011), refers to a person's ability to function appropriately and effectively in situations marked by cultural diversity, for example, study abroad or international business. Indeed, many businesses value the competences of employees who have participated in a study abroad program. In a 2013 study of 200 companies, 30% of them reported having missed out on international business opportunities due to a lack of employees who possess adequate international competences (Boix Mansilla & Jackson, 2013). 80% expected that their business would increase with more internationally competent employees. This finding suggests that there is significant room for growth in study abroad opportunities, based on current participation rates in the United States and the perceived needs of organizations.

Boix Mansilla and Jackson (2013) define the *globally competent student* as someone who is able to do the following:

1. investigate the world beyond their immediate environment, framing significant problems and conducting well-crafted and age-appropriate research;
2. recognize perspectives of others and their own, articulating and explaining such perspectives thoughtfully and respectfully;
3. communicate ideas effectively with diverse audiences, bridging geographic, linguistic, ideological, and cultural barriers; and
4. take action to improve conditions, viewing themselves as players in the world and participating reflectively.

Given such a definition, it is not surprising that companies hope to recruit internationally competent students who have had educational experiences abroad (University of California Merced, 2022).

Student Benefits and Expectations of Educational Experiences

Tamilla and Ledgerwood (2018) provide a thorough review of the literature on the reported benefits of study abroad, which they organize into four categories: cross-cultural exchanges, academic growth, professional development, and personal growth. Cross-cultural experiences are pertinent to any discussion of global education or global business. Tamilla and Ledgerwood refer to several studies reporting that students' cross-cultural skills increase from the experience of viewing/understanding their own culture through the lens of the host culture, which enables them to see their home culture in a more objective way. The study abroad experience also results in a reported increase in empathy, and positive changes in attitudes towards cultural differences. Students themselves consistently report increases in their sense of confidence and independence, as a result of navigating the inherent setbacks and ambiguities which are a part of interacting with a different culture.

Additionally, many studies point to academic growth which occurs as a result of studying abroad. While academic growth in linguistic and cultural areas which are related to the host country might be expected, many students also demonstrate an increased understanding of and interest in art, travel, history, and architecture—which contribute to an expansion of creative thinking more generally. A 2012 study (Lee et al., 2012) found that students who studied abroad generated more original ideas on both culture-specific and domain-general creativity tests, compared with students who had not studied abroad. Interestingly, Tamilla and Ledgerwood's (2018) study suggests that furthering academic knowledge is often not a main motivating factor in students' decisions to study abroad. Nonetheless, one could posit that the kind of learning which occurs in a cross-cultural setting might support, or function in tandem with, academic development.

In today's globalized economy, organizations expect new employees to be culturally aware and have the soft skills which are required to succeed in intercultural settings; such as communication, empathy, and adaptability. This expectation is consistent, regardless of whether or not a new employee will be working in a host culture or working from the home culture but interacting with colleagues or clients globally (Harder et al., 2015). Professional growth which results from international educational experiences is thus clearly tied to issues of employability and career development, in addition to more personal growth as individuals and citizens in a globally connected world (Marjanović & Križman Pavlović, 2018).

The Supply Side: Study-Abroad Programs and Their Types

A wide range of study abroad program types and lengths are available to students who seek an international education experience. Whether offered directly by an institution of higher education or by a third-party study abroad provider, the basic structures of the programs offered to students remain relatively similar. Below we provide a short description of some of the most common program types.

- *Instructor led.* An instructor-led program is led by instructors from a given institution of higher education and is generally short- or medium-term in length. In these programs, the curriculum is typically organized around one course or topic and often fulfills a requirement for the institute with which the instructor is associated. Students and instructors attend activities and events together, and often bond as a group. A pre-planned and structured itinerary provides significant support for students.
- *Intensive Language.* An intensive language program is most common during January-term or summer months and enables students to earn credits toward a foreign language requirement. Language programs are often partially or entirely linguistically and culturally immersive and include required and/or optional cultural excursions.
- *Semester or year abroad.* A semester-long or year-long program is one in which a student enrolls in a full-time course load, often earning transferable credits at an institution located abroad. Such programs might involve direct enrollment at a foreign institution of higher education, attendance at a satellite campus of the student's home institution located internationally, or enrollment at a local or American-based study abroad center which hires instructors (often local) to teach courses in various disciplines.
- *Internship abroad.* An internship program places students in full or part-time international internships in foreign companies, sometimes blending this experiential component with coursework. These internships are primarily unpaid, with students receiving course credit towards graduation requirements. Most internship abroad programs require students to enroll in a course which supports the internship experience, by mandating participation in structured opportunities for self-reflection and professional growth. This is a popular option for many professionally oriented students, or for students seeking a highly immersive cultural experience.
- *Community-based learning.* A community-based learning program provides students with volunteer placements in host-country public sector and nonprofit organizations, sometimes blending this experiential component with coursework. This is another avenue for students who seek a highly immersive cultural experience because it facilitates direct engagement with the local community.

THE EXPERIENCE ECONOMY: IMPLICATIONS FOR THE EDUCATION SECTOR

This section offers an overview of the concept of "experience" in the services sector and its relevance for education. The first section defines and provides some historical background on the notion of the experience economy; the second section focuses on service experiences and their role in the higher education sector.

Defining the Experience Economy

The concept of *customer experience* has roots in various fields (e.g., economics, sociology, psychology, & anthropology) and dates back to the 1980s—a period in which literature on consumer behavior was gaining increasing relevance (see Lemon & Verhoef, 2016). This was the moment in which customers began to be considered not only as rational decision-makers who seek to maximize utility, but also as human beings also driven by emotions. It is important to note that the concept of customer experience includes the role of emotions and emotional responses in the consumption behavior of individuals. In their pioneering article on this phenomenon, Holbrook and Hirschman (1982) define the customer experience as a "subjective state of consciousness with a variety of symbolic meanings, hedonic responses, and aesthetic criteria" (p. 132). Over a decade later, Pine and Gilmore (1998) introduced the term *experience economy* to characterize a new category of economic offering which succeeds the agrarian, industrial, and service economies. The experience economy urges (and challenges) managers to design and execute memorable events for their customers, because memories of these events have become the main outcomes which are sought by consumers.

A greater level of detail, along with some indications about how to craft such experiences in the business context, is provided by Schmitt (1999), who develops a conceptual framework for experiential marketing. Schmitt identifies five types of experiences which companies can deliver to their customers: sensing, feeling, thinking, acting, and relating. These can support companies in meeting (and exceeding) customers' expectations. This is particularly important, because "services, like goods before them, increasingly become commoditized... experiences have emerged as the next step in what we call the progression of economic value" (Pine & Gilmore, 1998, p. 97). Several subsequent studies—especially in the disciplines of marketing and management—have attempted to elaborate and shed further light on customer experiences as sources of value generation for both companies and their customers (see Addis & Holbrook, 2001; Carù & Cova, 2003; LaSalle & Britton, 2003).

Indeed, when in 2014 the *Harvard Business Review* suggested that crafting experiences would be one of the greatest challenges for enterprises in the immediate future, it anticipated a trend which was clearly manifest only a few years later (with the rise of experiential offerings such as Netflix in the entertainment sector, AirBnB in the travel industry, or large youth festivals such as Coachella). The new challenge on the frontier is now the development of experiences which extend beyond simple customer satisfaction, to meaningful customer engagement. This will be increasingly necessary for companies in order to sustain their business models in the long run (Rather, 2020).

Service Experiences and Their Role in the Higher Education Sector

Experiences play a particularly important role in the context of services because most services are experiential by nature (Lewis & Mitchell, 1990). In most instances, services are also co-created through joint efforts and exchanges between the provider (institution) and the customer (student; Hollebeek et al., 2019; Vargo & Lusch, 2008; Prahalad & Ramaswamy, 2004). For this reason, the concept of *service experience*—defined as the interaction between a company and its customers when a service is provided—has been described as the very core of a service offering, playing a central role in the design and delivery of the service itself (Zomerdijk & Voss, 2010).

In her comprehensive literature review on service experience in marketing research, Helkkula (2011) has further clarified the concept by identifying three categories of service experiences: the phenomenological service experience (subjective for each individual but often taking place in a collective setting and thus encompassing a relational component), the process-based service experience (a process entailing actions and multiple phases; Toivonen et al., 2007), and the outcome-based service experience (models which link a number of variables or attributes to specific outcomes). Service experiences are complex in design and manifold in their manifestation, since they are composed of different elements but experienced as a whole by customers (Gentile et al., 2007). For this reason, companies ought to strive to offer rich and smooth service experiences that customers can easily navigate and contribute to.

This aspect of an experiential service is of particular importance in the higher education sector, where the learning experience is co-created: by students and the institution, students and their instructors, students and administrators, and among students and their peers (Ng & Forbes, 2009). Indeed, the core service offered to the students is the *experiential learning opportunity* itself, which implies that the value is necessarily emergent, and the value generation process must account for the customer perspective. As early as 2005, Newby claimed that higher education institutions ought to be more customer focused. This is especially important in light of the steadily increasing demand for educational services, and in particular, educational services abroad (Enders, 2004), which are seen as the key to earning cultural competencies unlocking unique professional opportunities in today's global environment (Cant, 2004).

This growing interest—which is also expressed in extremely high private expenditure levels in the sector (OECD, 2017b)—urges educational service providers to understand the factors which influence the acquisition intention and perceived quality of prospective students, and the relationship between them (Cubillo et al., 2006). Because students' choices are necessarily influenced by the visible, tangible indicators of the services offered during their study abroad—which they use as markers of service experience quality (Johns & Howard, 1998)—it is important that study-abroad education providers become aware of these indicators and systematically account for them in their strategic decisions in order to be better positioned to leverage them and deliver unique and memorable student-oriented experiences. For example, cues, such as country and city image, can be largely independent of the education service provider, whilst other cues (e.g., in terms of quality and quantity of offered courses) are directly under the provider's control, such as institution image and program characteristics (Ng & Forbes, 2009). These latter cues ought to be investigated further, and mobilized to increase the likelihood of crafting positive, long-lasting learning experiences which are able to sustain the competitive advantage of education and study abroad providers in the long term (Ivy, 2001).

THE CASE OF A THIRD-PARTY AMERICAN STUDY ABROAD PROVIDER IN MILAN

In line with the goal of better understanding and identifying the critical success factors of intentional educational opportunities abroad, we conducted a case study with a qualitative inquiry method by following an exploratory logic and a grounded theory approach (Glaser & Straus, 1967/2017). This approach is particularly useful for identifying relevant patterns (decisions, priorities, strategies, etc.) of behavior of the various actors involved (Mitchell, 2014), making it particularly suitable for investigating the topic of experiential learning opportunities abroad, which requires deep understanding of students' needs and the attributes of the programs offered by providers.

In keeping with the iterative logic of qualitative research (Klag & Langley, 2013), we integrate both existing theoretical accounts and field evidence to identify education providers' critical success factors and key pillars upon which study abroad providers can strategically construct memorable experiential learning opportunities for students. We base our investigation on a relevant case (Yin, 2009) of a leading third-party study abroad provider (called "center" thereafter) which administers study abroad programs for

American college students. This provider is particularly useful for exploring the topic under investigation because it functions as a mediator among a consortium of American colleges and universities and international institutions, offering courses which are approved by the consortium schools but which are taught by local instructors. It also facilitates student enrollment in courses at local partner institutions. The provider offers programming throughout the academic year on a semester basis (fall, spring, and summer terms) with a wide array of courses and course-configurations in terms of content, duration, and service level. Its leading position in the market—together with an intermediary role which requires ongoing negotiation of the requirements of other educational institutions, students' needs, and the preservation of its own market positioning—make this provider particularly suitable for shedding light on the phenomenon of our research interest.

This third-party provider operates on a worldwide basis, with a common mission and vision but local adaptations and specificities. So, the chapter focuses on one specific center to allow for the investigation of the (best) practices at the operational level, thereby enabling the identification of critical success factors of study abroad. The center in focus is located in Milan. There are three reasons for this choice. First, the Milan center is one of the fastest growing among provider's centers in recent years, which calls for better understanding of its growth drivers (and thus, its critical success factors). Second, the center's program offerings are very broad in terms of disciplines, and it consequently hosts students with very different backgrounds (e.g., business, music, and humanities)—an element which allows us to obtain a more fine-grained understanding of how to match demand and supply. Third, Milan is one of the fastest developing cities in Europe, which permits investigation of the interdependencies and synergies between the provider's core service and its surrounding environment.

Through a series of field observations at the Milan center, interviews and conversations collected between 2018 and 2021 with the provider's instructors and staff members, and by leveraging the experience of the provider's alumni, we identified a set of critical success factors and key pillars according to which experiential learning opportunities in study abroad programs can be effectively and strategically crafted. The four critical success factors and three key pillars are visually summarized in our framework, which is represented in Figure 12.1.

COMBINING CRITICAL SUCCESS FACTORS TO OFFER EXPERIENTIAL LEARNING OPPORTUNITIES ABROAD

Our analysis of the data collected from both the supply-and-demand sides suggests that there are four different critical success factors which allow the

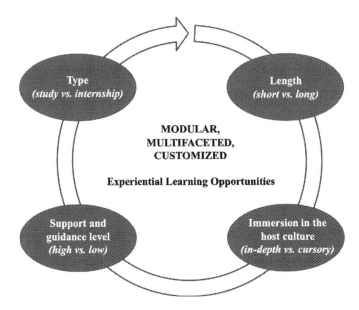

Figure 12.1 The critical success factors and key pillars of experiential learning opportunities.

center to craft attractive study abroad programs that stand out in the marketplace. We summarize these critical success factors as follows:

- *Type* of the study abroad program (study versus internship);
- *Length* (short, medium, or long);
- *Support and guidance level* (high versus low—the degree to which students' experiences are actively guided); and
- *Degree of immersion in the host culture* (in-depth versus cursory—the centrality of structured activities that encourage students to interact with the local culture).

What is crucial for the success of the center is that several variants of each content success factor are offered for each. Indeed, the fact that students are exposed to different program combinations in terms of type, length, support, and guidance level, and degree of immersion in the host culture provides multiple options, allowing them to make choices which best suit their needs.

First Critical Success Factor: Type

"I chose [the center] because [the alternative] didn't have an internship option."

"Even though I don't need any language credit, I wanted to start learning Italian, and [the center] forces you to take the language. If I wasn't forced to, I might have ended up taking something else instead."

Current study abroad programs at the center can be divided into the categories of full-time study and full-time internship, though the two share some overlapping elements. Full-time study requires 15–19 academic credits over the course of a 15-week semester. This format integrates experiential learning into the academic offering in a variety of ways, including:

- mandatory intensive language courses focused on a communicative approach, which helps students integrate into the local context;
- field studies in area studies courses which take students out of the classroom to learn about course concepts in real-world settings;
- an elective community-based learning placement which immerses students in the local community through part-time volunteer placements and a corresponding academic seminar which helps them reflect on their experiences and situate in a global context;
- an elective 3-credit part-time internship placement and academic seminar which helps students reflect on their internship experiences, position them within relevant theoretical frameworks, and develop the cultural intelligence and dexterity to adapt to their internship placements and situate their experiences within a larger context.

Students who select full-time study can also choose to enroll in up to two courses at a local partner institution in order to gain first-hand experience of the local academic culture and educational system, by taking courses alongside local students.

Full-time internship students, on the other hand, are required to spend a minimum of 300 hours at an internship placement per 15-week semester, or a minimum of 200 hours during an 8-week term, in addition to attending a mandatory 3-credit seminar course which helps them reflect on their internship experiences and develop the cultural intelligence and dexterity to adapt to their internship placements and situate their experiences within a larger context.

These two types of programs differ in their emphasis on academic- versus practice-focused learning, enabling students to choose how much academic credit or professional experience they would like to gain from their time abroad. There is some degree of overlap between these two categories however, because full-time study programs also allow students to participate in part-time internships, while some full-time internship programs allow students to elect additional academic coursework. The programs also differ in terms of cost, with full-time internship programs costing significantly less than full-time study programs, but still allowing students to have an experiential international learning experience.

Second Critical Success Factor: Length

> "I study Italian and wanted to actually have a chance to practice it and learn. Four months maybe isn't such a long time, but it's better than a shorter period. Plus, I need to use my summer to make money, so a semester program made more sense."

> "My major doesn't really leave much time for study abroad. I could only travel in the summer when I wouldn't get behind at school."

Current offerings at the center can be divided into short-term or semester-length programs. Short-term programs include 8-week summer programs or programs of various durations created *ad hoc* for colleges or universities to correspond to their specific academic calendars. Semester-length programs are 15-week programs with set arrival and departure dates which are standardized for all students, regardless of their home college or university calendars. The differing lengths allow students to choose programs in relation to time commitments and requirements which are dictated by their home institutions, majors, and academic or extracurricular schedules. Differing lengths also allow for a cost differential related to the duration of the stay abroad.

Third Critical Success Factor: Support and Guidance

> "I like the trips that they plan for us to places that maybe we wouldn't go by ourselves. Places that are off the beaten path. They feel more real and less touristy."

> "The staff is so responsive. When I needed to make a medical appointment...they sent someone with me to translate."

The center's programs can also be distinguished by the degree to which they facilitate student integration into the local culture through guidance, support, and structured activities. Programs can offer a high level of support in a variety of ways:

1. *Instructor guidance,* in the form of field studies or excursions led by locally based instructors and related to the content of specific courses which students take onsite, or in the form of U.S.-based instructors who accompany students abroad and provide supervision

from a 360-degree perspective (providing academic instruction and affective support while participating in cultural activities alongside students). This latter format is especially common in customized instructor-led programs, which typically correspond to a specific course or academic requirement at the instructor's American institution and offer students a person who can consistently facilitate critical engagement with their experiences as well as provide assistance and supervision. Because instructor-led programs combine academic and non-academic activities, they guide students in linking academic or theoretical concepts discussed in class or orientation sessions with real-world experiences.
2. *Staff support,* or local staff employed at the study abroad center who specialize in offering various types of services to students, including related to academic advising, student life, health and safety, housing, and internship placements. Staff typically run orientation sessions, organize events and activities which link student interest with the local community, coordinate services, and serve as a reference point for questions, problems, concerns, and policies. They constitute a connection between students and local laws, norms, instructors, and institutions.
3. *Resident assistants,* local university students or young professionals who support students primarily in their living accommodations, local lifestyles, and practical navigation of the new environment. These assistants usually focus on encouraging proper use of residential facilities, respect for local regulations and norms related to living spaces, integration into local neighborhoods and social activities, and cultivating a positive student community.

Fourth Critical Success Factor: Degree of Immersion in the Host Culture

> "I like more organized opportunities to meet locals. Not for class or as a requirement but informal things, like a social mixer. I would never approach an Italian student on my own, but in an organized setting it feels easier."

> "I have an internship, so I have lunch and coffee with my colleagues and feel like I know them. But most of my friends have been here several months and never really talk to Italians except for their teachers or the [center] staff."

The degree to which students are immersed in the host culture can vary based on the extent to which different programs adopt initiatives which are designed to facilitate engagement in the local culture. Programs at the center focus on in-depth cultural immersion by drawing from the following types of activities: intensive language learning; language exchange with local students; enrollment at local partner institutions; student residential placements with home-stay families; internship placements with local companies or organizations; community-based learning placements; academic field studies; local business visits; guest lectures by local instructors or professionals; resident assistants; cultural trips to nearby cities or regions (e.g., Tuscany or Liguria); and participation in local events (e.g., Milan Design Week or music festivals).

The number and type of activities chosen and the extent to which they are integrated structurally into a program strongly correlate to the degree of exposure that students have to the local culture. Enrollment at partner institutions, residing with home-stay families, internship placements, community-based learning opportunities, and interactions with resident assistants (which are prolonged in time, encourage students to build personal relationships with locals, and require them to develop skills in adaptation and integration) enable a *high degree* of local immersion. Intensive language learning and language exchanges, which facilitate students' engagement with locals, and encourage them to build personal relationships with instructors and local students (in a way which is more limited in time, and less academic in tone), promote a *moderate degree* of local immersion. Academic field studies, cultural trips, local business visits, local guest lectures, and participation in local events, which are all short in duration and less dependent on the development of personal relationships with local citizens, tend to promote a *lower degree* of local immersion.

Additionally, the amount of contact which students have with the various figures who provide support and guidance (instructors, staff members, etc.) and the length of their stay abroad, also influence the degree to which they are integrated into the host culture. Extensive interaction with locally based instructors, staff members, or resident assistants and longer-term programs tend to facilitate a higher degree of local immersion.

The criticality and success of these four success factors rest in the provider's capacity to offer several variations of each factor. Indeed, giving students the opportunity to choose among study abroad programs with different types (study vs. internship), for example, allows them to select the option which is most in line with their professional ambitions, academic requirements, and budgets. Having programs and courses of varying lengths also accommodates different student requirements and constraints, and in terms of spending power. Shorter programs give students the opportunity to gain international experience even when they lack the financial means to spend an entire semester in a different country. This helps to overcome barriers to accessibility. Likewise, the availability of different levels of support and guidance, and different degrees of immersion in the host culture, permit students to choose the kind of study abroad program which best suits their goals and personal traits along with their specific motivations for seeking an international experience. In other words, they can decide the extent to which understanding the host country's culture and learning new subject-related content is important to their experience, and the extent to which they need to be accompanied and guided throughout their time abroad.

KEY PILLARS OF EXPERIENTIAL LEARNING ABROAD

The study abroad provider's ability to combine the critical success factors mentioned above, therefore, is key to crafting successful learning outcomes for students. Study abroad providers ought to aim to develop modular, multifaceted, and customized educational programs which account for students' different needs and characteristics, and, consequently, achieve learning outcomes for different types of students.

Modularity means the study abroad provider ought to create an experience which allows for different combinations of the critical success factors. Offering *multifaceted* options means the provider ought to continuously update the specific options available (e.g., in terms of partner-institutions, field studies, and additional services offered) to build on strengths, while also integrating new components. *Customized* means the study abroad provider ought to envision students as co-creators (Vargo & Lusch, 2008) who can, and ought to, have an active role in determining the specific activities and content of their experience.

The following example clarifies how these three characteristics work in practice to contribute to successful study abroad opportunities for both students and the provider. Thanks to relationships with local companies, students in Milan can opt for a short (length) internship (aim) of just 2 months in the summer, so that they do not disrupt rigid pathways to graduation at their home institution. This internship can take place in either a company where English is the main language, or in a company in which Italian is the main language. In both cases, local habits and attitudes will be prominent (immersion in the host culture). Students provide indications of their fields of interest (co-creating their experience) but rely largely on the provider's local contacts and staff assistance (support and guidance).

CONCLUSION

The study of education-as-a-service is still underdeveloped (Ng & Forbes, 2009), and further investigation is required to understand consumption patterns within education (e.g., see the *Journal of Marketing Research*'s special issue of 2018 on education). The Milan center of the third-party study abroad provider which was presented in this chapter serves as an insightful case study for better understanding the critical success factors which global education providers can deploy to play a relevant role in the market, and to defend their positions in an increasingly competitive higher education environment.

The center focuses on these four critical success factors: type (study vs. internship), length (short vs. long), support and guidance level (high vs. low), and degree of immersion in the host culture (in-depth vs. cursory). The criticality and success potential of these factors lies in the provider's capability to offer several variations of each. As this chapter has emphasized, crafting modular, multifaceted, and customized study abroad programs are key to offering transformational study abroad opportunities—experiences which involve students in the decision-making process, engage them during their stays, and provide experiences which enable them to develop professional competences (University of California Merced, 2022).

In today's increasingly globalized world, the value of intercultural experiences like those offered by study abroad are gaining growing relevance. They help students in their development as professionals and citizens of a global, connected world, while unlocking learning opportunities which could hardly be achieved from the comfort of their home institutions (Prebys & Ricciardelli, 2017). Opportunities for global education are perhaps even more important in the so-called "new normal" after the COVID-19 pandemic, when students' interest in participating in study abroad programs will likely increase due to the need to make up for the lost time, and to a desire to return to in-person experiential learning. It is crucial, therefore, that study abroad providers get a clearer understanding of students' expectations, desires, and needs, while matching them with their own main affordances and characteristics. This approach is a successful way to deliver long-lasting and meaningful opportunities for study abroad programs.

CHAPTER 13

EXPLORING THE INTERCULTURAL CHALLENGES OF INTERNATIONALIZATION WITHIN HIGHER EDUCATION INSTITUTIONS IN THE UNITED KINGDOM

A Pilot Study

Cheryl Dowie

THE INTERNATIONALIZATION OF HIGHER EDUCATION: A HISTORICAL PERSPECTIVE

International influences and external forces have put enormous pressure on the higher education system to change and respond effectively to circumstances brought about by globalization and internationalization. The history of education is thus dependent on concerted strategic decisions requiring academic institutions to link their vision with the current challenges and highlight the gaps during moments of organic growth. A conceptual framework which links education theory and practice seems to be missing and does not offer educators sufficient opportunities to "practice their craft, consolidate their values, and persecute their ideals" (Goodman & Grosvenor, 2009, p. 606). On the other hand, the Anglo-Saxon/"Western" signposting which dominates higher education reform, fails to consider the educational and teaching practices, the diverse curriculum, policies, economic, political, and social structures, and so on. This poses a threat to the shared values which have underpinned universities, academic freedom, and institutional autonomy. A key example which highlights the growth and sustainability in higher education is Nalanda University, the world's first Buddhist university, founded in Northeastern India in 427 CE (more than half a millennium before Harvard and Yale were established). It housed 10,000 students in the university's heyday, accommodated 2,000 professors, and trained students in fine arts, medicine, astronomy, mathematics, politics, and the art of war (Buncombe, 2010; Garten, 2006). Scholars and students from China, Tibet, Indonesia, Persia, Turkey, Korea, and Japan studied and worked there (Buncombe, 2010) during their "sabbatical" period or "study" leave, which is an "integral" part of academic life but is not encouraged in higher education institutions today, as they focus more on research output or teaching. However, some of the reasons for the demise of Nalanda University were the decline of Buddhism in India, lack of financial support from successive monarchs, and corruption among university officials (Garten, 2006; "Nalanda: India's Ancient Buddhist," n.d.).

Given that the notions of globalization and knowledge production are concomitant, the accelerating rate of globalization has made universities progress towards internationalization. Various phases in the internationalization of higher education have emerged since medieval times (de Wit & Merkx, 2012). Daly (1999) distinguishes globalization and internationalization by stating that internationalization refers to the increasing salience of international trade, treaties, alliances, and so forth, while globalization refers to the economic integration of former national economies into one global economy, as a result of free trade, capital mobility, and unfettered migration.

Universities founded in the 18th and 19th centuries had a national focus (Buncombe, 2010), and mobility of students and scholars was not encouraged; and Latin—as the universal language of instruction—was displaced by vernacular languages (Hammerstein, 1996). In the early part of the 20th century, political events led to the development in 1919 of the Institute of International Education (IIE) in the United States; the Deutscher Akademischer Austauschdienst (DAAD) in Germany in 1925; and the British Council in the United Kingdom in 1934 (Thondhlana et al., 2020). When the European community strengthened as an economic and political power between 1950 and 1970, the European flagship program, ERASMUS, began to support student and staff mobility within Europe. The pilot program commenced in the early 1980s, and this was later restructured under the umbrella program SOCRATES in the 1990s, which later evolved into ERASMUS+ a broader program which embraced education, sports, and other youth programs, with a view toward nurturing a sense of European citizenship and observing international education as a cooperative initiative (de Wit, 2002). Though internationalization was not a new term even during this time, *international education* was still the favored term in some countries since the early 1980s (Knight, 2004).

The United Kingdom adopted a competitive model in 1981 under the Thatcher Government, where full-cost fee coverage was introduced for post-secondary education as a means of recruiting income-generating international students (de Wit, 2017; J. Lee et al., 2006; Mihut et al., 2017). Using international students as a source of revenue (De Vita & Case, 2003) and placing increasing emphasis on competition instead of cooperation eliminated the traditional approach to post-secondary education. Similar models soon followed in other English-speaking nations, and a competitive direction set the agenda for higher education institutions (HEIs) since the mid-1990s (de Wit, 2017). Around the same time, other terms such as *comparative education, multicultural education,* and *global education* were used indicating that internationalization was an evolving phenomenon (Harris, 2008). The driving forces of the contemporary university today are competitiveness, excellence, and performance, while knowledge seems to have been reduced to just information (Harris, 2008).

THE RESEARCH PROBLEM AND THE NEED FOR INTERNATIONALIZATION

From the pursuit of knowledge to the pursuit of revenue.
—Reisberg & Rumbley, 2014; p. 115).

In today's growth-based economy, there is the growing need to internationalize (Dolby & Rahman, 2008). Spurred by the contested globalization processes, the pressure to internationalize or to be international has intensified many aspects of education:

1. Global university rankings are driving the agendas of senior management in higher education institutes and national governments.
2. World rankings and regional rankings of universities place emphasis on reputation, accreditations, quality assurance, and other mechanisms which can help preserve the prestige and degrees of elite standing (Huisman et al., 2015) with frameworks in place that

favor the U.S. and U.K. higher education institutes (Hazelkorn, 2015; Marginson, 2002).
3. The ongoing competition among employers for the best brains and for universities to train the best brains (Kritz, 2006), have led to rich nations setting up government initiatives as part of their diplomatic efforts and developing incentives to compete for students globally (Tremblay, 2008).
4. Emerging nations are partnering with prestigious institutions to improve their global rankings (Guri-Rosenblit, 2015).
5. The restructuring of higher education systems has led to the enrollment of many international students and the recruitment of high-quality scholars, the latter also contributing to mutually beneficial scholarly collaborations (Guri-Rosenblit, 2015).

While the interest in internationalization has soared in conjunction with the process of globalization over the last 2 decades (de Wit, 2013), different countries carry diverse views about this broad and varied phenomenon, making the concept difficult to understand (Teichler, 2017). Key elements of internationalization such as international student mobility and knowledge transfer across borders seem to be taken for granted and are inadequately embedded in the internationalization of education (Teichler, 2017). Unevenly distributed opportunities in relatively wealthy countries which benefit from power and prestige seem to attract international students and scholars, thus undermining social and economic development in different regions of the world (Teichler, 2017). While the strategies and priorities for internationalization continue to change in conjunction with the environment in which the university operates, the first step to respond to this predicament is to re-conceptualize or interpret the terminology focusing on the core values and priorities which underpin the internationalization process among higher education providers. Conversely, the challenge here is to determine a comprehensive definition which can be universally applied to different countries, cultures, and education systems, and to apply the rationale in all aspects of education endeavor (Knight, 2014a). So, for this study, Knight's definition is used to observe this continuing process as "an international, intercultural, or global dimension into the purpose, functions, or delivery of post-secondary education" (Knight, 2003; p. 2). This definition effectively addresses the realities of today's context, as it considers the national/sector context, the institution context, and the diverse range of post-secondary education providers. It focuses on educational objectives and does not specify partnerships and cross-border education exchanges, stakeholders, benefits, outcomes, and collaborative scholarships, since these differ across nations and institutions, and it could raise new risks of being too dictatorial (Teichler, 2017). Given the myriad of conditions which influence the internationalization process, an inclusive definition can be the first step towards understanding the internationalization process, before addressing other key aspects within the U.K. higher education system. On a related note, since this study explores the intercultural challenges of internationalization, and given the many conceptualizations of culture, we define culture as a set of "shared and endured meanings, values, and beliefs which characterize national, ethnic, or other groups, and orient their behaviour" (Kersten et al., 2002; p. 88).

This study contributes to the literature on higher education, encouraging discourse on the international or global elements of internationalization relating to multicultural recruitment, teaching, research, and job satisfaction which have not been fully addressed. The pilot study consists of semi-structured interviews with instructors from the Global South, who work in the United Kingdom. Their perspectives on job satisfaction, interculturalism, teaching, and research are examined to find patterns and examples which could guide U.K. higher education providers to reflect on the international dimensions, leading them to radically reassess the institutional purposes, priorities, and processes in place. Clarification of the standards in the U.K. higher education system, can provide a productive platform which promotes a more multicultural university culture which is conducive to a critical stance as opposed to one which is developed by national prejudices. In the following section, we will provide an overview on the intercultural challenges of internationalization, focusing on the cultural drawbacks and benefits of internationalization for higher education institutes. This can help broaden cross-cultural knowledge, to better understand the implications for teaching and learning for international staff and students, and to encourage cross-cultural discourse. Consequently, this study outlines some of the opportunities and addresses some of the challenges faced by HEIs in the United Kingdom—to protect and sustain its important role as a trusted bank of knowledge to address global challenges and societal needs.

CULTURAL CHALLENGES OF INTERNATIONALIZATION WITHIN U.K. HIGHER EDUCATION

Attaining world-class status requires universities to operate under different strategies and infrastructure compared to those at the national level. Increasing interdependence among nations shows that international and interdisciplinary collaboration is key in solving global challenges (Knight, 2004). Economic, social, and political perspectives are to be considered in providing context to analyze conditions shaping the internationalization and globalization processes in the context of higher education. In the United Kingdom, international staff account for approximately a third of the academic community (Higher Education Staff Statistics, 2020). The United Kingdom is also the second most popular country in the world for attracting international students, and over 700,000 students obtain a post-secondary qualification through transnational education (Universities UK, 2018). Also, in the United Kingdom, international students from the top non-EU countries come from The People's Republic of China, India, Malaysia, the United States, and Nigeria (Madge et al., 2009). And from EU countries, the students mainly come from The Republic of Ireland, Greece, Germany, France, and Cyprus (Madge et al., 2009).

Nowadays, where internationalization and globalization are met with increasing skepticism, and are now facing the consequences of the global pandemic, advancing strategically at an operational level requires institutions to listen to diverse voices and reinforce unequal power relationships (Lee & Stensaker, 2021). While the body of scholarly literature on internationalization and higher education has increased, research in these areas is still dominated by countries like North America, Europe, and Australia (Kuzhabekova et al., 2015). This geographically limited literature analyzed by scholars can pose a threat by way of limiting the understanding of cultural differences and country-specific features which are vital to advance and make an impact on higher education in the years to come.

International students travel to the United Kingdom to experience a British (or Anglophone) culture which is influenced by Western liberalism (de Wit, 2017). In the United Kingdom, postgraduate programs are generally for 1 year and this relatively short period makes it difficult for students to get accustomed to the different cultural contexts, social differences, and the language of academic texts (Harris, 2008). There is the implied presumption that the host university will provide additional support to help with language problems, interacting with local learners, and the general academic expectations (Haigh, 2014). The ethnocentricity observed from such situations requires universities to occasionally request instructors to pass substandard work for fear that international student revenue might dry up if students fail (Haigh, 2014). Often, staff try to remedy these transitional difficulties by providing students with additional training and resources, focusing on language and culture, study skills, and the curricula (Collingridge, 1999; C. Li, 2008).

The consumerist approach to education in the West, where students are treated as customers and are required to pay for standardized qualifications, has pedagogical implications and is incompatible with the student–teacher relationship embedded within the education system in non-Western cultures (De Vita & Case, 2003). For instance, in the genesis of Hindu education, Vedic theory requires students to take responsibility for their own learning and respect the person from whom s/he is seeking knowledge (Patel, 1994). According to the Islamic education system, the teacher's role is to impart knowledge, while the student is expected to ask questions and seek knowledge (De Vita & Case, 2003). Another ongoing issue worth addressing is racism and other forms of cultural intolerance experienced by some international students, scholars, staff, and instructors throughout the world when compared to Caucasians from Canada, Australia, and European countries (Cantwell & Lee, 2010; Lee & Opio, 2011). While the focus of the study is to gain an international understanding of the higher education system, few studies have explored the lived experiences of international instructors from developing nations (Cantwell & Lee, 2010; Lee & Opio, 2011). Given the limited scholarly understanding in this area, this pilot study examines the expectations and lived experiences of international instructors from the Global South who work in the United Kingdom, to gain insight into the general trends with regards to their job satisfaction, cultural sensitivities, teaching, and research. Understanding the challenges faced by instructors can help universities plan more successfully and address obstacles which could hinder the activities associated with the internationalization process, such as academic mobility, international partnerships, delivery educational programs to other countries, scholarly collaborations and other research initiatives, and designing new curricula (Knight, 2004).

Complexities arising from cultural disconnection are difficult to resolve (Pherali, 2012) and pressures manifesting from changing educational priorities, opportunities, and regulatory environments are multifaceted. Supporting and sustaining a global world view requires decision-makers and leaders in HEIs to reframe their thinking and institutional strategies, to create structures and find solutions that meet basic logistical and administrative needs (e.g., through accreditations such as AACSB, AMBA, EQUIS; decolonizing the curriculum, and so on). Co-learning and co-working ought to align with the principles of responsible internationalization and not be based on the need to survive within a new context (Stallivieri, 2019). As internationalization and globalization continue to make an impact on the U.K. higher education system, the strategy of this study is to take a reflective approach on the intercultural challenges observed by communities from the Global South, with an effort to encourage scholarly debate and theoretical advancements which can better capture the current internationalization and globalization processes (Lee & Stensaker, 2021).

RESEARCH METHODOLOGY

After systematically reviewing the literature over the last 2 decades, a predetermined list of questions was developed to carry out semi-structured interviews with international instructors from the Global South who work at U.K. Universities. The questions for this study focus on their experience working in the United Kingdom, the support they received from their institutions as international staff, job satisfaction, cultural challenges associated with internationalization, and their understanding of the internationalization process. Our qualitative methodological approach helped to sensitively shed light on the global realities which exist and explore the challenges faced by international staff in adjusting to a new environment, while managing their professional life. It helped us capture in-depth insights into their lived experiences. The aim here is to contribute to the existing literature on higher education, to help U.K HEIs understand the measures which should be considered in their strategic planning for internationalization.

Data Collection

To examine the higher education environment in the United Kingdom, the pilot study comprised of 32 semi-structured interview questions with instructors who moved from the Global South to work in U.K. universities. The 5 participants who were interviewed were originally from India, China, and Turkey and worked as full-time instructors at autonomous, publicly funded business schools in the United Kingdom. The sample size is small for two reasons: Firstly, in this pilot study, we initially sought to understand the extent of the intercultural challenges faced by international instructors in the United Kingdom to see if the problem was worth exploring further; and secondly, the limitation was that only few interviewees were willing to come forward and share their experiences on this sensitive topic. On the other hand, the increased number of questions helped delve deeper into their experiences to understand the challenges and concerns they faced better.

Research Environment

The business schools, in which these instructors worked, have active research programs, developed undergraduate and postgraduate curricula, and extensive research facilities that attract a large number of students, instructors, and research staff from around the world. We believe the current mode of data collection helps us focus and gather data on the intercultural elements associated with internationalization, thus aiding us to reflect on the latter during the implementation stage, as this is essential for a university's success. Our data collection and analysis approach enables us to answer the following research question: "How has internationalization impacted instructors from the Global South who work in U.K. HEIs and what measures are taken to address intercultural challenges?"

Brief Overview of Findings

There were certain overlapping views in the data which were gathered during the semi-structured interviews. Out of the 5 participants, three of them identified themselves as early career researchers and two of them identified themselves as mid-career researchers. With regards to job satisfaction, all the 5 participants stated that they felt valued at the university because they had a supportive reporting manager. However, they did also mention that this would not be the case if their reporting managers were not supportive. They felt they had the academic freedom to carry out the research they wanted, and teaching was in line with the school and university's requirements. While they were satisfied with the current role and responsibilities, three of them mentioned that they might find the work too monotonous, and this might not be satisfying in 2- or 3-years' time. All 5 participants expressed that their salary was low in comparison to their impact on society. Two of them who moved to the United Kingdom after completing their PhD in Europe stated that the salary was three times higher in Europe as a PhD student. All 5 of them stated that their workload is generally manageable, but that they consistently work long hours during the week and over weekends. Four of them were satisfied with the last annual review that they had with their respective reporting managers, and one of them had not had an annual review meeting as of yet.

With regards to their intercultural experiences, all 5 participants had little understanding and awareness of the institutional policies and frameworks in place to support diversity, so very little information was shared around this area. On the other hand, 2 out of the 5 participants mentioned that the United Kingdom was more diverse than Europe and that it was an advantage that English was the medium of instruction in the United Kingdom as opposed to Europe, where European languages took precedence. This is one of the main reasons they moved to the United Kingdom.

With regards to the teaching and research areas, all 5 participants stated that they were given flexibility to deliver teaching activities; the organization provided them with a device (either laptop or screen) to carry out their work; and they did not think that the student evaluation/course evaluation forms provided an accurate and fair evaluation of their teaching. On the other hand, all 5 participants stated that there was room for embedding diversity and inclusion in the curriculum. They also felt that international students faced transitional challenges such as language barriers, interacting with local learners, and so on. This could put them at a disadvantage during the learning process. Four out of the 5 participants did not feel that their background put them at a disadvantage in obtaining research grants, however, one of them felt that receiving grants depended largely on whether they were successful in obtaining grants before and if they were at the early career stage, this could be disadvantageous. Two participants who moved from Europe stated that there was more freedom to carry out research in Europe than in the United Kingdom. One out of the 5 participants stated that their current U.K. university did not provide them with a research budget/allowance, whereas in Europe they had this opportunity and could use the budget for anything work-related. The remaining 4 participants stated that though their research budget was not much, they could still use the money to attend workshops and conferences, although at times this was open to scrutiny, approval, and in some cases, further clarification.

APPROACHES TO INTERNATIONALIZATION

Given the ever-changing world in which higher education providers are functioning and based on the empirical findings of this study it would be important to think about some generic advances to address aspects of internationalization, such as:

1. Initiating funded programs which allow instructors and students to engage in international activities such as research collaborations, joint research initiatives, staff development initiatives, encouraging students to attend branch campuses, twinning programs, and so forth, and other forms of academic and student mobility. This would expose staff and students to different lifestyles and contrasting ways of thinking. Developing geopolitical ties and economic relationships which can accentuate the linkages with other countries, would open opportunities for cross-border education. It would also create a global reputation/branding of their own institution and place them in a better position for competitive advantage.
2. Informing all instructors about the evolving phenomenon of internationalization instead of just treating it as an ad hoc initiative. This would also involve incorporating an international dimension into the teaching, research, and general functions within the institution. Streamlining the understanding of this concept is also important since there seem to be different variations of this concept among different academic units/schools within a university.
3. Revisiting the mission and vision statements at U.K. HEIs to determine whether or not they address the implications from internationalization. Taking an integrative approach to internationalization involves including information about this phenomenon in the policies and institutional frameworks to emphasize the importance of the intercultural dimension in all modes of post-secondary education, that is, face-to-face, online, e-learning, and blended learn-

ing formats. This would evolve based on the specific challenges and opportunities presented within the institution (Bartell, 2003).

While this is only a pilot study, it assists in recognizing the importance of the intercultural or global dimensions within internationalization. We hope that further studies will provide a clearer background on other emerging rationales for driving internationalization within HEIs in the United Kingdom. Deeper study will assist in the understanding of how best to incorporate an intercultural component in the curriculum—encouraging both local and international student engagement, in addition to redefining the teaching, learning, and research processes in line with an institutions' goal.

LIMITATIONS OF THE STUDY AND FUTURE TRAJECTORIES

Studies have empirically examined and critiqued English as the global language (Byun et al., 2011; Currie et al., 2003; Kuzhabekova et al., 2015). While this study is carried out in English, teaching in English is not synonymous to internationalization (de Wit, 2013) and so it would be useful to encourage scholars to review literature that pursues similar topics, published in other languages (Dolby & Rahman, 2008). Unfolding diversity in this field of research is an important driving factor in the management of internationalization. The second limitation of this pilot study was its small sample size. It would be useful to gather more evidence on these cultural challenges. Gaining insight into international academic's views on internationalization, can help understand the challenges and opportunities which could be faced by U.K. HEIs in the long run. Thirdly, while this study involved interviewing international instructors in the United Kingdom, gaining perspectives of internationalization from international students could also cater to the educational requirements of a more diverse global base—with the intention of contributing to quality education and research, and as a result, increasing their global ranking/status.

As research on internationalization matures in the 21st century, encouraging cross-border scholarship on this topic could bring about diverse views and shed light on possible rationales and implications for the restructuring of higher education. Secondly, it would be interesting to adapt future studies to explore the experiences faced by instructors from the Global North. A comparative study between instructors from the Global North and Global South could help facilitate an understanding of the realities and challenges of the current environment in the United Kingdom and other countries, recognize the misconceptions associated with internationalization, learn from different global standpoints, and rethink the internationalization efforts within HEIs. Furthermore, encouraging PhD students to undertake their doctoral studies on aspects of internationalization may allow for a more nuanced approach to its interpretation, helping to direct the new internationalization agenda.

CONCLUSION

In response to the pressures of the changing world, the emphasis on internationalization has created a shift in paradigm from a cooperative to a competitive stance, focusing on financial gain (Haigh, 2014). Counter-acts such as immigration bans, the BREXIT movement, challenges to academic freedom, and so on, have hampered equal and equitable educational opportunities for global citizens, making the internationalization strategy multifaceted. It seems that the value of education has not been adequately recognized along with the conception of internationalization which requires us to acknowledge the differences and remind ourselves that there is more than one culture. Given that culture cannot survive in a vacuum and needs exposure to external influences, it might be a good idea to re-examine the learning process to generate new ideas and ways of thinking (Harris, 2008). Encouraging discussion across different frameworks rather than within a particular paradigm can lead to progressive teaching approaches which can help students become more empowered and independent to make the most of the opportunities which present themselves, thereby contributing more to society (Harris, 2008).

While this study aims to re-examine the meaning of internationalization and think about strategies and approaches that could help HEIs identify some of the issues which could emerge during the internationalization process in the long-term, a comprehensive approach to internationalization will require a broader mix of views from international staff and students. This can help define the institutional strategies and functional priorities, to bring some radical reorganization of the way HEIs organize their operations (de Wit, 2013). Through this study, preliminary insights into the internationalization of the U.K. higher education sector are provided to understand how this can shape teaching, student curricula, and research. The hallmark of a world-class university is attracting high-quality international students (Russell Group, 2010; p. 7). And, to achieve this vision, a personal process of deconstruction and reconstruction is needed (Haigh, 2014) to indoctrinate both staff and students for global citizenship.

CHAPTER 14

LEGAL RISK ABROAD

Examining Trends in Extraterritoriality and the Application of U.S. Federal Law

Sara Easler
Susan Bon

Following 2 decades of steady growth, the 2018/2019 academic year marked the largest and most diverse in American international education with over 347,000 U.S. students studying abroad (Institute of International Education, 2020a). While the COVID-19 pandemic vastly impacted the once robust participation in study abroad and international education programs in 2020, early figures for the 2021/2022 academic year are indicative of a rebound with some institutions projecting record, pre-pandemic enrollments (Carrasco, 2022). In 2021 and in consideration of disruption to international education from the pandemic, the U.S. Department of Education and Department of State issued a joint statement committing support and a renewed focus on international education. In this joint statement, these U.S. federal agencies assert, "It is vital to reinforce our people-to-people relationships around the globe and to strengthen the infrastructure

---

The Internationalization of Higher Education:, pages 221–235
Copyright © 2023 by Information Age Publishing
www.infoagepub.com
All rights of reproduction in any form reserved.

and pathways that help prepare Americans in all sectors to engage with the world" (Carrasco, 2022, p. 3).

Institutions of higher education (HEI) are often educational pioneers in program designs, new-to-travel students, and efforts to expand globally in foreign locations. Initiatives to promote access and diversity in the cohorts of students who pursue study abroad opportunities have led to an increase of ethnic minorities and students with reported disabilities, who made up more than 10% of the 2018/2019 cohort (Institute of International Education, 2020b). Preparing students for the inherent risks of their destination, understanding their needs and specific academic accommodations, and guiding them through smooth transitions are all necessary functions in furtherance of the institutional goals of mitigating risks that are associated with the internationalization of education and educational experiences.

Managing and preparing for risks is especially complicated outside the United States in countries with different cultural perspectives on rights of individuals' to be free from discrimination and harassment in educational settings. For example, in countries with an Islamic law influenced penal code, which is vastly different from the U.S. criminal codes addressing such crimes, filing a sexual assault complaint could result in further harm or even criminal charges against the victim (Haddad, 2017). As a result, many of the increasingly diverse destinations selected by HEIs pose unique ethical and legal challenges.

In the American education system, the primary federal protections by the U.S. government afforded to higher education students are related to discrimination and equitable access to education. This chapter provides a review of federal anti-discrimination laws, select court decisions, and relevant administrative law rulings in the Office of Civil Rights (OCR)—opinions implicating decisions about the extraterritoriality of U.S. laws regarding institutional liability. Lessons from these laws and accompanying legal interpretations are instructive for international education and practitioners who must prepare for the anticipated and unanticipated challenges associated with increasing diversity among students and the study abroad locations.

The study abroad experience is an increasingly important aspect of the core mission for most institutions, thus higher education officials must be prepared and better informed about the responsibilities, limitations, and obligations of their roles. In particular, they must understand the associated risks and the necessary mitigation efforts to undertake as part of a high-quality and safe study abroad program. Before discussing the anti-discrimination laws, court cases, and OCR opinions, the chapter briefly reviews risk mitigation efforts, which have long been central to the successful expansion of international education.

RISKS AND MITIGATION

Study abroad professionals are generally adept at identifying mitigation strategies for threats to student safety. The underlying goal of such strategies is to consistently provide reasonably safe experiences, reducing the fears that might dissuade students and their parents from considering study abroad. Robust health and safety plans and student preparation for the possibility of risk are now standard and include routine outbound procedures (Fischer, 2010; Lee, 2010; Vossen, 2016). Study abroad professionals are trained and have extensive procedures to guide responses to external threats, most of which were heavily tested in the 2020 unprecedented recall of students due to the COVID-19 pandemic.

Beyond the external risks, American institutions of higher education are often met with a variety of "domestic" liability issues, not least of which is their vulnerability to litigation or penalty for non-compliance under U.S. federal laws and statutes. Not only do these issues pose risk to the institution's reputation, they also present a high risk of financial burden either from the loss of federal funding or through lengthy court proceedings, which could potentially end in high-figure damages awards by the courts or out of court settlements.

Universities and program providers have been sued for a number of reasons—negligence, breach of fiduciary duty, and discrimination—and in response, university offices of general counsel have advocated for "aggressive risk management and a well enforced set of policies and requirements" (Lee, 2010, p. 678) for departments offering study abroad programs (Johnson, 2006; Lee, 2010). While these claims have the potential to result in damages, they are brought at the state, not federal, level or in civil court. Study abroad officials must adopt risk mitigation measures for protecting the institution from a legal claim, which might jeopardize federal funding or tort litigation and could result in expensive damages. The success or failure of such litigation depends on a number of factors including the specific reach of the law, the location in which the case would be heard, and contractual obligations of those involved (Johnson, 2006). The university's vulnerability to litigation, however, depends on the nature of the complaint, the interpretation of general counsel, and the experience of compliance coordinators who are familiar with the nuances and context of the specific circumstances (The Forum on Education Abroad, 2017; Johnson, 2006).

Adherence to U.S. federal anti-discrimination laws is mandated based on receipt of federal funding. The Civil Rights Act of 1964, Title IX of the Education Amendments Act of 1972, Section 504 of the 1973 Rehabilitation Act, and the Americans With Disabilities Act (ADA)—specifically Title III of ADA—stipulate that recipients of federal funding are responsible for compliance with these statutes. The OCR states that it has the authority to enforce anti-discrimination standards through the suspension or revocation of federal funding (Setty, 1999).

Federal Anti-Discrimination Statutes

The following U.S. federal laws protect students from gender, race, and disability discrimination and apply to all higher education institutions that receive federal funding (Rothstein, 2014; Schaffer, 2004). The Civil Rights Act of 1964 protects students from racial discrimination; the Education Amendments of 1972 protects students from discrimination based on sex. The Americans With Disabilities Act of 1990, the Americans With Disabilities Amendment Act of 2008, and Section 504 of the Rehabilitation Act of 1973 protect students with disabilities (Title VI. Sec. 601, Civil Rights Act of 1964; Bull, 2017; Olivarius, 2014; 29 U.S.C. § 794(a)). Students have sought relief pursuant to these laws in federal courts based on claims of discrimination and other prohibited actions by public institutions and higher education officials in the domestic context, a controlled campus environment.

Yet it is not always clear which federal anti-discrimination laws reach beyond the territorial boundaries of the United States. The applicability of U.S. federal law to study abroad has typically hinged on the concept of extraterritoriality, which "concerns the operation of laws outside the boundary of a state or country" (The Law Dictionary, n.d.). In other words, when the alleged discrimination did not occur within the United States, courts examine the extraterritoriality of a law in determining whether an institution is liable for discrimination occurred in another country.

Extraterritoriality is complicated and widely disputed in our increasingly digital and global world where physical borders are progressively blurred. Many have asserted that the presumption is limited to those areas of American life that are specified in the statute, and in fact, this assumption has been tested time and again by the courts. Failure to amend the statute for any other purposes—namely education—has supported the argument that the statutes do not, in fact, apply extraterritorially, and that this is the explicit intent of Congress. In fact, in an effort to maintain the sovereignty of each nation's laws within their territorial bounds, courts tend to lean on the presumption against extraterritoriality as their default application of the legal concept.

While some degree of insight might be gleaned from legal precedents, Department of Education directives, or Office of Civil Rights (OCR), the court decisions vary from case-to-case and across the jurisdictions. Similarly, OCR guidance is prone to dramatic shifts based on the controlling political party; as observed with shifts in Title IX guidance during the last two presidential administrations (Anderson, 2020), with another iteration of guidance proposed by the current administration (Brown, 2021).

The OCR guidance, specifically the "Dear Colleague" letter issued on April 4, 2011, revealed changing views on sex discrimination and the ways in which the OCR has broadened the scope to include new ways in which harassment presents itself in modern society (Bull, 2017; Edwards, 2015; Hamill, 2012). Yet in September 2017, the DOE withdrew the April 4th guidance letter, noting its lack of due process and fundamental fairness (U.S. Department of Education, 2017). This move was further extended by the OCR in their 2020 guidance removing any such responsibility during study abroad (Anderson, 2020). While many presume additional Title IX guidance is forthcoming, the most recent guidance in June 2021 served to broaden the scope of protected persons to include the LGBTQ+ community (Yurcaba, 2021).

In the context of study abroad, the applicability of Title IX is unclear and might depend on the study abroad location as well as a variety of factors, such as the citizenship status and the student status of the victim and/or perpetrator. Applicability might also vary due to culturally acceptable differences across study abroad locations, the legal interpretations of whether the harassment or action is even a crime, or, have mandatory reporters met their obligation for the protection of victims and the educational environment. Additionally, under the newest application, one must determine how to respond to harassment on the basis of sexual orientation, considering, too, that homosexuality is potentially illegal or unaccepted in the host nation.

Although an in-depth search for case law related to study abroad has not revealed an extensive list of cases addressing the extraterritorial application of Title IX and the ADA, several high-profile cases were discovered that provide valuable insights. Namely, these cases provide lessons about litigation risks in study abroad related to Title IX compliance issues, disability rights and ADA protections, and negligence claims for failure to perform institutional duties.

Litigation Outcomes

A review of case law reveals that the number of complaints has steadily increased since 2000 (Easler, 2019). One possible explanation for the increase in Title IX litigation is the release in 1997 of Title IX guidance on sexual harassment, expanding the scope of students' protections to include violations by fellow students and even strangers (Bull, 2017; Hamill, 2012; Olivarius, 2014). Similarly, the 1990 ratification of the ADA made higher education and study abroad more accessible to students with disabilities (Bull, 2017; Hamill, 2012; Olivarius, 2014). Together, the policy guidelines and legislative enactment expanded students' rights and revealed litigation pathways to address discriminatory and harassing behaviors that interfere with an educational program or activity.

As highlighted in several cases filed under Title IX and the ADA, students have sought relief from the discriminatory and harassing behaviors of other students and instructors who participate in and lead university sponsored study abroad programs. The plaintiffs in these cases must overcome the presumption that U.S. statutes only apply in the territorial jurisdiction of the United States. As revealed in the following sample of cases, there is uncertainty regarding the evidence necessary to overcome a presumption against the extraterritorial application of Title IX and the ADA (see, e.g., *Smith v. United States*, 1993).

The crux of the dispute in *King v. Board of Control of Eastern Michigan University* (2002), is whether or not Title IX has extraterritorial application to actions outside the United States. It is undisputed that the actions took place during a faculty-led study abroad program in South Africa for students from Eastern Michigan University (EMU). The students were accompanied by an EMU instructor and teaching assistant (TA) who was hired by EMU to assist a disabled student and to serve as the instructor's assistant. During the program, six female students were sexually harassed by two male students who were in the program.

The harassment included entering the female student's rooms without permission, publicly using gender-specific slurs, exhibiting sexually explicit behavior, and soliciting South African women for sex. Seeking relief and an end to the harassment, the female students brought their complaints to the program's TA, who refused to intervene. They also contacted the instructor to share their complaints, but he failed to attend the established meeting, sending only the TA who had already dismissed the students' complaints.

A series of instances continued and culminated in a violent altercation between the male EMU students and a number of male South African students, allegedly because of the ongoing abuse of the female students. Following this clash, seven of the female students returned to the United States, cutting their program short by a week. The program instructor finished the program with the remaining students, six males and one female.

Six of the female students filed a claim under Title IX. The court explicitly ruled on the extraterritorial application of Title IX and on the applicability of Title IX to "any education program or activity" (Title IX, 1972). Specifically, the court determined that students are protected under Title IX even though the alleged harassment occurred as part of a study abroad educational program outside of the United States. According to the court, EMU had a duty to intervene and take steps to prevent sex discrimination from interfering with the females' access to the educational program, which was under their control even if the program was occurring outside U.S. territory.

Determining the extraterritorial application of Title IX similarly arose before the U.S. District Court for the District of Massachusetts in *Harbi v. Massachusetts Institute of Technology* (2017). Unlike the students in *King v. Board of Control of Eastern Michigan University* (2002), however, the student in *Harbi* resided permanently in France and her allegations involved online communications of a sexually explicit nature from her physics course instructor. The instructor, Walter Lewin was a professor emeritus and had been hired by MIT to teach the introductory physics course.

Although the student complainant never met Professor Lewin in person, their online communications became increasingly explicit and sexual in nature. Harbi did not end the relationship out of fear that it would jeopardize her successful completion of the course as a result of Lewin's requests for continued correspondence. As a result of the correspondence, Harbi became distressed to the point of needing hospitalization. She eventually reported the conduct to MIT, and an investigation was launched. The investigation determined that Lewin had violated MIT policies and severed ties with Lewin, prohibiting him from accessing university resources.

Further distinguishing the present case from the court's ruling in *King v. Board of Control of Eastern Michigan University* (2002), the Massachusetts district court determined that Harbi was not a "person in the United States" as plainly stated in Title IX. Consequently, the court refused to extend the protections of Title IX extraterritorially to Harbi in spite of her participation in an education program or activity. As an interesting aside, the court commented, "Title IX may well be outdated. Online learning is a relatively new phenomenon, and the statute was promulgated in 1972, in a much different technological environment" (*Harbi v. Massachusetts Institute of Technology*, 2017, p. 9). Nonetheless, the court refused to undertake the worthy goal of revising an outdated statute, a duty that falls squarely on the U.S. Congress and not the U.S. Judiciary.

In one of the most frequently cited cases in study abroad disability-based discrimination litigation, *Bird v. Lewis & Clark* (2002), the Ninth Circuit Court sidestepped the issue of extraterritorial application of U.S. legislation after affirming the lower court's denial of equitable relief to the student, Bird. Specifically, in a terse footnote reference, the court refused to determine if Title III of the Americans With Disabilities Act or Section 504 of the Rehabilitation Act apply extraterritorially to overseas programs.

Although the issue of extraterritorial application was not resolved in Bird, much can be learned from the court's discussion and resolution of the primary issue, whether the college provided reasonable accommodations for the student's disabilities as required by the ADA and Rehabilitation Act. In *Bird v. Lewis & Clark* (2002), a wheelchair-bound student on a faculty-led program in Australia claimed that the college failed to reasonably accommodate her disabilities in compliance with ADA and the Rehabilitation Act.

The college argued that when the program was considered in its entirety, reasonable accommodations were provided to ensure the student's participation, such as the hiring of TAs to assist her, arranging for alternate transportation, arranging alternate activities, and providing alternate accessible housing. As determined by the district court, and affirmed by the Ninth Circuit, the college presented ample evidence of accommodations, such as hiring two helpers; purchasing special flights solely for Bird; and paying for numerous additional items solely for accommodating Bird's disabilities (*Bird v. Lewis & Clark College*, 2003). Additionally, Bird's lodgings were wheelchair-accessible and many of the programming activities were altered to provide Bird benefit from the semester abroad program.

Although the issue of extraterritorial application did not arise in the negligence claim by a student who was raped while studying internationally, this case reveals important lessons for higher education leaders who have ethical and legal obligations to proactively mitigate risks and promote student safety. In this case, *Doe v. Rhode Island School of Design* (2021), a female student, Jane Doe, asserted that her rape by a fellow student was the direct result of RISD's negligence during the sponsored 3-week art program in Ireland (*Doe v. Rhode Island School of Design*, 2021). In her claims against RISD, she identified the absence of workable locks on the bedroom doors as evidence that RISD failed to provide safe housing, which directly led to the rape and significant trauma she suffered. Negligence claims are likely to succeed if the plaintiff proves (a) a legally recognized duty; (b) breach of this duty; (c) proximate cause between the conduct and injury; and (d) actual loss, harm, or damages. As a result of the rape, the court concluded that the student suffered and continues to suffer permanent injuries. As such, the court reached a ruling of negligence in favor of Jane and awarded her $2,500,000 as compensatory damages, also including interest and costs (Anderson, 2021).

In addition, a number of study abroad penalties levied on institutions are not solely a result of litigation outcomes. In fact, numerous cases end in costly settlement agreements, both in terms of financial costs and reputational impacts on the institutions. As revealed in several of the settlement agreements below, the financial impacts might be significant, but the reputational impacts are possibly longer lasting.

Settlement Agreements

Often HEIs and their general counsel prefer to settle disputes through arbitration or mediation rather than be faced with a costly alternative (Lee, 2010). Many consider settling out of court (Baldwin & Ferron, 2006; Johnson, 2006) because they are motivated to reduce the fallout from the exposure of a federal violation. Avoiding public scrutiny is another motivating factor that influences an institutional decision to settle out of court, especially when a clear error has been made or if similar recent incidents have occurred.

Although many settlement agreements related to international education experiences are not publicly released, the initial cases are often reported in the media and include upsetting details about student harms, reflecting poorly on HEIs. For example, an Earlham College student's claim that she was raped by her host in Japan in 1996 was settled out of court approximately a year after being filed in the U.S. District Court of Connecticut (Reisberg, 1998); the University of Connecticut settled a Title IX complaint for $25,000 in 2013 (Thomas, 2013); in November 2018, the University of Minnesota settled a student's rape claim from a study abroad program in Cuba for $137,000 (*U.S. News & World Report*, 2018); and a Clemson University student settled a Title IX case related to his sexual encounter with a male program instructor during a study abroad program in Peru for $40,000 (Latos, 2021; Simon, 2019)—to name a few.

A settlement typically accompanies a non-disclosure agreement, and so the full scope and financial impact of such cases, and certainly others not reported in the media, may never fully be known. For example, the University of South Carolina paid an undisclosed amount in damages to a former student (*Dunavant v. University of South Carolina*, 2018) who claimed that she was sexually harassed in violation of Title IX and treated poorly by the instructor who was leading the university-sponsored study abroad program (Butler, 2018); and as recently as August 2021, a University of North Carolina Charlotte student's claim of sexual misconduct by an instructor during an abroad program in Israel were settled for an undisclosed amount in damages (Latos, 2021). The transparency of violation claims and their investigation outcomes is further limited by recent changes in OCR reporting; in March 2018, they announced that the details of resolved sexual-violence investigations would no longer be made publicly available (*Chronicle of Higher Education*, 2021).

LITIGATION LESSONS

Although only select case and settlement agreement outcomes were highlighted in the previous discussion, these examples illustrate the nature of risks from study abroad related litigation under anti-discrimination laws, specifically Title IX and the ADA. Notwithstanding the ethical and legal implications, the failure to engage in sound risk mitigation planning can have significant financial impact, as revealed in the RISD court-ordered damages of $2.5m. As the internationalization of higher education programming and activities increase, past litigation and settlement agreement outcomes ought to guide institutional efforts to mitigate future risks and provide safe learning and working environments for university affiliated instructors, students, and staff members.

Forecasting Future Risks

As reported in 2015 by the U.S. Department of Education, post-secondary OCR complaints most frequently involve disability and sex-based discrimination allegations, accounting for nearly three-quarters of all complaints (U.S. Department of Education, 2015). It is perhaps not surprising that these same types of complaints are also the most likely to be litigated in study abroad at nearly the same rate (72%), particularly given the level of attention in the media to tracking such investigations. Title IX cases made up 28% of OCR investigations in 2015, or nearly 3,000 complaints. In higher education that year, the number of sexual violence complaints alone grew to 164, the figure five times higher than only three years prior (U.S. Department of Education, 2015).

As of September 2021, there were nearly 250 open investigations into sexual violence or harassment in higher education (U.S. Department of Education, 2021). The *Chronicle of Higher Education* has an entire project page dedicated to the daily tracking and posting of sexual assault complaints and the subsequent outcomes of Title IX investigations on university campuses (*Chronicle of Higher Education*, 2021). These cases have proven challenging in the domestic context, and yet, even more so when occurring abroad.

According to the highlighted cases and settlement agreements, when disability discrimination and sex-based harassment occur during university-sponsored study abroad programs, institutions might be vulnerable to litigation or OCR investigations. As the interpretation of Title IX evolves, with recent statutory guidance and case law expanding protections on the basis of sex to include sexual orientation, officials planning study abroad opportunities will need to consider how to mitigate risks of discrimination and harassment on the basis of sexual orientation and identity. To reduce vulnerability to litigation while mitigating risks of harm to participating students, university administrators and study abroad professionals ought to be informed of the laws and attitudes of their host destinations and begin proactive discussions with international partners and providers about the evolving Title IX interpretations.

Vulnerability of University Administrators

In the vast majority of cases, the complaining students name a university administrator (77%; Easler, 2019) as the violator of their federally protected rights. In ADA cases, claims were typically centered on the administrator's inability or unwillingness to meet accommodation requests by the student. The Title IX claims were usually brought by students based on inadequate or lack of response to their claims of sexual violence or harassment occurring abroad, real or perceived.

Although most higher education institutions engage in risk mitigation strategies with respect to on campus student activities, the study abroad field exposes vulnerability given the nature and international settings of these activities. As noted previously, with appropriate planning and predefined processes for managing discrimination cases, university administrators will be better able to avoid being named in a lawsuit.

Administrators play a significant role in responding appropriately to discrimination complaints. As the front-line, administrators are responsible for protecting students from possible discrimination. They also need to be informed legally regarding the nature of study abroad discrimination claims so they can implement procedures and measures to mitigate risk before claims arise. Adopted protocols, established specific safety measures and checks to be completed for every study abroad experience, and partnerships with sound in-country providers could decrease harmful and costly errors that lead to student harm.

For example, a university employee's actions, such as failing to ensure workable locks on bedroom doors (*Doe v. Rhode Island School of Design*, 2021) on a program for which RISD had full programmatic control, led to the harm of a student during a study abroad program. The administrator's use of a protocol, such as a safety checklist for study abroad housing, would have decreased the risk of harm significantly in this case. The case law demonstrates that the actions of administrators can and will be examined as part of any investigation emerges and that their role in the incident will be scrutinized. Moreover, the negative outcomes for students who were harmed during their study abroad experiences could be prevented by administrators and employees who are trained to make legally sound decisions and to reduce liability through adherence to risk mitigation safety protocols.

Liability Based on Level of Programmatic Control

The presumption against extraterritoriality is not a blanket protection for institutions engaging in international education. It cannot be expected to be applied in all cases, and the circumstances of the incidences do matter. In *King v. Board of Control of Eastern Michigan University* (2002), where the university had full programmatic control and sexual harassment was brazen, the liability risk increased. As discussed in *King v. Board of Control of Eastern Michigan University* (2002), the study abroad program lacked appropriate university oversight and intervention, thus extraterritoriality was overruled because allowing such overt discrimination in an environment where the university could and ought to have better protected its female students would undoubtedly have led to future discrimination and impeded access to educational programs.

The level of control that an institution has over study abroad programming directly impacted the resolution of disability-based claims as well. For example, an OCR complaint against Arizona State University (ASU) involved circumstances for which the universities had more of a hands-off approach to the programming. ASU's role in connecting the student to the opportunity, not administering it, was a consideration in their decision to not support the accommodation request while abroad (Hebel, 2001). The OCR ruled in favor of ASU's decision in this case.

Extraterritoriality at its core seeks to confine rulings to the American context and to not overstep the boundaries of U.S. laws. This perceived boundary of control can be observed in these cases—the more control of programmatic aspects by a U.S. HEI, the greater the likelihood of application of the law despite the physical location of program delivery. *King v. Board of Control* (2002) was indeed an extraordinary circumstance where the HEI failed its students. While it creates a bit of a legal abnormality, it was undeniably the suitable outcome based on the specific circumstances of that case. Few cases have challenged the longstanding legal theory.

Further clarification by legislation or a higher court such as the U.S. Supreme Court, however, would be welcomed. Yet, there are no signs that such clarification is forthcoming. An opportunity for such a review of the law was denied in 2003. Following her unsuccessful appeal in 2002 for insufficient accommodations based on her disability, Bird filed a petition for writ of *certiorari*, or a request for the U.S. Supreme Court to review a lower court's ruling. This writ was denied, leaving the matter unaddressed to date and continuing the ambiguity of the application of these statutes to abroad locations (*Bird v. Lewis & Clark*, 2003).

RECOMMENDATIONS FOR PRACTICE

Considering the important and yet risky nature of such programming, the need for ongoing professionalization of the field becomes increasingly evident. HEIs must recognize the need for skill and training of professionals in international positions regardless of the size of the institution or their scope of internationalization. By failing to recognize the important role that these professionals play in their organization and the added vulnerability of limited staffing, training, and funding of such professional departments include upsetting details about student harms, reflecting poorly on HEIs.

Through the professional organizations dedicated to the advancement of international education such as the Forum and NAFSA, adequate materials and professional development resources exist to educate practitioners on the risks and resources related to federal legislation and discrimination abroad. By learning and considering such ADA language as "reasonable accommodation" and "undue burden," for example, those same professionals can assess more critically the programs they are developing and/or in which they are involved. Access to these memberships and conferences may be viewed as costly from a budgetary perspective, but might help to insure an institution from even costlier legal expenses and media scrutiny.

These same organizations also serve to inform practitioners of changes in the statutes and their interpretations through their newsletters and updates. However, in addition, practitioners ought to also consider how domestic issues might influence interpretation while abroad. Staying abreast of higher education news through known and reputable outlets such as the *Chronicle of Higher Education* can help international education professionals stay attuned to important developments in leadership and in the current events that are shaping the broader landscape of American higher education.

Further, beyond the training needed for practitioners, is additional training and resources for students and instructors. Depending on the length and type of program, training needs might vary, but the development of institutional-level modules can help students to understand their rights and responsibilities while abroad. Of note, perhaps, is that of the recent settlement cases mentioned, the majority were the result of instructor misconduct as opposed to administrative deficiency. Reiterating the expectations for acceptable conduct while abroad can also reinforce the role of the university in enforcing standards regardless of the student's whereabouts. It also reinforces the intent of the endeavor as educational at its core and can serve to remind students of the goals and reasons for their participation.

Similarly, instructors leading programs must engage in regular and robust training opportunities in an effort to help them become aware of the responsibility they have undertaken, the process to follow ought any issues arise during a program, and the university expectations for their behavior and response. HEIs ought to note that those programs with the greatest level of control of the study abroad programming, such as faculty-led programs, are most susceptible to successful litigation. Therefore, these programs, which are now the most popular and subscribed to from study abroad program portfolios, are the most vulnerable. The importance of the selection and training of the instructors of such programs cannot be understated. For many instructors, their involvement in programs abroad is a small piece of their teaching and research responsibilities, and in many cases, is seen as a perk of their appointment; however, articulation of their important role in successful outcomes is absolutely necessary.

Recognition of the limitations of a study abroad office or of an instructor's planning capabilities is also critical. In cases where adequate resources cannot be dedicated to finer details of program planning, institutions might want to consider sharing these responsibilities with a trusted study abroad provider. Capable of providing in-country support from the planning to the execution stage, these partnerships can also overlay additional risk and safety protocols and facilitate the response to an in-country incident.

Finally, the need for coordination between study abroad offices, offices of disability services, and offices of general counsel is highly important in the facilitation of positive student outcomes. By working together, all institutional stakeholders can better understand the opportunities and limitations of international education. They can work together to identify appropriate locations for study abroad on a case-by-case basis which addresses each student's specific needs, they can coordinate with any host institution or study abroad advisor in advance, and perhaps most importantly, they can work with the student to help manage expectations for what might or might not be possible. By identifying all possible solutions and narrowing the gap between accommodation expectation and delivery, students have an opportunity to be partners in the process of designing the experience that is best for them. In working with the office of general counsel, collaboration on risk management can occur both before, during, and after any incidences abroad. Not only is it important for international education professionals to understand the scope and limitations of their HEI's legal team, the general counsel can also better understand the programming that is in place and advise on any areas of vulnerability.

CONCLUSION

In the absence of clear court and OCR guidance, interpretation has been left to professional organizations, individual institutions, international education professionals, and campus general counsel. Not only is this approach troublesome for students who are unsure about their legal rights and protections while participating in study abroad, institutions are similarly unsure about their obligations and duties—financial and otherwise—to ensure protections outside of the territorial United States. Understanding the reach and scope of federal regulation, particularly in situations where institutions might have limited control over all program aspects, will help institutions develop appropriate programming that addresses the demand for increased participation while protecting its students, instructors, and staff from overreaching their legal limitations.

Similarly, study abroad professionals must recognize that not all cases are resolved in court, thus they ought to review settlement agreements that offer additional insights about the nature of study abroad disputes and resolutions. The costs of not being fully prepared are not purely financial, in fact, the harms to students can be significant. Efforts must be undertaken to stay informed not only to mitigate against the litigation risks, but also to ensure the legal protections of students while abroad.

CHAPTER 15

INTERNATIONALIZATION OF HIGHER EDUCATION

The Challenges of Facilitating Critical Thinking Among Culturally Diverse Student Populations

Andriy Kovalenko
Rosemary Richards

Education might once have been a predominately localized activity which serviced the needs and aspirations of the immediate communities, societies, and nations in which it was embedded. While local communities continue to benefit, with rapid technological advances, and the worldwide exchange of goods, services, people, and information, higher education in the 21st century has increased. The globalization of higher education is an ever-evolving phenomenon, and the economic and social value for students, educators, and host countries has been well documented (Allen, 2018; Wu et al., 2015)—as has the role of international higher education in "fostering students' competencies to act in international environments" (Teichler, 2017, p. 181) and become global citizens (New Zealand Government, 2018).

With the global interconnectedness comes the internationalization of education, which traditionally involves global mobility of students and faculty members alongside knowledge transfer, such as media and publications, and international research and collaborations (Teichler, 2017). These notions speak of values of partnership, cooperation, academic, and social purposes, but at the same time internationalization is associated with economic, political, and status-raising rationales for the universities (Knight, 2014a). Indeed, for the small nation of around five million, international education was New Zealand's fifth largest export industry and second largest export service sector in 2018 (New Zealand Government, 2018). New Zealand's Higher Education Institutes (HEIs) include universities, wānanga (tertiary institutions providing education in a Māori cultural environment), private training establishments, and Institutes of Technology and Polytechnics (ITPs). The ITPs, the context in which the authors operate, experienced a 17% increase of international students between 2014 and 2015, and a further 5% in 2016 (Education New Zealand, 2016, 2018). The COVID-19 pandemic, which involves border-crossing, has significantly disrupted internationalization, and the associated income streams. This facilitated high-level discussions about what the future of international education might look like, and how the internationalization of higher education might operate.

The prospect of gaining post-study work visas and settling families in New Zealand, has undoubtedly been a drawcard for immigrant students. However, COVID-19 border restrictions disrupted these aspirations making students transition to other options, such as studying internationally online. Whilst an examination of these challenges is outside the scope of this chapter, the way New Zealand presents itself to the world is as a place of quality education, premised on being "world-class, responsive, and student-centered" (New Zealand Government, 2018, p. 10), and placing high value on critical thinking, inquiry, and adaptability. For example, the New Zealand immigration website states, "As a student here you'll be encouraged to be questioning, flexible, and to seek your own answers by thinking for yourself" (New Zealand Immigration, 2021). New Zealand's higher education graduates are expected to have well-developed critical thinking skills, and graduate profile outcomes of HEIs are likely to include the ability to critically evaluate personal practice, critique challenges and issues within specialist fields and develop solutions to solve problems, and critically evaluate existing research and work as reflective practitioners. These aspirations align with what employers might expect of tertiary graduates, such as the ability to make well-justified decisions (Anderson & Reid, 2013). As such, critical thinking (CT) is one of the main skills graduates of HEIs are expected to possess (Liu et al., 2014). The essence of this skill has largely been defined by the European school of thought, making CT in its Western understanding quite ethnocentric. With internationalization of higher education comes the challenge of teaching CT to students, whose cultural backgrounds are different, and who, consequently, have different approaches to, understanding of, and logic for, this type of critical thinking.

In a New Zealand-based qualitative research study in an ITP, with 12 international higher education students and 10 instructors it was evident that students experienced cultural disconnections between their previous home-based tertiary experiences and the expectations in New Zealand. In New Zealand students were expected to participate in problem-solving, inquiry-based learning, critical thinking, critical discussions, and written assignments (Richards et al., 2020). At the same time, students expressed high satisfaction with the applicability of their higher education studies to their professional fields, and development as critical thinkers. The disconnection between international students' previous educational experiences and those that are expected in the Western-influenced HEIs, has been observed in other research with international students in New Zealand (Li, 2016; Ryan et al., 2019; Skyrme, 2007; Zhiheng & Bruton, 2007) and elsewhere (Allen, 2018; Glass et al., 2015; Wang, 2009; Wolf & Lihn, 2019; Zhang, 2018; Zhu & Bresnahan, 2018).

Thus, while CT can be a core concept of Westernized higher education (Moore, 2013), many international students might be unfamiliar with CT in its Western understanding and struggle to engage in this type of critical reading and thinking (Wilson, 2016). In turn, academics who are mired in Anglo-Saxon conventions of CT might assume that such practices are either known by students, or ought to be, and such assumptions contribute to internationalization of education which is centrally Westernized (Vandermensbrugghe, 2004).

Rather than being innate, CT is a learned skill (Cottrell, 2017), and in many Western countries, teachers and students are guided in the pedagogy of critical thinking (Delamain & Spring, 2021). In New Zealand, young children are supported as critical thinkers, and encouraged to value "innovation, inquiry, and curiosity, by thinking critically, creatively, and reflectively" (Ministry of Education, 2017, p. 10)—an expectation which carries through to higher education and life in general. However, these socially and culturally embedded practices contrast with the experiences of students in some East Asian HEIs (Egege & Kutieleh, 2004). Nevertheless, they are expected to use CT in their assessments, writing, and learning activities in Westernized HEIs and, as a result, when students employ different approaches to CT tasks this adversely affects their academic performance (Shaheen, 2016).

CRITICALLY REFLECTING ON CT AND THE INTERNATIONALIZATION OF HIGHER EDUCATION

Whilst critical thinking has become an essential feature of the internationalization of Western higher education, teachers are often unaware of the CT systems which dominate their teaching practices, and might regard international students' different approaches as deviations from the norm (Egege & Kutieleh, 2004). Notions of CT vary, and the way thinking is constructed influences social and cognitive functioning. Nisbett et al. (2008) note two significant systems of CT: analytic (related to Ancient Greek philosophy, promoting personal agency and debate) and holistic (based on teachings of Confucius, promoting collective agency and ethical obligations). Westerners tend towards the analytic, and these approaches to CT might unconsciously dominate their teaching practices, and lead to seeing Westernized education systems as unquestionably superior (Vandermensbrugghe, 2004), which creates "conceptual colonialism" (Biggs, 1997, as cited in Egege & Kutieleh, 2004, p. 76). To avoid these biases and discriminations, Hammersley-Fletcher and Hanley (2016) suggest that HEI students and educators ought to develop critical perspectives which are open to challenge and debate around "all aspects of critical activity, including the nature of reasoning, the self, and our relations with others" (p. 979). Yet, the practice of CT and such debates by international students, might be compounded by the complexity of argumentation skills, when English is a second language (Vandermensbrugghe, 2004).

Discipline-based CT practices can also be ingrained, and while educators might be aware of their practices, they might be less aware of other CT approaches. Research in an Australian HEI, which investigated 17 academics' ideas about critical thinking within three disciplines, found that those teachers had varied definitions of CT which they conveyed to students, and these diverse disciplinary lenses appeared to impact students' understanding of CT (Moore, 2013). This research supports the hypothesis that, in addition to cultural traditions that underpin dominant notions of CT, academics learn the CT principles through their professional practice.

Discipline-based understanding of CT among academics can be one of the reasons for the lack of consensus regarding its essence. There are some aspects of CT, nevertheless, which recur in many definitions. For example, many studies suggest that critical thinkers do not just seek flaws in others' arguments, they also question and evaluate their own and other's assumptions with an open-minded, fair, and inquisitive disposition (see Barnet et al., 2017). In other words, critical thinkers identify the most relevant information, evaluate it, and, thereby, transform it into meaningful knowledge, which enables them to determine the optimal course of action (Flores et al., 2012). This ability to make well-justified decisions is reportedly one of the most desired skills expected from college graduates by employers (Anderson & Reid, 2013). Noting critical thinking as an essential feature of internationalized higher education creates a second consideration—that is, the relationships between learners and teachers. Non-Western CT traditions were developed in societies with a high level of power distance (the level of tolerance to the unequal distribution of power), where students regarded teachers as authority figures whose expertise was respected and unchallenged, and learning was based on teacher-centered instructions, such as lectures (Fell & Lukianova, 2015). In contrast, in New Zealand and other Westernized nations, efforts are made in higher education to reduce the power distance between learners and teachers. The principles of adult learning, such as those proposed by Knowles et al. (2015), place the individual student as central to learning, and their needs, self-concepts, prior knowledge, readiness to learn, and orientation to learning are respected and supported.

Treating students as active-learners, rather than passive recipients of information, places emphasis on how learning is experienced, as well as what is learned. However, this too can be problematic in culturally diverse student populations. For example, research suggests that some groups of international students are largely focused on academic performance rather than on the process of learning (Iannelli & Huang, 2014). Furthermore, although assured that it is fine to argue in a classroom, students might still perceive teachers as the dominant authority due to their involvement in the process of assessment (Hinett, 2002, as cited in Moon, 2008).

In addition to this conundrum, research has shown that international students often struggle to present their arguments in their second language (Egege & Kutieleh, 2004), especially in writing (Rear, 2017). Students' limited English proficiency can be one of the reasons, though differences between English and non-English written discourse might play a certain role as well. The indirect, somewhat repetitive and non-assertive writing style of many non-native English speakers is in stark contrast to the Anglo-American writing style with its deductive, linear, and intolerance of digressions in the presentation of arguments (MacKenzie, 2015). Requiring non-native English speakers to change their discourse patterns when presenting ideas in English is viewed as an infringement of human rights by some authors (Clyne, 2004). Western educators can mitigate such power imbalance by recognizing the epistemological diversity of their students' educational background and by decolonizing Eurocentric curricula of the Global North HEIs (de Sousa Santos, 2020).

Higher education students having a sense of voice and empowerment, and valuing learning processes, are essential in New Zealand's student-centered approaches, which promote knowledge construction through such things as critical discussions, problem-solving, and purposeful interactions between learners and teachers. These approaches can be unfamiliar and somewhat subversive for some international students, especially if public debate of different propositions is considered to undermine social harmony (Hook et al., 2009).

Being able to justify decisions requires insights into one's own thinking processes. In research in the United States, which investigated the fostering of CT through effective pedagogy, Tsui (2002) noted that passive-learning instructions, such as lectures, coupled with large student cohorts, teaches students what to think, rather than how to think. On the other hand, CT can be fostered more effectively in smaller classes and through students' engagement in writing and re-writing exercises, in which they get constructive feedback having been exposed to analytical writing across disciplinary boundaries, discussions, and questions between students, and student study groups. Overall, knowledge construction through the interaction between teachers and learners has become a common trend in global north HEIs. Moving towards a more student-centered, active-learning approach is also consistent with New Zealand's aspirations for effective higher education. This is why students from the traditional teacher-led environments might experience challenges in becoming fully fledged critical thinkers. For these students, it can be quite difficult to question arguments and opinions of others, especially those perceived as figures of authority. These conditions can stifle their ability to critically process available information and, thereby, reduce effectiveness of their decision-making. Likewise, the influx of international students to countries such as New Zealand prior to the pandemic, has resulted in large classes and therefore, challenges to implementing student-centered active learning. Indeed, in higher education, students are expected to engage in self-directed and student-centered learning, which can create significant challenges for both international students and academic staff (Richards et al., 2020).

In the ITP, in which the authors teach and research, each course outline has a clear statement on internationalization:

> Respectful, inclusive, and collaborative engagement with a broad range of cultures is a fundamental part of working in an increasingly globalized world. Teaching and learning throughout this course will incorporate international perspectives, and ensure the identity and culture of all students are embraced within the learning environment.

Such statements are likely applicable to many HEIs and whilst sincere efforts are made to adhere to this statement, some Western educators appear to disregard international students' prior learning experiences (Egege & Kutieleh, 2004), which includes different perspectives on CT.

The mindset of Western educators has been shaped by education which stems from neoliberalism—the ideology that favors the free market exchange over state intervention. In free markets, not only businesses but also HEIs are expected to sustain themselves by competing for limited resources with their counterparts (Davies & Bansel, 2007). The competition makes control over the implementation of performance goals imperative, and many curriculums aim at preparing students for the neoliberal workplace (Martin-Sanchez & Flores-Rodriguez, 2018). For example, graduates ought to be capable of making independent decisions in their entrepreneurial endeavors (W. Brown, 2003). CT is thought to contribute to the development of such skills (Calma & Davies, 2021), which can explain why the development of CT "has become an explicit goal of HEIs in the West" (Rear, 2017, p. 18).

Operating within neoliberal education system can create, reproduce, and legitimate specific forms of critical thinking and critical thinkers (Danvers, 2021, p. 1), which might constrain educators willingness to entertain CT approaches that are noncompliant with the postulates of the neoliberal. Ironically, in such environments, people who teach how to be open-minded critical thinkers can become quite conservative in applying CT in their practices.

SYNERGIES IN CT AND INTERNATIONAL HIGHER EDUCATION

The pandemic and subsequent drop in the cross-border movement of students and academics, demands innovation in terms of which courses are offered and the manner in which they are delivered. Some institutions have already shifted from focusing primarily on small populations of financially privileged on-campus international students towards more inclusive collaborative online international learning (COIL) programs, which allow students to attend online courses delivered jointly by partner institutions. COIL might make it possible to achieve international and intercultural learning outcomes in a less elitist and more cost-effective manner (de Wit & Altbach, 2021). Implementing COIL curriculum necessitates HEIs to internationalize the courses and learning experiences, incorporating international and intercultural dimensions in learning outcomes, assessment tasks, teaching techniques, and support services (Leask, 2015). If such synergies are accomplished, the needs and interests of individual HEIs can be satisfied and, thereby, the true internationalization at home can be achieved (Knight, 2014b).

Higher education curricula almost universally aims at the development of CT skills (Thompson, 2011) and if these curricula are to be internationalized, there is a need to look at how the concept of CT is perceived in different education systems. The popular idea about CT being a uniquely Western approach to knowledge acquisition (Cuypers, 2004) fails to embrace the cultural, social, or historical complexity of ways of thinking which have supported development of cultures and societies. It is believed that CT originated in the works of ancient Greek philosophers and has become a truth-seeking endeavor of individuals relying on abstract and linear thinking (Tan, 2017). These ideas of autonomous truth-thinking and self-fulfillment can be quite foreign for the representatives of collectivist and high-power distance cultures. For example, people belonging to Confucian cultures might value CT as an activity and skill which benefits not only an individual, but also the communities in which the critical thinker belongs (Tan, 2017). Notions of power distance, can influence how knowledge about, and engagement with, CT is enacted among people. In Dharmic cultures, knowledge is acquired through attentive and uninterrupted listening to teachers who transfer the content necessary for becoming an educated person (Reagan, 2004). As previously noted, this teacher-directed transfer of knowledge approach is in contrast with dialogic teaching, which is widespread in Western education from an early age.

Despite these cultural differences in understanding the goal of CT and how it is taught, there are synergies across cultural perspectives on what it involves. For example, deductive syllogistic reasoning is viewed as part of CT in its Western tradition (West et al., 2008), and in Hindu educational thought, the development of arguments through the use of syllogism is also a common practice (Organ, 1998). Analogical reasoning, or comparison of two phenomena sharing similar characteristics, is another feature of CT introduced in Hindu philosophical thought much earlier than in the West (Klostermaier, 2007). Identifying a missing premise in an argument is also a common practice in Hindu CT (Reagan, 2004), which is quite similar to the one employed by Western critical thinkers in argument assessment (Bowell et al., 2020).

Several elements of Western CT align with traditional Confucian thought. Although adherence to *Dao* or the Way of Heaven—which prescribes how to behave—plays a central role in the teachings of Confucius, these prescriptions can be modified based on the judgment of those who apply Dao to their daily life experiences (Brindley, 2011). Evaluating alternative ways of behavior in given situations requires logic and problem-solving skills, which are also indispensable for exercising CT in its Western understanding. Because of its emphasis on conformity and reproduction of arguments, some argue that the use of judgment is not common in the modern-day Confucian education systems, however, much current research "challenges the idea that Confucian cultures produce learners who are passive, unquestioning and lacking in CT skills" (Floyd, 2011, p. 299). There is also evidence that Chinese students are familiar with Daoism and believe that its use can help them to be rational and creative (Paton, 2011).

FACILITATING AND ASSESSING CRITICAL THINKING

Despite the synergies between various constructs of CT, research suggests that many international students in Western HEIs, from places such as India and China, have felt ill-equipped to apply CT to assessments, when their previous home country assessments were largely examination-based and relied on recall (Paton, 2011). More recently, curriculum reform in several Asian countries has seen a move towards student-centered approaches which promote students' critical and creative thinking, so judging student ability to engage in CT in their assessments cannot be assumed based on stereotypes. Given the importance placed on CT as graduate outcomes in internalized higher education, which has diverse student populations, HEI academics need to use CT throughout the entire process of assessment, beginning with judgments about what and how to assess. Noting also that various disciplines unconsciously expect certain types of CT relevant to their fields, assessment developers might also need to elaborate on how elements of CT can be integrated in the assessment of learning objectives that might not be directly connected to CT.

To facilitate more involvement of students in assessment, instead of the traditional peer-review of course assessments prior to implementation, student representatives from diverse backgrounds could be involved in assessment development. If this input were from current students, this would require a move away from fully pre-prescribed content in course outlines to negotiated understandings of assessment tasks, criteria, and purpose. *Ako* is a Māori term referring to reciprocity between learners and teachers, and is valued in New Zealand. Consequently, learners are teachers and teachers are learners.

Such approaches not only empower students, but also broaden the perspectives and expectations of academics who straddle multiple social and cultural contexts when facilitating and assessing learning in the era of internationalization of education. Through negotiated understandings of CT and how CT is applied within assessments, provision is made for decolonizing CT in higher education, building a better understanding for students of what they are expected to do, simultaneously developing their CT skills by evaluating assessment criteria, analyzing multiple perspectives and thinking about alternative methods of assessment. This is not to suggest that the academics do not take a lead role in providing a well-considered model of assessment, but rather that if students suggest changes to assessments, they will need to justify their arguments by discussing them with their classmates and teachers.

Building on this point, in-class discussion of assessment criteria can be considered as a formative assessment of students' ability to clearly present and justify their arguments orally, while asking students to critique assessments in writing can be a part of summative assessments. In particular, a question about challenges and how to improve assessment tasks (thereby asking students to use their CT) can be added to other questions about the course content.

Facilitating students' diverse perspectives in assessment development can also benefit academics in terms of understanding the needs and expectations of international students. The perceived power distance between students and teachers, coupled with difficulties presenting ideas in a second language, can discourage active participation in discussions, so students must be convinced that their ideas matter. Such discussions can help students and teachers identify historical and cultural assumptions behind concepts of CT, and how they might be utilized to meet the requirements of the assessment.

Embedding real-world scenarios and problem-solving tasks in assignments might support the development of CT skills among students accustomed to pragmatic CT. Students can further improve their practical CT skills if they are involved in work-integrated projects, simulated work experiences, and work placements, which can help students to learn through practice and interaction with practitioners. Although, for some international students in on-campus courses, visa restrictions, cultural differences, the lack of prior work experience, and insufficient language proficiency can make this learning experience very stressful for some international students (Goodwin & Mbah, 2019), but skillful supervisors or mentors can alleviate such stress by providing critical feedback about how to improve their performance (Barton et al., 2017). Those involved in COIL programs might benefit from home-based work-integrated projects, where language might not present significant issues.

Discussion and exchange of ideas and views are central to CT, so teachers' and peer students' feedback can improve understanding of CT principles and motivate to develop CT skills (Cajander et al., 2014). However, negative feedback can discourage students, especially if they regarded themselves as "good" students in their home country (Fakunle et al., 2016). Students can be unpleasantly surprised with the feedback and low marks due to the discrepancy between their own and their assessor's understanding of assessment criteria. This can also happen if students are simply instructed about what CT is, without any effort made to explain how CT skills can be developed and used.

CT is a complex mental process that cannot be observed externally. As a result, educators need to articulate as clearly as possible what students ought to do to be a critical thinker. To understand the essence of CT, Golding (2011) suggests using thought-encouraging questions (e.g., "What does it mean?" or "What is the difference?"), which do not lead to predetermined answers, but promote using arguments supported by convincing evidence.

These questions might lead to online student discussions, although international students might expect clear guidance and input from educators, to steer discussion towards the correct responses (Zhang, 2013). CT aims to question established knowledge using arguments supported by convincing evidence. Good questioning skills and facilitated discussion can model the critiquing of the taken-for-granted ideas and practices that have been a part of CT tradition in students' respective societies. Thus, in Confucian cultures, the operating principles of the world (Dao), which are not static, might be adjusted to the changing reality by exercising judgment (Tan, 2017). This means that there can be multiple truths in how reality is interpreted (Xu, 2010).

While discussions play an important role in developing negotiated understandings and application of CT, in HEIs, CT is commonly expressed and assessed in writing. English academic writing style is quite rigid and rule-bound in comparison to academic writing in other cultures (Bennett, 2009) and those familiar with the language and conventions are at an advantage to those who are not. Internationalization of HE, has led to continued emphasis on "written communication plus a growing emphasis on oral communication" (Sawir, 2005, p. 567), which doubly impacts those with limited prior experience of written and oral English. Performing cognitive tasks in a second language creates cognitive overload, which can temporarily hinder task accomplishment. Consequently, to reduce the impact of such cognitive overload, avoid jargon and local slang in course materials and assessments.

With the internationalization of higher education, many international students have been attracted to higher education qualifications, where the expectation for proficiency in CT is evident. Most course descriptors and learning outcomes at postgraduate level, for example, refer to different types of CT skills (e.g., critical understanding and critical awareness of issues in a field of study; NZQA, 2021). Achievement of such learning outcomes often involves summary and critical evaluation of studies related to a specific topic and research questions (Jesson et al., 2011). This makes the creation of literature reviews (LRs) one of the most commonly used types of CT assessment in higher-level studies. Whilst many international students might have prior experience writing LRs in their first language, and be skilled in describing and summarizing relevant literature, the Western understanding of these tasks require a critical evaluation of a range of studies and their contextualization around a specific topic or theme (the use of CT skills). Thus, as the authors have found, for many international students, the writing of a critical LR becomes a more formidable task. There are not only issues with expressing complex ideas in English, but also cultural reservations which can hamper students' critical writing. For example, the perceived power imbalance between a student as a junior-researcher, and showing respect for the authors in reputable journals can explain some students' reluctance to critically evaluate the literature (Qian & Krugly-Smolska, 2008). Extended discussions of the essence of CT, and how its understanding can vary in different cultures, ought to help students be more comfortable with the idea of critical evaluation.

Writing an LR requires good paraphrasing skills, which international students might not possess or are reluctant to use when the original source has clear language and is difficult for them to present differently and accurately (Gunnarsson et al., 2014).

To a certain extent, paraphrasing can contribute to the development of CT. However, using paraphrasing exercises, without engaging metacognitive higher-level planning and evaluating strategies, limits mastering of CT skills (Ku & Ho, 2010). The writing of an LR in higher education requires critical evaluation and problem-solving, as existing knowledge is applied to a specific context, which requires planning and CT. As writing progresses, the writing plan, and the LR itself, adjusts in response to new details emerging from external sources. This flexibility and adjustments in the LR are part of the CT process, which academics might expect of their higher education students. Insights from small scale research with four Chinese students writing an LR, found that these students planned their writing of LR and either stuck to the plan or revised it to accommodate new information (Qian & Krugly-Smolska, 2008). However, having a plan might not be that beneficial if its quality is questionable. If academics foster practices that value the critical input of students and teachers, then students might feel supported in sharing their plans for critique by others. As noted earlier, this is not an opportunity to abdicate responsibility as a facilitator of learning, but rather an opportunity to foster CT within a community of learners, and provide formative assessment and feedback, which might lead to the development of CT and more successful achievement in summative assessments and graduate outcomes.

CONCLUSION

Internationalization of higher education is a well-established and enduring phenomenon which despite its neoliberal objectives (Bamberger et al., 2019), might diversify to cater for global conditions and needs of culturally and socially diverse peoples. What appears to be steadfast is the place of critical thinking in higher education curriculum and the aspirations for graduates to be critical thinkers. Notions and practice of CT are culturally constructed, and as the internationalization of higher education is predominantly Westernized, biases and unexamined assumptions can dominate approaches to CT in HEIs. This can have a detrimental effect on international students, working against the goals espoused in CT and the value of internationalized higher education. The challenges which might be met include greater awareness of the CT systems which dominate higher education curriculum and how these promote and constrain ways of thinking and being, especially among culturally diverse student populations; and recognition of how power–distance relationships can impact student experience and CT practices, learner-centered education, and reciprocal teacher–learner relations (*Ako*). Honoring the synergies which can exist across CT systems and approaches to higher education can be a starting point for facilitating and assessing CT in internationalized education, and can lead to CT processes which are integral to supporting critical discussions, assessment development, authentic learning experiences, and robust research practices.

REFERENCES

53% of International Students Pondering Delay or Switch. (2020, October 24). University World News. https://www.universityworldnews.com/post.php?story=20201024060349906

Aasen, P., & Stensaker, B. (2007). Balancing trust and technocracy? Leadership training in higher education. *International Journal of Educational Management, 21*(5), 371–383. https://eric.ed.gov/?id=EJ800408

Ableser, J., & Moore, C. (2018, September 10). Universal design for learning and digital accessibility: Compatible partners or a conflicted marriage. *Educause Review, 10.* https://er.educause.edu/articles/2018/9/universal-design-for-learning-and-digital-accessibility-compatible-partners-or-a-conflicted-marriage

Addis, M., & Holbrook, M. (2001). On the conceptual link between mass customisation and experiential consumption: An explosion of subjectivity. *Journal of Consumer Behaviour: An International Research Review, 1*(1), 50–66. https://doi.org/10.1002/cb.53

Adnett, N., & Davies, P. (2003). Schooling reforms in England: From quasi-markets to co-opetition? *Journal of Education Policy, 18*(4), 393–406. https://doi.org/10.1080/0268093032000106848

Agostinelli, A. (2021). Teaching international students in Western universities: A literature review. *Journal of Comparative & International Higher Education, 13*(4). https://doi.org/10.32674/jcihe.v13i4.1846

Aizawa, I., & Rose, H. (2018). An analysis of Japan's English as medium of instruction initiatives within higher education: The gap between meso-level policy and micro-level practice. *Higher Education, 77*(6), 1125–1142. https://doi.org/10.1007/s10734-018-0323-5

Aizawa, I., Rose, H., Thompson, G., & Curle, S. (2020). Beyond the threshold: Exploring English language proficiency, linguistic challenges, and academic language skills of Japanese students in an English medium instruction programme. *Language Teaching Research.* https://doi.org/10.1177/1362168820965

Alderman, G. (2001). The globalization of higher education: Some observations regarding the free market and the national interest. *Higher Education in Europe, 26*(1), 47–52. https://doi.org/10.1080/03797720120054175

Aleles, J. (2015). Japan's global 30 program: The push and pull factors of international student mobility. *International Journal of Learning, Teaching, and Educational Research, 13*(2). http://www.ijlter.org/index.php/ijlter/article/view/420/0

Alexiadou, N., Kefala, Z., & Rönnberg, L. (2021). Preparing education students for an international future? Connecting students' experience to institutional contexts. *Journal of Studies in International Education, 25*(4), 443–460. https://doi.org/10.1177/1028315321998498

Ali, F., Zhou, Y., Hussain, K., Nair, P. K., & Ragavan, N. A. (2016). Does higher education service quality effect student satisfaction, image, and loyalty? A study of international students in Malaysian public universities. *Quality Assurance in Education, 24*(1), 70–94. https://eric.ed.gov/?id=EJ1087392

Allen, S. (2018). Creative diversity: Promoting interculturality in Australian pathways to higher education. *Journal of International Students, 8*(1), 251–273. https://doi.org/10.32674/jis.v8i1.164

Almond, N., & Mangione, D. (2015). The flying faculty: Internationalising curriculum in an Arabic context. In W. Green & C. Whitsed (Eds.), *Critical perspectives on internationalising the curriculum in disciplines* (pp. 91–105). Brill Sense.

Alon, S. (2009). The evolution of class inequality in higher education: Competition, exclusion, and adaptation. *American Sociological Review, 74*(5), 731–755. https://doi.org/10.1177/000312240907400503

Alonderiene, R., & Klimavičiene, A. (2013). Insights into Lithuanian students' choice of university and study program in management and economics. *Management: Journal of Contemporary Management Issues, 18*(1), 1–22. https://hrcak.srce.hr/104235

Altbach, P. (1998a). The university as center and periphery. In P. Altbach (Ed.), *Comparative higher education: Knowledge, the university and development* (pp. 19–36). Ablex.

Altbach, P. (1998b). Gigantic peripheries: India and China in the world knowledge system. In P. Altbach (Ed.), *Comparative higher education: Knowledge, the university, and development* (pp. 133–146). Ablex.

Altbach, P. (2003a). Centers and peripheries in the academic profession: The special challenges of developing countries. In P. Altbach (Ed.), *The decline of the guru: The academic profession in developing and middle-income countries* (pp. 1–21). Palgrave MacMillan.

Altbach, P. (2003b). Globalisation and the university: Myths and realities in an unequal world. *Journal of Educational Planning and Administration, 17*(2), 227–247. https://doi.org/10.1080/13583883.2004.9967114

Altbach, P. (2007). Twinning and branch campuses: The professorial obstacle. *International Higher Education, 48,* 2–3. https://doi.org/10.6017/ihe.2007.48.7976

Altbach, P. (2010). Why branch campuses may be unsustainable. *International Higher Education, 2010*(58), 2–3.
Altbach, P. (2016). *Global perspectives on higher education*. JHU Press.
Altbach, P., & Davis, T. (1999). Global challenge and national response: Note for an international dialogue on higher education. *International Higher Education, 14*. https://doi.org/10.6017/ihe.1999.14.6471
Altbach, P., & de Wit, H. (2015). Internationalization and global tension: Lessons from history. *Journal of studies in international education, 19*(1), 4–10. https://doi.org/10.1177/1028315314564734
Altbach, P., & Knight, J. (2007). The internationalization of higher education: Motivations and realities. *Journal of studies in international education, 11*(3–4), 290–307. https://doi.org/10.1177/1028315307303542
Altbach, P., & Reisberg, L. (2018). Global trends and future uncertainties. *Change: The Magazine of Higher Learning, 50*(3–4), 63–67. https://doi.org/10.1080/00091383.2018.1509601
Altbach, P., & Yudkevich, M. (2017). Twenty-first century mobility: The role of international faculty. *International Higher Education, 90*, 8–10. https://doi.org/10.6017/ihe.2017.90.9995
Anandakrishnan, M. (2008). Promises and perils of globalized higher education. *Journal of Educational Planning and Administration, 22*(2), 199–211. http://www.niepa.ac.in/New/download/Publications/JEPA_(15%20years)/JEPA%202008_Vol-22%20(1-4)/JEPA_APR-2008-VOL22_2%20Final.pdf#page=85
Anderson, B., & Maharasoa, M. (2002). The internationalisation of higher education: Facilitating partnerships between universities. *South African Journal of Higher Education, 16*(1), 15–21. https://doi.org/10.4314/sajhe.v16i1.25267
Anderson, G. (2020, May 12). *Location-based protection*. Inside Higher Ed. https://www.insidehighered.com/news/2020/05/12/new-title-ix-regulation-sets-location-based-boundaries-sexual-harassment-enforcement
Anderson, G. (2021, February 10). *R. I. School of Design ordered to pay alumna $2.5M*. Inside Higher Ed. https://www.insidehighered.com/quicktakes/2021/02/10/ri-school-design-ordered-pay-alumna-25m
Anderson, P., & Reid, J. (2013). The effect of critical thinking instruction on graduates of a college of business administration. *Journal of Higher Education Theory and Practice, 13*(3/4), 149–167. http://t.www.na-businesspress.com/JHETP/ReidJR_Web13_3__4_.pdf
Ang, S., Van Dyne, L., & Tan, M. L. (2011). "Cultural intelligence." In R. J. Sternberg & S. B. Kaufman (Eds.), *Cambridge handbook on intelligence* (pp. 582–602). Cambridge University Press. https://doi.org/10.1017/CBO9780511977244.030
Ang, Z., & Massingham, P. (2007). National culture and the standardization versus adaptation of knowledge management. *Journal of Knowledge Management, 11*(2), 5–21. http://dx.doi.org/10.1108/13673270710738889
Ansari, S. (2020, September 18). *Can Canada's universities survive COVID?* MacLean's. September 18. https://www.macleans.ca/education/can-canadas-universities-survive-covid/
Ansari, S., Fiss, P., & Zajac, E. (2010). Made to fit: How practices vary as they diffuse. *Academy of Management Review, 35*(1), 67–92. https://doi.org/10.5465/AMR.2010.45577876

Anthony, C., & Tripsas, M. (2016). Organizational identity and innovation. In M. Pratt, M. Schultz, B. Ashforth, & D. Ravasi (Eds.), *The Oxford handbook of organizational identity* (pp. 417–435). Oxford University Press.

Apaydin, M. (2014). The full circle: Case teaching and writing in business courses. *European Journal of Educational Sciences, 1*(3), 26–38. https://files.eric.ed.gov/fulltext/EJ1236649.pdf

Applebaum, B. (2019). Remediating campus climate: Implicit bias training is not enough. *Studies in Philosophy and Education, 38*(2), 129–141. https://doi.org/10.1007/s11217-018-9644-1

Arnold, P. (2005). Disciplining domestic regulation: The World Trade Organization and the market for professional services. *Accounting, Organizations and Society, 30*(4), 299–330. https://doi.org/10.1016/j.aos.2004.04.001

Arnold, P. (2009). Global financial crisis: The challenge to accounting research. *Accounting, Organizations and Society, 34*(6–7), 803–809. https://doi.org/10.1016/j.aos.2009.04.004

Arregui-Pabollet, E., Doussineau, M., & Dettenhofer, M. (2018). *An analytical framework to assess the governance of universities and their involvement in smart specialisation strategies* (EUR 29306 EN). European Commission, Joint Research Centre. https://data.europa.eu/doi/10.2760/760453

Askin, N., & Bothner, M. S. (2016). Status-aspirational pricing: The "chivas regal" strategy in US higher education, 2006–2012. *Administrative Science Quarterly, 61*(2), 217–253. https://doi.org/10.1177/00018392166296

Association of Chartered Certified Accountants. (2016). *ACCA integrated report for the year ended 31st March 2016.* https://www.accaglobal.com/content/dam/ACCA_Global/disc/agm-annual-review/2016/ACCA-integrated-report-2015-16.pdf

Association of Chartered Certified Accountants. (2020). *ACCA Integrated Report for the year ended 31st March 2020.* https://annualreport.accaglobal.com/mediaLibrary/other/english/ACCA-Integrated-Report-2020.pdf

Aydinli, E., & Mathews, J. (2021). Searching for larger status in global politics: Internationalization of higher education in Turkey. *Journal of Studies in International Education, 25*(3), 247–265. https://doi.org/10.1177/10283153209323

Ayoubi, R. M., & Massoud, H. K. (2007). The strategy of internationalization in universities: A quantitative evaluation of the intent and implementation in UK universities. *International Journal of Educational Management, 21*(4), 329–349. https://doi.org/10.1108/09513540710749546

Baker, S. (2020, January 23). UK universities 'increasingly reliant' on Chinese fee income. *Times Higher Education.* https://www.timeshighereducation.com/news/uk-universities-increasingly-reliant-chinese-fee-income

Baldwin, G., & Ferron, J. (2006). Quantitative research strategies. In R. Mawdsley & S. Permuth (Eds.), *Research methods for studying legal issues in education* (pp. 53–86). Education Law Association.

Baldwin, G., & James, R. (2000). The market in Australian higher education and the concept of student as informed consumer. *Journal of Higher Education Policy and Management, 22*(2), 139–148. https://doi.org/10.1080/713678146

Baltagi, B. (2013). *Econometric analysis of panel data* (5th ed.). John Wiley & Sons.

Bamberger, A., Morris, P., & Yemini, M. (2019). Neoliberalism, internationalisation and higher education: Connections, contradictions and alternatives. *Discourse: Studies in the Cultural Politics of Education, 40*(2), 203–216. https://doi.org/10.1080/01596306.2019.1569879

Barblan, A., Ergüder, Ü., & Gürüz, K. (2008). *Case studies higher education in Turkey: Institutional autonomy and responsibility in a modernising society*. Bononia University Press.

Barnet, S., Bedau, H., & O'Hara, J. (2017). *Critical thinking, reading, and writing: A brief guide to argument* (9th ed.). Bedford/St Martin's.

Barnett, G., Lee, M., Jiang, K., & Park, H. (2016). The flow of international students from a macro perspective: A network analysis. *Compare: A Journal of Comparative and International Education, 46*(4), 533–559. https://doi.org/10.1080/03057925.2015.1015965

Bartell, M. (2003). Internationalization of universities: A university culture-based framework. *Higher Education, 45*(1), 43–70. https://www.jstor.org/stable/3447513

Barton, G., Hartwig, K., Bennett, D., & Cain, M. (2017). Work placement for international student programmes (WISP): A model of effective practice. In G. Barton & K. Hartwig (Eds.), *Professional learning in the workplace for international students* (pp. 13–34). Springer.

Basiri, M. (2021, January 6). *ApplyInsights: Forecast for International Education in 2021*. ApplyBoard. https://www.applyboard.com/blog/applyinsights-forecast-for-international-education-in-2021

Battilana, J., Besharov, M., & Mitzinneck, B. (2017). On hybrids and hybrid organizing: A review and roadmap for future research. In R. Greenwood, C. Oliver, T. B. Lawrence, & R. E. Meyer (Ed.), *The SAGE handbook of organizational institutionalism, 2*, 133–169.

Battilana, J., & Lee, M. (2014). Advancing research on hybrid organizing—Insights from the study of social enterprises. *Academy of Management Annals, 8*(1), 397–441. https://doi.org/10.1080/19416520.2014.893615

Bedenlier, S., Kondakci, Y., & Zawacki-Richter, O. (2018). Two decades of research into the internationalization of higher education: Major themes in the *Journal of Studies in International Education* (1997–2016). *Journal of Studies in International Education, 22*(2), 108–135. https://doi.org/10.1177/1028315317710

Bengtsson, M., Eriksson, J., & Wincent, J. (2010). Co-opetition dynamics—An outline for further inquiry. *Competitiveness Review: An international business journal, 20*(2), 194–214. https://doi.org/10.1108/10595421011029893

Bengtsson, M., & Kock, S. (2014). Coopetition—Quo vadis? Past accomplishments and future challenges. *Industrial Marketing Management, 43*(2), 180–188. https://doi.org/10.1016/j.indmarman.2014.02.015

Bengtsson, M., & Kock, S. (2000). "Coopetition" in business networks—to cooperate and compete simultaneously. *Industrial Marketing Management, 29*(5), 411–426. https://doi.org/10.1016/S0019-8501(99)00067-X

Bengtsson, M., Kock, S., Lundgren-Henriksson, E., & Näsholm, M. (2016). Coopetition research in theory and practice: Growing new theoretical, empirical, and methodological domains. *Industrial Marketing Management, 57*, 4–11.

Bennett, K. (2009). English academic style manuals: A survey. *Journal of English for Academic Purposes, 8*(1), 43–54. https://doi.org/10.1016/j.jeap.2008.12.003

Benneworth, P., Culum, B., & Farnell, T. (2018). *Mapping and critical synthesis of current state-of-the-art on community engagement in higher education.* TEFCE. http://pascalobservatory.org/sites/default/files/scribd/tefce_publication-1.pdf

Bentil, N. L. (2019, April 8). *Africa: Vital to CEIBS' internationalisation strategy.* Graphic Online. https://www.graphic.com.gh/features/features/ghana-news-africa-vital-to-ceibs-internationalisation-strategy.html

Bess, J., & Dee, J. (2007). *Understanding college and university organization: Dynamics of the system.* Stylus Publishing, LLC.

Beugelsdijk, S., Kostova, T., Kunst, Spadafora, E., & Van Essen, M. (2018). Cultural distance and firm internationalization: A meta-analytical review and theoretical implications. *Journal of Management, 44*(1), 89–130. https://doi.org/10.1177/0149206317729027

Bickerstaff, G., & Wood, M. (2012). Lessons from China: John Quelch interview. *EFMD Global Focus, 6*(2), 8–11. https://issuu.com/efmd/docs/global_focus_vol_06_issue_02_online

Bird v. Lewis & Clark College, 303 F.3d 1015 (9th Cir. 2002).

Bird v. Lewis & Clark College, 538 U.S. 923 LEXIS 2217 (2003).

Blankenberger, B., & Williams, A. (2020). COVID and the impact on higher education: The essential role of integrity and accountability. *Administrative Theory & Praxis, 42*(3), 404–423.

Blumenthal, D., Causino, N., Campbell, E., & Louis, K. (1996). Relationships between academic institutions and industry in the life sciences—An industry survey. *New England Journal of Medicine, 334*(6), 368–374.

Boix Mansilla, V., & Jackson, A. (2013). Educating for global competence: Learning redefined for an interconnected world. In H. Jacobs (Ed.), *Mastering global literacy, contemporary perspectives.* Solution Tree.

Bok, D. (2020). *Higher expectations: Can colleges teach students what they need to know in the 21st century?* Princeton University Press.

Bolton, D., & Nie, R. (2010). Creating value in transnational higher education: The role of stakeholder management. *Academy of Management Learning & Education, 9*(4), 701–714. https://www.jstor.org/stable/25782058

Bordogna, C. (2018). Transnational higher education partnerships and the role of operational faculty members: Developing an alternative theoretical approach for empirical research. *Journal of Studies in International Education, 22*(1), 3–19. https://doi.org/10.1177/102831531772455

Bothwell, E. (2020, April 3). Most prospective overseas students 'not shifting plans.' *Times Higher Education.* https://www.timeshighereducation.com/news/most-prospective-overseas-students-notshifting-plans

Bound, J., Braga, B., Khanna, G., & Turner, S. (2021). The globalization of postsecondary education: The role of international students in the US higher education system. *Journal of Economic Perspectives, 35*(1), 163–184. https://doi.org/10.1257/jep.35.1.163

Bourgeault, I. L., Wrede, S., Benoit, C., & Neiterman, E. (2016). Professions and the migration of expert labour: Towards an intersectional analysis of transnational mobility patterns and integration pathways of health professionals.

In M. Dent, I. L. Bourgeault, J.-L. Denis, E. Kuhlmann (Eds.), *The Routledge companion to the professions and professionalism* (pp. 313–330). Routledge.

Bowell, T., Cowan, R., & Kemp, G. (2020). *Critical thinking: A concise guide* (5th ed.). Routledge.

Bradford, A. (2016). Toward a typology of implementation challenges facing English-medium instruction in higher education: Evidence from Japan. *Journal of Studies in International Education, 20*(4), 339–356. https://doi.org/10.1177/1028315316647165

Bradford, A. (2019). It's not all about English! The problem of language foregrounding in English-medium programmes in Japan. *Journal of Multilingual and Multicultural Development, 40*(8), 707–720. https://doi.org/10.1080/01434632.2018.1551402

Branch, J. D. (2017). *A praxiography of the transnationalization of the Stockholm school of economics* [Unpublished doctoral dissertation]. https://deepblue.lib.umich.edu/handle/2027.42/136151

Brandenburger, A., & Nalebuff, B. (2011). *Co-opetition.* Crown.

Bratianu, C., & Pinzaru, F. (2015, November 12–13). *University governance as a strategic driving force* [Paper presentation]. The European Conference on Management, Leadership, & Governance.

Brindley, E. (2011). Moral autonomy and individual sources of authority in the analects. *Journal of Chinese Philosophy, 38*(2), 257–273. https://doi.org/10.1111/j.1540-6253.2011.01648.x

Briston, R., & Kedslie, M. (1997). The internationalization of British professional accounting: The role of the examination exporting bodies. *Accounting, Business & Financial History, 7*(2), 175–194. https://doi.org/10.1080/095852097330702

British Council. (2015). *Bridging the gap: Enabling effective UK-Africa university partnerships.* British Council.

British Council. (2021). *Local impact of transnational education.* Retrieved from https://www.britishcouncil.org/sites/default/files/bc_tne_report_final_120421.pdf

Brotherhood, T., Hammond, C., & Kim, Y. (2020). Towards an actor-centered typology of internationalization: A study of junior international faculty in Japanese universities. *Higher Education, 79*(3), 497–514. https://doi.org/10.1007/s10734-019-00420-5

Brown, H. (2017). Why and why now? Understanding the rapid rise of English-medium instruction in higher education in Japan. *Journal of International Studies and Regional Development, 8*, 1–16. https://www.academia.edu/32208571/Why_and_Why_Now_Understanding_the_Rapid_Rise_of_English_medium_Instruction_in_Higher_Education_in_Japan

Brown, R. (2010). The march of the market. In M. Molesworth, R. Scullion, & E. Nixon (Eds.), *The marketization of higher education and the student as consumer* (pp. 25–38). Routledge.

Brown, S. (2021, May 13). Higher ed under Biden-Harris: Biden nominates former education dept. official known for aggressive Title IX enforcement. *The Chronicle of Higher Education.* https://www.chronicle.com/blogs/higher-ed-under-biden-harris/biden-nominates-education-dept-official-known-for-aggressive-title-ix-enforcement

Brown, W. (2003). Neo-liberalism and the end of liberal democracy. *Theory & Event, 7*(1), 37–59. https://doi.org/10.1353/tae.2003.0020

Brusca, I., Cohen, S., Manes-Rossi, F., & Nicolò, G. (2019). Intellectual capital disclosure and academic rankings in European universities: Do they go hand in hand? *Meditari Accountancy Research.*

Buckner, E. (2019). The internationalization of higher education: National interpretations of a global model. *Comparative Education Review, 63*(3), 315–336. https://doi.org/10.1086/703794

Buckner, E., Lumb, P., Jafarova, Z., Kang, P., Marroquin, A., & Zhang, Y. (2021). Diversity without race: How university internationalization strategies discuss international students. *Journal of International Students, 11*(S1), 32–49. https://doi.org/10.32674/jis.v11iS1.3842

Bull, B. K. (2017). Raped abroad: Extraterritorial application of Title IX for American university students sexually assaulted while studying abroad. *Northwestern University Law Review, 111*(2), 439–482.

Buncombe, A. (2010, August 4). Oldest university on earth is reborn after 800 years. *The Independent.* https://www.independent.co.uk/news/world/asia/oldest-university-on-earth-is-reborn-after-800-years-2042518.html

Burgess, C., Gibson, I., Klaphake, J., & Selzer, M. (2010). The 'Global 30' project and Japanese higher education reform: An example of a 'closing in' or an 'opening up'? *Globalisation, Societies and Education, 8*(4), 461–475. https://doi.org/10.1080/14767724.2010.537931

Butler, A. (2018, May 15). *Recent USC grad files lawsuit against university, professor following study abroad trip.* WACH Fox57. https://wach.com/news/local/recent-usc-grad-files-lawsuit-against-university-professor-following-study-abroad-trip

Byun, K., Chu, H., Kim, M., Park, I., Kim, S., & Jung, J. (2011). English-medium teaching in Korean higher education: Policy debates and reality. *Higher Education, 62*(4), 431–449. https://www.jstor.org/stable/41477877

Cajander, Å., Daniels, M., Peters, A., & McDermott, R. (2014, October 22–25). Critical thinking, peer-writing, and the importance of feedback. In *Proceedings of the IEEE frontiers in education conference (FIE 2014): Opening innovations and internationalization in engineering education*, Madrid, Spain. https://doi.org/10.1109/FIE.2014.7044234

Calma, A., & Davies, M. (2021). Critical thinking in business education: Current outlook and future prospects. *Studies in Higher Education, 46*(11), 2279–2295. https://doi.org/10.1080/03075079.2020.1716324

Campbell, A., Cameron, P., Klein, M., McCormack, C., & Wilson, K. (Eds.). (2000). *Proceedings of the offshore 2000 conference: Education and training in an elearning world: Boom or doom?* Centre for the Enhancement of Learning, Teaching, and Scholarship, University of Canberra.

Campbell, J. (2012). Higher educational reform values and the dilemmas of change: Challenging secular neo-liberalism. In H. Cuadra-Montiel (Ed.), *Globalization: Education and management agendas* (pp. 23–44). IntechOpen. https://doi.org/10.5772/45739

Cant, A. (2004). Internationalizing the business curriculum: Developing intercultural competence. *Journal of American Academy of Business & Economics, 5*(1/2), 177–182. http://www.jaabc.com/jaabcv5n2preview.html

Cantwell, B., & Lee, J. (2010). Unseen workers in the academic factory: Perceptions of neoracism among international postdocs in the United States and the United Kingdom. *Harvard Educational Review, 80*(4), 490–517. https://doi.org/10.17763/haer.80.4.w54750105q78p451

Cantwell, B., Luca, S., & Lee, J. (2009). Exploring the orientations of international students in Mexico: Differences by region of origin. *Higher Education, 57*(3), 335–354. https://www.jstor.org/stable/40269126

Carneiro, J., Rocha, A., & Silva, J. (2008). Challenging the Uppsala internationalization model: A contingent approach to the internationalization of services. *BAR-Brazilian Administration Review, 5*(2), 85–103. https://doi.org/10.1590/S1807-76922008000200002

Carrasco, M. (2022, January 20). *Study abroad programs resume after pandemic hiatus*. Inside Higher Ed. https://www.insidehighered.com/news/2022/01/20/students-venture-back-study-abroad-programs

Carù, A., & Cova, B. (2003). Revisiting consumption experience: A more humble but complete view of the concept. *Marketing Theory, 3*(2), 259–278. https://doi.org/10.1177/147059310300320

Çetinsaya, G. (2014). *Büyüme, kalite, uluslararasıla?ma: Türkiye yükseköğretimi için bir yol haritası* [Growth, quality, internalization: A roadmap for higher education in Turkey] (2nd ed.). Yükseköğretim Kurulu.

Chan, D., & Ng, P. (2008). Similar agendas, diverse strategies: The quest for a regional hub of higher education in Hong Kong and Singapore. *Higher Education Policy, 21*(4), 487–503. https://doi.org/10.1057/hep.2008.19

Charles, M. (2019). Effective teaching and learning: Decolonizing the curriculum. *Journal of Black Studies, 50*(8), 731–766. https://doi.org/10.1177/0021934719885631

CHEA. (2005). *Sharing quality higher education across borders: A statement on behalf of higher education institutions worldwide*. Retrieved from www.chea.org/pdf/StatementFinal0105.pdf.

Chen, P. (2015). Transnational education: Trend, modes of practices, and development. *International Journal of Information and Education Technology, 5*(8), 634–637. https://doi.org/10.7763/IJIET.2015.V5.582

Chen, T., & Barnett, G. (2000). Research on international student flows from a macro perspective: A network analysis of 1985, 1989, and 1995. *Higher Education, 39*(4), 435–453. https://doi.org/10.1023/A:1003961327009

Chen, Y., & Van Ullen, M. (2011). Helping international students succeed academically through research process and plagiarism workshops. *College & Research Libraries, 72*(3), 209–235. https://doi.org/10.5860/crl-117rl

Cheung, P. (2006). Filleting the transnational education steak. *Quality in Higher Education, 12*, 283–285.

Chien, H. (2016). Role of the public sector in agricultural coopetition: Place-based marketing in post-WTO rural Taiwan. *Journal of Management and Strategy, 7*(1), 65–80. https://doi.org/10.5430/jms.v7n1p65

Childress, H. (2019). *The adjunct underclass: How America's colleges betrayed their faculty, their students and their mission*. University of Chicago Press.

Chim-Miki, A., & Batista-Canino, R. (2017). Tourism coopetition: An introduction to the subject and a research agenda. *International Business Review, 26*(6), 1208–1217.

Chipchase, L., Davidson, M., Blackstock, F., Bye, R. Colthier, P. Krupp, N., Dickson, W., Turner, D., & Williams, M. (2017). Conceptualising and measuring student disengagement in higher education: A synthesis of the literature. *International Journal of Higher Education, 6*(2), 31–42. https://doi.org/10.5430/ijhe.v6n2p31

Chita-Tegmark, M., Gravel, J., Maria De Lourdes, B., Domings, Y., & Rose, D. (2012). Using the universal design for learning framework to support culturally diverse learners. *Journal of Education, 192*(1), 17–22. https://eric.ed.gov/?id=EJ1054593

Cho, J., & Yu, H. (2015). Roles of university support for international students in the United States: Analysis of a systematic model of university identification, university support, and psychological well-being. Journal of Studies in International Education, 19(1), 11–27. https://doi.org/10.1177/1028315314533606

Choudaha, R. (2020). Addressing the affordability crisis for international students. *Journal of International Students, 10*(2), iii–v. https://doi.org/10.32674/jis.v10i2.1969

Chowdhury, A., & Rahman, Z. (2021, March 31). Global ranking framework & indicators of higher educational institutions: A comparative study. *Library Philosophy and Practice* (e-journal), 5268. https://digitalcommons.unl.edu/libphilprac/5268

Chronicle of Higher Education. (2021). *Title IX: Tracking sexual assault investigations.* Retrieved from https://projects.chronicle.com/titleix/.

Clyne, M. (2004). Toward an agenda for developing multilingual communication with a community base. In J. House & J. Rehbein (Eds.), *Multilingual Communication* (pp. 19–39). https://doi.org/10.1075/hsm.3.02cly

Coelen, R., & Gribble, C. (Eds.). (2019). *Internationalization and employability in higher education*. Routledge.

Coelho, A., & Braga, A. (2016). Organization communication: A critical discourse analysis of the inter-institutional agreement for academic international cooperation. *The ESPecialist, 37*(2). https://revistas.pucsp.br/index.php/esp/article/view/20380

Collingridge, D. (1999). Suggestions on teaching international students: Advice for psychology instructors. *Teaching of Psychology, 26*(2), 126–128. https://doi.org/10.1207/s15328023top2602_11

Coleman, D. (2003). Quality assurance in transnational education. *Journal of Studies in International Education, 7*(4), 354–378. https://doi.org/10.1177/1028315303255597

Collins, F. (2012). Organizing student mobility: Education agents and student migration to New Zealand. *Pacific Affairs, 85*(1), 137–160. https://doi.org/10.5509/2012851137

Committee to Strengthen the Accountancy Profession. (2014). *Report on the strengthening of the accountancy profession in Malaysia*. Securities Commission of Malaysia.

Competition & Markets Authority. (2015, June 24). *Competition and regulation in higher education in England*. Gov.UK. https://www.gov.uk/cma-cases/competition-and-regulation-in-higher-education-in-england

Cottrell, S. (2017). *Critical thinking skills: Effective analysis, argument and reflection* (3rd ed.). Bloomsbury Publishing.

Council of Europe & UNESCO Lisbon Recognition Convention. (2007). *Revised code of good practice in the provision of transnational education*. https://www.enic-naric.net/fileusers/REVISED_CODE_OF_GOOD_PRACTICE_TNE.pdf

Cousin, G., & Cureton, D. (2012). *Disparities in student attainment (DiSA): The university of Wolverhampton final report*. The Higher Education Academy. https://wlv.openrepository.com/handle/2436/621968

CPA Australia. (2015). *Leading the accounting profession into tomorrow: CPA Australia 2015 integrated report*. https://www.cpaaustralia.com.au/-/media/project/cpa/corporate/documents/about-cpa/our-organisation/annual-report/annual-report-2015.pdf?rev=9656150ecf624dbbbc25adfeea3ee084

Cross, J. G., & Goldenberg, E. N. (2009). *Off-track profs: Nontenured teachers in higher education*. MIT Press.

Cross-Border Education Research Team. (2017). *Fast Facts*. http://cbert.org/

Cubillo, J., Sánchez, J., & Cerviño, J. (2006). International students' decision-making process. *International Journal of Educational Management, 20*(2), 101–115. https://doi.org/10.1108/09513540610646091

Cudmore, G. (2005). Globalization, internationalization, and the recruitment of international students in higher education, and in the Ontario Colleges of Applied Arts and Technology. *The Canadian Journal of Higher Education, 35*(1), 37–60. https://doi.org/10.47678/cjhe.v35i1.183491

Cureton, D., & Gravestock, P. (2019). We belong: Differential sense of belonging and its meaning for different ethnicity groups in higher education. *Compass: Journal of Learning and Teaching, 12*(1). https://doi.org/10.21100/compass.v12i1.942

Curran, P., Lee, T., Howard, A., et al. (2012). Disaggregating within-person and between-person effects in multilevel and structural equation growth models. In J. Harring & G. Hancock (Eds.), *Advances in longitudinal methods in the social and behavioral sciences* (pp. 217–253). Information Age Publishing.

Currie, J., & Newson, J. (1998). *Universities and globalization: Critical perspectives*. SAGE Publications.

Currie, J., DeAngelis, R., Boer, H., & De Boer, H. (2003). *Globalizing practices and university responses: European and Anglo-American differences*. Greenwood Publishing Group.

Cuypers, S. (2004). Critical thinking, autonomy, and practical reason. *Journal of philosophy of education, 38*(1), 75–90. https://doi.org/10.1111/j.0309-8249.2004.00364.x

Dagen, T., Doušak, M., Fink-Hafner, D., Hafner-Fink, M., & Novak, M. (2019). Defining internationalisation, globalisation and europeanisation in higher education. *Teorija in praksa, 56*(2), 643–659. https://www.fdv.uni-lj.si/docs/default-source/tip/tip_02_2019_dagen_idr.pdf?sfvrsn=0

Dagnino, G. B., & Padula, G. (2002). *Coopetition strategy: A new kind of interfirm dynamics for value creation*. Paper presented at the second annual European

Institute for Advanced Studies in Management (EIASM) conference "Innovative Research in Management," Stockholm, May 9–11.

Dagnino, G., & Rocco, E. (Eds.). (2009). *Coopetition strategy: Theory, experiments and cases*. Routledge.

Dahl, J., Kock, S., & Lundgren-Henriksson, E-L. (2016). Conceptualizing coopetition strategy as practice: A multilevel interpretative framework. *International Studies of Management & Organization, 46*(2–3), 94–109. https://doi.org/10.1080/00208825.2015.1093794

Dai, H. (2019). Performance of universities in the United States of America. *International Journal of Information and Education Technology, 9*(6). http://www.ijiet.org/vol9/1235-M0801.pdf

Dalpiaz, E., Rindova, V., & Ravasi, D. (2016). Combining logics to transform organizational agency: Blending industry and art at Alessi. *Administrative Science Quarterly, 61*(3), 347–392. https://doi.org/10.1177/0001839216636103

Dal-Soto, F., & Monticelli, J. (2017). Coopetition strategies in the Brazilian higher education. *Revista de Administração de Empresas, 57*(1), 65–78. https://doi.org/10.1590/S0034-759020170106

Daly, H. (1999). Globalization versus internationalization implications. *Ecological Economics, 31*(1), 31–37.

Dalton, E. M., Lyner-Cleophas, M., Ferguson, B. T., & McKenzie, J. (2019). Inclusion, universal design and universal design for learning in higher education: South Africa and the United States. *African Journal of Disability, 8*(1), 1–7. https://doi.org/10.4102/ajod.v8i0.519

Danvers, E. (2021). Individualised and instrumentalised? Critical thinking, students and the optics of possibility within neoliberal higher education. *Critical Studies in Education, 62*(5), 641–656. https://doi.org/10.1080/17508487.2019.1592003

Davie, S. (2020, June 24). NTU ranked world's top young university for seventh year running. *The Straits Times*. https://www.straitstimes.com/singapore/education/ntu-ranked-worlds-top-young-university-for-seventh-year-running

Davies, B., & Bansel, P. (2007). Neoliberalism and education. *International Journal of Qualitative Studies in Education, 20*, 247–259. https://doi.org/10.1080/09518390701281751

Davies, S., & Zarifa, D. (2012). The stratification of universities: Structural inequality in Canada and the United States. *Research in Social Stratification and Mobility, 30*(2), 143–158. https://doi.org/10.1016/j.rssm.2011.05.003

Day, T., Chang, I., Chung, C., Doolittle, W., Housel, J., & McDaniel, P. (2021). The immediate impact of COVID-19 on postsecondary teaching and learning. *The Professional Geographer, 73*(1), 1–13. https://doi.org/10.1080/00330124.2020.1823864

de Sousa Santos, B. (2020). Decolonizing the university. In B. de Sousa Santos & M. Meneses (Eds.), *Knowledges born in the struggle: Chacha-warmi: Another form of gender equality, from the perspective of Aymara culture* (pp. 219–240). Routledge.

De Freitas, G. (1992). Malaysian accountancy: Waking the sleeping tiger. *Certified Accountant*, June, 12–15.

De Ngo, D., & Okura, M. (2008). Coopetition in a mixed duopoly market. *Economics Bulletin, 12*(20), 1–9. http://hdl.handle.net/10069/20724

de Ridder-Symoens, H. (1992). Mobility. In H. de Ridder-Symoens (Ed.), *A history of the university in Europe* (pp. 280–304). Cambridge University Press.

De Vita, G., & Case, P. (2003). Rethinking the internationalisation agenda in UK higher education. *Journal of Further and Higher Education, 27*(4), 383–398. https://doi.org/10.1080/0309877032000128082

de Wit, H. (2002). *Internationalization of higher education in the United States of America and Europe: A historical, comparative, and conceptual analysis*. Greenwood Publishing Group.

de Wit, H. (2013). *An introduction to higher education internationalisation*. Vita e Pensiero.

de Wit, H. (2017). Internationalization of higher education, historical perspective. In J. D. Shin & P. N. Teixeira (Eds.), *Encyclopedia of international higher education systems and institutions* (pp. 1–4). Springer.

de Wit, H. (2018). Internationalization in higher education, a critical review. *SFU Educational Review, 12*(3), 9–17. https://doi.org/10.21810/sfuer.v12i3.1036

de Wit, H. (2019). Internationalization in higher education: A critical review. *SFU Educational Review, 12*(3), 9–17. https://doi.org/10.21810/sfuer.v12i3.1036

de Wit, H. (2020). Internationalization of higher education: The need for a more ethical and qualitative approach. *Journal of International Students, 10*(1), i–iv. https://doi.org/10.32674/jis.v10i1.1893

de Wit, H., & Altbach, P. (2021). Internalisation in higher education: Global trends and recommendations for its future. *Policy Reviews in Higher Education, 5*(1), 28–46. https://doi.org/10.1080/23322969.2020.1820898

de Wit, H., & Deca, L. (2020). Internationalization of higher education, challenges and opportunities for the next decade. In A. Curaj, L. Deca, & R. Pricopie (Eds.), *European Higher Education Area: Challenges for a New Decade* (pp. 3–11). Springer.

de Wit, H., Hunter F., Howard L., & Egron-Polak E. (Eds.) (2015). *Internationalisation of higher education*. European Parliament, Brussels.

de Wit, H., & Merkx, G. (2012). The history of internationalization of higher education. In *The SAGE handbook of international higher education* (pp. 43–59). SAGE Publications. https://dx.doi.org/10.4135/9781452218397.n3

Dearden, J., Grewal, R., & Lilien, G. (2019). Strategic manipulation of university rankings, the prestige effect, and student university choice. *Journal of Marketing Research, 56*(4), 691–707. https://doi.org/10.1177/0022243719831258

Deem, R. (2001). Globalisation, new managerialism, academic capitalism and entrepreneurialism in universities: Is the local dimension still important? *Comparative Education, 37*(1), 7–20. https://www.jstor.org/stable/3099730

Delamain, C., & Spring, J. (2021). *Teaching critical thinking skills: An introduction for children aged 9–12*. Routledge.

Delgado-Márquez, B., Escudero-Torres, M., & Hurtado-Torres, N. (2013). Being highly internationalised strengthens your reputation: An empirical investigation of top higher education institutions. *Higher Education, 66*(5), 619–633.

Delgado-Márquez, B., Hurtado-Torres, N., & Bondar, Y. (2011). Internationalization of higher education: Theoretical and empirical investigation of its influence on university institution rankings. *International Journal of Educational*

Technology in Higher Education, 8(2), 265–284. https://doi.org/10.7238/rusc.v8i2.1069
Dimmock, C., & Tan, C. (2013). Educational leadership in Singapore: Tight coupling, sustainability, scalability, and succession. Journal of Educational Administration, 51(3), 320–340. http://dx.doi.org/10.1108/09578231311311492
Dirlik, A. (2012). Transnationalization and the university: The perspective of global modernity. Boundary 2, 39(3), 47–73. https://doi.org/10.1215/01903659-1730617
Doe v. Rhode Island School of Design, 516 F. Supp. 3d 188 (D.R.I. 2021)
Dolby, N., & Rahman, A. (2008). Research in international education. Review of Educational Research, 78(3), 676–726. https://doi.org/10.3102/0034654308320291
Dudden, A. (2020). Matthew Perry in Japan, 1852–1854. In S. Haggard & D. Kang (Eds.), East Asia in the world: Twelve events that shaped the modern international order (pp. 188–205). Cambridge University Press.
Duke, B. C. (2009). The history of modern Japanese education: Constructing the national school system, 1872–1890. Rutgers University Press.
Dunavant v. University of South Carolina (2018). Retrieved from https://www.scribd.com/document/379353517/ALLISON-DUNAVANT-V-USC?secret_password=Ndim8f7SWtuFE7UYxhqX#from_embed
Dunn, L., & Wallace, M. (2004). Australian academics teaching in Singapore: Striving for cultural empathy. Innovations in education and teaching international, 41(3), 291–304. https://doi.org/10.1080/14703290410001733285
Dunn, L., & Wallace, M. (2006). Australian academics and transnational teaching: An exploratory study of their preparedness and experiences. Higher Education Research & Development, 25(4), 357–369. https://doi.org/10.1080/07294360600947343
Dunn, M., & Jones, C. (2010). Institutional logics and institutional pluralism: The contestation of care and science logics in medical education, 1967–2005. Administrative Science Quarterly, 55(1), 114–149. https://doi.org/10.2189/asqu.2010.55.1.114
Earley, P., & Ang, S. (2003). Cultural intelligence: Individual interactions across cultures. Stanford University Press.
Easler, S. (2019). A litigation analysis of the extraterritoriality of US federal laws in international education [Doctoral dissertation, University of South Carolina]. https://scholarcommons.sc.edu/etd/5121/
Eaton, J. (2012). Toward internationalizing quality assurance. AUDEM: The International Journal of Higher Education and Democracy, 3(1), 55–70. https://www.muse.jhu.edu/article/500243
Edelman, L. (1992). Legal ambiguity and symbolic structures: Organizational mediation of civil rights law. American Journal of Sociology, 97(6), 1531–1576.
Education New Zealand. (2016). New Zealand international education snapshot: 2015 full year report. https://enz.govt.nz/assets/Uploads/Final-January-August-2015-snapshot.pdf
Education New Zealand. (2018). Beyond the economic—How international education delivers broad value for New Zealand. http://www.researchnz.com/pdf/Media%20Releases/2018/Beyond-the-economic-How-international-education-delivers-broad-value-for-New-Zealand.pdf

Edwards, J. (2007). Challenges and opportunities for the internationalization of higher education in the coming decade: Planned and opportunistic initiatives in American institutions. *Journal of Studies in International Education, 11*(3–4), 373–381.

Edwards, S. (2015). The case in favor of OCR's tougher Title IX policies: Pushing back against the pushback. *Duke Journal of Gender Law & Policy, 23*, 121–144. https://scholarship.law.duke.edu/djglp/vol23/iss1/5

Egege, S., & Kutieleh, S. (2004). Critical thinking: Teaching foreign notions to foreign students. *International Education Journal, 4*(4), 75–85. https://files.eric.ed.gov/fulltext/EJ903810.pdf

Elken, M. (2017). Standardization of (higher) education in Europe – Policy coordination 2.0? *Policy and Society, 36*(1), 127–142. https://doi.org/10.1080/14494035.2017.1278873

Enders, J. (2004). Higher education, internationalisation, and the nation-state: Recent developments and challenges to governance theory. *Higher education, 47*(3), 361–382. https://doi.org/10.1023/B:HIGH.0000016461.98676.30

Engwall, L., Kipping, M., & Üsdiken, B. (2016). *Defining management: Business schools, consultants, media* (1st ed.). Routledge. https://doi.org/10.4324/9781315851921

Eriksson, P. (2008a). Achieving suitable coopetition in buyer–supplier relationships: The case of AstraZeneca. *Journal of Business-to-Business Marketing, 15*(4), 425–454. https://doi.org/10.1080/15470620802325674

Eriksson, P. (2008b). Procurement effects on coopetition in client-contractor relationships. *Journal of construction Engineering and Management, 134*(2), 103–111. https://doi.org/10.1061/(ASCE)0733-9364(2008)134:2(103)

Estermann, T., Pruvot, E., & Stoyanova, H. (2021). *The governance models of the European University Alliances: Evolving models of university governance I. Briefing.* European University Association.

Fakunle, L., Allison, P., & Fordyce, K. (2016). Chinese postgraduate students' perspectives on developing critical thinking on a UK education masters. *Journal of Curriculum and Teaching, 5*(1), 27–38. https://eric.ed.gov/?id=EJ1157530

Faulconbridge, J., & Muzio, D. (2012). The rescaling of the professions: Towards a transnational sociology of the professions. *International Sociology, 27*(1), 109–125. https://doi.org/10.2139/ssrn.2074125

Fell, E. V., & Lukianova, N. A. (2015). British universities: International students' alleged lack of critical thinking. *Procedia-Social and Behavioral Sciences, 215*, 2–8. https://doi.org/10.1016/J.SBSPRO.2015.11.565

Ferlie, E., Musselin, C., & Andresani, G. (2008). The steering of higher education systems: A public management perspective. *Higher Education, 56*(3), 325–348. https://www.jstor.org/stable/40269080

Ficarra, F., Ficarra, V., & Ficarra, M. (2011). New technologies of the information and communication: Analysis of the constructors and destructors of the European educational system. In F. Ficarra, C. Lozano, & M. Jimenez (Eds.), *International conference on advances in new technologies, interactive interfaces, and communicability* (pp. 71–84). Springer.

Fiss, P.C., Cambré, B., & Marx, A. (2013). Configurational theory and methods in organizational research. *Research in the Sociology of Organizations, 38*, 1–22.

Fischer, K. (2010, May 26). Study-abroad missteps remind colleges of need to train trip leaders. *The Chronicle of Higher Education.* chronicle.com/article/study-abroad-missteps-remind-colleges-of-need-to-train-trip-leaders/

Flammia, M., Sadri, H., & Mejia, C. (2019). An internalization project to develop global competency across the disciplines. International Journal of Teaching and Learning in Higher Education, *31*(2), 332–345. https://files.eric.ed.gov/fulltext/EJ1224379.pdf

Fleet, C., & Kondrashov, O. (2019). Universal design on university campuses: A literature review. *Exceptionality Education International, 29*(1), 136–148. https://eric.ed.gov/?q=source%3A%22Exceptionality+Education+International%22&id=EJ1225650

Fligstein, N. (2010). Politics, the reorganization of the economy, and income inequality, 1980–2009. *Politics & Society, 38*(2), 233–242. https://doi.org/10.1177/0032329210365047

Flores, K., Matkin, G., Burbach, M., Quinn, C., & Harding, H. (2012). Deficient critical thinking skills among college graduates: Implications for leadership. *Educational Philosophy and Theory, 44*(2), 212–230. https://doi.org/10.1111/j.1469-5812.2010.00672.x

Floyd, C. (2011). Critical thinking in a second language. *Higher Education Research & Development, 30*(3), 289–302. https://doi.org/10.1080/07294360.2010.501076

Fornauf, B., & Erickson, J. (2020). Toward an inclusive pedagogy through universal design for learning in higher education: A review of the literature. *Journal of Postsecondary Education and Disability, 33*(2), 183–199.

Forstorp, P., & Mellström, U. (2018). *Higher education, globalization and eduscapes: Towards a critical anthropology of a global knowledge society.* Springer.

Fovet, F. (2014, April 30–May 1). Social model as catalyst for innovation in design and pedagogical change. In *Widening Participation Through Curriculum Open University 2014 Conference Proceedings* (pp. 135–139). Milton Keynes, United Kingdom.

Fovet, F. (2018). Making do with what we have: Using the built in functions of a learning management system to implement UDL. *The Ahead Journal: A Review of Inclusive Education & Employment Practices,* 7. https://www.ahead.ie/journal/Making-do-with-what-we-have-using-the-built-in-functions-of-a-Learning-Management-System-to-implement-UDL

Fovet, F. (2019). Not just about disability: Getting traction for UDL implementation with International Students. In S. Bracken & K. Novak (Eds.), *Transforming Higher Education Through Universal Design for Learning* (pp. 179–200). Routledge.

Fovet, F. (2020a). Beyond novelty: "Innovative" accessible teaching as a return to fundamental questions around social justice and reflective pedagogy. In S. Palahicky (Ed.), *Enhancing learning design for innovative teaching in higher education* (pp. 22–42). IGI Global.

Fovet, F. (2020b). Universal design for learning as a tool for inclusion in the higher education classroom: Tips for the next decade of implementation. *Education Journal, 9*(6), 163–172. https://doi.org/10.11648/j.edu.20200906.13

Fovet, F. (2021a). Developing an ecological approach to the strategic implementation of UDL in higher education. *Journal of Education and Learning, 10*(4), 27–39. https://doi.org/10.5539/jel.v10n4p27

Fovet, F. (2021b, April). Embracing equity in a public health emergency: The role of UDL in guiding instructors as they adapt to an unprecedented reliance on online and hybrid teaching [Paper presentation]. *AHEAD Conference 2021, Reconnection—Placing inclusion at the heart of online learning and support* [online].

Freeman, K., & Li, M. (2019). We are a ghost in the class: First year international students' experiences in the Global Contact Zone. *Journal of International Students, 9*(1), 19–38. https://doi.org/10.32674/jis.v9i1.270

Freeman, R. (1984). *Strategic management: A stakeholder theory.* Pitman.

Freudenreich, B., Lüdeke-Freund, F., & Schaltegger, S. (2020). A stakeholder theory perspective on business models: Value creation for sustainability. *Journal of Business Ethics, 166*(1), 3–18. https://doi.org/10.1007/s10551-019-04112-z

Friga, P. (2020, April 20). Under COVID-19, University Budgets Like We've Never Seen Before. *The Chronicle of Higher Education.* chronicle.com/article/under-covid-19-university-budgets-like-weve-never-seen-before/

Furedi, F. (2010). Introduction to the marketisation of higher education and the student as consumer. In M. Molesworth, R. Scullion, & E. Nixon (Eds.), *The marketisation of higher education and the student as consumer* (pp. 15–22). Routledge.

Gacel-Avila, J. (2005). The internationalisation of higher education: A paradigm for global citizenry. *Journal of Studies in International Education, 9*(2), 121–136. https://doi.org/10.1177/1028315304263795

Garcia, C., & Velasco, C. (2002, May 9–11). Co-opetition and performance: Evidence from European biotechnology industry [Paper presentation]. *Second European Academy of Management Annual Conference*, Stockholm. https://www.sciencedirect.com/science/article/abs/pii/S0166497203000609

Garrett, R., Kinser, K., Lane, J., & Merola, R. (2017). *International branch campuses: Success factors of mature IBCs, 2017.* Observatory on Borderless Higher Education and Cross-Border Education Research Team.

Garrett, R., & Verbik, L. (2004a). *Transnational delivery by UK Higher Education, Part 1: Data and missing data.* The Observatory on Borderless Higher Education. https://www.obhe.org/resources?sort=date%3Adesc&q=transnational&from=&to=&tags=&page=1

Garrett, R., & Verbik, L. (2004b). *Transnational delivery by UK higher education, Part 1: Innovation & competitive advantage.* Observatory on borderless higher education. https://www.obhe.org/resources?sort=date%3Adesc&q=transnational&from=&to=&tags=&page=1

Garten, J. (2006, December 9). Really old school. *New York Times.* http://spinup-000d1a-wp-offload-media.s3.amazonaws.com/faculty/wp-content/uploads/sites/31/2019/06/2006-12-NYT-Really-Old-School.pdf

Gelb, C. (2012). Cultural issues in the higher education classroom. *Inquiries Journal, 4*(7), 1–3. http://www.inquiriesjournal.com/articles/661/cultural-issues-in-the-higher-education-classroom

Gendron, Y., & Barrett, M. (2004). Professionalization in action: Accountants' attempt at building a network of support for the WebTrust Seal of Assurance.

Contemporary Accounting Research, 21(3), 563–602. https://doi.org/10.1506/H1C0-EU27-UU2K-8EC8

Gentile, C., Spiller, N., & Noci, G. (2007). How to sustain the customer experience: An overview of experience components that co-create value with the customer. *European Management Journal, 25*(5), 395–410. https://doi.org/10.1016/j.emj.2007.08.005

Georgallis, P., & Lee, B. (2020). Toward a theory of entry in moral markets: The role of social movements and organizational identity. *Strategic Organization, 18*(1), 50–74. https://doi.org/10.1177/1476127019827472

Ghemawat, P. (2001). Distance still matters: The hard reality of global expansion. *Harvard Business Review, 79*(8), 137–147.

Ghemawat, P. (2007). *Redefining global strategy: Crossing borders in a world where differences still matter.* Harvard Business Press.

Ghemawat, P. (2008). The globalization of business education: Through the lens of semiglobalization. *Journal of Management Development, 27*(4), 391–414. https://doi.org/10.1108/02621710810866741

Gibson, I. (2011). Nationalistic tendencies and tensions within the Japanese educational system. *Ritsumeikan Annual Review of International Studies, 10,* 95–119.

Gill, A. (2009). Digitizing the past: Charting new courses in the modeling of virtual landscapes. *Visual Resources, 25*(4), 313–332. https://doi.org/10.1080/01973760903331809

Gill, M. (2014). The possibilities of phenomenology for organizational research. *Organizational Research Methods, 17*(2), 118–137. https://doi.org/10.1177/1094428113518348

Gioia, D., Patvardhan, S., Hamilton, A., & Corley, K. (2013). Organizational identity formation and change. *Academy of Management Annals, 7*(1), 123–193. https://doi.org/10.1080/19416520.2013.762225

Glaser, B., & Strauss, A. (2017). *The discovery of grounded theory: Strategies for qualitative research.* Aldine. (Original work published 1967)

Glass, C., Godwin, K., & Helms, R. (2021). *Toward greater inclusion and success: A new compact for international students.* American Council on Education.

Glass, C., Gómez, E., & Urzua, A. (2014). Recreation, intercultural friendship, and international students' adaptation to college by region of origin. *International Journal of Intercultural Relations, 42,* 104–117. https://doi.org/10.1016/j.ijintrel.2014.05.007

Glass, C., Kociolek, E., Wongtrirat, R., Lynch, R. J., & Cong, S. (2015). Uneven experiences: The impact of student–faculty interactions on international students' sense of belonging. *Journal of International Students, 5*(4), 353–367. https://doi.org/10.32674/jis.v5i4.400

Global Citizenship Education. (n.d.). Maastricht University. https://www.maastrichtuniversity.nl/global-citizenship-education/global-citizenship-education

Glynn, M. (2000). When cymbals become symbols: Conflict over organizational identity within a symphony orchestra. *Organization Science, 11*(3), 285–298. https://doi.org/10.1287/orsc.11.3.285.12496

Goering, S. (2015). Rethinking disability: The social model of disability and chronic disease. *Current Reviews in Musculoskeletal Medicine, 8*(2), 134–138. https://doi.org/10.1007/s12178-015-9273-z

Golden, P. (2011). *Central Asia in world history*. Oxford University Press.
Goldenberg, E., & Cross, J. (2011). *Off-track profs: Nontenured teachers in higher education*. MIT Press.
Golding, C. (2011). Educating for critical thinking: Thought-encouraging questions in a community of inquiry. *Higher Education Research & Development, 30*(3), 357–370. https://doi.org/10.1080/07294360.2010.499144
Goodman, J., & Grosvenor, I. (2009). Educational research—History of education a curious case? *Oxford Review of Education, 35*(5), 601–616. https://doi.org/10.1080/03054980903216325
Goodman, R. (2010) The rapid redrawing of boundaries in Japanese higher education. *Japan Forum,* (22)1–2, 65–87. https://doi.org/10.1080/09555803.2010.488944
Goodman, R., & Oka, C. (2018). The invention, gaming, and persistence of the hensachi ('standardised rank score') in Japanese education. *Oxford Review of Education, 44*(5), 581–598. https://doi.org/10.1080/03054985.2018.1492375
Goodrick, E., & Salancik, G. (1996). Organizational discretion in responding to institutional practices: Hospitals and cesarean births. *Administrative Science Quarterly,* 1–28. https://doi.org/10.2307/2393984
Goodwin, K., & Mbah, M. (2019). Enhancing the work placement experience of international students: towards a support framework. *Journal of Further and Higher Education, 43*(4), 521–532. https://doi.org/10.1080/0309877X.2017.1377163
Graham, G. (1999). *The Internet: A philosophical inquiry*. Routledge.
Greckhamer, T., Furnari, S., Fiss, P., & Aguilera, R. (2018). Studying configurations with qualitative comparative analysis: Best practices in strategy and organization research. *Strategic Organization, 16*(4), 482–495.
Green, H. (2016). Top global soft power? Japanese higher education and foreign policy goals. *Toyo University Repository for Academic Resources, 60*(1), 89–101. https://toyo.repo.nii.ac.jp/?action=repository_action_common_download&item_id=8496&item_no=1&attribute_id=22&file_no=1
Greenwood, R., Raynard, M., Kodeih, F., Micelotta, E. R., & Lounsbury, M. (2011). Institutional complexity and organizational responses. *Academy of Management Annals, 5*(1), 317–371. https://doi.org/10.5465/19416520.2011.590299
Grönroos, C., & Ravald, A. (2011). Service as business logic: Implications for value creation and marketing. *Journal of Service Management, 22*(1), 5–22. https://doi.org/10.1108/09564231111106893
Group of Eight Australia. (2014). *International students in higher education and their role in the Australian economy*. http://hdl.voced.edu.au/10707/301736
Guilhon, A. (2015). SKEMA: The story of a merger. *EFMD Global Focus, 9*(3), 46–49. https://globalfocusmagazine.com/wp-content/uploads/2015/10/Issue__3_2015_SKEMA.pdf
Gunnarsson, J., Kulesza, W., & Pettersson, A. (2014). Teaching international students how to avoid plagiarism: Librarians and faculty in collaboration. *The Journal of Academic Librarianship, 40*(3–4), 413–417. https://doi.org/10.1016/j.acalib.2014.04.006
Guo, Y., & Guo, S. (2017). Internationalization of Canadian higher education: Discrepancies between policies and international student experiences. *Studies in*

Higher Education, 42(5), 851–868. https://doi.org/10.1080/03075079.2017.1293874

Guri-Rosenblit, S. (2015). Internationalization of higher education: Navigating between contrasting trends. In A. Curai, J. Salmi, L. Matei, L., et al. (Eds.), *The European higher education area* (pp. 13–26). Springer.

Hacker, J., & Pierson, P. (2010). Winner-take-all politics: Public policy, political organization, and the precipitous rise of top incomes in the United States. *Politics & Society, 38*(2), 152–204. https://doi.org/10.1177/0032329210365042

Haddad, M. (2017, May 9). Victims of rape and law: How the laws of the Arab world protect rapists, not victims. *Jurist: Legal News & Commentary*. https://www.jurist.org/commentary/2017/05/mais-haddad-arab-world-laws-protect-the-rapist-not-the-victim/

Haigh, M. (2014). From internationalisation to education for global citizenship: A multi-layered history. *Higher Education Quarterly, 68*(1), 6–27. https://doi.org/10.1111/hequ.12032

Hall, E. (1989). *Beyond culture*. Anchor Books.

Hamill, N. (2012). *Legal issues & study abroad*. OSAC College & University Health, Safety, and Security Seminar, Santa Barbara, CA.

Hammersley-Fletcher, L., & Hanley, C. (2016). The use of critical thinking in higher education in relation to the international student: Shifting policy and practice. *British Educational Research Journal, 42*(6), 978–992. https://doi.org/10.1002/berj.3246

Hammerstein, N. (1996). The enlightenment. In H. de Ridder-Symoens & W. Ruegg (Eds.), *A history of the university in Europe* (pp. 436–439). Cambridge University Press.

Hammond, C. (2016). Internationalization, nationalism, and global competitiveness: A comparison of approaches to higher education in China and Japan. *Asia Pacific Education Review, 17*(4), 555–566. https://doi.org/10.1007/s12564-016-9459-0

Han, H., & Zhang, L. (2021). Critical pedagogy in Hong Kong: Classroom stories of struggle and hope. *Journal of International Students, 11*(1), 274–277. https://doi.org/10.32674/jis.v11i1.3258

Han, X., & Appelbaum, R. (2018). China's science, technology, engineering, and mathematics (STEM) research environment: A snapshot. *PloS One, 13*(4), Article e0195347. https://doi.org/10.1371/journal.pone.0195347

Harbi v. Massachusetts Institute of Technology et al. (2017). United States District Court, District of Massachusetts. https://www.plainsite.org/dockets/download.html?id=246494636&z=dcdb6629

Harder, A., Andenoro, A., Roberts, T. G., Stedman, N., Newberry III, M., Parker, S. J., & Rodriguez, M. T. (2015). Does study abroad increase employability? *NACTA Journal, 59*(1), 41–48. https://www.nactateachers.org/index.php/vol-59-1-mar-2015/2266-does-study-abroad-increase-employability

Harris, S. (2008). Internationalising the university. *Educational Philosophy and Theory, 40*, 346–357. https://doi.org/10.1111/j.1469-5812.2007.00336.x

Harvard Business Review. (2014). *Lessons from the leading edge of customer experience management* [A report by Harvard Business Review Analytic Service]. https://www

.sas.com/content/dam/SAS/en_us/doc/whitepaper2/hbr-leading-edge-customer-experience-mgmt-107061.pdf

Haslet, A. (2020, November 5). *Survival-lessons learned through movement and healing*. [Keynote speech at APTA National Student Conclave 2020]. American Physical Therapy Association. https://apta.confex.com/apta/nsc2020/meetingapp.cgi/Session/10043

Hawawini, G. (2017, April 28). Outward internationalisation in action at INSEAD. *University World News*. https://www.universityworldnews.com/post.php?story=20170411174847366

Hayes, S. (2019). *The labour of words in higher education: Is it time to reoccupy policy?* Brill. https://doi.org/10.1163/9789004395374

Hazelkorn, E. (2015). *Rankings and the reshaping of higher education: The battle for world-class excellence*. Springer.

Healey, N. (2015). Towards a risk-based typology for transnational education. *Higher Education, 69*(1), 1–18. https://doi.org/10.1007/s10734-014-9757-6

Healey, N., & Bordogna, C. (2014). From transnational to *multinational* education: Emerging trends in international higher education. *Internationalisation of Higher Education, 3*, 33–56. https://www.researchgate.net/publication/297758065_From_transnational_to_multinational_education_emerging_trends_in_international_higher_education

Hebel, S. (2001, December 14). Advocates for students with disabilities concerned about decision in study-abroad case. *The Chronicle of Higher Education*. https://www.chronicle.com/article/Advocates-for-Students-With/109704

Heffernan, T., & Poole, D. (2004). "Catch me I'm falling": Key factors in the deterioration of offshore education partnerships. *Journal of Higher Education Policy and Management, 26*(1), 75–90. https://doi.org/10.1080/1360080042000182546

HE Global. (2016). *The scale and scope of UK higher education transnational education*. British Council. https://www.britishcouncil.org/sites/default/files/scale-and-scope-of-uk-he-tne-report.pdf

Helkkula, A. (2011). Characterising the concept of service experience. *Journal of Service Management, 22*(3), 367–389. https://doi.org/10.1108/09564231111136872

Helms, R. (2015). *International higher education partnerships: A global review of standards and practices*. CIGE Insights. American Council on Education

Hénard, F., & Mitterle, A. (2010). *Governance and quality guidelines in Higher Education. A review of governance arrangements and quality assurance*. OECD.

Heng, T. (2018). Different is not deficient: Contradicting stereotypes of Chinese international students in US higher education. *Studies in higher education, 43*(1), 22–36. https://doi.org/10.1080/03075079.2016.1152466

Henry, F., Dua, E., Kobayashi, A., James, C., Li, P., Ramos, H., & Smith, M. S. (2017). Race, racialization and Indigeneity in Canadian universities. *Race Ethnicity and Education, 20*(3), 300–314. https://doi.org/10.1080/13613324.2016.1260226

Higher Education Staff Statistics. (2020, January 23). HESA. https://www.hesa.ac.uk/news/23-01-2020/sb256-higher-education-staff-statistics

Hiles, R. (2015, July 14). *TNE data collection: Reflections from a UK perspective*. Observatory on Borderless Higher Education. https://www.obhe.org/resources/tne-data-collection-reflections-from-a-uk-perspective

Hiles, R. (2016a, July 7). *Out of 'site,' out of mind? Overseas degree delivery and the student experience.* WONKHE. https://wonkhe.com/blogs/comment-out-of-site-out-of-mind-overseas-degree-delivery-and-the-student-experience/

Hiles, R. (2016b, October 12). *The rise of TNE: If you can't import students, export degrees instead.* WONKHE. https://wonkhe.com/blogs/analysis-rise-of-tne-cant-import-students-export-degrees/

Hills, R. (2017). *Out of 'site', out of mind? Overseas degree delivery and the student experience.* Wonkhe. Retrieved from https://wonkhe.com/blogs/comment-out-of-site-out-of-mind-overseas-degree-delivery-and-the-student-experience/

Hlib, P. (2019). *Financial support of higher education institutions. A comparative study of universities in Ukraine and Norway* [Master's thesis, Nord universitet]. https://nordopen.nord.no/nord-xmlui/bitstream/handle/11250/2621151/PolianovskyiHlib.pdf?sequence=1&isAllowed=y

HM Government. (2019). *International education strategy: Global potential, global growth* [Policy paper]. Department for International Trade & Department for Education. https://www.gov.uk/government/publications/international-education-strategy-global-potential-global-growth

Hofmeyr, A. S. (2021). Rethinking the concept of global human resources in the Japanese higher education context. *Asia Pacific Journal of Education*, 1–17. https://doi.org/10.1080/02188791.2021.1889970

Hofstede, G. (2001). *Culture's consequences: Comparing values, behaviors, institutions, and organizations across nations.* SAGE Publications.

Hofstede, G., Hofstede, G. J., & Minkov, M. (2010). *Cultures and organizations: Software of the mind* (3rd. ed.). McGraw-Hill.

Holbrook, M., & Hirschmann, E. (1982). The experiential aspects of consumption: Consumer fantasies, feelings, and fun. *Journal of Consumer Research*, 9(2), 132–140. https://www.jstor.org/stable/2489122

Hollebeek, L., Srivastava, R., & Chen, T. (2019). S-D logic–informed customer engagement: Integrative framework, revised fundamental propositions, and application to CRM. *Journal of the Academy of Marketing Science*, 47(1), 161–185. https://doi.org/10.1007/s11747-016-0494-5

Hook, J., Worthington Jr., E., & Utsey, S. (2009). Collectivism, forgiveness, and social harmony. *The Counseling Psychologist*, 37(6), 821–847. https://doi.org/10.1177/0011000008326546

Horner, R. (2020). Towards a new paradigm of global development? Beyond the limits of international development. *Progress in Human Geography*, 44(3), 415–436. https://doi.org/10.1177/0309132519836158

Houshmand, S., Spanierman, L., & Tafarodi, R. (2014). Excluded and avoided: Racial microaggressions targeting Asian international students in Canada. *Cultural Diversity and Ethnic Minority Psychology*, 20(3), 377. https://doi.org/10.1037/a0035404

Huang, F. (2003). Transnational higher education: A perspective from China. *Higher Education Research, & Development*, 22, 193–203.

Huisman, J., De Boer, H., Dill, D., & Souto-Otero, M. (Eds.). (2015). *The Palgrave international handbook of higher education policy and governance.* Springer.

Humphrey, C., Loft, A., & Woods, M. (2009). The global audit profession and the international financial architecture: Understanding regulatory relationships

at a time of financial crisis. *Accounting, Organizations and Society, 34*(6–7), 810–825. https://doi.org/10.1016/j.aos.2009.06.003
Humphrey, O., & Lowe, T. (2017). Exploring how a 'Sense of Belonging' is facilitated at different stages of the student journey in Higher Education. *The Journal of Educational Innovation, Partnership and Change, 3*(1), 172–188. https://doi.org/10.21100/jeipc.v3i1.583
Iannelli, C., & Huang, J. (2014). Trends in participation and attainment of Chinese students in UK higher education. *Studies in Higher Education, 39*(5), 805–822. https://doi.org/10.1080/03075079.2012.754863
Inelmen, K., Selekler-Goksen, N., & Yildirim-Öktem, Ö. (2017). Understanding citizenship behavior of academics in American- vs continental European-modeled universities in Turkey. *Personnel Review, 46*(6), 1142–1164. https://doi.org/10.1108/PR-06-2015-0182
Institute for Academic Development. (2020). *Moderation guidance*. The University of Edinburgh. https://www.ed.ac.uk/institute-academic-development/learning-teaching/staff/assessment/moderation-guidance
Institute of International Education. (2020a). *Percent of U.S. study abroad students by field of study, 2000/01–2018/19: Open doors report on international educational exchange*. https://opendoorsdata.org/
Institute of International Education. (2020b). *Profile of U.S. study abroad students, 2006/07–2018/19: Open doors report on international educational exchange*. https://opendoorsdata.org/
International Association of Universities, Association of Universities and Colleges of Canada, American Council on Education, & Council for Higher Education Accreditation. (2005). *Sharing quality higher education across borders: A statement on behalf of higher education institutions worldwide*. https://www.iau-aiu.net/IMG/pdf/statement_sharing_quality-2.pdf
International Students Generate Global Economic Impact of US$300 Billion. (2019, August 28). icef Monitor. https://monitor.icef.com/2019/08/international-students-generate-global-economic-impact-of-us300-billion/
Irarrázaval, L. (2020). A phenomenological paradigm for empirical research in psychiatry and psychology: Open questions. *Frontiers in Psychology, 11*, 1399. https://doi.org/10.3389/fpsyg.2020.01399
Iredale, R. (2001). The migration of professionals: Theories and typologies. *International migration, 39*(5), 7–26. https://doi.org/10.1111/1468-2435.00169
Ishikawa, J. (2012). Leadership and performance in Japanese R&D teams. *Asia Pacific Business Review, 18*(2), 241–258. https://doi.org/10.1080/13602381.2010.532907
Ishikawa, M. (2009). University rankings, global models, and emerging hegemony: Critical analysis from Japan. *Journal of Studies in International Education, 13*(2), 159–173. https://doi.org/10.1177/1028315308330853
Ito, H. (2014). Challenges towards employability: Higher education's engagement to industrial needs in Japan. *Higher Education Studies, 4*(2), 1–8. https://doi.org/10.5539/hes.v4n2p1
Ivy, J. (2001). Higher education institution image: A correspondence analysis approach. *International Journal of Educational Management, 15*(6/7), 276–282. https://doi.org/10.1108/09513540110401484

Japan Student Services Organization. (2019). *Result of an annual survey of international students in Japan 2019*. Retrieved from https://studyinjapan.go.jp/en/_mt/2020/08/date2019z_e.pdf

Jaramillo, A. (2012). *Benchmarking university governance*. The World Bank.

Jesson, J., Matheson, L., & Lacey, F. (2011). *Doing your literature review: Traditional and systematic techniques*. SAGE Publications.

Jin, L., & Schneider, J. (2019). Faculty views on international students: A survey study. Journal of International Students, 9(1), 84–99. https://doi.org/10.32674/jis.v9i1.268

Johanson, J., & Vahlne, J. (1977). The internationalization process of the firm–A model of knowledge development and increasing foreign market commitments. *Journal of International Business Studies, 8*(1), 23–32. https://doi.org/10.1057/palgrave.jibs.8490676

Johns Hopkins University. (n.d.). *A brief history of JHU*. http://webapps.jhu.edu/jhuniverse/information_about_hopkins/about_jhu/a_brief_history_of_jhu

Johns, N., & Howard, A. (1998). Customer expectations versus perceptions of service performance in the foodservice industry. *International Journal of Service Industry Management, 9*(3), 248–265. https://doi.org/10.1108/09564239810223556

Johnson, T., & Caygill, M. (1971). The development of accountancy links in the Commonwealth. *Accounting and Business Research, 1*(2), 155–173. https://doi.org/10.1080/00014788.1971.9728562

Johnson, V. (2006). Americans abroad: International educational programs and tort liability. JC & UL, 32, 309–360. https://commons.stmarytx.edu/cgi/viewcontent.cgi?article=1418&context=facarticles

Jon, J., & Kim, E. (2011). What it takes to internationalize higher education in Korea and Japan: English-mediated courses and international students. In J. Palmer, A. Roberts, Y. Ha Cho, & G. Ching (Eds.), *The internationalization of East Asian higher education* (pp. 147–171). Springer.

Jørgensen, M. T., & Brogaard, L. (2021). Using differentiated teaching to address academic diversity in higher education: Empirical evidence from two cases. *Learning and Teaching, 14*(2), 87–110. https://doi.org/10.3167/latiss.2021.140206

Jumakulov, Z., Ashirbekov, A., Sparks, J., & Sagintayeva, A. (2019). Internationalizing research in Kazakhstan higher education: A case study of Kazakhstan's state program of industrial innovative development 2015 to 2019. *Journal of Studies in International Education, 23*(2), 234–247. https://doi.org/10.1177/1028315318786445

Kalafatelis, E., de Bonaire, C., & Alliston, L. (2018, May). *Beyond the economic—How international education delivers broad value for New Zealand*. https://www.researchnz.com/assets/resources/Featured1.pdf

KAM. (2015). *Yükseköğretimin uluslararasıla?ması çerçevesinde Türk üniversitelerinin uluslararası öğrenciler için çekim merkezi haline getirilmesi* [Turning Turkish universities into a center of attraction for international students within the framework of internationalization of higher education]. Kalkınma Bakanlığı.

Karwowska, E., & Leja, K. (2018). Is there any room for improvement for university social responsibility? Coopetition as a catalyst. *E-MENTOR, 3*, 4–13. https://doi.org/10.15219/em75.1357

Kehm, B., & Teichler, U. (2007). Research on internationalisation in higher education. *Journal of Studies in International Education, 11*(3–4), 260–273. https://doi.org/10.1177/1028315307303534

Kennedy, M., & Fiss, P. (2009). Institutionalization, framing, and diffusion: The logic of TQM adoption and implementation decisions among US hospitals. *Academy of Management Journal, 52*(5), 897–918. https://doi.org/10.5465/amj.2009.44633062

Kennette, L. N., & Wilson, N. A. (2019). Universal design for learning: What is it and how do I implement it. *Transformative Dialogues: Teaching & Learning Journal, 12*(1), 1–6.

Kernohan, D. (2019, December 6). *We have no idea how much education related exports are worth to the UK.* WONKHE. https://wonkhe.com/blogs/we-have-no-idea-how-much-education-related-exports-are-worth-to-the-uk/

Kerr, C. (1994). *Higher education cannot escape history: Issues for the twenty-first century.* SUNY Press.

Kersten, G., Kersten, M., & Rakowski, W. (2002). Software and culture: Beyond the internationalization of the interface. *Journal of Global Information Management, 10*(4), 86–101.

Khoshlessan, R. (2013). Is there a relationship between the usage of active and collaborative learning techniques and international students' study anxiety? *International Research and Review, 3*(1), 55–80.

Kieran, L., & Anderson, C. (2019). Connecting universal design for learning with culturally responsive teaching. *Education and Urban Society, 51*(9), 1202–1216. https://doi.org/10.1177/0013124518785012

Kim, T., Shin, D., & Jeong, Y. (2016). Inside the "hybrid" iron cage: Political origins of hybridization. *Organization Science, 27*(2), 428–445. https://www.jstor.org/stable/24763311

King v. Board of Control of Eastern Michigan Univ., 221 F. Supp. 2d 783 (E.D. Mich. 2002)

King, R., Marginson, S., & Naidoo, R. (Eds.). (2011). *Handbook on globalization and higher education.* Edward Elgar Publishing.

King's College London. (n.d.). *King's strategic vision 2029.* https://www.kcl.ac.uk/about/assets/pdf/Kings-strategic-vision-2029.pdf

Kirkpatrick, A. (2011). *Internationalization or Englishization: Medium of instruction in today's universities.* https://www.researchgate.net/publication/225083938_Internationalization_or_Englishization_Medium_of_Instruction_in_Today's_Universities

Klag, M., & Langley, A. (2013). Approaching the conceptual leap in qualitative research. *International Journal of Management Reviews, 15*(2), 149–166. https://doi.org/10.1111/j.1468-2370.2012.00349.x

Klostermaier, K. (2007). *A survey of Hinduism.* SUNY Press.

Knaus, C. (2019, October 11). Murdoch University sues whistleblower after comments on international students. *The Guardian.* https://www.theguardian.com/australia-news/2019/oct/11/murdoch-university-sues-whistleblower-after-comments-on-international-students

Knight, J. (2003). Updated definition of internationalization. *International Higher Education, 33.* https://doi.org/10.6017/ihe.2003.33.7391

Knight, J. (2004). Internationalization remodeled: Definition, approaches, and rationales. *Journal of Studies in International Education, 8*(1), 5–31. https://doi.org/10.1177/1028315303260832

Knight, J. (2008a). Borderless, offshore, transnational and cross-border education: Are they different? In *Higher education in turmoil: The changing world of internationalization* (pp. 81–96). Brill. https://doi.org/10.1163/9789087905224_006

Knight, J. (2008b). Internationalisation: Key concepts and elements. In M. Gaebel, L. Purse, B. Wächter, & L. Wilson (Eds.), *Internationalisation of European Higher Education. An EUA/ACA Handbook* (pp. 2–21). Raabe.

Knight, J. (Ed.). (2013a). *International education hubs: Student, talent, knowledge-innovation models*. Springer Science & Business Media.

Knight, J. (2013b). The changing landscape of higher education internationalisation—for better or worse? *Perspectives: Policy and practice in higher education, 17*(3), 84–90. https://doi.org/10.1080/13603108.2012.753957

Knight, J. (2014a). Is internationalisation of higher education having an identity crisis? In A. Maldonado & R. Bassett (Eds.), *The forefront of international higher education* (pp. 75–87). Springer Netherlands.

Knight, J. (2014b). Three generations of cross-border higher education: New developments, issues, and challenges. In B. T. Streitwieser (Ed.), *Internationalisation of higher education and global mobility* (pp. 43–58). Symposium Books.

Knight, J. (2015). Meaning, rationales and tensions in the internationalisation of higher education. In *Routledge handbook of international education and development* (pp. 345–359). Routledge.

Knight, J. (2016). Transnational education remodeled: Toward a common TNE framework and definitions. *Journal of Studies in International Education, 20*(1), 34–47. https://doi.org/10.1177/1028315315602927

Knight, J., & Altbach, P. (2007). The internationalization of higher education: Motivations and realities. *Journal of Studies in International Education, 11*, 290–307.

Knight, J., & de Wit, H. (1995). Strategies for internationalization of higher education: Historical and conceptual perspectives. In H. de Wit (Ed.), *Strategies for internationalization of higher education: A comparative study of Australia, Canada, Europe and the United States of America* (pp. 5–33). European Association for International Education.

Knight, J., & Morshidi, S. (2011). The complexities and challenges of regional education hubs: Focus on Malaysia. *Higher Education, 62*(5), 593–606. https://doi.org/10.1007/s10734-011-9467-2

Knowles, M. S., Holton III, E. F., & Swanson, R. A. (2015). *The adult learner: The definitive classic in adult education and human resource development* (8th ed.). Routledge.

Kodeih, F., & Greenwood, R. (2014). Responding to institutional complexity: The role of identity. *Organization Studies, 35*(1), 7–39. https://doi.org/10.1177/0170840613495333

Komotar, M. (2019). Comprehensive internationalisation of Slovenian higher education? The rhetoric and realities. *Higher Education, 77*(5), 871–887. https://doi.org/10.1007/s10734-018-0306-6

Kondakci, Y. (2011). Student mobility reviewed: Attraction and satisfaction of international students in Turkey. *Higher Education, 62*(5), 573–592. https://doi.org/10.1007/s10734-011-9406-2

Kondakci, Y., Bedenlier, S., & Zawacki-Richter, O. (2018). Social network analysis of international student mobility: Uncovering the rise of regional hubs. *Higher Education, 75*(3), 517–535. https://www.jstor.org/stable/26449092

Kraatz, M., & Block, E. (2008). Organizational implications of institutional pluralism. In R. Greenwood, C. Oliver, R. Suddaby, & K. Sahlin (Eds.), *The SAGE handbook of Organizational Institutionalism* (pp. 243–275). SAGE Publications.

Kraatz, M., Ventresca, M., & Deng, L. (2010). Precarious values and mundane innovations: Enrollment management in American liberal arts colleges. *Academy of Management Journal, 53*(6), 1521–1545.

Kritz, M. (2006, June 28–30). Globalization and internationalization of tertiary education [Paper presentation]. *International Symposium on International Migration and Development*, Turin, Italy. https://www.un.org/en/development/desa/population/events/pdf/other/turin/P02_Kritz.pdf

Ku, K., & Ho, I. (2010). Metacognitive strategies that enhance critical thinking. *Metacognition and Learning, 5*(3), 251–267. https://doi.org/10.1007/s11409-010-9060-6

Kubota, R. (2009). Internationalization of universities: Paradoxes and responsibilities. *The Modern Language Journal, 93*(4), 612–616. https://www.jstor.org/stable/25612236

Kumar, P., & Aithal, P. (2020). Internationalization of higher education: A stakeholder approach. *Scholedge International Journal of Business Policy & Governance, 7*(6), 84–93. https://doi.org/10.19085/sijbpg070601

Kuzhabekova, A., Hendel, D., & Chapman, D. (2015). Mapping global research on international higher education. *Research in Higher Education, 56*(8), 861–882. https://doi.org/10.1007/s11162-015-9371-1

Kylänen, M., & Rusko, R. (2011). Unintentional coopetition in the service industries: The case of Pyhä-Luosto tourism destination in the Finnish Lapland. *European Management Journal, 29*(3), 193–205. https://doi.org/10.1016/j.emj.2010.10.006

Lanvers, U., & Hultgren, A. (2018). The Englishization of European education: Foreword. *European Journal of Language Policy, 10*(1), 1–11. https://doi.org/10.3828/ejlp.2018.1

Larsen, K., & Vincent-Lancrin, S. (2002). The learning business: Can trade in international education work? *OECD Observer*, 235, 26–29. https://go.gale.com/ps/i.do?p=AONE&u=googlescholar&id=GALE%7CA98136441&v=2.1&it=r&sid=AONE&asid=d14ae205

Larsen, K., Martin, J., & Morris, R. (2002). Trade in educational services: Trends and emerging issues. *World Economy, 25*(6), 849–868. https://doi.org/10.1111/1467-9701.00466

LaSalle, D., & Britton, T. (2003). *Priceless: Turning ordinary products into extraordinary experience*. Harvard Business School Press.

Latos, A. (2021, August 13). *Settlement reached between UNCC, former student in sexual misconduct lawsuit*. WSOC-TV. https://www.wsoctv.com/news/local/

lawsuit-accuses-uncc-professor-sexual-misconduct/BLPXKGLNKRGMHN6F R7FNJDHQIM/

Lawton, W. (2018, June 1). *The pppassage to India*. WONKHE. https://wonkhe.com/blogs/the-pppassage-to-india/

Lawton, W., & Jensen, S. (2015). *An early-warning system for TNE understanding the future global network connectivity and service needs of UK higher education*. The Observatory on Borderless Higher Education.

Layne, C. (2012, April 25). *The global power shift from West to East*. The National Interest. https://nationalinterest.org/article/the-global-power-shift-west-east-6796

Leask, B. (2015). *Internationalizing the curriculum*. Routledge.

Lee, B. A. (2010). Fifty years of higher education law: Turning the kaleidoscope. *Journal of College and University Law, 36*(3), 649–690.

Lee, C., Therriault, D., & Linderholm, T. (2012). On the cognitive benefits of cultural experience: Exploring the relationship between studying abroad and creative thinking. *Applied Cognitive Psychology, 26*(5), 768–778. https://doi.org/10.1002/acp.2857

Lee, H. (2012). Affirmative action in Malaysia: Education and employment outcomes since the 1990s. *Journal of Contemporary Asia, 42*(2), 230–254. https://doi.org/10.1080/09500782.2012.668350

Lee, H., & Khalid, M. (2016). Discrimination of high degrees: Race and graduate hiring in Malaysia. *Journal of the Asia Pacific Economy, 21*(1), 53–76. https://doi.org/10.1080/13547860.2015.1055948

Lee, J. (2008). Beyond borders: International student pathways to the United States. *Journal of Studies in International Education, 12*(3), 308–327. https://doi.org/10.1177/1028315307299418

Lee, J., & Opio, T. (2011). Coming to America: Challenges and difficulties faced by African student athletes. *Sport, Education and Society, 16*(5), 629–644. https://doi.org/10.1080/13573322.2011.601144

Lee, J., & Stensaker, B. (2021). Research on internationalisation and globalisation in higher education—Reflections on historical paths, current perspectives and future possibilities. *European Journal of Education, 56*(2), 157–168. https://doi.org/10.1111/ejed.12448

Lee, J., Liu, K., & Wu, Y. (2020). Does the Asian catch-up model of world-class universities work? Revisiting the zero-sum game of global university rankings and government policies. *Educational Research for Policy and Practice, 19*(3), 319–343. https://doi.org/10.1007/s10671-020-09261-x

Lee, J., Maldonado-Maldonado, A., & Rhoades, G. (2006). The political economy of international student flows: Patterns, ideas, and propositions. In J. C. Smart (Ed.), *Higher Education: Handbook of theory and research* (pp. 545–590). Springer.

Lehmann, H. (2010). International information systems in the literature. In The dynamics of international information systems (pp. 9–17), Springer. https://doi.org/10.1007/978-1-4419-5750-4_2

Lehmann, T., Saulich, C., & Wohlgemuth, V. (2018). Transnational student consultancy—An integrated approach to business students' learning. In *Proceedings of the 4th International Conference on Higher Education Advances* (HEAd'18;

pp. 303–311). http://ocs.editorial.upv.es/index.php/HEAD/HEAD18/paper/view/7983

Lemon, K., & Verhoef, P. C. (2016). Understanding customer experience throughout the customer journey. *Journal of Marketing, 80*(6), 69–96. https://doi.org/10.1509/jm.15.0420

Leonor, I. (2020). A phenomenological paradigm for empirical research in psychiatry and psychology: Open questions. *Frontiers in Psychology, 11*, 1399. https://doi.org/10.3389/fpsyg.2020.01399

Leung, M., & Waters, J. (2017). Educators sans frontières? Borders and power geometries in transnational education. *Journal of Ethnic and Migration Studies, 43*(8), 1276–1291. https://doi.org/10.1080/1369183X.2017.1300235

Lewis, B., & Mitchell, V. (1990). Defining and measuring the quality of customer service. *Marketing Intelligence & Planning, 8*(6), 11–17. https://doi.org/10.1108/EUM0000000001086

Leydesdorff, L., Bornmann, L., & Wagner, C. (2019). The relative influences of government funding and international collaboration on citation impact. *Journal of the Association for Information Science and Technology, 70*(2), 198–201. https://doi.org/10.1002/asi.24109

Li, C. (2008). Why are you giggling? An exploratory investigation of communication educators' interactions with international students. *PRism, 5*(1–2), 1–11. https://www.prismjournal.org/uploads/1/2/5/6/125661607/v5-no1-2-a3.pdf

Li, M. (2016). Developing skills and disposition for lifelong learning: Acculturative issues surrounding supervising international doctoral students in New Zealand Universities. *Journal of International Students, 6*(3), 740–761. https://doi.org/10.32674/jis.v6i3.354

Liu, O., Frankel, L., & Roohr, K. (2014). *Assessing critical thinking in higher education: Current state and directions for next-generation assessment* (ETS RR–14-10). ETS Research Report Series. https://files.eric.ed.gov/fulltext/EJ1109287.pdf

Lofgren, J., & Leigh, E. (2017). The Mikkeli programme: International education and flagship response to globalisation. In Nygaard, C., Horsted, A., & Branch, J. (Eds.), *Globalisation of Higher Education: Political, institutional, cultural, and personal perspectives* (pp. 167–194). Libri Publishing.

Lofgren, J., Pavlov, O., & Hoy, F. (2019). Higher education as a service: The science of running a lean program in international business. In H. Yang & R. Qiu (Eds.), *Advances in service science: Proceedings of the 2018 INFORMS International Conference on Service Science* (pp. 53–60). Springer.

Loft, A., Humphrey, C., & Turley, S. (2006). In pursuit of global regulation: Changing governance and accountability structures at the International Federation of Accountants (IFAC). *Accounting, Auditing, & Accountability Journal, 19*(3), 428–451. https://doi.org/10.1108/09513570610670361

Loudenback, T. (2016, September 26). *International students are now 'subsidizing' public American universities to the tune of $9 billion a year*. Business Insider. https://www.businessinsider.com/foreign-students-pay-up-to-three-times-as-much-for-tuition-at-us-public-colleges-2016-9

Lowrie, A., & Hemsley-Brown, J. (2011). This thing called marketisation. *Journal of Marketing Management, 27*(11–12), 1081–1086. https://doi.org/10.1080/0267257X.2011.614733

Luchilo, L., & Albornoz, M. (2008). Universities and global competition for graduate students: Scenarios for Latin America. *Technology Analysis & Strategic Management, 20*(3), 351–367. https://doi.org/10.1080/09537320802000120

Lumby, J., & Foskett, N. (2016). Internationalization and culture in higher education. *Educational Management Administration & Leadership, 44*(1), 95–111. https://doi.org/10.1177/1741143214549978

Lund University. (n.d.). *Strategic plan: 2017–2026 | Lund University*. https://www.lunduniversity.lu.se/sites/www.lunduniversity.lu.se/files/strategic_plan_2017-2026-updated030517.pdf

Luo, J., & Jamieson-Drake, D. (2013). Examining the educational benefits of interacting with international students. *Journal of International Students, 3*(2), 85–101. https://files.eric.ed.gov/fulltext/EJ1056457.pdf

Macaro, E., Curle, S., Pun, J., An, J., & Dearden, J. (2018). A systematic review of English medium instruction in higher education. *Language Teaching, 51*(1), 36–76.

Macgregor, A., & Folinazzo, G. (2018). Best practices in teaching international students in higher education: Issues and strategies. *TeSoL Journal, 9*(2), 299–329. https://doi.org/10.1002/tesj.324

MacKenzie, I. (2015). Rethinking reader and writer responsibility in academic English. *Applied Linguistics Review, 6*(1), 1–21. https://doi.org/10.1515/applirev-2015-0001

Madge, C., Raghuram, P., & Noxolo, P. (2009). Engaged pedagogy and responsibility: A postcolonial analysis of international students. *Geoforum, 40*(1), 34–45. https://doi.org/10.1016/j.geoforum.2008.01.008

Malaysian Institute of Accountants. (1987). *Malaysian Institute of Accountants: 1987 Reports and Accounts*.

Malaysian Institute of Certified Public Accountants. (2016). *MICPA 2016 annual report*. https://mia.org.my/annual-report-2016

Malsch, B., & Gendron, Y. (2011). Reining in auditors: On the dynamics of power surrounding an "innovation" in the regulatory space. *Accounting, Organizations and Society, 36*(7), 456–476. https://doi.org/10.1016/j.aos.2011.06.001

Manning, K. (2018). *Organizational theory in higher education*. Routledge.

Marginson, S. (2002). Nation-building universities in a global environment: The case of Australia. *Higher Education, 43*(3), 409–428. https://www.jstor.org/stable/3447524

Marginson, S. (2004). Competition and markets in higher education: A 'glonacal' analysis. *Policy Futures in Education, 2*(2), 175–244. https://doi.org/10.2304/pfie.2004.2.2.2

Marginson, S. (2006). Dynamics of national and global competition in higher education. *Higher Education, 52*(1), 1–39. https://doi.org/10.1007/s10734-004-7649-x

Marginson, S. (2011). Higher education in East Asia and Singapore: Rise of the Confucian model. *Higher Education, 61*(5), 587–611. https://doi.org/10.1007/s10734-010-9384-9

Marginson, S. (2012). International education in Australia: The roller coaster. *International Higher Education*, 68, 11–13. https://doi.org/10.6017/ihe.2012.68.8626

Marginson, S. (2013). The impossibility of capitalist markets in higher education. *Journal of Education Policy*, 28(3), 353–370. https://doi.org/10.1080/02680939.2012.747109

Marginson, S. (2018). Higher education and science in the age of Trump, Brexit and Le Pen. In A. Veiga, A. Magalhães, M. da Rosa, & P. Teixeira (Eds.), *Under pressure* (pp. 17–36). Brill.

Marginson, S., & Considine, M. (2000). *The enterprise university: Power, governance and reinvention in Australia*. Cambridge University Press.

Marginson, S., & Rhoades, G. (2002). Beyond national states, markets, and systems of higher education: A glonacal agency heuristic. *Higher Education*, 43(3), 281–309. https://doi.org/10.1023/A:1014699605875

Mariani, M. (2007). Coopetition as an emergent strategy: Empirical evidence from an Italian consortium of opera houses. *International Studies of Management & Organization*, 37(2), 97–126. https://www.jstor.org/stable/40397699

Maringe, F., Foskett, N., & Woodfield, S. (2013). Emerging internationalisation models in an uneven global terrain: Findings from a global survey. *Compare: A Journal of Comparative and International Education*, 43(1), 9–36. https://doi.org/10.1080/03057925.2013.746548

Marjanović, B., & Križman Pavlović, D. (2018). Factors influencing the high school graduates' decision to study abroad: Toward a theoretical model. *Management*, 23(1), 221–240. https://doi.org/10.30924/mjcmi/2018.23.1.221

Martin-Sanchez, M., & Flores-Rodriguez, C. (2018). Freedom and obedience in Western education. *Journal of Pedagogy*, 9(2) 55–78. https://doi.org/10.2478/jped-2018-0011

Martirosyan, N., Bustamante, R., & Saxon, D. (2019). Academic and social support services for international students: Current practices. *Journal of International Students*, 9(1), 172–191. https://doi.org/10.32674/jis.v9i1.275

Martirosyan, N., Hwang, E., & Wanjohi, R. (2015). Impact of English proficiency on academic performance of international students. *Journal of International Students*, 5(1), 60–71. https://files.eric.ed.gov/fulltext/EJ1052835.pdf

Massaro, V. (2022). Global citizenship development in higher education institutions: A systematic review of the literature. *Journal of Global Education and Research*, 6(1), 98–114. https://doi.org/10.5038/2577-509X.6.1.1124

McBurnie, G., & Ziguras, C. (2001). The regulation of transnational higher education in Southeast Asia: Case studies of Hong Kong, Malaysia and Australia. *Higher Education*, 42(1), 85–105. https://www.jstor.org/stable/3448084

Mellors-Bourne, R., Fielden, J., Kemp, N., R. Middlehurst, & S. Woodfield. (2014). *The value of transnational education to the UK* (BIS Research Paper Number 194). Department for Business Innovation & Skills. https://assets.publishing.service.gov.uk/government/uploads/system/uploads/attachment_data/file/387910/bis-14-1202-the-value-of-transnational-education-to-the-uk.pdf

Merton, R. (1968). The Matthew effect in science: The reward and communication systems of science are considered. *Science*, 159(3810), 56–63. https://doi.org/10.1126/science.159.3810.5

Meschi, P., & Riccio, E. (2008). Country risk, national cultural differences between partners and survival of international joint ventures in Brazil. *International Business Review, 17*(3), 250–266. https://doi.org/10.1016/j.ibusrev.2007.11.001

MEXT. (2013). *Report and statistics* [Graphics]. http://www.mext.go.jp/en/publication/statistics/title01/detail01/1373636.htm#05

MEXT. (2014, September). *Selection for the FY2014 top global university project* [Press release]. http://docplayer.net/16379288-Selection-for-the-fy-2014-top-global-university-project-we-hereby-announce-the-selectionof-universities-for-the-top-global-university-project.html

MEXT. (2016). *Statistical abstract 2016 edition.* https://www.mext.go.jp/en/publication/statistics/title02/detail02/1379369.htm

MEXT. (2017). *Top global university project.* https://tgu.mext.go.jp/en/about/index.html

Mihut, G., Altbach, P., & de Wit, H. (Eds.). (2017). *Understanding higher education internationalization: Insights from key global publications.* Springer.

Miloloža, H. (2015). Differences between Croatia and EU candidate countries: The CAGE distance framework. *Business Systems Research: International Journal of the Society for Advancing Innovation and Research in Economy, 6*(2), 52–62. https://doi.org/10.1515/bsrj-2015-0011

Mizikaci, F. (2010). Isomorphic and diverse institutions among Turkish foundation universities. *Eğitim ve Bilim, 35*(157), 140–151.

Minett-Smith, C., & Davis, C. (2019). Widening the discourse on team-teaching in higher education. *Teaching in Higher Education,* (25), 579–594. https://www.tandfonline.com/doi/full/10.1080/13562517.2019.1577814

Ministry of Education. (2017). *Te Whāriki: He whāriki mātauranga mō ngā mokopuna o Aotearoa: Early childhood curriculum* [The blanket: An educational mat for the children of New Zealand]. Ministry of Education, New Zealand. https://www.education.govt.nz/assets/Documents/Early-Childhood/ELS-Te-Whariki-Early-Childhood-Curriculum-ENG-Web.pdf

Mitchell, W. (2014, August). Grounded theory, with or without priors. *Strategic Management Journal, 36*(5), 637–639.

Mohajeri Norris, E., & Gillespie, J. (2009). How study abroad shapes global careers: Evidence from the United States. *Journal of Studies in International Education, 13*(3), 382–397. https://doi.org/10.1177/1028315308319740

Mongkhonvanit, J. (2014). *Coopetition for regional competitiveness: The role of academe in knowledge-based industrial clustering.* Springer.

Moon, J. (2008). *Critical thinking: An exploration of theory and practice.* Routledge.

Moore, T. (2013). Critical thinking: Seven definitions in search of a concept. *Studies in Higher Education, 38*(4), 506–522. https://doi.org/10.1080/03075079.2011.586995

Moriña, A. (2017). Inclusive education in higher education: Challenges and opportunities. *European Journal of Special Needs Education, 32*(1), 3–17. https://doi.org/10.1080/08856257.2016.1254964

Moriña, A., Perera, V., & Carballo, R. (2020). Training needs of academics on inclusive education and disability. *SAGE Open, 10*(3). https://doi.org/10.1177/2158244020962758

Morris, C., Milton, E., & Goldstone, R. (2019). Case study: Suggesting choice: Inclusive assessment processes. *Higher Education Pedagogies, 4*(1), 435–447. https://doi.org/10.1080/23752696.2019.1669479

Morshidi, S. (2006). Transnational higher education in Malaysia: Balancing benefits and concerns through regulations. *RIHE International Publication Series, 10*, 109–126.

Muijs, D., & Rumyantseva, N. (2014). Coopetition in education: Collaborating in a competitive environment. *Journal of Educational Change, 15*(1), 1–18.

Naidoo, V. (2009). Transnational higher education: A stock take of current activity. *Journal of Studies in International Education, 13*(3), 310–330. https://doi.org/10.1177/1028315308317938

Naidoo, V., & Wu, T. (2014). Innovations in marketing of higher education: Foreign market entry mode of not-for-profit universities. *Journal of Business & Industrial Marketing, 29*, 546–558. https://doi.org/10.1108/JBIM-07-2013-0153

Nalanda: India's Ancient Buddhist—And the World's—University. (n.d.). Facts and Details. https://factsanddetails.com/india/Places/sub7_11d/entry-7119.html

Nanda, V. (2006). The "good governance" concept revisited. *The ANNALS of the American Academy of Political and Social Science, 603*(1), 269–283. https://doi.org/10.1177/0002716205282847

National Commission on Excellence in Education. (1983). *A nation at risk: The imperative for educational reform.* https://edreform.com/wp-content/uploads/2013/02/A_Nation_At_Risk_1983.pdf

National Science Board. (2016). *Science & engineering indicators.* https://www.nsf.gov/nsb/publications/2016/nsb20161.pdf

Naudé, P. (2021). *Contemporary management education: Eight questions that will shape its future in the 21st century.* Springer Nature.

Naumovska, I., Gaba, V., & Greve, H. (2021). The diffusion of differences: A review and reorientation of 20 years of diffusion research. *Academy of Management Annals, 15*(2), 377–405. https://doi.org/10.5465/annals.2019.0102

Naumovska, I., Zajac, E., & Lee, P. (2021). Strength and weakness in numbers? Unpacking the role of prevalence in the diffusion of reverse mergers. *Academy of Management Journal, 64*(2), 409–434. https://doi.org/10.5465/amj.2018.0716

Neave, G. (2001). The European dimension in higher education: An excursion into the modern use of historical analogues. In J. Huisman, G. Huisman, & P. Maassen (Eds.), *Higher education and the nation state: The international dimension of higher education* (pp. 13–73). Elsevier.

New Zealand Government. (2018). *International education strategy: He Rautaki Mātauranga a ao, 2018–2030.* https://enz.govt.nz/assets/Uploads/International-Education-Strategy-2018-2030.pdf

New Zealand Immigration. (2021). *Study in New Zealand.* https://www.immigration.govt.nz/new-zealand-visas/options/study

Newby, H., Weko, T., Breneman, D., Johanneson, T., & Maassen, P. (2009). *OECD reviews of tertiary education: Japan.* Retrieved from http://www.oecd.org/dataoecd/44/12/42280329.pdf

Newfield, C. (2011). *Unmaking the public university: The forty-year assault on the middle class.* Harvard University Press.

Ng, I., & Forbes, J. (2009). Education as service: The understanding of university experience through the service logic. *Journal of Marketing for Higher Education, 19*(1), 38–64. https://doi.org/10.1080/08841240902904703

Nisbett, R. E., Peng, K., Choi, I., & Norenzayan, A. (2008). Culture and systems of thought: Holistic versus analytic cognition. In J. E. Adler & L. J. Rips (Eds.), *Reasoning: Studies of human inference and its foundations* (pp. 956–985). Cambridge University Press.

NZQA. (2021). *Understanding New Zealand qualifications framework (NZQF).* https://www.nzqa.govt.nz/studying-in-new-zealand/understand-nz-quals/

O'Dwyer, B., Owen, D., & Unerman, J. (2011). Seeking legitimacy for new assurance forms: The case of assurance on sustainability reporting. *Accounting, Organizations and Society, 36*(1), 31–52. https://doi.org/10.1016/j.aos.2011.01.002

OECD. (2003). Changing patterns of governance in higher education. In *Education policy analysis* (pp. 59–78). https://doi.org/10.1787/19991517

OECD & World Bank. (2007). *Cross-border tertiary education: A way towards capacity development.* http://hdl.handle.net/10986/6865

OECD. (2017a). *Benchmarking higher education system performance: Conceptual framework and data.* Enhancing Higher Education System Performance, OECD Paris.

OECD. (2017b). *Education at a glance 2017: OECD indicators.* OECD, Paris. https://www.oecd-ilibrary.org/education/education-at-a-glance-2017_eag-2017-en

OECD. (2021). *The state of higher education: One year into the COVID-19 pandemic.* https://doi.org/10.1787/83c41957-en

Okyar, O. (1968). Universities in Turkey. *Minerva, 6*(2), 213–243. https://doi.org/10.1007/BF01096555

Oleksiyenko, A. (2014). Socio-economic forces and the rise of the world-class research university in the post-Soviet higher education space: The case of Ukraine. *European Journal of Higher Education, 4*(3), 249–265. https://doi.org/10.1080/21568235.2014.916537

Olier, E., Valderrey, F., & García-Coso, E. (2021). University governance models across regions: Europe. In M. A. Khan, A. J. Dieck-Assad, R. G. Castillo-Villar, T. K. Henderson-Torres (Eds.), *Governance models for Latin American universities in the 21st century* (pp. 73–95). Palgrave Macmillan.

Olivarius, A. (2014). *A brief guide to Title IX compliance for study abroad* [Paper presentation]. The Association of American Study Abroad Programmes Meeting United Kingdom.

Olssen, M., & Peters, M. (2005). Neoliberalism, higher education and the knowledge economy: From the free market to knowledge capitalism. *Journal of Education policy, 20*(3), 313–345. https://doi.org/10.1080/02680930500108718

Öncü, A. (1993). Academics: The West in the discourse of university reform. In M. Heper, H. Kramer, & A. Oncu (Eds.), *Turkey and the West: Changing political and cultural identities* (pp. 142–176). I. B. Tauris.

Open University. (2014). *Welcome to the Open University Business School.* http://business-school.open.ac.uk/about

Ordorika, I., & Lloyd, M. (2015). International rankings and the contest for university hegemony. *Journal of Education Policy, 30*(3), 385–405.

Organ, T. (1998). *The Hindu quest for the perfection of man.* Wipf and Stock Publishers.

Ota, H. (2018). Internationalization of higher education: Global trends and Japan's challenges. *Educational Studies in Japan, 12*, 91–105. https://doi.org/10.7571/esjkyoiku.12.91

Padula, G., & Dagnino, G. (2007). Untangling the rise of coopetition: The intrusion of competition in a cooperative game structure. *International Studies of Management & Organization, 37*(2), 32–52.

Page, A., & Chahboun, S. (2019). Emerging empowerment of international students: How international student literature has shifted to include the students' voices. *Higher Education, 78*(5), 871–885. https://doi.org/10.1007/s10734-019-00375-7

Park, S., Han, S., Hwang, S., & Park, C. (2019). Comparison of leadership styles in Confucian Asian countries. *Human Resource Development International, 22*(1), 91–100. https://doi.org/10.1080/13678868.2018.1425587

Patel, N. (1994). A comparative exposition of Western and Vedic theories of the institution of education. *International Journal of Educational Management, 8*(6), 9–14. https://doi.org/10.1108/09513549410069158

Paton, M. (2011). Asian students, critical thinking and English as an academic lingua franca. *Analytic Teaching and Philosophical Praxis, 32*(1), 27–39. https://journal.viterbo.edu/index.php/atpp/article/view/1063/877

Pavlov, O., & Hoy, F. (2019). Toward the service science of education. In P. P. Maglio, C. A. Kieliszewski, J. C. Spohrer, K. Lyons, L. Patricio, & Y. Sawatani (Eds.), *Handbook of Service Science, Volume II* (pp. 545–566). Springer.

Pearson, M. (2015). Modeling universal design for learning techniques to support multicultural education for pre-service secondary educators. *Multicultural Education, 22*(3–4), 27–34. https://files.eric.ed.gov/fulltext/EJ1078698.pdf

Pease, P. (2001). *Transnational education and quality assurance for online learning*. Abstract retrieved from http://www.oecd.org/edu/skills-beyond-school/1853930.pdf

Pelkonen, A., & Nieminen, M. (2015). *Korkeakoulujen ja tutkimuslaitosten yhteistyö ja yhteistyön esteet* (Cooperation and barriers to cooperation between universities and research institutes). Teaching and Ministry of Culture's publications. http://urn.fi/URN:ISBN:978-952-263-335-4

Pessoa, S., Miller, R., & Kaufer, D. (2014). Students' challenges and development in the transition to academic writing at an English-medium university in Qatar. *International Review of Applied Linguistics in Language Teaching, 52*(2), 127–156. http://www2.ryanmiller.org/wp-content/uploads/2017/12/Pessoa-Miller-Kaufer-2014-IRAL.pdf

Petitmengin, C., Remillieux, A., & Valenzuela-Moguillansky, C. (2019). Discovering the structures of lived experience: Towards a micro-phenomenological analysis method. *Phenomenology and the Cognitive Sciences, 18*(4), 691–730. https://doi.org/10.1007/s11097-018-9597-4

Pherali, T. (2012). Academic mobility, language, and cultural capital: The experience of transnational academics in British higher education institutions. *Journal of Studies in International Education, 16*(4), 313–333. https://doi.org/10.1177/1028315311421842

Phillips, D., & Zuckerman, E. (2001). Middle-status conformity: Theoretical restatement and empirical demonstration in two markets. *American Journal of Sociology, 107*(2), 379–429. https://doi.org/10.1086/324072

Pine, J., & Gilmore, G. (1998). Welcome to the experience economy. *Harvard Business Review, 76*(4), 97–105. https://hbr.org/1998/07/welcome-to-the-experience-economy

Pino, M., & Mortari, L. (2014). The inclusion of students with dyslexia in higher education: A systematic review using narrative synthesis. *Dyslexia, 20*(4), 346–369. https://doi.org/ 10.1002/dys.1484

Pitard, J. (2019). Autoethnography as a phenomenological tool: Connecting the personal to the cultural. In P. Liamputtong (Ed.), *Handbook of Research Methods in Health Social Sciences* (Vol. 3, pp. 1829–1846). Springer.

Podolny, J. (1993). A status-based model of market competition. *American Journal of Sociology, 98*(4), 829–872. http://pascal-francis.inist.fr/vibad/index.php?action=getRecordDetail&idt=6118560

Pokarier, C. (2010). Japanese higher education: Seeking adaptive efficiency in a mature sector. In C. Findlay & W. G. Tierney (Eds.), *Globalisation and tertiary education in the Asia-Pacific: The changing nature of a dynamic market* (pp. 255–284). Stallion Press.

Postiglione, G., & Altbach, P. (2017). Global: Professors: The key to internationalization. In G. Mihut, H. de Wit, & A. Altbach (Eds.), *Understanding Higher Education Internationalization* (pp. 247–249). Sense Publishers.

Prahalad, C., & Ramaswamy, V. (2004). *The future of competition: Co-creating unique value with customers*. Harvard Business Press.

Pratt, M., & Foreman, P. (2000). Classifying managerial responses to multiple organizational identities. *Academy of Management Review, 25*(1), 18–42. https://doi.org/10.2307/259261

Prebys, P., & Ricciardelli, F. (Eds.). (2017). A tale of two cities: Florence and Rome from the grand tour to study abroad. In *Proceedings of the Conference held in Florence, Palazzo Vecchio, Salone dei Cinquecento, on March 9, 2016*. Ferrara, Edisai. https://aacupi.files.wordpress.com/2017/09/taleoftwocities-florence.pdf

QAA. (2012). *Review of TNE in China, 2012*. Retrieved from https://www.qaa.ac.uk/docs/qaa/international/tne-china-overview-(1).pdf?sfvrsn=e43ff481_2

QAA. (2018). *The revised UK quality code for higher education* (UKSCQA/02). https://www.qaa.ac.uk/docs/qaa/quality-code/revised-uk-quality-code-for-higher-education.pdf?sfvrsn=4c19f781_8

QAA. (2021). *The quality evaluation and enhancement of UK transnational higher education provision 2021–22 to 2025–26*. https://www.qaa.ac.uk/docs/qaa/guidance/qe-tne-handbook-21.pdf?sfvrsn=3ec7d281_10

QAA. (2021). *Transnational education*. https://www.qaa.ac.uk/international/transnational-education

Qian, J., & Krugly-Smolska, E. (2008). Chinese graduate students' experiences with writing a literature review. *TESL Canada Journal, 26*(1), 68–86. https://doi.org/10.18806/tesl.v26i1.391

Quacquarelli Symonds. (2022). QS world university rankings: Methodology. Retrieved September 12, 2021 from https://www.topuniversities.com/qs-world-university-rankings/methodology

Raffaelli, R., & Glynn, M. (2014). Turnkey or tailored? Relational pluralism, institutional complexity, and the organizational adoption of more or less customized practices. *Academy of Management Journal, 57*(2), 541–562. https://www.jstor.org/stable/43589270

Rampelt, F., Orr, D., & Knoth, A. (2019). *Bologna digital 2020 – White paper on digitalisation in the European higher education area.* https://www.researchgate.net/publication/333520288_Bologna_Digital_2020_-_White_Paper_on_Digitalisation_in_the_European_Higher_Education_Area

Ranking Web of Universities. (2019). https://www.webometrics.info/en/node/54

Rao, K., & Meo, G. (2016). Using universal design for learning to access academic standards. *SAGE Open, 6*(4), 1–18. https://doi.org/10.1177/2158244016680688

Rathburn, M., & Lexier, R. (2016). Global citizenship in Canadian universities: A new framework. *Journal of Global Citizenship & Equity Education, 5*(1), 1–25. https://journals.sfu.ca/jgcee/index.php/jgcee/article/view/149/210

Rather, R. (2020). Customer experience and engagement in tourism destinations: The experiential marketing perspective. Journal of Travel & Tourism Marketing, 37(1), 15–32. https://doi.org/10.1080/10548408.2019.1686101

Reagan, T. (2004). *Non-Western educational traditions: Alternative approaches to educational thought and practice.* Routledge.

Rear, D. (2017). Reframing the debate on Asian students and critical thinking: Implications for Western universities. *Journal of Contemporary Issues in Education, 12*(2), 18–33. https://doi.org/10.20355/C5P35F

Reisberg, L. (1998, September 28). Earlham college settles suit by exchange student who said she was raped in Japan. *The Chronicle of Higher Education.* https://www.chronicle.com/article/earlham-college-settles-suit-by-exchange-student-who-said-she-was-raped-in-japan/

Reisberg, L., & Rumbley, L. (2014). Redefining academic mobility: From the pursuit of scholarship to the pursuit of revenue. In A. Maldonado-Maldonado & R. Bassett (Eds.), *The forefront of international higher education* (pp. 115–126). Springer.

Rhee, J., & Sagaria, M. (2004). International students: Constructions of imperialism in the Chronicle of Higher Education. *The Review of Higher Education, 28*(1), 77–96. https://doi.org/10.1353/rhe.2004.0031

Richards, R., Emery, T., & France, L. (2020). Internationalisation of NZ tertiary education: Supporting international students' adjustments to learner-centred education. In J. Fox, C. Alexander, & T. Aspland (Eds.), *Teacher education in globalised times* (pp. 53–73). Springer.

Rindova, V., Martins, L., Srinivas, S., & Chandler, D. (2018). The good, the bad, and the ugly of organizational rankings: A multidisciplinary review of the literature and directions for future research. *Journal of Management, 44*(6), 2175–2208.

Ritala, P. (2010). *Coopetitive advantage—How firms create and appropriate value by collaborating with their competitors.* Lappeenranta University of Technology. https://lutpub.lut.fi/handle/10024/61790

Rivers, D. (2010). Ideologies of internationalisation and the treatment of diversity within Japanese higher education. *Journal of Higher Education Policy and Management, 32*(5), 441–454. https://doi.org/10.1080/1360080X.2010.511117

Robertson, S., Bonal, X., & Dale, R. (2002). GATS and the education service industry: The politics of scale and global reterritorialization. *Comparative Education Review, 46*(4), 472–496. https://doi.org/10.1086/343122

Robinson-Pant, A., & Magyar, A. (2018). The recruitment agent in internationalized higher education: Commercial broker and cultural mediator. *Journal of Studies in International Education, 22*(3), 225–241. https://doi.org/10.1177/1028315318762485

Robson, K., Humphrey, C., Khalifa, R., & Jones, J. (2007). Transforming Audit technologies: Business risk audit methodologies and the audit field. *Accounting, Organizations and Society, 32*(4–5), 409–438. https://doi.org/10.1016/j.aos.2006.09.002

Rose, H., & McKinley, J. (2018). Japan's English-medium instruction initiatives and the globalization of higher education. *Higher Education, 75*(1), 111–129. https://doi.org/10.1007/s10734-017-0125-1

Rothstein, L. (2014). Forty years of disability policy in legal education and the legal profession: What has changed and what are the new issues. *American University Journal of Gender, Social Policy & the Law, 22*, 519–650. https://digitalcommons.wcl.american.edu/cgi/viewcontent.cgi?referer=&httpsredir=1&article=1639&context=jgspl

Rowley, C., Oh, I., & Jang, W. (2019). New perspectives on East Asian leadership in the age of globalization: Local grounding and historical comparisons in the Asia Pacific Region. *Asia Pacific Business Review, 25*(2), 307–315. https://doi.org/10.1080/13602381.2018.1557424

Rusko, R. (2012). Perspectives on value creation and coopetition. *Problems and Perspectives in Management, 10*(2), 60–72. https://www.businessperspectives.org/index.php/journals?controller=pdfview&task=download&item_id=4601

Rusko, R. (2018). Coopetition for destination marketing: The scope of forging relationships with competitors. In M. Camilleri (Ed.), *Tourism planning and destination marketing* (pp. 75–98). Emerald Publishing Limited.

Rusko, R. (2019). Is coopetitive decision-making a black box? Technology and digitisation as decision-makers and drivers of coopetition. *Technology Analysis & Strategic Management, 31*(8), 888–901. https://doi.org/10.1080/09537325.2019.1573981

Rusko, R., Alatalo, L., Hänninen, J., Riipi, J., Salmela, V., & Vanha, J. (2018). Technological disruption as a driving force for coopetition: The case of the self-driving car industry. *International Journal of Innovation in the Digital Economy, 9*(1), 35–50. https://doi.org/10.4018/IJIDE.2018010104

Russell Group. (2010). *Staying on top: The challenge of sustaining world-class higher education in the UK*. Russell Group Papers–Issue 2. https://russellgroup.ac.uk/media/5255/staying-on-top-the-challenge-of-sustaining-world-class-higher-education-in-the-uk.pdf

Rust, V., & Kim, S. (2012). The global competition in higher education. *World Studies in Education, 13*(1), 5–20.

Rutherford, J. (2001, January 26). Scholars squeezed by market muscle. *Times Higher Education Supplement*. https://www.businessperspectives.org/index.php/journals?controller=pdfview&task=download&item_id=4601

Ryan, J., Rabbidge, M., Wang, Y., & Field, J. (2019). Satisfiers and Dissatisfiers for International Vocational Education Students: A Case Study Using Narrative Frames. *Journal of International Students, 9*(3), 795–814. https://doi.org/10.32674/jis.v9i3.751

Ryans, J., Griffith, D., & White, D. (2003). Standardization/adaptation of international marketing strategy: Necessary conditions for the advancement of knowledge. *International Marketing Review, 20*(6), 588–603. https://doi.org/10.1108/02651330310505204

Sabzalieva, E., Chacón, E., & Morales, D. (2021). *Thinking higher and beyond: Perspectives on the futures of higher education to 2050.* UNESCO.

Saito, K., & Kim, S. (2019). Internationalization of Japanese higher education: Effective organization of internationally cooperative higher education programs. *Higher Learning Research Communications, 9*(1), 47–63. https://doi.org/10.18870/hlrc.v9i1.441

Sakhiyya, Z., & Rata, E. (2019). From 'priceless' to 'priced': The value of knowledge in higher education. *Globalisation, Societies and Education, 17*(3), 285–295. https://doi.org/10.1080/14767724.2019.1583089

Samsonova-Taddei, A., & Humphrey, C. (2014). Transnationalism and the transforming roles of professional accountancy bodies: Towards a research agenda. *Accounting, Auditing & Accountability Journal, 27*(6), 903–932. https://doi.org/10.1108/AAAJ-05-2013-1345

Sanders, J. (2019). National internationalisation of higher education policy in Singapore and Japan: Context and competition. *Compare: A Journal of Comparative and International Education, 49*(3), 413–429. https://doi.org/10.1080/03057925.2017.1417025

Sauder, M., Lynn, F., & Podolny, J. (2012). Status: Insights from organizational sociology. *Annual Review of Sociology, 38*, 267–283. https://doi.org/10.1146/annurev-soc-071811-145503

Sawir, E. (2005). Language difficulties of international students in Australia: The effects of prior learning experience. *International Education Journal, 6*(5), 567–580. https://files.eric.ed.gov/fulltext/EJ855010.pdf

Schaffer, S. (2004, April 15). Do United States laws prohibiting discrimination on the basis of disability apply to study abroad programs [Paper presentation]. *Nonprofit Forum*, New York, NY. https://www.law.nyu.edu/sites/default/files/npf/Schaffer%20April%202004.pdf

Schmitt, B. (1999). Experiential marketing. Journal of Marketing Management, 15(1–3), 53–67. https://doi.org/10.1362/026725799784870496

Schott, T. (1988). International influence in science: Beyond center and periphery. *Social Science Research, 17*(3), 219–238. https://doi.org/10.1016/0049-089X(88)90014-2

Scott, P. (1995). *The meanings of mass higher education.* The Society for Research Into Higher Education & Open University Press.

Scott, P. (2000). Globalisation and higher education: Challenges for the 21st century. *Journal of Studies in International Education, 4*(1), 3–10. https://doi.org/10.1177/102831530000400102

Scott, P. (Ed.). (1998). *The globalization of higher education.* Open University Press.

Seeber, M., Cattaneo, M., Huisman, J., & Paleari, S. (2016). Why do higher education institutions internationalize? An investigation of the multilevel determinants of internationalization rationales. *Higher Education, 72*(5), 685–702. https://doi.org/10.1007/s10734-015-9971-x

Seidel, H. (1991). Internationalisation: A new challenge for universities. *Higher Education, 21*, 289–296. https://doi.org/10.1007/BF00132721

Selvaratnam, V. (1988). Ethnicity, inequality, and higher education in Malaysia. *Comparative Education Review, 32*(2), 173–196. https://doi.org/10.1086/446755

Selvi, A. (2014). The medium-of-instruction debate in Turkey: Oscillating between national ideas and bilingual ideals. *Current Issues in Language Planning, 15*(2), 133–152. https://doi.org/10.1080/14664208.2014.898357

Setty, S. (1999). Leveling the playing field: Reforming the Office for Civil Rights to achieve better Title IX enforcement. *Columbia Journal of Law & Social Problems, 32*(4), 331–358. https://digitalcommons.law.wne.edu/cgi/viewcontent.cgi?referer=&httpsredir=1&article=1156&context=facschol

Shaheen, N. (2016). International students' critical thinking–related problem areas: UK university teachers' perspectives. *Journal of Research in International Education, 15*(1), 18–31. https://doi.org/10.1177/1475240916635895

Shaheer, N., & Li, S. (2020). The CAGE around cyberspace? How digital innovations internationalize in a virtual world. *Journal of Business Venturing, 35*(1), Article 105892. https://doi.org/10.1016/j.jbusvent.2018.08.002

Shams, F., & Huisman, J. (2012). Managing offshore branch campuses: An analytical framework for institutional strategies. *Journal of Studies in International Education, 16*(2), 106–127. https://doi.org/10.1177/1028315311413470

Shams, S. M. (2016). Transnational education and total quality management: A stakeholder-centred model. *Journal of Management Development, 36*(3), 376–389. https://doi.org/10.1108/JMD-10-2015-0147

Sharipov, F. (2020). Internationalization of higher education: Definition and description. *Mental Enlightenment Scientific-Methodological Journal, 2020*(1), 127–138. Article 47.

Sharma, M., & Portelli, J. (2014). Uprooting and settling in: The invisible strength of deficit thinking. *LEARNing Landscapes, 8*(1), 251–267. https://doi.org/10.36510/learnland.v8i1.684

Shemshack, A., & Spector, J. (2020). A systematic literature review of personalized learning terms. *Smart Learning Environments, 7*(1), 1–20. https://doi.org/10.1186/s40561-020-00140-9

Shields, R. (2013). Globalization and international student mobility: A network analysis. *Comparative Education Review, 57*(4), 609–636. https://doi.org/10.1086/671752

Shils, E. (1988). Center and periphery: An idea and its career, 1935–1987. In L. Greenfeld & M. Martin (Eds), *Center: Ideas and institutions* (pp. 250–282). University of Chicago Press.

Siegel, D., & Leih, S. (2018). Strategic management theory and universities: An overview of the special issue. *Strategic Organization, 16*(1), 6–11. https://doi.org/10.1177/1476127017750776

Simon, M. (2019, May 20). Lawsuit details alleged sexual harassment of Clemson University student by a professor. *The Greenville News.* https://www.greenville

online.com/story/news/2019/05/20/clemson-university-student-lawsuit-details-alleged-sexual-harassment/3731295002/

Simpson, E. (1949). Measurement of diversity. *Nature, 163*(4148), 688–688. http://dx.doi.org/10.1038/163688a0

Skyrme, G. (2007). Entering the university: The differentiated experience of two Chinese international students in a New Zealand University. *Studies in Higher Education, 32*(3), 357–372. https://doi.org/10.1080/03075070701346915

Skyrme, G., & McGee, A. (2016). Pulled in many directions: Tensions and complexity for academic staff responding to international students. *Teaching in Higher Education, 21*(7), 759–772. https://doi.org/10.1080/13562517.2016.1183614

Slaughter, S., & Cantwell, B. (2012). Transatlantic moves to the market: The United States and the European Union. *Higher Education, 63*(5), 583–606. https://www.jstor.org/stable/41429102

Slaughter, S., & Leslie, L. (1997). *Academic capitalism: Politics, policies, and the entrepreneurial university.* John Hopkins University Press.

Smart, D., & Ang, G. (1993). Exporting education: From aid to trade to internationalization? *Institute of Public Affairs Review, 46*(1), 31–33. https://search.informit.org/doi/abs/10.3316/iclapa.930808990

Smith v. United States, 507 U.S. 197, 122 L. Ed. 2d 548, 113 S. Ct. 1178 (1993).

Smith, C., Zhou, G., Potter, M., & Wang, D. (2019). Connecting best practices for teaching linguistically and culturally diverse international students with international student satisfaction and student perceptions of student learning. *Advances in Global Education and Research, 3,* 252–265. https://scholar.uwindsor.ca/educationpub/24

Smith, K. (2014). Exploring flying faculty teaching experiences: Motivations, challenges and opportunities. *Studies in Higher Education, 39*(1), 117–134. https://doi.org/10.1080/03075079.2011.646259

Soler, J. (2019). Language policy and the internationalization of universities: A focus on Estonian higher education. *Language and Social Life* (Vol. 15). https://doi.org/10.1515/9781501505898

Soliman, S., Anchor, J., & Taylor, D. (2019). The international strategies of universities: Deliberate or emergent? *Studies in Higher Education, 44*(8), 1413–1424. https://doi.org/10.1080/03075079.2018.1445985

Spencer-Oatey, H., & Dauber, D. (2017). *Internationalisation and the development of 'global graduates': Hearing the students' voices.* GlobalPAD Working Papers. https://warwick.ac.uk/fac/soc/al/globalpad-rip/openhouse/interculturalskills/internationalisation_gg_student_voices.pdf

Spohrer, J., Maglio, P., Bailey, J., & Gruhl, D. (2007). Steps toward a science of service systems. *Computer, 40*(1), 71–77. https://doi.org/10.1109/MC.2007.33

Stallivieri, L. (2019, August 31). *Making the case for responsible internationalisation.* University World News. https://www.universityworldnews.com/post.php?story=20190829092237117

Statista. (2019). *Number of universities worldwide in 2018, by country.* https://www.statista.com/statistics/918403/number-of-universities-worldwide-by-country

Stein, S., Andreotti, V., Bruce, J., & Suša, R. (2016). Towards different conversations about the internationalization of higher education. *Comparative and International Education, 45*(1), 2–20.

Steunpunt Inclusief Hoger Onderwijs. (2021, March 18). *Webinar 4–The potential of universal design to create inclusive classroom practices with international students.* Towards genuinely inclusive universities: An international perspective on best practices in the implementation of universal design series. https://www.siho.be/nl/publicaties/webinars-inclusive-universities

Stier, J. (2004). Taking a critical stance toward internationalization ideologies in higher education: Idealism, instrumentalism and educationalism. *Globalisation, Societies and Education, 2*(1), 1–28. https://doi.org/10.1080/1476772042000177069

Straker, J. (2020). Object in view: Understanding international students' participation in group work. *Journal of International Students, 10*(4), 1040–1063. https://doi.org/10.32674/jis.v10i4.1370

Strang, D., & Soule, S. (1998). Diffusion in organizations and social movements: From hybrid corn to poison pills. *Annual Review of Sociology, 24*(1), 265–290. https://doi.org/10.1146/annurev.soc.24.1.265

Suddaby, R., Cooper, D., & Greenwood, R. (2007). Transnational regulation of professional services: Governance dynamics of field level organizational change. *Accounting, Organizations and Society, 32*(4–5), 333–362. https://EconPapers.repec.org/RePEc:eee:aosoci:v:32:y:2007:i:4-5:p:333-362

Susela, D. (1999). "Interests" and accounting standard setting in Malaysia. *Accounting, Auditing & Accountability Journal, 12*(3), 358–387. https://doi.org/10.1108/09513579910277410

Susela, D. (2010). The Malaysian accountancy profession and its imperial legacy (1957–1995). In C. Poullaos & S. Sian (Eds.), *Accountancy and empire: The British legacy of professional organization* (Chapter 5). Routledge.

Szkornik, K. (2017). Teaching and learning on a transnational education programme: Opportunities and challenges for flying faculty in geography and related disciplines. *Journal of Geography in Higher Education, 41*(4), 521–531. https://doi.org/10.1080/03098265.2017.1337735

Takayama, K. (2017). Imagining East Asian education otherwise: Neither caricature, nor scandalization. *Asia Pacific Journal of Education, 37*(2), 262–274. https://doi.org/10.1080/02188791.2017.1310697

Tamilla, C., & Ledgerwood, J. R. (2018). Students' motivations, perceived benefits and constraints towards study abroad and other international education opportunities. *Journal of International Education in Business, 11*(1), 63–78. http://dx.doi.org.ezproxy.lib.utexas.edu/10.1108/JIEB-01-2017-0002

Tamrat, W., & Teferra, D. (2018). Internationalization of Ethiopian higher education institutions: Manifestations of a nascent system. *Journal of Studies in International Education, 22*(5), 434–453. https://doi.org/10.1177/1028315318786425

Tamtik, M. (2017). Policy coordination challenges in governments' innovation policy—The case of Ontario, Canada. *Science and Public Policy, 44*(3), 417–427.

Tan, C. (2017). A Confucian conception of critical thinking. *Journal of Philosophy of Education, 51*(1), 331–343. https://doi.org/10.1111/1467-9752.12228

Tang, L. (2019). Five ways China must cultivate research integrity. *Nature, 575,* 589–591. https://doi.org/10.1038/d41586-019-03613-1

Taras, V., Kirkman, B., & Steel, P. (2010). Examining the impact of culture's consequences: A three-decade, multilevel, meta-analytic review of Hofstede's cultural value dimensions. *Journal of Applied Psychology, 95*(3), 405–439. https://doi.org/10.1037/a0018938

Tawfik, S. (2021). Phenomenological narrative in the art of autobiography: In theory and personal experience. *American Journal of Art and Design, 6*(4), 112–119. https://doi.org/10.11648/j.ajad.20210604.11

Tayar, M., & Jack, R. (2013). Prestige-oriented market entry strategy: The case of Australian universities. *Journal of Higher Education Policy and Management, 35*(2), 153–166. https://doi.org/10.1080/1360080X.2013.775924

Teekens, H. (2003). The requirement to develop specific skills for teaching in an intercultural setting. *Journal of Studies in International Education, 7*(1), 108–119. https://doi.org/10.1177/1028315302250192

Teichler, U. (1996). Comparative higher education: Potentials and limits. *Higher Education, 32*(4), 431–465. https://doi.org/10.1007/BF00133257

Teichler, U. (2017). Internationalisation trends in higher education and the changing role of international student mobility. *Journal of International Mobility, 1*, 177–216. https://doi.org/10.3917/jim.005.0179

Tenzer, H., & Pudelko, M. (2016). Media choice in multilingual virtual teams. *Journal of International Business Studies, 47*(4), 427–452. https://www.jstor.org/stable/43907582

Tham, S. (2013). Internationalizing higher education in Malaysia: Government policies and university's response. *Journal of Studies in International Education, 17*(5), 648–662. https://doi.org/10.1177/1028315313476954

Thang, N., & Quang, T. (2007). International briefing 18: Training and development in Vietnam. *International Journal of Training and Development, 11*(2), 139–149. https://doi.org/10.1111/j.1468-2419.2007.00275.x

The Forum on Education Abroad. (2017). *Sexual misconduct, education abroad and Title IX / Clery Act.* The Forum on Education Abroad Standards Committee Title IX/Clery Act Working Group. https://forumea.org/wp-content/uploads/2017/02/ForumEA-Sexual-Misconduct-Education-Abroad-and-Title-IXClery-Act-Updated-Feb-2017.pdf

The Law Dictionary. (n.d.). *EXTRATERRITORIALITY definition & legal meaning.* https://thelawdictionary.org/extraterritoriality/

Thomas, J. (2013, November 1). Uconn students file federal lawsuit over university's handling of sexual assaults. *The CT Mirror.* https://ctmirror.org/2013/11/01/uconn-students-file-federal-lawsuit-over-universitys-handling-sexual-assaults/

Thomas, L. (2012). *Building student engagement and belonging in higher education at a time of change: A summary of findings and recommendations from the What Works? Student Retention & Success programme.* PHF, HEFCE, The Higher Education Academy, Action on Access.

Thompson, C. (2011). Critical thinking across the curriculum: Process over output. *International Journal of Humanities and Social Science, 1*(9), 1–7. http://www.ijhssnet.com/journals/Vol._1_No._9_Special_Issue_July_2011/1.pdf

Thondhlana, J., Garwe, E., de Wit, H., Gacel-Ávila, J., Huang, F., & Tamrat, W. (Eds.). (2020). *The Bloomsbury handbook of the internationalization of higher education in the global south.* Bloomsbury Publishing. https://www.bloomsbury.com/us/bloomsbury-handbook-of-the-internationalization-of-higher-education-in-the-global-south-9781350139251

Tidström, A. (2008), Perspectives on coopetition on actor and operational levels. *Management Research, 6*(3), 207–217. https://doi.org/10.2753/JMR1536-5433060304

Tidström, A., & Rajala, A. (2016). Coopetition strategy as interrelated praxis and practices on multiple levels. *Industrial Marketing Management, 58*, 35–44. https://doi.org/10.1016/j.indmarman.2016.05.013

Tight, M. (2021). Globalization and internationalization as frameworks for higher education research. *Research Papers in Education, 36*(1), 52–74. https://doi.org/10.1080/02671522.2019.1633560

Tirgar, A., Sajjadi, S., & Aghalari, Z. (2019). The status of international collaborations in compilation of Iranian scientific articles on environmental health engineering. *Globalization and Health, 15*(1), 1–9. https://doi.org/10.1186/s12992-019-0460-3

Title IX. Education Amendments of the Civil Rights Act, 92 P.L. 318, 86 Stat. 235; 20 USC § 1972. https://www.justice.gov/crt/fcs/TitleIX-SexDiscrimination

Title VI. Sec. 601, Civil Rights Act of 1964; 78 Stat. 252; 42 USCS § 2000d. https://www.justice.gov/crt/fcs/TitleVI-Overview#:~:text=Overview%20of%20Title%20VI%20of,activities%20receiving%20federal%20financial%20assistance

Toh, G. (2014). English for content instruction in a Japanese higher education setting: Examining challenges, contradictions and anomalies. *Language and Education, 28*(4), 299–318. https://doi.org/10.1080/09500782.2013.857348

Toivonen, M., Tuominen, T., & Brax, S. (2007). Innovation process interlinked with the process of service delivery: A management challenge in KIBS. *Economies et Sociétés, 41*(3), 355–384. https://research.aalto.fi/en/publications/innovation-process-interlinked-with-the-process-of-service-delive

Tonini, D., Burbules, N., & Gunsalus, C. (2016). New models of hybrid leadership in global higher education. *Educational Considerations, 43*(3), 37–46. https://doi.org/10.4148/0146-9282.1019

Topaler, B., & Üsdiken, B. (2021). Diffusion of pure and hybrid forms of a practice: Language of instruction in Turkish universities, 1983–2014. *European Management Review, 18*(2), 173–185. https://doi.org/10.1111/emre.12439

Torres-Olave, B., Brown, A., Franco Carrera, L., & Ballinas, C. (2020). Not waving but striving: Research collaboration in the context of stratification, segmentation, and the quest for prestige. *The Journal of Higher Education, 91*(2), 275–299. https://doi.org/10.1080/00221546.2019.1631074

Tracey, P., Phillips, N., & Jarvis, O. (2011). Bridging institutional entrepreneurship and the creation of new organizational forms: A multilevel model. *Organization Science, 22*(1), 60–80. https://www.jstor.org/stable/20868847

Tran, L., & Nguyen, N. (2015). Re-imagining teachers' professional roles and identity under the condition of internationalisation. *Teachers and Teaching: Theory and Practice, 21*(8), 958–973. https://doi.org/10.1080/13540602.2015.1005866

Tremblay, K. (2008). Internationalisation: Shaping strategies in the national context. In E. Arnal, E. Basri, P. Santiago (Eds.), *Tertiary education for the knowledge society* (Vol. 3, pp. 53126). OECD.

Trends in U.S. Study Abroad. (n.d.). NAFSA. https://www.nafsa.org/policy-and-advocacy/policy-resources/trends-us-study-abroad

Trenkic, D., & Warmington, M. (2019). Language and literacy skills of home and international university students: How different are they, and does it matter? *Bilingualism: Language and Cognition, 22*(2), 349–365. https://doi.org/10.1017/S136672891700075X

Trompenaars, F. (1993). *Riding the waves of culture.* Nikolas Brealey Publishing.

Tsang, E., & Yip, P. (2007). Economic distance and the survival of foreign direct investments. *Academy of Management Journal, 50*(5), 1156–1168.

Tsui, L. (2002). Fostering critical thinking through effective pedagogy: Evidence from four institutional case studies. *The Journal of Higher Education, 73*(6), 740–763.

Übi, J. (2014). *Methods for coopetition and retention analysis: An application to university management.* Docotral Dissertation. Tallinn University of Technology.

U.S. Department of Education. (n.d.). *Centers for international business education.* https://www2.ed.gov/programs/iegpscibe/index.html

U.S. News & World Reports. (2018). U of Minnesota settled student's Cuba rape lawsuit for $137K. *U.S. News & World Reports.* Retrieved from https://www.us-news.com/news/best-states/minnesota/articles/2018-11-28/u-ofminnesota-settled-students-cuba-rape-lawsuit-for-137k

Uchihara, T., & Harada, T. (2018). Roles of vocabulary knowledge for success in English-medium instruction: Self-perceptions and academic outcomes of Japanese undergraduates. *Tesol Quarterly, 52*(3), 564–587. https://doi.org/10.1002/tesq.453

UNESCO. (2020, March 24). *COVID-19 education in the time of disruption and response.* https://www.unesco.org/en/articles/covid-19-educational-disruption-and-response?TSPD_101_R0=080713870fab200068a1eefb4ac66a98203db798c228e78d1957db1a41ff9e7aa1a933f761ae9f9f088eb014af14300027e13d9a5502ab4910d411bfb9105ed0f9e9ff645395c78f489ea63793919797ada1582b38331e50dc369fac40a1835b

University of Bonn. (2022). *Rectorate. University of Bonn. 2025 Internationalization Strategy.* https://www.uni-bonn.de/en/international/international-profile/2025-internationalization-strategy/university-of-bonn_2025-internationalization-strategy.pdf

United States Department of Education. (2015). *Delivering justice: Report to the president and secretary of education.* U.S. Department of Education Office of Civil Rights. https://www2.ed.gov/about/reports/annual/ocr/report-to-president-and-secretary-of-education-2015.pdf

United States Department of Education. (2016). *Programs: Centers for international business education.* Retrieved from https://www2.ed.gov/programs/iegpscibe/index.html

United States Department of Education. (2017). *Department of Education issues new interim guidance on campus sexual misconduct.* https://content.govdelivery.com/accounts/USED/bulletins/1b8b87c

United States Department of Education. (2021). *Pending cases currently under investigation at elementary-secondary and post-secondary schools.* https://www2.ed.gov/about/offices/list/ocr/docs/investigations/open-investigations/tix.html

United States. Department of Health, Education, and Welfare. Office for Civil Rights. (1978). *Section 504 of the Rehabilitation act of 1973: Fact sheet: Handicapped persons rights under Federal law*. Washington: Dept. of Health, Education, and Welfare, Office of the Secretary, Office for Civil Rights. https://www.hhs.gov/sites/default/files/ocr/civilrights/resources/factsheets/504.pdf

Universities UK. (2018). *International facts and figures 2018*. UUKI Publications. https://www.universitiesuk.ac.uk/universities-uk-international/insights-and-publications/uuki-publications/international-facts-and-figures-2018

Universities UK. (2020). *The scale of UK higher education transnational education 2018–19*. https://www.universitiesuk.ac.uk/universities-uk-international/insights-and-publications/uuki-publications/scale-uk-higher-education-transnational-1

University of Bonn (2021). *2025 internationalization strategy*. https://www.uni-bonn.de/en/international/international-profile/2025-internationalization-strategy/internationalization-strategy

University of California Merced. (2022). *What statistics show about study abroad students*. https://studyabroad.ucmerced.edu/study-abroad-statistics/statistics-study-abroad

University of Oxford. (n.d.). *International applicants*. https://www.ox.ac.uk/admissions/graduate/international-applicants

Üsdiken, B. (2011). Transferring American models for education in business and public administration to Turkey, 1950–1970. In B. Criss, S. Esenbel, T. Greenwood, & L. Mazzari (Eds.), *American Turkish encounters: Politics and culture, 1830–1989* (pp. 316–330). Cambridge Scholars Publishing.

Üsdiken, B. (2014). Centres and peripheries: Research styles and publication patterns in 'Top' US journals and their European alternatives, 1960–2010. *Journal of Management Studies, 51*(5), 764–789. https://doi.org/10.1111/joms.12082

Üsdiken, B., Topaler, A., & Koçak, Ö. (2013). Diversity in types of law, market and organization: Universities in Turkey after 1981. *Journal of Ankara University Faculty of Political Sciences, 68*(3), 187–223. https://research.sabanciuniv.edu/id/eprint/21867

Üsdiken, B., & Wasti, S. (2009). Preaching, teaching and researching at the periphery: Academic management literature in Turkey, 1970–1999. *Organization Studies, 30*(10), 1063–1082. https://doi.org/10.1177/0170840609337952

Vale, K., & Littlejohn, A. (2014). Massive open online courses: A traditional or transformative approach to learning? In A. Littlejohn & C. Pegler (Eds.), *Reusing open resources: Learning in open networks for work, life and education* (pp. 138–153). Routledge.

van der Wende, M. (2007). Internationalization of higher education in the OECD countries: Challenges and opportunities for the coming decade. *Journal of Studies in International Education, 11*(3–4), 274–289. https://doi.org/10.1177/1028315307303543

van der Wende, M. (2010). Internationalization of higher education. In P. Peterson, E. Baker, & B. McGraw (Eds.), *International encyclopedia of education* (pp. 540–545). Elsevier Science.

van Vught, F. (2008). *Benchmarking in European higher education: Findings of a two-year EU-funded project*. http://www.ehea.info/media.ehea.info/file/Transparency/75/1/benchmarking_report_1101_607751.pdf

Vandermensbrugghe, J. (2004). The unbearable vagueness of critical thinking in the context of the Anglo-Saxonisation of education. *International Education Journal, 5*(3), 417–442. https://files.eric.ed.gov/fulltext/EJ903866.pdf

Vargo, S., & Lusch, R. (2008). Service-dominant logic: Continuing the evolution. *Journal of the Academy of Marketing Science, 36*(1), 1–10. https://doi.org/10.1007/s11747-007-0069-6

Vedder, R. (2019). *Restoring the promise: Higher education in America.* Independent Institute.

Velayutham, S. (1998). The chartered accountant in New Zealand: From professional qualification to franchised brand. *Accounting Forum, 22*, 230–251. University of South Australia.

Velayutham, S. (1999). The professional accounting body in the 21st century: The global franchise. *Pacific Accounting Review, 11*(2), 163–173. https://doi.org/10.1108/eb037939

Venaik, S., & Midgley, D. (2019). Archetypes of marketing mix standardization—Adaptation in MNC subsidiaries: Fit and equifinality as complementary explanations of performance. *European Journal of Marketing, 53*(2), 366–399. https://doi.org/10.1108/EJM-11-2017-0861

Verma, S., & Gray, S. (2006). The creation of the institute of chartered accountants of India: The first steps in the development of an indigenous accounting profession post-independence. *Accounting Historians Journal, 33*(2), 131–156. https://www.jstor.org/stable/40698344

Video: Global Virtual Teams Course Challenges Students From Seven Global Network Schools to Work Across Borders. (2019, April 24). Yale School of Management. https://som.yale.edu/news/2019/04/video-global-virtual-teams-course-challenges-students-to-work-across-borders

Vincent-Lancrin, S. (2005). *Building capacity through cross-border tertiary education.* Observatory on Borderless Higher Education. https://www.obhe.org/resources/building-capacity-through-cross-border-tertiary-education

Vossen, J. (2016). *At risk abroad: Lessons from higher ed claims.* EduRisk by United Educators Risk Research Bulletin. Retrieved from: https://www.ue.org/uploadedFiles/RRB%20At%20Risk%20Abroad.pdf

Walker, A., & Dimmock, C. (2002). Moving school leadership beyond its narrow boundaries: Developing a cross-cultural approach. In K. Leithwood & P. Halinger (Eds.), *Second international handbook of educational leadership and administration* (pp. 167–202), Springer.

Wallerstein, I. (1974). The rise and future demise of the world capitalist system: Concepts for comparative analysis. *Comparative Studies in Society and History, 16*(4), 387–415. https://www.jstor.org/stable/178015

Walley, K., & Custance, P. (2010). Coopetition: Insights from the agri-food supply chain. *Journal on Chain and Network Science, 10*, 185–192. https://doi.org/10.3920/JCNS2010.x187.

Wang, J. (2009). A study of resiliency characteristics in the adjustment of international graduate students at American universities. *Journal of Studies in International Education, 13*(1), 22–45. https://doi.org/10.1177/1028315307308139

Watson, K., & McGowan, P. (2019). Rethinking competition-based entrepreneurship education in higher education institutions: Towards an affectuationinformed coopetition model. *Education+ Training, 62*(1), 31–46. https://doi.org/10.1108/ET-11-2018-0234

Webb, A., & Welsh, A. (2019). Phenomenology as a methodology for scholarship of teaching and learning research. *Teaching & Learning Inquiry, 7*(1), 168–181. https://doi.org/10.20343/teachlearninqu.7.1.11

West, C. (2015). *Japan looks to take flight: Through various initiatives, Japan is working to make internationalization soar nationwide.* Retrieved from https://www.nafsa.org/sites/default/files/ektron/files/underscore/ie_marapr15_supplement.pdf

West, R., Toplak, M., & Stanovich, K. (2008). Heuristics and biases as measures of critical thinking: Associations with cognitive ability and thinking dispositions. *Journal of Educational Psychology, 100*(4), 930–941. https://doi.org/10.1037/a0012842

Westwood, R., & Jack, G. (2007). Manifesto for a post-colonial international business and management studies: A provocation. *Critical Perspectives on International Business, 3*(3), 246–265. https://doi.org/10.1108/17422040710775021

Wheeler Campbell Limited. (1993). *A new strategy for the New Zealand Society of Accountants: A discussion paper.* NZSA.

Whieldon, J. (2019). "Are they ready to fly?" Flying faculty preparedness and professional learning: An exploratory study of transnational education staff perspectives [Unpublished doctoral thesis, University of Wolverhampton]. https://wlv.openrepository.com/bitstream/handle/2436/622708/Whieldon_Doctorate.pdf?sequence=6&isAllowed=y

Whitsed, C., & Volet, S. (2013). Positioning foreign English language teachers in the Japanese university context. *Teachers and Teaching, 19*(6), 717–735. https://doi.org/10.1080/13540602.2013.827459

Wilkins, S., & Huisman, J. (2012). The international branch campus as transnational strategy in higher education. *Higher Education, 64*(5), 627–645. https://www.jstor.org/stable/23275717

Wilkins, S., & Urbanovič, J. (2014). English as the lingua franca in transnational higher education: Motives and prospects of institutions that teach in languages other than English. *Journal of Studies in International Education, 18*(5), 405–425. https://doi.org/10.1177/1028315313517267

Willekens, F. (2008). Demography and higher education: The impact on the age structure of staff and human capital formation. In *Higher education to 2030. Volume 1: Demography* (pp. 105–124). OECD.

Wilson, K. (2016). Critical reading, critical thinking: Delicate scaffolding in English for academic purposes (EAP). *Thinking Skills and Creativity, 22,* 256–265. https://doi.org/10.1016/j.tsc.2016.10.002

Winspear, J. (2016). "We talk about globalization today as if…" [Quote]. https://www.brainyquote.com/quotes/quotes/j/jacqueline498087.html

Wohlgemuth, V., Saulich, C., & Lehmann, T. (2019, June). Internationalising education—Cross-country co-teaching among European higher education institutions. In proceedings of *5th International Conference on Higher Education Advances (HEAd'19)* (pp. 1035–1042). https://doi.org/10.4995/HEAD19.2019.9185

Woicolesco, V., Morosini, M., & Marcelino, J. (2021). COVID-19 and the crisis in the internationalization of higher education in emerging contexts. *Policy Futures in Education, 20*(4). https://doi.org/10.1177/14782103211040913

Wolf, D., & Phung, L. (2019). Studying in the United States: Language learning challenges, strategies, and support services. *Journal of International Students, 9*(1), 211–224. https://doi.org/10.32674/jis.v9i1.273

Wong, Y., Tsai, P., Liu, T., et al. (2014). Male Asian international students' perceived racial discrimination, masculine identity, and subjective masculinity stress: A moderated mediation model. *Journal of Counseling Psychology, 61*(4), 560–569. https://doi.org/10.1037/cou0000038

Worthington, E., & Taylor, K. (2019, October 10). *Four corners whistleblower sued by Murdoch University after raising concerns about international students*. ABC News. https://www.abc.net.au/news/2019-10-11/murdoch-university-sues-four-corners-whistleblower/11591520

WOW Room Takes IE's Commitment to Technology Immersion in Learning Environments to the Next Level. (2016, October 20). IE University. https://www.ie.edu/university/news-events/news/wow-room-takes-ies-commitment-to-technology-immersion-in-learning-environments-to-the-next-level/

Wu, H., Garza, E., & Guzman, N. (2015). International student's challenge and adjustment to college. *Education Research International, 2015*, Article ID 202753. https://doi.org/10.1155/2015/202753

Xiao-lin, L. (2010). On university coopetition. *Journal of Xiangtan University (Philosophy and Social Sciences), 2010*(5), 153–156.

Xu, K. (2010). Chinese "dao" and Western "truth": A comparative and dynamic perspective. *Asian Social Science, 6*(12), 42–49. https://ccsenet.org/journal/index.php/ass/article/view/6483

Yang, R. (2008). Transnational higher education in China: Contexts, characteristics and concerns. *Australian Journal of Education, 52*(3), 272–286. https://doi.org/10.1177/000494410805200305

Yayasan Peneraju Pendidikan Bumiputera. (n.d.). *Professional Accounting Programmes*. http://www.yayasanpeneraju.com.my/program-program-profesional-perakaunan.php

Yefanova, D., Montgomery, M., Woodruff, G., Johnstone, C., & Kappler, B. (2017). Instructional practices facilitating cross-national interactions in the undergraduate classroom. *Journal of International Students, 7*(3), 786–805. https://doi.org/10.5281/zenodo.570034

Yeh, E., Sharma, R., Jaiswal-Oliver, M., & Wan, G. (2021). Culturally responsive social emotional learning for international students: Professional development for higher education. *Journal of International Students, 12*(1), 19–41. https://doi.org/10.32674/jis.v12i1.2976

Yemini, M., & Sagie, N. (2016). Research on internationalisation in higher education—Exploratory analysis. *Perspectives: Policy and Practice in Higher Education, 20*(2–3), 90–98. https://doi.org/10.1080/13603108.2015.1062057

Yıldırım, S., Bostancı, S., Yıldırım, D., & Erdoğan, F. (2021). Rethinking mobility of international university students during COVID-19 pandemic. *Higher Education Evaluation and Development, 15*(2), 98–113. https://pesquisa.bvsalud.org/global-literature-on-novel-coronavirus-2019-ncov/?lang=pt&q=au:

%22Y%C4%B1ld%C4%B1r%C4%B1m,%20D.%20%C3%87a%C4%9Fr%C4%B1,%20Erdo%C4%9Fan,%20Fatma%22

Yin, R. (2009). *Case study research: Design and methods* (Vol. 5). SAGE Publications.

Yokoyama, K. (2006). Entrepreneurialism in Japanese and UK universities: Governance, management, leadership, and funding. *Higher Education, 52*(3), 523–555. https://doi.org/10.1007/s10734-005-1168-2

Yokoyama, K. (2008). Neo-liberal 'governmentality' in the English and Japanese higher education systems. *International Studies in Sociology of Education, 18*(3–4), 231–247. https://doi.org/10.1080/09620210802492815

Yonezawa, A. (2010). Much ado about ranking: Why can't Japanese universities internationalize? *Japan Forum, 22*(1–2), 121–137. https://doi.org/10.1080/09555803.2010.488948

Yonezawa, A. (2018). Higher education research in Japan: Seeking a connection with the international academic community. In J. Jung, H. Horta, & A. Yonezawa (Eds.), *Researching higher education in Asia: History, development and future* (pp. 113–130). Springer.

Yonezawa, A. (2020). Challenges of the Japanese higher education amidst population decline and globalization. *Globalisation, Societies and Education, 18*(1), 43–52. https://doi.org/10.1080/14767724.2019.1690085

Yonezawa, A., Akiba, H., & Hirouchi, D. (2009). Japanese university leaders' perceptions of internationalization: The role of government in review and support. *Journal of Studies in International Education, 13*(2), 125–142. https://doi.org/10.1177/1028315308330847

Yonezawa, A., Neubauer, D., & Meerman, A. (2012). Multilateral initiatives in the East Asian arena and the challenges for Japanese higher education. *Asian Education and Development Studies, 1*(1), 57–66. https://doi.org/10.1108/20463161211194469

Yonezawa, A., & Shimmi, Y. (2015). Transformation of university governance through internationalization: Challenges for top universities and government policies in Japan. *Higher Education, 70*, 173–186. https://doi.org/10.1007/s10734-015-9863-0

Yonezawa, Y. (2017). Internationalization management in Japanese universities: The effects of institutional structures and cultures. *Journal of Studies in International Education, 21*(4), 375–390. https://doi.org/10.1177/1028315317706412

Yu, J. (2021). Lost in lockdown? The impact of COVID-19 on Chinese international student mobility. *Journal of International Students, 11*(S2), 1–18. https://doi.org/10.32674/jis.v11iS2.3575

Yükseköğretim Bilgi Yönetim Sistemi (Higher Education Management Information System of Turkey). (2020). https://istatistik.yok.gov.tr/

Yurcaba, J. (2021, June 16). *Education department says Title IX protects LGBTQ students.* NBC News. https://www.nbcnews.com/nbc-out/education-department-says-title-ix-protects-lgbtq-students-rcna1202

Zacharia, Z., Plasch, M., Mohan, U., & Gerschberger, M. (2019). The emerging role of coopetition within inter-firm relationships. *The International Journal of Logistics Management, 30*(2), 414–437. https://doi.org/10.1108/IJLM-02-2018-0021

Zapp, M., & Lerch, J. (2020). Imagining the world: Conceptions and determinants of internationalization in higher education curricula worldwide. *Sociology of Education, 93*(4), 372–392. https://doi.org/10.1177/0038040720929304

Zelenková, A., & Hanesová, D. (2019). Intercultural competence of university teachers: A challenge of internationalization. *Journal of Language and Cultural Education, 7*(1), 1–18. https://doi.org/10.2478/jolace-2019-0001

Zeng, W., & Resnik, D. (2010). Research integrity in China: Problems and prospects. *Developing World Bioethics, 10*(3), 164–171. https://doi.org/10.1111/j.1471-8847.2009.00263.x

Zhang, Y. (2013). Power distance in online learning: Experience of Chinese learners in US higher education. *International Review of Research in Open and Distributed Learning, 14*(4), 238–254. https://doi.org/10.19173/irrodl.v14i4.1557

Zhang, Y. (2017). *Visitors or stakeholders? Engaging international students in the development of higher education policy* [Unpublished master's thesis, University of Prince Edward Island]. https://islandscholar.ca/islandora/object/ir%3A21180/datastream/PDF/view

Zhang, Y. (2018). Using Bronfenbrenner's ecological approach to understand academic advising with international community college students. *Journal of International Students, 8*(4), 1764–1782. https://doi.org/10.32674/jis.v8i4.230

Zhiheng, Z., & Brunton, M. (2007). Differences in living and learning: Chinese international students in New Zealand. *Journal of Studies in International Education, 11*(2), 124–140. https://doi.org/10.1177/1028315306289834

Zhu, Y., & Bresnahan, M. (2018). "They make no contribution!" versus "We should make friends with them!"—American domestic students' perception of Chinese international students' reticence and face. *Journal of International Students, 8*(4), 1614–1635. https://doi.org/10.32674/jis.v8i4.221

Zomerdijk, L., & Voss, C. (2010). Service design for experience-centric services. *Journal of Service Research, 13*(1), 67–82. https://doi.org/10.1177/1094670509351960

Zuckerman, E. (1999). The categorical imperative: Securities analysts and the illegitimacy discount. *American Journal of Sociology, 104*(5), 1398–1438. https://doi.org/10.1086/210178

ABOUT THE CONTRIBUTORS

Annette Ammeraal is senior lecturer at Avans University of Applied Sciences in Utrecht, Netherlands.

Marina Apaydin is associate professor of management at the School of Business of the American University in Cairo, Egypt.

Íñigo Arbiol is associate professor in the Department of International Relations and Humanities at the University of Deusto in Bilbao, Spain.

Susan Bon is interim associate dean for Research and Faculty Affairs and affiliate professor in the School of Law at the University of South Carolina in Colombia.

John D. Branch is clinical associate professor of Business Administration and co-director of the Yaffe Initiative for Digital Media at the Stephen M. Ross School of Business, at the University of Michigan in Ann Arbor.

Laura Colm is researcher of marketing and sales at SDA Bocconi School of Management in Milan, Italy.

Bradley D. F. Colpitts is associate lecturer in the School of Policy Studies at Kwansei Gakuin University in Nishinomiya, Japan.

Brandi DeMont is lecturer at the University of Texas at Austin.

The Internationalization of Higher Education: , pages 303–305
Copyright © 2023 by Information Age Publishing
www.infoagepub.com
All rights of reproduction in any form reserved.

Michael M. Dent is professor and head of the Department of Marketing, Strategy, and Innovation at Sunway Business School in Petaling Jaya, Malaysia.

Cheryl Dowie is lecturer in the School of Business at the University of Aberdeen in Aberdeen, Scotland.

Sara Easler is director of international programs and study abroad at the Haslam College of Business at the University of Tennessee in Knoxville.

Aleksandar Erceg is adjunct professor in the Faculty of Economics at Josip Juraj Strossmayer University of Osijek in Osijek, Croatia.

Frederic Fovet is associate professor in the School of Education and Technology at Royal Roads University in Victoria, Canada.

Eun Sun Godwin is senior lecturer in International Business in the Business School at the University of Wolverhampton in Wolverhampton, England.

Jenni Jones is senior lecturer in Human Resources Management in the Business School at the University of Wolverhampton in Wolverhampton, England.

Andriy Kovalenko is postgraduate research supervisor in the Faculty of Business, Design, and Service Industries at Toi Ohomai Institute of Technology in New Zealand.

Adriana Kudrnová Lovera is EQUIS manager at EFMD Global in Prague, Czech Republic.

Tine Lehmann is professor at HTW Berlin University of Applied Sciences in Berlin, Germany.

Joan Lofgren is director of the BScBA program in international business at Aalto University School of Economics in Mikkeli, Finland.

Tanya Mpofu is a doctoral student in corporate governance in the Business School at the University of Wolverhampton in Wolverhampton, England.

Sunčica Oberman Peterka is professor in the Faculty of Economics at Josip Juraj Strossmayer University of Osijek in Osijek, Croatia.

Michael Osbaldeston is emeritus professor at the Cranfield School of Management at Cranfield University in Cranfield, England.

Oleg V. Pavlov is associate professor of economics and system dynamics at Worcester Polytechnic Institute in Worcester.

About the Contributors • **305**

Rosemary Richards is postgraduate research supervisor in the Faculty of Health, Education, and Environment at Toi Ohomai Institute of Technology in New Zealand.

Rauno Rusko in university lecturer of management and organizations in the Faculty of Social Sciences at the University of Lapland in Rovaniemi, Finland.

Amanda Swain is assistant director at IES abroad in Milan, Italy.

Mike Szymanski is associate professor of strategy at Moscow School of Management Skolkovo in Moscow, Russia.

Başak Topaler is assistant professor in the faculty of economics, administrative and social sciences at Kadir Has University in Istanbul, Turkey.

Menno de Lind van Wijngaarden is senior lecturer in organization studies at HU University of Applied Sciences Utrecht in Utrecht, Netherlands.

Ajantha Velayutham is PhD candidate in accounting at the Auckland University of Technology Business School in Auckland, New Zealand.

Sivakumar Velayutham is professor and dean of the Faculty of Business, Hospitality, and Humanities at Nilai University in Nilai, Malaysia.

Francisco Valderrey is professor at Tecnologico de Monterey in León, Mexico.

Joshua Whale is lecturer in enterprise and entrepreneurship in the Business School at the University of Wolverhampton in Wolverhampton, England.

Veit Wohlgemuth is professor at HTW Berlin University of Applied Sciences in Berlin, Germany.